The Eichmann Tapes

My Role in the Final Solution

by

Adolf Eichmann

The Eichmann Tapes

My Role in the Final Solution

by

Adolf Eichmann

Original German edition:
Ich, Adolf Eichmann
Ein historischer Zeugenbericht
© Druffel Verlag
Leoni am Starnberger See

Black House Publishing Ltd

Kemp House

152 City Road

London

United Kingdom

EC1V 2NX

www.blackhousepublishing.com
Email: info@blackhousepublishing.com

The Eichmann Tapes

My Role in the Final Solution

by

Adolf Eichmann

Translated by
Dr. Alexander Jacob

Contents

Introduction

Dr. Alexander Jacob

Adolf Eichmann (1906-1962) was born in Solingen in Germany to Adolf Karl Eichmann and Maria Eichmann, née Schefferling. After his mother died in 1914, his family moved to Linz in Austria. Eichmann began working in his father's mining company in 1923 and, from 1925 to 1927, worked as a sales clerk for the Oberösterreichische Elektrobau company. He also served as district agent in the Vacuum Oil Company.

As a young man, Eichmann joined the German Austrian Young Frontline Soldiers' Association, which was the youth wing of the paramilitary Frontline Soldiers' Association of Hermann Hiltl. On the advice of his family friend Ernst Kaltenbrunner, he joined the Austrian branch of the NSDAP and was enlisted as a member of the SS in 1932. Shortly after the National Socialists came to power in January 1933, Eichmann was dismissed from the oil company and so he devoted all his time to working with the National Socialist party. He was promoted to SS Scharführer in November 1933 and served in the administrative staff of the Dachau concentration camp. In 1934 he moved to the Security Service and, after briefly working in the Freemasonry department, moved to the Jewish department in Berlin in November 1934.

In 1937, he travelled with his superior Herbert Hagen to the British Mandate territory of Palestine to assess the possibility of Jewish emigration from Germany to Palestine. In 1938, after the Anschluss, Eichmann was posted in Vienna and was entrusted with the establishment of a Central Office for Jewish Emigration. In the course of this assignment Eichmann developed numerous contacts with Jewish authorities who helped him speed up the emigration of Jews from Austria. In December 1939, he was made head of the Gestapo division IV-B4 of the newly formed Reich Security Head Office (RSHA) and worked, under Heinrich Müller, on Jewish matters. By 1941 Eichmann had been promoted to SS Obersturmbannführer (Lieutenant Colonel) and was entrusted with the organisation of the deportation of the European Jews to various concentration camps in the Greater German Reich.

5

Introduction

Though arrested at the end of the war by the U.S. army, Eichmann succeeded in escaping from U.S. custody early in 1946 and lived unnoticed in Germany and Austria until 1950, when he travelled to Argentina, through Italy, under the false name of Ricardo Klement. For the next ten years he worked at mechanical jobs in Buenos Aires and, in 1952, brought his family over to Argentina from Germany. However, in 1953, Simon Wiesenthal obtained a letter to an Austrian baron Mast from a German officer in Argentina who reported that he had met Eichmann, who was working at that time in a power plant near Buenos Aires. Although this information was conveyed to the Israeli consul in Vienna as well as to Dr. Nahum Goldmann of the World Jewish Congress in New York, it was 1957 before the Mossad was involved in the search for Eichmann. Walter Eyan of the Israeli Foreign Ministry was informed by the German public prosecutor Fritz Bauer that Eichmann was living in Argentina and he then relayed this information to Isser Harel, the head of Mossad, whose agents succeeded in tracing Eichmann in Argentina and capturing him, three years later, on May 11, 1960. On May 21 he was flown to Israel, where he was tried by the Israeli Court in 1961, found guilty and hanged on May 31, 1962.

In Argentina, from 1951 until 1959, Eichmann made a series of tape-recorded interviews with the former SS Dutchman Willem Sassen. When the Israeli prosecutor Gideon Hausner wished to have the full Sassen transcripts admitted into evidence during Eichmann's trial in 1961, Eichmann opposed this claiming that this record was mere "pub talk" since he had been drinking red wine during the interview and Sassen had constantly encouraged him to embellish his accounts for journalistic sensation and had even falsely transcribed the interview. Portions of the Sassen interview were sold by Sassen to Life magazine, which published them in December 1960 (*Life*, Vol.49, no.22, November 28, 1960 and no.23, December 5, 1960), that is, when Eichmann had already been taken to Israel.

Another copy of the transcription of Eichmann's original recordings and handwritten notes, was taken by Eichmann's widow Veronika to the Nuremberg lawyer, Dr. Rudolf Aschenauer, whom she commissioned to act on her behalf in regards to their publication. This edition was published by the German publisher Druffel Verlag as *Ich, Adolf Eichmann: ein historischer Zeugenbericht*

In the Foreword and Preface to this edition, Eichmann declares that this is indeed the only testimony that he wishes to be considered as genuine and not dictated under duress.

The Eichmann Tapes

After his courtroom testimony, in August 1961, Eichmann wrote another handwritten testimony that he called "Götzen" (False Gods). This record was for many years guarded in the Israeli State Archives and was released only briefly during the Irving-Lipstadt trial in London in 2000. My English translation of this manuscript, *False Gods*, is also published by Black House Publishing, and is a companion to the present edition.

This edition of Eichmann's memoirs supplies a detailed account of Eichmann's career in the SS and Gestapo as the divisional head in charge of the numerous deportations of the European Jews, and establishes the scope of the anti-Jewish measures undertaken in the Third Reich and points out the gradual development of these measures from emigration to concentration to finally the large-scale liquidations that took place after Hitler had issued his orders in 1942, when Germany moved from offensive to defensive operations in the war against the USSR.

What is also noteworthy in this account is the enormous organisational framework of this undertaking involving hundreds of political, military and police officials, across the continent. At the same time, Eichmann highlights his own constant efforts to help the Jews find an independent home territory – even, indeed, during his last posting in Hungary towards the end of the war. The reader of Eichmann's memoirs will thus obtain not only a vivid impression of the extensive police operations of the Third Reich but also a glimpse into the ideological and political motivations of these actions, motivations that were perhaps not fully shared by Eichmann himself.

Dr Alexander Jacob.

Foreword

To the living and coming generations, I wish to provide an account of a frightful chapter of the past war. I shall speak only the complete truth – I shall not conceal anything, nor shall I gloss over anything.

I submit this account of these events at a time in which I am in full possession of my mental powers and physical freedom, neither influenced nor forced by anybody.

This testament of mine overrides any explanation deviating from this which I may give in the future before a hostile forum or tribunal.

Martinez, 9 February 1959

Adolf Eichmann

SS-Obersturmbannführer Adolf Eichmann 1906-1962.

Preface

Thoughts Under US Imprisonment

It is December 1945. I am an American prisoner in the Oberdachstetten camp and I stand in one of those frightful latrines that represent the international sign of all such prison camps. In my mouth I feel the poison capsule. A few months ago, it apparently took the life of my second highest chief, the SS Reichsführer Heinrich Himmler. The capsule has not left me since the end of the war; I have preserved it through a number of camps and numerous inspections. Now I have to decide: life or death. I choose death when I think that the Reich, the dream and content of my life, is defeated, and in ruins. I choose death when I think that I do not know how long I can hide my true identity from the officials of the CIC – but I choose life when I think of my family, who have a right to their life, and to mine. My conscience forces me to death; for I know that I had a difficult and cruel mission, which I did not choose, and to whose fulfilment however, obedience and dedication to duty categorically forced me.

So I choose life and throw the poison capsule into the latrine. Then a short, severe desperation overcomes me. I have taken an initiative and must think further – act further – logically. I must get out of this camp, I must escape; for only in this way can I avoid the risk of identification. So I decide to escape.

However – if I had known at that time that in a short time not a single one of my direct and highest superiors would be alive, and that only I would be left behind to give evidence of the truth, if I had been able at that time to know that the propagandist would make of me a mass murderer, a Caligula[1] dripping with blood, and that my decision to live would impose on my shoulders the responsibility to tell the truth

---

1   Caius Caesar Germanicus Caligula, from A.D. 37-41 Roman emperor, murdered by a Praetorian tribune. His character sketch has been partially distorted in the historical records. The concept of "imperial madness" is associated with Caligula.

11

German prisoners of war in the Ober-Dachstetten PoW Camp.

of these historical events, under circumstances and in a world ruled completely by the enemy and all the means standing at his disposal for the moulding of public opinion, if I had known of the superhuman task of speaking out against a world of enemies without any moral support, not even the support of one's own people, I would perhaps have chosen death!

Since I chose life at that time, I must now speak. The generations still living and those to come have a right to it. It may be that in these years even my own people, to whom I was and am blindly dedicated, may spit me out – cast me away like a poisonous viper. Even this most painful of all circumstances cannot prevent me from serving the truth and therewith the true history of the Greater German Reich.

I have never been able to live without god, I have seen him in Nature and even traced him in the play of clouds. I appeal to this god, so that he may stand with me, test me on my honour and conscience and lend me the power to build a pathway to the truth and to decry falsehood.

A Review: Zionism and the Final Solution

When I was under American captivity, I read a small pamphlet entitled "The Nuremberg Trial" or something similar, in which it said that Judge Jackson[2] had described me as the "darkest figure of this century", especially since I had clearly recognised the outcome of the war a long time before. It is true that in Paris in 1940, when Field Marshal General Bock[3] reviewed the troop parade, the confidence in victory of the Germans was at its high point. At this time, my humble self, Walther Huppenkothen,[4] and three other comrades, met every Thursday in the private house of Group Leader Müller:[5] In all the five departmental leaders of Gestapo Office IV.[6] They were casual evenings, during which we played chess; and only on occasion did we discuss service-related matters.

On the evening of the victory parade in Paris I thought I should express my concerns, for around this time I began to become pessimistic on account of my anxiety for the future of Germany, so I said to Huppenkothen: "I believe that if it continues like this, we shall lose the war". Huppenkothen was the official in charge of the "National Opposition". Among the daily reports on my desk I read the "Moods within the Reich", the efforts of our opponents and so on. I pointed out to Huppenkothen the internal situation because he was responsible for it. He contradicted me severely and indeed objected to the word "pessimism"; because we National Socialists should not be pessimistic. There then arose a small argument between us, and I said to him: "We who stand in the midst of it, we have the right to pessimism; for if we are not seized with pessimism, we shall never have the power and the possibility to judge and sentence those of our opponents who spread pessimism. Naturally I may not communicate my own pessimism to any third person, only to those who, like us

---

2   Robert H. Jackson, Chief Prosecutor in the IMT trial of Nuremberg against Göring, etc., Judge in the Federal Supreme Court of the USA.

3   Feder von Bock, Field Marshal General, Senior Commanding Officer of the Central Army in the campaign against the Soviet Union (1941).

4   Walther Huppenkothen, born 1907, active in different offices, Prosecutor against Canaris, sentenced in 1955 to 7 years' imprisonment.

5   Heinrich Müller, SS Obergruppenführer, Head of Department IV of the Reich Security Head Office, thereby Eichmann's superior.

6   In September 1939 the Gestapo (Secret State-Police) was designated as Office IV of the RSHA, Reich Security Head Office, which was led by Reinhard Heydrich.

Adolf Hitler and military leaders tour Paris in 1940.

stand in the midst of it, and because of anxiety for the Reich!" Müller
then entered the conversation, he agreed partly with me, partly with
Huppenkothen. So I said to my immediate superior Müller that we
must first place half a million Germans against the wall before we
have the right to destroy the enemy. So long as we could not do that we
would have no right to it. Müller did not either agree or disagree, but
only smiled rather paternally. The half million Germans represent the
saboteurs as we saw them. For example, the "Rote Kapelle" resistance
in Berlin,[7] the "Pressespiegel",[8] and the many others. During this
discussion there arose before me an image that caused me to say:
"God, there is so much trouble in the country – why don't we finally
just destroy it?"

To know exactly what was happening in the Reich was the task
of Internal Security Intelligence Office III, which was under Otto
Ohlendorf.[9] Huppenkothen also received the reports of Office III. Office

---

7   'The Red Orchestra' was a Soviet espionage ring operating in German
    occupied Europe.

8   The name of a news digest.

9   Otto Ohlendorf, Ministerial Director in the Reich Economics Ministry, Head

III compiled all the reports, dealt with them, determined the manner of dealing with the enemy and then passed its recommendations on to the Gestapo and to all concerned offices of the Reich Security Head Office.

It is from this context that my attitude to the solution of the Jewish question must be considered. My basic attitude to the Jewish question – in relation to our people – is based on an understanding and knowledge of history. It is enough here to point briefly to the beginning and end of the development: living for centuries in a diaspora, Jewry was in the beginning practically ghettoised and (for religious reasons) prevented from practising certain professions (within its Christian host nations). Thus the Jews, concentrated on certain sectors, for example, trade, finance and the loan-interest economy. If we take – for Germany – 1932 as the end point of this development, we must declare that Jewry ruled an incredible percentage compared to their numbers in the total population. In all important fields, the Jews were to be found in key positions.

Numerous people both within and outside of Germany, including me, thought more in terms of the separation of the Jews from their host peoples; for even within Jewish, especially Zionist circles, first under Herzl, the Jews themselves had also endorsed this solution. There could only be a political solution; a political solution, and by political solution I do not mean breaking their shop windows, dragging them into slavery, or killing them – a *political solution means only territorial separation.* That was of course attempted already long before National Socialism came to power; at that time the German was not the driving force behind this desire for separation, but the Jew himself, and indeed the programme was called separation of Jews and non-Jews in general and not just in relation to the Germans!

If I had had the opportunity to determine things and the authority to carry through a solution, I would have carried out that which I have already attempted in a rudimentary fashion, that is, to give the Jews first of all a certain autonomy so that they acquired an administrative training to be able in this way to maintain and lead themselves. At that time and even today I believe, that the Jewish question can only be resolved if the Jews have their own homeland. The "where" is a task for the politicians.

---

of Office III in the Reich Security Head Office (Internal Security), from July 41 to April 42 Chief of the Einsatz Group D. In April 1948 sentenced to death by the US Military Tribunal in Nuremberg. On 8 June 1951 hanged in the Landsberg/Lech prison.

I had recognised early that Jewry in intellectual as well as in party political matters are divided into dozens of groups – just like every other people. Even from this recognition did I conclude that *only a political solution could bring about a "final solution of the Jewish question"*. There is an abundance of examples at hand to illustrate this; the Jews are a people like any other, only they have in the course of a history of many thousands of years, especially through their dispersal throughout the world, been transformed in such a way that they unfortunately operate in any host nation in an irksome manner. The Jew could be highly esteemed by us – on condition that he live in some distant country, as far away from us as possible.

It is a paradox that the Jews of all people returned to their so-called ancestral homeland: they left it 2,000 years ago, in revolt against the Roman authority, but they now try to annex it through cunning and violence – that is contradictory to history; for if one has abandoned a country for a period of two thousand years one no longer possesses a right to it.

We offered the Jews Madagascar or some such region, for in the Middle East they would naturally always come into conflict with the Arabs. Two thousand years cannot be thrust aside in this manner as if it had not existed. In this time other peoples have settled and rooted themselves in the ancestral homeland of the Jews; those who can prove such a long period of actual settlement are the true owner.

What I Want

In these explanations of mine on events that have already become a part of history, I intend to sit in judgement on myself publicly in order that I may prove that I am neither a murderer, nor indeed a mass murderer. I do not think of glossing over anything in order to justify myself or to attempt to diminish the scope of the operations carried out by me according to my orders. No, I wish to produce clarity, to denounce both our and our enemy's lies! I do not in any way wish to appear better than I am. On the contrary: I am convinced that, in the case of a possible character evaluation, I would come through with no more than an average of merits along with many shortcomings. The actions and motives of a man consist indeed of a large number of errors and misunderstandings; only through reflection can one progress. However, every time when I believed that I had to go on this path, the path of reflection, this intention was disturbed. From

1945 to today, events always came up which indeed contradicted in a completely flagrant manner the questionable norms that arose in the "International Court" in Nuremberg.

Those who considered the new "legal conception" of Nuremberg as a new panacea and practised it immediately on the German people, in no way applied the law to their own activities and efforts. I would accept without argument the punishment that a just and competent international court would impose upon me, for I confess without hesitation that, acting upon orders, I am "guilty" of "assisting in the killing" of men during the war. I would voluntarily set myself before such a court because Germans, like Jews, have a right to have the events clarified.

But I would only be ready to present myself voluntarily if *the other nations too* including the Jewish nation were ready to declare that all of their own state members who have – by following orders – made themselves, during the war or from May 1945 to today, guilty of "assisting in the killing" of men, and to send them also to a just international court.

Apart from the government of the Greater German Reich, there are many governments which both during the second World War and also after the end of the war maintained security units or offices which had and have to fulfil precisely the same tasks as my office. Through the normal official channels I received from my superior chiefs' offices communicated in the form of orders and directives whatever arose within the government as law, decree, ordinance, instruction and order.

Yes, other governments had and have offices and security units whose task coincided precisely with mine. There is only a single difference: I had in the service of the Greater German government to deal with one aspect of the Jewish affairs, *but I never had to carry out an order for their annihilation.* I wish however to declare clearly and objectively here that if I had received, during the war, orders of my superiors to kill enemies of the Reich, my oath to service would have forced me naturally to carry out that order. Fate clearly did not wish that. I am for that reason neither thankful nor ungrateful; it was certainly already written in the stars long before my birth ...

Among my "colleagues" are those working for Polish, Czech, Yugoslav and Soviet men who have collected and deported millions of Germans from the German eastern territories, ... "colleagues" who have collected and expelled millions of ethnic Germans from Poland, Romania, Hungary, Yugoslavia and Czechoslovakia. Soviet Russian "colleagues" who have led Soviet citizens by the millions into camps and death,... Israeli "colleagues" who have consigned entire Arab tribes, settled for 1400 years in Palestine, to death and expulsion ..., exactly as I *collected and deported, on orders, and during the war, over a million Jews.* I do not want any pardon: *I want justice, the same justice for all concerned,* for whatever side they may have performed their service.

No man can seriously suppose that for such a high regulatory authority as the International Court of Nuremberg only the *Vae victis* the "woe of the defeated" – is valid. But if one does not find my "colleagues" on the other side guilty, if one does not punish them for their deportation work and methods, if their governments even grants them honours and decorations for fulfilling their duty, even though it is a question exactly as in our case of the fulfilment of a sad duty, if one promotes them, and they are able to enjoy their well-deserved state pension in peace and security – then there is not an equitable law! Of course I would gladly give up distinctions and promotion; there is no question of that.

How much longer fate gives me to live I do not know. But I do know that there must be somebody who must give information about these events to the still living and coming generations, information of such a sort that it is possible for present and future historians to form a rounded and truthful picture. If only they may be objective enough not to deviate from the truth laid down here! I give these explanations at a time in which, as mentioned, I am in full possession of my physical powers and psychological freedom, neither influenced or forced by anybody.

I

From My life

When I Was Not Yet A National Socialist

In the twenties I was an employee of the Austrian branch of the Vacuum-Oil Company, I received a salary that was large for the conditions of that time and lived happily and carefree. In 1930 I was introduced by a former senior lieutenant of the Imperial and Royal Army, who was at the same time an official at the oil company, to the "Schlaraffia" in Linz which had in the club-house an extremely nice cellar room. I became acquainted there with all sorts of people, for example, doctors from the General Hospital in Linz, actors, big businessmen, all from Linz.

As part of the welcome ceremony I was instructed to bow before a stuffed eagle owl which sat in a corner halfway up the club-house room, and then I was greeted by all those present. The arch chancellor then gave a sign, whereupon music was struck up on a spinet-like instrument and all put on their dunce-caps hung with all sorts of coloured trinkets. Near one of the members stood a swastika; to my question why, he said "But naturally – we do not accept any Jews!" That made a great impression on me. I was expected to give an entry speech as best as I could, humorous but intellectually substantial; I had therefore already decided what subject I would choose. Finally, as the evening progressed, we went to the Café Central, and because I was, as a young man of 23, in a good mood I ordered a round of a fine variety of wine for the table. At the same table sat the dialect poet Franz Resel. After some moments he left the café somewhat enraged with a remark to the effect that I did not need to come back henceforth. Why? Simply because I had mentioned that I was a member of the German-Austrian Frontline Soldiers' Association, which was composed of two different

19

Franz Josef-Platz in the Austrian city of Linz, 1931

groups, one monarchist in attitude and the other nationalist, which was especially anti-Marxist.

At that time, the Republikaner Schutzbund[1] ruled the streets and, along with it, on the basis of a privilege of the German-Austrian government, the Frontline Soldiers' Association under the leadership of Colonel Hiltl.[2] Because I came from the association of the monarchist party, I was immediately accepted in the "German Austrian Young Frontline Soldiers' Association". In the Monarchist Club we had among our peers officials as well as sons and daughters of officers. In the Frontline Soldiers' Association there were officers with many high decorations, Austrian corps men, commanders, sergeants, ordinary guards; they were all united under the banner of anti-Marxism. In the Upper Austria section, the Major General von Ehrenwald well-known from the first World War had a certain place of honour; his wife was dead; one of his former commanders from a traditional regiment was his servant, who while wearing white cotton gloves had the task of shuffling the glasses to and from his master and the few guests.

---

1   A paramilitary organisation established in 1923 by the Sozialdemokratische Arbeiterpartei Österreichs (Social Democratic Workers' Party of Austria).

2   The Frontline Soldiers' Association was an Austrian paramilitary organisation founded by the military officer Hermann Hiltl (1872-1930) along the lines of the German Stahlhelm (League of Frontline Soldiers). It was an anti-Semitic organisation that favoured the unification of Austria with Germany.

On many a Sunday afternoon we travelled by tram to the Ebelsberg near Linz where there was a large shooting range. The Frontline Soldiers' Association had been granted permission to even shoot with military weapons. The Major General, pressed into my hand for the first time in my life a military carbine and exhorted me to fire the weapon. The Major General always carried – even in radiant sunshine – an umbrella and narrated to everybody that he met, some small episode from a battle, where it was not at all important if one understood any of it or even paid any attention to it. The Major General brandished his umbrella around in the air, rolled his eyes, twirled his moustache and gesticulated; and once he tried to describe a situation especially vividly with a torrent of words so that everybody understood: now the General is standing in the midst of battle! That naturally impressed us boys very strongly; and we often sought the company of this worthy old gentleman.

The Monarchist Club provided the opportunity for convivial meetings where we could meet one another, have a small drink and chat a little about Bismarck. In the German-Austrian Frontline Soldiers' Association there prevailed a rather more militant atmosphere. I had in any case, alongside my pleasant and well-paying job, political views which may be characterised as "nationalist"; for the principle of the Frontline Soldiers' Association was the general welfare of the nation. I was anti-Marxist because, well, one was in our circles, but I did not understand politics in any real depth. Occasionally our Major General clarified things for us.

At this time I had become engaged to the daughter of a senior officer of the constabulary. When we had nothing better to do in her father's parlour we frequently sprawled on the windowsill and looked out on the street. A hundred metres from the barracks there was an inn, the "Märzen Cellar", where at certain seasons there was a good bock beer; in this inn members of the National Socialist German Workers' Party would frequently hold meetings. In our circles we used to say that the NDSAP consisted only of idiots and the frustrated. This local branch was led by a man called Andreas Boleck,[3] who was the "Gauleiter",[4] as one called it, of Upper Austria. After the first World War, Bolek came to Linz as a former lieutenant of the Imperial and Royal Army and

---

3   Andreas Bolek (1894-1945) was an Austrian NSDAP leader who served as Gauleiter of Upper Austria from 1927 to 1934. In 1937 he joined the SS and was appointed President of the Magdeburg Police in 1938.

4   A Gauleiter was a National Socialist head of a county.

had married the daughter of a local butcher. Later he got a position in the Linz Tramway and Electricity Company, where my father was a director.

At that time the NSDAP meant nothing in Upper Austria. When I and my fiancée looking out through the window, saw troops of twenty to twenty five men – partly in brown shirts, partly with swastika bands and partly without any insignia at all – marching past singing, I felt as if something rushed into my blood from these songs. They marched "differently" from the Republikanischer Schutzbund, they sang "differently" and, when my fiancé once said to me: "These idiots!", I answered her: "But they have order and discipline – and they march well!" My fiancée soon left me, especially when I told her that I admired these men, for they had fought for their fatherland, and were idealists.

At that time I used to go every forenoon to a certain coffee-house to drink my black coffee, and read the *Linzer Tagespost* and the *Volksstimme,* and to wait until the only copy of *Völkischer Beobachter*[5] that was available in the pub became free, which the waiter Franz always brought me for a small tip. There I read how at that time SA and SS men were killed and borne to the grave in a demonstration of their faith: "They died for something great!"[6] I read also how even the funeral processions were attacked by their opponents in the local community. All that infuriated me immeasurably and caused to develop in me an inclination and even friendship towards those "idiots" who marched singing freedom songs through the streets past the police barracks.

I Became A National Socialist

One evening I received an invitation from Gauleiter Bolek to a meeting of the NSDAP in the "Märzen Cellar". I went there. After Bolek had spoken I came upon Ernst Kaltenbrunner;[7] who was wearing the SS

---

5   The *Nationalist Observer*, the party organ of the NSDAP.

6   Eichmann refers to the contemporary civil war-like situation at the end of the Weimar Republic, when especially SA, SS Stahlhelm, Reichsbanner and Red Front fighters (KPD) increasingly engaged in street and meeting hall fights.

7   Ernst Kaltenbrunner, Director of the Reich Security Head Office, successor of Heydrich, who was assassinated in Prague on 5 June 1942. Before 1933 Kaltenbrunner was a lawyer in Austria. He was hanged in Nuremberg on 16 October 1946, after the IMT had sentenced him to death.

uniform which I saw here for the first time. Then he said to me the words that I still remember: "You ... you belong to us!" Then he drew out a sheet of paper, filled it in, and I only needed to sign it. I still remember that I did not ask any further questions, but was happy and proud to belong now, like Kaltenbrunner, to the SS. That was in 1931.

Kaltenbrunner's father and my father were business friends in Linz so we knew each other quite well. Kaltenbrunner himself was at that time active in a legal position in his father's office. So I became an SS man.

Kaltenbrunner and I then spoke about the Jews and Freemasons; and he said in this connection: "The Schlaraffen[8] organisation was a preliminary stage to Freemasonry; these are enemies of the Reich". I expressed my own opinion, but Kaltenbrunner did not agree with me, and he became quite adamant so that I felt as if I was half a criminal because I had myself been part of these Schlaraffen. When I then told him that I had anyway been expelled, he laughed; then we drank a beer together.

As an SS man I had now to hold watch every Friday evening in the "Brown House" in Linz. Since many of my SS comrades were unemployed, I ordered in the Café Bahnhof sandwiches and beer for everybody. During this time we had to participate in some debates, also once in the Volksgarten Hall, where Bolek was supposed to speak and the Communists had already in the afternoon filled the hall with up to 2,000 men in order to make the meeting impossible for us. Although we had rented the hall, the police gave only Bolek and 25 SS men permission to enter. So we went in; the speech by Gauleiter Bolek was short, he could only say: "My German national comrades ..." and already an enormous racket broke out, I heard Kaltenbrunner calling "Get the guys", for the Communists placed their women right in front of the podium, and behind them collected the men, mostly bellowing, drunken shipyard workers. We all stood on the podium and had to protect our Gauleiter from the charging people with our boots and shoulder straps strengthened with leaden knots. After we had done this successfully we withdrew, but with losses. So, for example, the kidneys of the later adjutant of the SS Reichsführer,[9] staff sergeant Breuer, were battered; the voluntary fire brigade took him to the

---

8   The Schlaraffen was a men's cultural organisation founded in 1858 in Prague which bore some resemblance to Freemasonry.

9   Leader of the SS, Heinrich Himmler.

hospital. The "Volksgarten" Hall was smashed up – to the last glass and the last mirror.

One day a delegate of the engineering team, apparently a technical sergeant, came to me and in a serious tone gave me the leadership of the Motor Squadron unit of the 37th SS Standard. I was thus "Motorsturmführer",[10] but I had no idea what was required of me. So I asked for a job description in order to become acquainted with the command. There was another man who wished to become an adjutant of mine, but I thought that I must first organise motor vehicles, which could also cost me some money. I still continued my service at the oil company, and at work I wore my insignia of the NSDAP.

I became a missionary for the NSDAP, and preached everywhere, even to my customers. As a result of this the oil company transferred me to Salzburg. I had obtained my post at the company partly through the help of a Jew and was able to get along with any Jews whom I met. In Salzburg a Jew became a technical inspector at the oil company, but in spite of advice against doing so, I wore my SS insignia even during business meetings; I was after all single and I had no responsibilities of any sort. On Whitsun 1933 I was dismissed.

The German consul prepared for me a letter with the content that I was dismissed "from the Vacuum Oil Company on account of my membership in the SS". Kaltenbrunner sent me to Germany with the commission of reporting to the "boss" in Passau, the Gauleiter Bolek, who had in the meanwhile moved there. I packed my brown shirt, riding breeches and boots into my bag.

With the Austrian Legion

Bolek lived in the Bahnhof street in Passau as the Gauleiter of Upper Austria. There it was suggested to me that a military education would not hurt; I was to go to Dachau, but the motor team leader, who had named me Motorsturmführer at one time, took command of me in Passau: that was Major von Pichl. I was then promoted to SS Sergeant and received my first medal. It was my task to watch over, with my eight men, a certain section of the German-Austrian border in accord with the chief of the border police station of Passau.

---

10   Motor squadron leader.

1933, it took the Jewish lobby six years to achieve their war against Germany.

I had to lead National Socialists who for some reason had to flee from Austria over the "green line", even smuggle our propaganda material in the same way into Austria; the NSDAP had been for a long time prohibited in Austria. I got a motorcycle and did service in the Bayerische Wald.

Christmas 1933 we celebrated in Passau. The city councillors came to us, eight people who had left Austria and we were on this evening absolutely regaled in the then flourishing Passau. We had placed our heavy machine-gun at a stream, near which in our quarters stood the Christmas tree.

In the first months of 1934 I received an order to report to the battalion of the "Austrian Legion" SS-I in Dachau. I arrived at the barracks as a civilian there with a bag, borne by a porter, and an umbrella ... I never saw the bag or umbrella again. First I received many things – like blue-white chequered bed linen – some sneakers were also thrown at my head which I was however able to catch in time. But it was still better than in the Lechfeld Cloister, where I waited for two months before I succeeded in obtaining so much as an SS tie rod. There we were in a really old first World War army camp and we even had to pick out the pieces of meat and potatoes with our fingers because there were neither knives nor forks nor spoons. We slept on straw. I moistened my handkerchief and placed it as a filter on my nose against the dust. But one got accustomed even to that.

From My life

In Dachau on the other hand everything was very orderly. I passed my shooting exercises and belonged to SS unit Sturm 13[11]. We were subdivided into infantry and combat patrol: to the infantry belonged the narrow-chested tall ones, to the combat patrol the "athletically" built; I went to the combat patrol. The Sturmführer was a former staff sergeant of the Bavarian Provincial Police, a feared "slave-driver" whom we hated like sin. In spite of my preparedness for self-denial – I could after all have led a better life at home – and in spite of my natural joy in everything, my life was now nourished only on murderous thoughts. When in the mornings the bugle sounded, fury rose high in me. I got used to waking up a quarter of an hour earlier in order to be able to dress in ease before the awful bugle signal sounded. We then did twenty minutes of early morning exercises on the double; from there we went to a water tap. Hardly did we reach this water tap to dash a few drops of water onto our faces than we would already be shouted to the coffee table; hardly had we stuck the bread in our mouths and gulped the cold coffee sludge, when we had to fall in line and report for roll-call. The Sturmführer greeted us in a friendly manner with "Good morning people", then the badgering began once again. I escaped only into "murderous thoughts" against this former police chief.

The training-camp parade ground was on the "Schinder meadow", where prickly grass and gravel tore our boots. Half the company reported to the parade ground. I had myself bound with gauze and plaster – but in the first minutes of crawling on hands and knees everything came off and was bloody again. Years later I mentioned that staff-seargent and my days at the training camp to my bosses, Heydrich, Kaltenbrunner and Müller, to anybody who wanted to listen. Only through the pleasure of imagining the "murder" of this member of the provincial police was I able to survive that period and do service to this slave-driver.

In the end there remained in all only eight or ten men. When I was in this way more or less at the end of my strength, I was ordered to report to a petty officer. It emerged that our "slave-driver" had received orders to propose a certain number of petty officers for a "strenuous march" since the SS Reichsführer was to urgently form some new regiments. So I was promoted and could then pin on my new SS medals.

---

11   "Sturm", an SS company.

So that was National Socialism, such as I experienced it at first hand. Nothing could rob me any longer of my fanaticism because I constantly heard from the Goebbels press of the heroic struggle of the individual soldier. That fascinated me, and I said to myself if men could die in this way for their fatherland, it must be for something great. In this way everything else became irrelevant. I was grateful to my parents that they had let me go wherever it drew me. The first stage of the education the old Major General von Ehrenwald had given me; for I had never before had a weapon in my hand. He had also taught us why "spit and polish" was necessary to defend the sanctity of the fatherland! Prior to joining the NSDAP I only knew National Socialism from gossip as something despicable, for in our circles it was considered as "coarse" to get together with these people who did not belong to one's "class" and that many of them were unemployed.

What I felt at that time (in Linz) and later experienced in Passau and Dachau was the unconditional comradeship, the staying together and never to surrender in order to achieve something greater. It was worth it indeed to allow oneself to be killed for something great. There must indeed have been something in it, to be borne by one's friends to the grave to the beating of drums. And then how Goebbels would get carried away with enthusiasm for the dead comrade in the *Völkischer Beobachter* or in the *Angriff* and, on the other hand, kindled a hatred against all of our enemies! There were few National Socialists, the enemies were many – and I said to myself "Where there are few, there you belong – and where there are many you are superfluous!" These thoughts occupied and formed me just as my friends too formed me, although many of my friends at that time stood politically in other camps.

The Step to the Security Service

In late summer 1934 I was transferred from the SS troop to the Security Service, where I was *occupied for a fortnight with filing cards.* Many years later Heydrich[12] once said to me after a discussion – and it was like a contented reflection on what had been accomplished up to then – that he could remember the time when in Munich he used to make filing cards in a small attic room on Brienner Street ... That

---

12   Reinhard Heydrich, was Chief of the Security Police and SD, Deputy Protector in Bohemia and Moravia. On 5 June 1942 he died as a result of an assassination attempt made against him by Czechs on contract to the English.

Adolf Hitler, Goering, Goebbels and Hess at NSDAP rally 1934.

was the time the Security Service was born. That was around 1930; it was considered the great merit of Heydrich. Although it is completely possible that Heydrich entered this office of the Party Information Service through Canaris,[13] he distinguished himself from the start through his work and initiative.

Even before Hitler came to power the Security Service, or "SD" as it had become known, had performed important tasks for the party. In the summer of 1934, the Secret Service, was moved from Munich, the "city of the movement" to Berlin and received as its headquarters the mansion at 102 Wilhelm Street, which was connected through a park to the Prinz Albert Palais, where the Gestapo were accommodated.

When I went to the SD, I was given the number 54 or 59. Around this time the SD began to grow stronger. Large funds must have flowed into the department, for the party had no desire to let its powerful information apparatus slip from its hands. Certainly the NSDAP had the means to finance the SD, but I can nevertheless

---

13   Wilhelm Canaris, Admiral, Chief of the German Defence from 1935-1944, was sentenced to death on 9 April 1945 in the Flossenbürg concentration camp and hanged there.

remember that in September 1934 there was a problem for months with the salaries. We worked but were not paid anything because the SD had at that time little money. Once our office chief lent each of us ten marks! Only many days after the first of the month did we receive our money until one day the big shot at the cashier's office, a sergeant named Wettich, said: "Now we can be sure that we will receive our pay punctually". All state organs watched over their affairs carefully, whether it was the Reich army, the police or the defence office, all scented in the SD an unpleasant competition. But the party naturally wanted to prevent a state sector from taking this important information service from it.

At that time my service office was called "Security Service Head Office". Later many of my comrades were transferred to the Security Police, others remained at the SD. My first fortnight at the SD I spent, as mentioned, with filing cards. In a large hall of the Palais new heavy trays had been set up, twenty or thirty pieces, in which lay columns of filing cards. Every filing card was approximately the size of a book page. There was a Freemasonry filing card, a card of the U.O.B.B the "Independent B'nai Brith, 'sons of the Covenant', Order",[14] then filing cards of the so-called secret leagues and also a small number of Jewish cards. The filing cards of the Freemasons were yellow, those of the U.O.B.B. pink to crimson. Together with my comrade Jänisch, later my external office chief, I went into this filing card hall, where six or seven comrades were also working. We had to arrange these 100,000 or perhaps 200,000 filing cards in alphabetical order. If eight men had to work around a fortnight to arrange everything alphabetically, there must indeed have been quite a respectable number of filing cards. Later, all personal records, events, among other things, from the Service circulation were analysed and stacked in the large card drums. Everything that ever appeared in relation to the state police, in terms of official records or personal information, was filed in the card index. We also compiled the personal details from membership records of the opposition organisations. In this hall there worked, among others, an SS man called Paul Nordmann, who at that time met with a fatal accident. We transported him to his Westphalian homeland, where his father, a lawyer, was well-known as an opponent of National Socialism. The very dignified burial made a great impression on the population. Shortly after, a SD convalescent home, some seventy kilometres from Berlin, was set up and inaugurated under the name of "the Paul Nordmann House".

---

14   B'nai Brith, a Jewish "order" founded in 1848 in New York.

1	2	3	4	5	6	7	8	9	10	11	12	13	14	15	16	17	18	19	20

Name: (bei Frauen auch Geburtsname)
A d e n a u e r

Wohnung:
unbekannt

Bildverme

Vorname:
Konrad

A 67

Geboren:
5.1.1876 Köln

Familienstand:

Beruf: Oberbürgermeister a.D.

Deck- Name:
Adresse:

Glaubensbekenntnis:

Personalakten: 440

Staatsangehörigkeit: RD

Politische Einstellung:

Angelegt: 14.11.35

	Zeit	Ort	Tat	rechtskräftige Gerichtsentscheidung	Staatsanwaltschaft und Aktenzeichen	Polizeiakte
Strafen						

KOBLENZ — Heffrand

Post war West German leader Konrad Adenauer's SD card from 1935.

At that time many visitors came to us who were sent partly by the SS Reichsführer, partly by Heydrich, and partly by my immediate superior, Sturmbannführer[15] Brandt. Even Streicher visited our filing card hall once, and, since it was one of the best loved jokes that visitors might name anybody at random who would be immediately looked up, Streicher was also invited to do so. He named the name of his adjutant. When we had pulled out the card, it emerged that his adjutant was a former member of a freemason lodge – thereupon Streicher terminated his visit.

When I joined there already existed a huge card index on Freemasonry, so my predecessors must have been industrious. Nevertheless it seemed to me even at that time the danger of Freemasonry was grossly overestimated. On the card the "master of the chair"[16] and even the minor brothers of the lodge were listed, and we were already preparing difficulties for them, but if Freemasonry ever became an instrument of international Jewry – which we saw happen later – the minor members knew nothing about it.

---

15 SS major; Sturmbann (literally 'assault unit') is a battalion.

16 The chairman of a Masonic lodge.

The filing cards also had an international dimension; already many countries were recorded in cards. The cards constantly increased; for example, at long tables people worked on membership directories that had been confiscated by the regional state police and state police head offices. The members of the different organisations or the subscribers to the different newspapers were recorded in filing cards, these drawn up not only according to person, but also according to organisation. The filing cards were constantly edited and grew correspondingly bigger. When I was transferred in 1935 to another department the apparatus of the filing card authority had grown in the meantime to twenty or thirty men. At that time my later chief, the engineer and at that time Untersturmführer[17] Mildenstein,[18] designed two huge filing card wheels which worked automatically and could be maintained by two people. These two men sat as if before a harmonium and could in an instant automatically pull out the necessary filing cards, which were now smaller and thinner and besides perforated. Although huge amounts of filing cards were in these drums, I do not believe the claim that the entire German nation was recorded therein. After the first fortnight in the filing card hall I was sent to the "museum" department and for a whole year there I did nothing but arrange and examine Freemasonic seals, and undertake similar boring museum work.

There existed in 1934 and/or 1935 an SD Head Office, which was the Security Service of the SS Reichsführer. Under it stood the SD sectors and higher sectors. On the other hand, the Gestapo (Secret State Police) Office and the Reich Criminal Police Office belonged to the Security Police Head Office. The first was led by Müller, the second by Nebe.[19] Under the Secret State Police Office stood the Stapo[20] and the Stapo Control Offices, Secret State Police and the Secret State Police Offices set up in the provinces. Under the Reich Criminal Police Office stood the Criminal Police (Kripo) and the Kripo-Control Centres set up in

---

17   SS second lieutenant.

18   Leopold von Mildenstein, Esq. (1902-1968) was an Austrian SS officer who favoured the Zionist emigration plans to Israel and headed the Jewish department of the SDHA from 1934 but was removed from this post in 1936 as a result of a dispute with Heydrich. He was replaced by Kuno Schroeder and in 1939 Eichmann himself assumed the post.

19   Arthur Nebe, as Reich criminal directo, Head of the Reich Criminal Office, old National Socialist, up to October 1941 chief of Einsatz group B in the rear army area of the Central Army, as member of the circle of 20 July 1944 sentenced to death by the People's Court and then killed.

20   Staatspolizei, State Police.

the provinces. The SDHA was comprised of many offices, which were led at that time by Brandt, Oberg,[21] Ohlendorf and others, whose chief in this sector was Heydrich, who was also the chief of the Security Police Head Office. Above Heydrich was the SS Reichsführer, under whom stood all the head offices. Under the Regular Police Head Office were the Fire Protection Police and others. In terms of pay the SDHA was under the Reich Treasurer Schwarz[22] insofar as it concerned the appointment of its administrative chief and the administrative chief of the party. The chief of the financial administration had in every sector and higher sector of the SD his administrative "bosses" who had under them all financial matters and the administration of buildings. Whereas this sector was a pure party apparatus and did not have anything to do with state offices, the Gestapo with the Stapo offices and the Reich Kripo with the Kripo offices and Kripo control centres were of a purely state character; they were also paid by the state. Around this time we wore an arm-stripe with the inscription "SDHA". In the museum, which was under Office VII, I did my work under the museum director Richter from Berlin. I had to arrange the Freemason seal collection, compile and organise it all onto filing cards. We were thereby quite removed from the activity of the SD. At best we had visits from HJ,[23] BDM[24] and other organisations to look at the museum. Sturmbannführer Brandt, the later police president of Graz, was my immediate superior, Heydrich our chief.

For the Christmas celebration 1934 the SS Reichsführer Heinrich Himmler had announced to us that he wished to celebrate Christmas with us – we were indeed a small sworn group. The SS Reichsführer came somewhat late with his wife Margarete, whom I saw there for the first and last time. She gave the impression of a sympathetic, modest, south-Bohemian peasant woman. It was a very nice, intimate evening; we sang a couple of folk-songs. Near me sat Darré, the Agriculture

---

21   Karl Oberg, SS Obergruppenführer, Senior SS and Police Chief of Paris, after 1945 sentenced to death, pardoned by General de Gaulle, regiment comrade of General Heinrich von Stülpnagel, who was Military Commanding Officer in France from 1942-44. Oberg contributed to the fact that the quelling of the putsch of 20 July 1944 remained largely without consequences for the participants in Paris. Oberg made a farewell visit to Heinrich von Stülpnagel, accompanied only by his chauffeur, after 20 July 1944, in the Verden hospital. Stülpnagel was sentenced to death by the People's Court in Berlin and killed.

22   Franz-Xaver Schwarz, Reich Chief of the NSDAP, Reich Treasurer of the NSDAP office in Munich.

23   Hitler Jugend, Hitler Youth.

24   Bund deutscher Mädel, League of German girls.

Minister.[25] Each of us received a book from the SS Reichsführer. I requested him to autograph the "Kaiser Wilhelm" edition of *The Red Earth* by Hermann Löns.[26] This was the first time I had spoken to the SS Reichsführer. I had seen him often for at that time he personally conducted the Gauleiter, minister or national leader through the museum when Heydrich could not represent him. Jewish questions were not at all touched upon that Christmas evening, though world-view questions were discussed, whereby the Reichsführer assured himself of the internal solidarity of his people in the SDHA.

At one stage I met for the first and last time in my life the Grand Mufti.[27] On the next day three Iraqi officers were sent to me for information. If I remember right, one of them was a nephew of the Grand Mufti. I heard later, that it must have been he who had shot King Abdullah[28] and thereafter had killed himself. This nephew was, after the victory of the German army in north Africa, considered as a sort of "Heydrich of the Middle East". The three Iraqi officers each held the rank of major; I had orders to grant them access to our records and to guide them through my entire special field. I took personal care of these three gentlemen; one of them spoke German quite well, while another only managed a few fragments. My meeting with them was in no way a social get-together but a regular office introduction, so that they obtained a comprehensive overview of my work. I know that they also went through several other departments which interested them in some way. The Iraqi majors were remarkably quick to learn and studied our entire procedures eagerly.

In summer 1936 I took over the Freemasonry department from von Mildenstein, which dealt with the Jewish question, if not in a special way, still partly. Mildenstein had visited me in the seal collection of the museum[29] and was thereby able to awaken my interest in his

---

25   Walter Darré, Reich Minister of Food from 1933-42.

26   Hermann Löns (1866-1914) was a German writer who celebrated in his poems and novels the North German moors, especially the Lüeberg Heath in Lower Saxony. He was killed fighting in the first World War and was championed by the National Socialists as a representative of the "blood and soil" ideology.

27   El Huseini, Grand Mufti of Jerusalem.

28   Abdullah, Emir of Transjordan, plays a role in the Palestinian-Jordanian Federation Plan.

29   Large filing room of the Security Service Head Office – Editor.

newly established Jewish department, and I was glad of this change after the monotonous museum service. After my transfer to the new department I was "Specialist Compiler for the World Zionist Organisation".[30] Around this time Mildenstein was transferred to the Speer Service Office[31] where he travelled to the USA to study their highway system. For a few weeks his former department had been led by the most senior-ranking specialist compiler. When the latter moved to the army, Dieter Wisliceny[32] came to replace him, under whose leadership the department for Jewish affairs was first properly established, and the specialist compilers were promoted to consultants.

Already under Mildenstein I had begun to study the Jewish problem thoroughly. The first book I studied that was of fundamental significance was called *The Jewish State* by Adolf Böhm. [33] This book was the basis of the article that I wrote for *Leitheft*[34] on the World Zionist Organisation. My first article for *Leitheft* comprised around thirty to forty pages and was printed and distributed by the educational head of the SD sectors and higher sectors. I wrote other *Leitheft* articles in which I proposed the Jews be given the greatest possible support in their efforts to emigrate. As a consequence of these *Leitheft*'s articles naturally a work programme had to be given for the Jewish specialist compilers in the SD sectors so that they knew

---

30 Zionist executive. After the first World War, its seat was London, later Jerusalem.

31 Albert Speer, successor of the Reich Minister Dr. Todt who died on 7 February 1942, On 9 February 1942 Speer was appointed Reich Miniser for Armaments and Munition, as well as General Inspector for the German Penal System and for Water and Energy. Sentenced to 20 years' imprisonment by the IMT in Nuremberg. After the completion of the sentence, released from the Berlin-Spandau prison.

32 Dieter Wisliceny, Eichmann's colleague. Adviser on the Jewish question during the second World War in Slovakia. Sentenced to death in Preßburg in 1948 and hanged.

33 In a sworn declaration of Moritz Fleischmann, relating to 1938, given in London on 8 June 1960, it says: "When Eichmann allowed himself to use our name and our connection with Jewish actions, he was immediately struck by the name of Adolf Böhm. He asked him if he was the author of the *Geschichte des Zionismus* the first volume of which had appeared some months earlier. When Adolf Böhm affirmed this, Eichmann said that he had studied this work with special interest. One particular section aroused in him special interest, on a certain page, and he began to cite the entire page "by heart" … He said further that he had not yet found time to study the second volume which had appeared three weeks earlier, but he would do this as soon as possible."

34 The *Leitheft* (Leadership Magazine) of the SS.

how they had to conduct themselves. It was a matter of focusing the individual sectors on the same goal, so that sector leaders could orient the Gauleiters in an appropriate manner. That was also true of the representatives of the individual central authority offices. I wrote everything under the motto "Greatest possible promotion of Jewish emigration". Such *Leiheft*'s were never published under the name of the compiler, only in the accompanying letter, along with the print number, the sign of the specialist compiler was given, but then only when the office chief wished it. I studied religious philosophy and made an effort also to study Hebrew. During this time of study and the search for constructive solutions I stood strongly under the influence of the old, extremely lovable and very humble Prof. Dr. Schwarz-Bostumitch. He came from Kiev and did service with us as an SS Major. He was a mystic, and I considered him as my superior and teacher.

Personally I did not think much of mysticism at all, but I respected my teacher nevertheless very much. I clung to what was then obvious, namely ensuring that our descendants could live properly and to forge our weapons according to the strength of our enemies. But above all I stressed the unity of the nation! For that we gave up everything, youth and freedom and many even their life. That is why it infuriates me today when one represents National Socialism as something "criminal": it was pure both in its idealism and in its intentions.

In summer 1937, Wisliceny was replaced as department head by SS Senior Company Leader Herbert Hagen,[35] a confidant of Dr. Six's,[36] who was in charge of the general study of the counter world-view. In autumn 1937, I travelled with Hagen to Egypt and Palestine.

Around this time the Nuremberg legislation had already been brought into effect, that is, the "Reich citizenship law" and the "Law for the protection of German blood and German honour". Personally I did

---

35   Herbert Hagen, SS Sturmbannführer, appointed Commander of the Security Police in Paris during the second World War. After 1945 sentenced *in absentia* in France to death. In Cologne in 1980 sentenced to 12 years' imprisonment on account of his participation in the Jewish deportations in France.

36   Dr. Franz Six, SS Oberführer, temporarily Chief of Office VII of the RSHA, chief of the SS "Moscow" advance commando. Sentenced by the US Military Tribunal in the trial against Ohlendorf and others to 20 years' imprisonment. Penalty reduced in January 1951 to 10 years. Dr. Six was released on 30 September 1952 from imprisonment in the Landsberg/Lech prison. He died in Eppan/South Tyrol.

Two Germans accused of having violated the law against sexual relations between Jews and Gentiles. The woman's sign: "At this place I am the greatest swine for I laid with a Jew" The man's sign: "As a Jewish youth I take only German girls to my room"

not have anything to do with these matters, but like everybody at that time, I felt the definite atmosphere which was evoked by them. I think that these two laws arose in discussions at the highest level, between Goebbels, Göring, Himmler, Hitler and Frick[37], and also his state secretary Dr. Stuckart[38] were certainly included.

The propaganda preparation was effected by Streicher and Goebbels; the chancellery of the Führer was certainly involved in the creation of the initiatives. Only from 1940 was IV-B4 gradually involved in the executive consequences of these laws.

That this legislation could in general arise is explicable in a fundamental way. So why did National Socialism take up the Jewish question in its programme already during the period of the party's

---

37   Dr. Wilhelm Frick, Reich Minister of the Interior up to the appointment of Himmler in 1944. Sentenced to death by the IMT in Nuremberg and hanged there on 16 October 1946.

38   Dr. Wilhelm Stuckart, SS Obergruppenführer, State Secretary in the Reich Ministry of the Interior. In April 1949 sentenced by the US Military Tribunal to a term of imprisonment that had been served by his pretrial detention and he was immediately released, He died in Hannover in 1952.

struggle? The Jewish population had in percentage terms relative to the rest of the population a disproportionately high share in the management of the economy, in the free professions, in the press, in the radio, in the theatre, etc. So the enmity between host people and guests, between the Jewish part and the non-Jewish part of the population grew to such an extent that this would have doubtless led at some point to an explosion That was why the leadership was concerned to reduce the tension in an orderly, normal and legal way. This enmity had been present already for a long time in the German population, because the Jews had been able to enrich themselves with brutality and violence, and to let the German people starve. Especially during the period of hyperinflation dramatic events had arisen and the Jews themselves partially admit that they had enriched themselves at the expense of the German people, their host people.

Contacts Abroad

When I had already grappled with Hebrew and studies on Zionism for years and worked on the legal and illegal immigration to Palestine, I came upon an article on Jewish underground military organisations, thus also on the Haganah,[39] in which the Jewish army was to later be incorporated. My colleagues from the Schellenberg Office[40] had close contacts with the Arabs. At this time Mussolini[41] also had proclaimed himself "the "Sword of Islam". Obviously it interested me to know how far Jewry in Palestine maintained itself as a minority, while infiltrating the population there. The Jews were only waiting to reach a numerical majority in order to appropriate this land. So I was extremely interested in whether and when this new Jewish state would be established.

---

39 Haganah, Hebrew "Defence", armed self-defence organisation of the Jews during the British Mandate in Palestine. Participating in the battle for the creation of Palestine sic along with all that that involved.

40 Walter Schellenberg, SS Gruppenführer, Chief of Office IV in the Reich Security Head Office, succeeded Canaris as Chief of the Germany Army. In April 1949 sentenced by the US Military Tribunal to 6 years' imprisonment, pardoned in December 1950, died in summer 1952.

41 Benito Mussolini, Duce of the Partito Nazionale Fascista, Prime Minister of Italy from 1922 to 1945 (interruption 1944), finally government chief of the Reppublica Sociale Italiana, murdered in 1945 by Communist partisans with his friend Clara Petacci.

The Step to the Security Service

In Palestine Jewish uprisings were quite frequent. I heard through a friend of Mildenstein's, a Mr. von Bodelschwingh, who had been settled a long time in Palestine, of the arrival of a leading Jew from Palestine in Berlin. He was active in an influential position within the Jewish military organisation. Through Mr. von Bodelschwingh an invitation was issued to this Jew to meet us as a guest of the SD Head Office in Berlin. I met him several times, and we ate together in the "Traube" and spoke about things in general. He did not really beat about the bush, but narrated to me some interesting things which I edited in a report to my superior service office. Heydrich marked this report as "good", a sign that he was interested in it; for if something did not attract his interest he crossed the whole thing out with his blue pencil. Later this Jew sent me an invitation to Palestine, so in autumn 1937 I travelled in the company of SS-Oberscharführer Hagen through Poland, Romania and Syria to Palestine, then further to Egypt. We came to Haifa, where the representative of the German news agency, Dr. Reichert, received us.

At that time there were a couple of bomb attacks in Palestine so it was not a safe place, and only with the greatest effort did I obtain permission to stay there 24 hours. I made full use of the single day, admired buildings and city sights and became acquainted with an extremely impressive landscape. After all I had indeed read so much about Palestine that I was glad to get to know this land. Then I travelled directly to Alexandria, where we were guests of the president of the Young Arab lawyers for three days. Here once again Dr. Reichert waited for us, this time in the company of Mr. Genz, the representative of the DNB (German News Agency) in Egypt. Through the mediation of Dr. Reichert my former Jewish guest in Berlin also came to Cairo. We met in the Menz house, where he proposed among other things a German aviation line to Palestine within the scope of general cooperation, also especially in relation to emigration.

I wanted indeed to visit the Grand Mufti and had made an appointment with my former Jewish guest for a new meeting in Haifa or Tel Aviv. My writer's identification card from the *Berliner Tageblatt* did not at all work with the English passport authorities in Cairo, and on account of ongoing bombing attacks I was told there: "I'm sorry ...", and that was the end of the matter. Even during our journey there the timing of our Palestine visit had turned out as unfavourably as possible, but that we could not know in advance. Peaceful times would have been better and more favourable to a thorough study of such things. It would be many years before I was able to become personally acquainted with the Grand Mufti; that happened during the war, when he came to Berlin from Italy for the treatment of an eye ailment. At that time he was under the protection of the Schellenberg Office and I was invited to a dinner at his guest house, to which the other department heads who had something to do with the Arabs were also invited.

As a gift Dr. Reichert gave me a mail bag belonging to the British Mandate's Aviation Society in Palestine that had been stolen by the Arabs. In it were, among other things, some important letters, for example, addressed to the High Commissioner and to the English Lord Chief Justice of the Mandate power. These letters were passed on by us to the Foreign Office. When on 1 September 1939 the war with Poland broke out, they were published on the first page of the *Völkischer Beobachter*; for the documents contained evidence that the cooperation of the Mandate with the official Jewish offices operated to the disadvantage and harm of the Arabs. However, these questions did not interest me generally for I was not responsible for them.

Furthermore, a visit to the then king Abdullah was also prepared for me. I was advised in the case of a chess-game to lose, for that was the custom. With the Arab or Jewish rebels we did not in general have any contact during our travel. I travelled back to Berlin and thereby stepped on Austrian soil again for the first time in years, though it was only a few metres when, on the return journey through Italy to the border between Austria and Switzerland near the Bodensee, I had the pleasure of breathing the air of my homeland for a few minutes. I had never returned to Austria, until my professional order to Vienna in Spring 1938.

Continuation Of My SS Work In The Reich

After my return, I continued my study of Jewish affairs with increased eagerness. Slowly I grew used to my task and acquired a certain feel for my subject. What historical development every individual type of our enemies underwent was traced deep into the past, what had branded him as an enemy, what goals he pursued at that time and now, how he disguised himself, who helped him directly or indirectly. If any other office needed help, they contacted Office VII. But already the predecessor of Office VII, "Office J", had by itself sought through the *Leitheft*'s to place an armoury of information at the disposal of the other offices of the SD. If any V-man (informer) for example, stationed somewhere in France encountered a Jewish institution with which he was not acquainted, then he inquired at the Schellenberg Office. If he could not obtain any information there, the enquiry was passed to Office VII; from here one obtained, in every case, the necessary information in the shortest possible time.

From 1937 I came into contact with Heydrich more often. He ordered me to hold talks in the SD school at Bernau on my field of specialisation, whereby I was then slowly but surely raised above the others and, although I was only an SS First Sergeant, I enjoyed certain favours which otherwise were allowed only to the senior ranks, such as, for example, the use of a car for service travels. I was increasingly incorporated in services positions and service tasks. Heydrich called me to his office quite often. I did not need to wait long in the antechamber, but Heydrich's antechamber was always very interesting, because one met all types of people with whom one would not easily have come into contact. In all, up to Heydrich's death, I was perhaps called to his office fifty times. There were times in which I went to him perhaps three times in a fortnight, when special matters were at hand, and then again there were times when I saw him once a month. I noted that independent tasks were assigned to me, for example, shortly before my departure for the Near East, the briefing of SS 2nd Lieutenant Rösler as Jewish specialist in Upper Silesia. So I took with me comprehensive materials, for there existed a special situation for the Jews in Upper Silesia on account of an agreement between Germany and Poland. I reported to the Service Office in Breslau[42]; the chief there kept me waiting for three days. Then he received me and thundered at me: "If you come from the Head Office to spy on me, then I shall place you against the wall". I made it clear to him that I had not received any such "spying mission" from anybody, but only had an order to instruct his advisors on Jewish matters.

A short time previously I had slipped on the parquet floor and fell on my right hand in such a way that I broke it in two places. it was then placed in a cast, and I got used to giving my signature with the left hand. In Berlin Dannecker[43] sat near me as specialist on assimilationist Jewry. I was now very angry that, while leaving, I had to make my salute with my left hand; I disappeared in as dignified a manner as possible from the office and promptly met one of his Captains by

---

42   Now Wrocław

43   Theodor Dannecker, SS Hauptsturmführer, Eichmann's colleague in the RSHA, in the Jewish department in France 1942, Bulgaria 1943, Italy 1944.

whom I was taken to task on account of my unorthodox salutation. The week of my transfer to Breslau was filled with difficulties; I wrote a report every day to my superior Wisliceny. Promptly after a week I travelled back to Berlin without having accomplished much. Later this all-powerful Major was dismissed. I met him again later when I was by then a Lieutenant Colonel but he was still a Major. It was at some lecture. He tried to be friendly with me, but I had nothing more to do with him – for me, the matter was over.

While I was still conducting my scientific research in Office VII on world-view counter warfare, there was already a department within the Gestapo which concerned itself with Jewish affairs. It was at that time led by government councillor Friedrich Lange,[44] whose successor was governmental advisor Kurt Lischka.[45] Already at that time there existed the "Reich Union of Jews". It acquired shape and form under the two mentioned government councillors. The basis of this Reich Union of Jews was established legally and the Chief of the Security Police was appointed as its supervisory authority. Ever new by-laws were issued to this Reich Union, which grew steadily. The leader of this Reich Union in Germany was Dr. Eppstein.[46] As the specialist for the "World Zionist Union" and the Jewish orthodoxy within Office VII, I was frequently asked for clarification on many issues. I was the only one in Office VII who dealt with Jewish functionaries, but even at that time I did not exercise any executive powers of any sort within the SD.

Stronger Contacts with the Jews

At that time a criminal district inspector, Kuchmann, was a junior official in the Gestapo Office. These people had hardly any idea what a Zionist was, nor did they know Zionism's ideological characteristics, it's strategy and aims. They had made it very easy for themselves by simply demanding the necessary information from Office VII, to which I

---

44   Dr. Friedrich Lange, SS Sturmbannführer, Commander of the Security Police for the General district of Latvia in the second World War.

45   Kurt Lischka, during the second World War, Commander of the Security Police in Paris, sentenced *in absentia* in France to death, in Cologne to 10 years' imprisonment.

46   Dr. Paul Eppstein was appointed by Eichmann to serve as Jewish Elder in Theresienstadt, where his deputies were Jakob Edelstein and Benjamin Murmelstein. He was shot in Theresiestadt in 1944.

Germans reading Der Stürmer newspaper in Berlin 1933.

belonged at that time. Soon such requests occurred no longer in writing but by telephone. I was asked to come over for a discussion on obscure cases, and so I went to the office of Kuchmann and was present at the interrogations that he had to carry out when his departmental head had ordered him, for example, to interrogate Dr. Eppstein. In this way I got together with other offices too; this was advantageous both for the Gestapo which I could serve through my theoretical knowledge and also for me personally, because these discussions extended my knowledge of Jewry in Germany and throughout the world. Besides I could always request through Kuchmann to speak to Rabbi So-and-so, if I hoped to obtain useful information from him. The first meeting I had with Dr. Eppstein, and the Chief Rabbi Dr. Leo Baeck[47] Kuchmann mediated for me. I then discussed in depth with Dr. Baeck the problems of orthodoxy and with Dr. Eppstein the current practical questions of Zionist politics.

In general I could recognise if my conversation partners were not divulging the full facts, because I also had the reports from our informants and agents. These reports I could test through my conversations with the Jews and vice-versa the opinions of my Jewish conversation partners through our informers and agents. That was a typical method of the SD with its possibility of double checking.

---

47   Dr. Leo Baeck, Chief rabbi, Chairman of the Reich Association of German Jews, was sent to the Theresienstadt camp and freed from there in 1945.

Dr. Eppstein was an extraordinarily skilled, educated and well-bred lawyer; exactly like Dr. Löwenherz[48] and he didn't have in the least degree anything "obsequious" about him. He spoke freely and openly – and indeed with courage, whereby it may have been decisive that these Jewish knew that no sympathy would be given to them on the basis of these conversations. I had instructed my guards and waiting-room people to arrange the visits of these Jewish functionaries in such a way that they would not lose any unnecessary waiting time. They came, were treated by the guards politely and courteously and allowed in without much ado, since they were indeed regular visitors. They took a seat and we spoke and acted as is customary among gentlemen.

When one deals for a long time with an enemy it is unavoidable that one obtains an insight into their attitude, just through the conversation which now and then also touches upon the personal, and thus there arises a personal relationship. That was true of both sides, just as they could read from my face, so I could from theirs. In the beginning they may have allowed caution to rule, but after they had ascertained that I never harboured any devious thoughts, they got used in the course of the conversation to speaking quite openly. Indeed they also knew – and I have never made a secret of that – that I did not foster any prejudice and hatred against the individual Jew. I saw, and see, the necessity and the indispensability of the battle, but only in the political field. Streicher's[49] views were already at that time far from finding even the least approval in me. Already the word "anti-Semitism" did not please me. After my return from the Near East I expressly warned against the use of this word. In precisely the same way I did not wish ever to hear of so-called Jewish ritual murder. Streicher and his circle very much liked to use this term.

The teacher Wurm, whom I liked very much personally, occupied a special place with Streicher; I said to them: "Children, what then do you wish with your "ritual murder" ... what sort of nonsense is that? Perhaps this occurred once in the Middle Ages, but then there occurred also other things like witch-burnings on the part of the Catholic Church – only because these women were blond! But today

---

48   Josef Richard Löwenherz (1884-1960) was an Austrian Zionist whom Eichmann made the office director of the revived Jewish Religious Community in Vienna.

49   Julius Streicher, Gauleiter of Central Franconia, publisher of the weekly *Der Stürmer*. He fell from grace with Adolf Hitler through an accusation of self-enrichment through the Aryanisation programme. The IMT in Nuremberg sentenced him to death in 1946.

there is not any orthodox Jew who wishes a ritual murder. These are all fairy-tales exactly like the "Elders of Zion" who lead and direct everything. From a healthy standpoint all that has nothing to do with the world-view counter-battle!" I knew that the SS Reichsführer subscribed to these mysterious and half-mystical ideas and Streicher always had a "handle" on him when he could narrate this subject that consolidated these old ideas. When later, during the war, a book was published on Jewish ritual murder and the SS Führer wished to bring this story into the newspapers, naturally nobody could publicly contradict the content of this book, the Jews themselves least of all. If there had been ritual murders by Jews once, that was all so long ago that it is irrelevant to the present. That is my view.

A Political Solution Through Emigration

Dr. Six headed Office VII at that time and developed the counter-battle on a purely scientific basis. He had eyes and ears everywhere and knew precisely who headed this or that institution, who this or that person was. It is clear that under such an office chief we flatly denied fairy-tales like "The Elders of Zion" or Jewish ritual murders. For us it was a question of collecting information and this task of Office VII was in full swing before the war. After the beginning of the war the research work decreased, especially since the specialists were transferred to other more important war tasks.

In January 1938 I was promoted to 2nd Lieutenant. The annexation of Austria tore me out of my research work. Up to this time I had practically nothing at all to do with the executive aspects of the Jewish question or the Jewish legislation.

Many weeks before the annexation we had prepared the Austria action on filing cards, insofar as it concerned Office VII. Regardless of service rank or position we proceeded in twenty-four hour three-shift work in accordance with the information requirement of the SD and Gestapo. We included the Jewish functionaries and Freemasons in all world-view fields. We sat like schoolboys on benches and wrote the filing cards, and then they were arranged alphabetically, ordered according to spelling. With this filing card material the first wave of the SD swept into Austria.

According to an established plan Sipo and SD spread out over Austria. In the meantime I was held back in Berlin to prepare myself for my first practical task: the reorganisation of the Jewish organisational life with a view to emigration. A fortnight after the annexation I suddenly received the order to go without delay to Vienna and to report there to the commanding officer of the Sipo and the SD, SS Oberführer Dr. Stahlecker,[50] who was later replaced by Dr. Rasch.[51] Naturally I was glad to be in Austria once again, and insofar as the service allowed it, I also made some personal visits.

With Second Lieutenant Pfeiffer, who at that time worked on the problem of the Austrian "legitimists"[52] in Vienna, I undertook a journey to Sonntagsberg. There nearby there was a Habsburg castle where the Hohenbergs lived. In the Schleiten castle in Strengberg lived the Baroness Scoda. As a boy I had many motorbike accidents, one of them in the vicinity of Strengberg, where I lay with a concussion and was brought to an inn of this castle. When the Baroness Marianne Scoda learnt of this, she visited me at the inn, and had me taken to the castle where she looked after me for a couple of days. The Scodas are relatives of the Hohenbergs. Back in Austria I obtained the commission to visit the different SD sectors and especially within the scope of the Jewish question. Pfeiffer drove with me in the black Rothschild limousine.

On the way from Vienna to Linz we spent the night in Strengberg. In the castle I was received very ungraciously because I wore the black SS uniform. I gave the baroness my explanation for my visit while her mother, an old lady of around eighty, did not listen to or hide her contempt. Baroness Marianne then requested my intervention for some relative who had been taken into custody as a "legitimist". I said to her that I neither could, nor wanted to, intervene. Pfeiffer was surprised by my harshness, especially since he was himself the specialist responsible for this. In reality I later interested myself in the fate of this person. What I experienced there gave further evidence of the fact that some higher personalities, even of the Gestapo or other offices, could interfere in others' territories. I heard later, that the

---

50   Dr. Franz Stahlecker, SS Brigadeführer, Commanding Officer of the Security Police and SD in Vienna and Prague, chief of the Einsatz group A in the Baltic during the German-Soviety war. In March 1942 killed by partisans in Krasnogvardejsk.

51   Dr. Otto Rasch, SS Brigadeführer, chief of Einsatz group C during the German-Soviet war, declared in the Einsatz Group trial in Nuremberg to be unfit to stand trial.

52   The Austrian legitimists supported Otto von Habsburg against Adolf Hitler.

archduke was taken to Mauthausen concentration camp and ordered to constantly push a block of stone up a hill; once arrived at the top he had to let the stone hurtle down again. The order to do this apparently came from Göring through the SS Führer to Pohl,[53] and from Pohl to the commandant at the Mauthausen camp.

When I came to Vienna it became clear to me that it had obviously been forgotten to set a Jewish specialist to work. During this fortnight the Jewish political life had already been fully smashed and I went about rebuilding the Jewish organisations once again and at the same time – I belonged still to Office VII – securing the scientifically interesting archive and library materials, having them packed in crates under my supervision, and myself numbering crates and preparing a list of contents. The library was packed cleanly according to subjects and went in wagons to Berlin, where it was then preserved in the cellar of Office VII. The interesting material of the Jewish organisations left Vienna in this way, but I left to the Israelite Religious Community in Vienna their library because these people needed it partly for their work. In the SD sectors of Klagenfurt, Innsbruck, Graz, Linz, etc. the same material was likewise collected, but on a much smaller scale, from the local offices of the SD, transported to the Vienna central office and transferred to a Viennese forwarding company. For this company there worked two furniture packers who came into contact with the SD in this way. One day they requested to be accepted into the SD. One was two metres tall and hefty, the other small and very meek. This small, meek furniture packer then later became caretaker in the office building of the SD. Thus indeed was it with us, each could become blessed in his own way.

After two years' service in the SD Head Office, I decided to leave the church, voluntarily, it was my own decision and my church membership had no influence on my promotion.

---

53   Oswald Pohl, SS Gruppenführer, Chief of the SS Economic Administration Head Office (WVHA), sentenced to death by the US Military Tribunal in Nuremberg to death on 3 November 1946. Hanged on 8 June 1951 in the Landsberg/Lech prison.

For a Greater Emigration of the Jews

My chief task in Vienna was to encourage Jewish emigration. In my role as a specialist in Zionist world-organisations I must have seemed to the chief of the Sipo and the SD, Heydrich, as the specialist most suited for this. First of all I had discussions with the official Dr. Ebener,[54] who still wore the Austrian Commissioner uniform and dragged around a heavy sabre. Later this Dr. Ebener was to become the permanent representative of the Stapo control office in Vienna. I also held talks with Dr. Stahlecker on my programme and my intention of reviving first of all the Jewish organisations that had been shattered in these days, and indeed insofar as I needed them for the emigration of the Jews from Austria. I made it clear to him that I needed an orderly, workable Jewish central structure which I would later hand over to a suitable Jewish functionary. I could count on the understanding and approval of Dr. Stahlecker, I then formulated my goals in writing in the form of a memorandum, had this signed and had the authority of the superior of the Stapo office in Vienna that I would proceed in this manner and not otherwise. The Stapo was also instructed to take all my wishes into consideration and to make things easy for me.

I asked Dr. Ebener to bring to me the former leaders of the Jewish organisations in Austria who had been imprisoned. I had an office in the Metropol Hotel to which these were summoned. Dr. So-and-so, who was too old, Dr. So-and-so, who was too slow and infirm, Dr. So-and-so, who was too polite and servile to me. Then came Dr. Josef Löwenherz, who had already been active as the official of the Israelite Religious Community. I posed the usual questions about personal data, etc. Löwenherz did not indeed know me and he lied to me in some instances in his anxiety and distress. Thereupon I lost my composure and boxed him on the ear. That was the first and last time in my entire period of Jewish work that I attacked a Jew. Later in the presence of my subordinate I apologised emphatically and officially to Dr. Löwenherz for my lack of self-control. In the course of the coming years I was able to work excellently with him.

I made it clear to Dr. Löwenherz that the Jewish organisational life must be rebuilt and the situation whereby Jews were imprisoned and thus all Jewish life is crippled must stop. For it was now a matter of ensuring Jewish emigration took place in an efficient manner. Therefore I suggested to him that the reorganisation should especially aim at the

---

54   Dr. Ebner was a Gestapo official.

Josef Löwenherz (Left), in the parish hall of the Jewish Community of Vienna on March 18, 1938.

strengthening of the Zionist organisations and thereby promote Jewish emigration. For this the assimilationist Jews did not interest me, whereas on the other hand the Israelite Religious Community in Vienna should be the focus of a markedly Zionist political agenda in Austria.

I intended to make Löwenherz the office director of the Israelite Religious Community and therefore I gave him paper and pencil in his cell and the task of describing to me the organisational structure of the Jewish life in Vienna and in Austria, along with his plans of working and his ideas on resolving the practical issues. I outlined to him my own plan and ideas, especially in relation to Jewish emigration. Thereupon Löwenherz went back into his cell and I instructed him that he perhaps would have to remain in custody but was no longer to be regarded as a prisoner. I also felt that Löwenherz had the intellectual aptitude to be able to lead such a large apparatus.

The next day he came back from his cell, and he read me his proposals. I was very surprised that it corresponded entirely to my own opinion. It lay also fully in line with my discussions with the commanding officer of the Sipo and the SD. Löwenherz said to me that his watch and something else had been taken from him. I said to Dr. Ebener that Löwenherz must have his watch and his things back. I then released Löwenherz and sent him home.

Now Löwenherz was the office director, he "unearthed" a large number of colleagues and incorporated them into the Israelite Religious Community. Even Dr. Storfer,[55] a commercial councillor, who had been an Austro-Hungarian officer during the first World War, began to work more closely with me, along with Dr. Neumann, a very well-known surgeon. They intervened for imprisoned Jews and because the apparatus of the Israelite Religious Community needed a large number of officials, I complied in some cases with the wishes expressed. So there soon spread the myth that Storfer was the man who had at his disposal "connections in high places" and that, by virtue of these connections, he could let imprisoned Jews go free. Storfer was a wealthy man, but he certainly never took a penny from his Jewish comrades. Through his long relationship with us there arose a degree of trust.

The commercial councillor and I met frequently, and he also befriended Dr. Löwenherz. He swung back and forth between Dr. Löwenherz and Dr. Rothenberg who were also among the leading figures of the Religious Community. I must admit that I had a liking for this councillor of commerce, Dr. Storfer, a liking that my colleague, SS Major Hans Günther,[56] could not understand at all. Storfer once showed me a book that his army chief, a field marshal, had published. It contained many photographs. On one page was a photo of Storfer as administrative major of the Imperial and Royal Army. He had a very nice and orderly manner about him, and I never waved him away; for he was like me. He betrayed nobody, did special commissions for me and communicated any difficulties to me that could arise in the case of any of our offices, and was to a certain extent a sort of agent, but not against the Jews. He was an agent whom I could even install in our own apparatus to get information.

Neither in Vienna, nor in Prague or Berlin did I ever appoint a single Jewish office director who would have said "of course" or "as you order" to all that I proposed. Other "compliant instruments" may perhaps have been appointed, by regional departmental heads of the Stapo or Stapo control offices, but I never did that. Naturally, subordinate offices of the Jews were anyway provided with instructions and guidelines by

---

55   Dr. Berthold Storfer (1880-1944) was a Jewish Austrian commercial councillor who helped organise the transport of Jews from the Reich to Palestine.

56   Hans Günther, SS Sturmbannführer, Eichmann's colleague, presumably killed on 10 May 1945.

their Central Office and were only implementing organs. But I could not have anything to do with "yes men" in such important roles; the Jewish organisation would not have functioned and the Jewish offices would have needed ten or twenty times more personnel. Precisely because I placed Jewish personalities at the top, the organisation was clear and transparent. The Israelite Religious Community in Vienna worked with around four hundred officials. They had their own registries, and corresponding office directors whom I protected personally from any attack. These Jewish personalities continuously contradicted me and had their "if"s and "but"s. Such people of distinction are conscious of their importance, which they wish to see preserved even in front of the service's supervisory authority and all the subordinate officials, and are therefore not at all easy, but are so much the more valuable, colleagues.

Through the reconstruction of the Jewish organisational life in Vienna and my direct task of promoting emigration by all possible means, there was finally founded the *"Central Office for Jewish Emigration"*. In order to emigrate the Jew needed an incredible amount of papers: a tax clearance certificate, a criminal record certificate, a whole series of documents which were necessary for the acquisition of a passport. For example, the tax clearance certificate, which was most difficult to obtain and was valid only for six to eight weeks. The Jews had to wait at the government offices until the normal working hours had almost come to an end; if he then finally had the good fortune and opportunity to speak to the counter clerks this was an exceptional case. As a rule he had to come back three or four times. If he managed to finally obtained this tax clearance certificate, then he had to stand in a long queue, at a number of other offices. Even then it could still be that "Jews wait", according to the pleasure and mood of the counter clerks. The consequence of this was that the six or eight weeks validity of the tax clearance certificate had expired and he had to start again at the beginning whereas, in the mean time, other papers became invalid.

Then Dr. Rothenberg and Dr. Löwenherz came to me one day and said: "Sturmführer, this cannot go on. What else should the Jews do to be able to emigrate? If it is not possible to grant the Jews preferential treatment, then you will not be free of them even though the Jew is willing to emigrate". They described to me in detail the existing difficulties; thereupon I gave it some thought. I presented everything to the commanding officer of the Sipo and the SD, Dr. Stahlecker, and made a proposal of concentrating all these counter clerks who had to do with emigration under our control in a single building that the Sipo would give me. There the Jews could be dealt with by a conveyor belt system and granted everything necessary for emigration. I had the good fortune of having in Dr. Stahlecker a superior who understood the problem immediately and he went with me on the same day to see the Reich Commissioner Bürckel.[57] The Reich Commissioner was enthusiastic and prepared on the same evening an order relating to this.

This story is an example of how right it was not to appoint as office director any compliant "yes-men" in the hands of the Security Police", but people of merit who were assertive. People without distinction would in this case have come crawling, whimpering and trying to gloss over the problems. In this way a major problem was identified, an appropriate solution sought, and resolved in the shortest time.

Löwenherz visited me almost daily or at the least twice a week. Even later I made it my custom to receive the high Jewish functionaries on a regular basis. They made their submission to me and requested a decision. Everybody who came to me to get a decision or to communicate his measures and ordinances presented me with a memo drawn up in duplicate. Either I approved or refused, and at the next meeting I then gave them back the memo with my marginal notes, provided with an approval or refusal and other notes. In order to avoid unnecessary paperwork the Jews received the original. I retained the carbon copy. Thus I remember that Dr. Löwenherz had an entire lever-arch file with such memos, and soon even three. Naturally I also made it my duty to hold discussions in the building of the Israelite Religious Community in Vienna. At such discussions the divisional heads and the departmental chiefs of the Jewish organisations were present. I myself brought along some particular specialist of my office. I then sat next to the office chief who led the discussion, and in this way many purely functional work conferences were conducted with full attendance. In this way the service supervision incumbent on the chief of the Sipo and the SD was also carried out.

The proposal of a "Central Office for Jewish Emigration" in Vienna came from me. When Heydrich came to Vienna after a fairly long time, the Central Office was already running quite satisfactorily. Heydrich went over it a whole afternoon. shortly after I was ordered to Berlin.

---

57   Josef Bürckel, Gauleiter of the Pfalz, later of Vienna, finally of Saarland-Lothringen, committed suicide in September 1944.

The Jews in Vienna and in Austria in general had great respect for Dr. Löwenherz, and I did my bit to reinforce this respect. Dr. Löwenherz led his four hundred Jewish officials and employees in an excellent manner. I left him his regular registrars who had the same rights and duties as an official employed by the state. Even in the eyes of those Jews who were politically hostile to him Dr. Löwenherz possessed authority, and they did not dare to cause difficulties for him. They indeed saw that this man was a *"persona grata"*[58] among the representatives of the Chief of the Security Police and the SD, and I think until today that few men could handle any authority with such generosity and such openness as Dr. Löwenherz, and later his colleagues in Prague and Berlin. The collaboration with the Jewish organisations was later made a principle policy by Heydrich but the idea was born on the day that I saw Löwenherz returning to his cell with pencil and paper.

The Night of Broken Glass

The "Night of Broken Glass" surprised me like a clap of thunder from a bright sky with its retributions for the assassination of the German diplomat von Rath in Paris, by the Polish Jew Grynszpan[59]. After the occupation of France Grynszpan was delivered to us; I personally conducted the final interrogation with him. After that it was certain to me that this young Jew clearly had no men behind him but carried out the act through his own motivation. Nevertheless I must make an important reservation: Grynszpan lived for a long time in solitary confinement and although no purely physical illness occurred to him, one can no longer consider a man after a long solitary confinement as being fully independent in terms of negotiations.

The "Night of Broken Glass" raged also in Vienna. I arrived there precisely when an SS Brigadeführer[60] sought to set aflame the synagogue near the building of the Jewish Religious Community. I saw a typewriter that had been flung on the ground. I confronted the Brigadeführer even though I was of a much lower rank, but after

---

58 A fully acceptable person

59 Herschel Grynspan killed the embassy counsellor Ernst von Rath in Paris on 7 November 1938. His intention was to kill the German Ambassador in Paris, Count Johannes von Moltke.

60 SS Brigadier General

all I was a responsible official. I put an end to this riot as quickly as possible. A number of Jews in Vienna came running agitatedly to me and asked for protection. I let them camp and sleep in my office. The next day they went back to their homes. This whole "Night of Broken Glass" was in total opposition to our wishes and our goal. The Jews themselves must have recognised this, for why else would they have "crawled into the jaws of the lion"! by seeking refuge in an office of the Sipo and the SD. The Jews must have known that we were absolutely against it. I myself knew nothing about it and had received not a single instruction or order.

Throughout the day as well as the night there stood a guard before the Palais to whom I gave strict instructions to allow nobody in. The synagogue was ablaze, but I also effected in the quickest way the exit of the people from the building of the Israelite Religious Community and set a policeman on guard until the mania had passed. I shuddered at the fate of the comprehensive inventory of filing cards held in the Religious Community on which our entire migration capability was recorded. They were essential to maintain the tempo of some thousand emigrants per day. If they had been destroyed I would have need months to reconstruct them.

Who may have had a hand in the "Night of Broken Glass" I cannot say. In any case, it was not through any official offices of the Reich! Neither the SD nor the Gestapo had anything to do with it. They were on the contrary infuriated, because they had, in accordance with the instructions of the SS Führer, through the most painstaking detailed work, built up organisations and offices which were ruthlessly attacked and destroyed.

Now, just when we were trying to let the organisational tasks of these Jewish functionaries run undisturbed as far as possible, these institutions were smashed, just as the Jewish businesses were. We were speechless. The SD was an extended arm of the German police. These rabble acts did not suit the character of the police. These excesses certainly also did not have the sympathy of Goebbels, for from my discussions at that time with officials of his ministry, I know that they too were shocked. Naturally the "Night of Broken Glass" must have been directed and led somehow, but I really have no idea by whom; perhaps by Ley,[61] but I do not know.

---

61   Robert Ley, Reich Organisational leader of the NSDAP, leader of the German Work Front, took his own life in Nuremberg in 1945.

The Night of Broken Glass on 9 November 1938 resulted in the destruction of many Jewish owned shops and offices.

Not only the above mentioned filing cards were preserved in the Religious Community but also the Jewish functionaries performed the entire preparatory work, the correspondence with foreign representatives in Austria or abroad in order to develop new emigration possibilities. They worked on the acquisition of foreign exchange and were orderly people, for the most part, Zionists, who themselves wished to emigrate anyway. For that reason I strove to neutralise the negative consequences of the "Night of Broken Glass" as quickly as possible and not interrupt the normal office operations. Even the examination of the emigration questionnaires was partly undertaken by the officials of the Religious Community to whom I delegated as much responsibility as possible because this was in the interests of the smooth performance of my task.

The "Reich Union of Jews in Germany" had the right to issue ordinances for the Jews, but only after these ordinances had been previously discussed and approved by the responsible departmental head in Gestapo Office IV. In practice this meant that the chief of the Reich Union, Dr. Eppstein, until 1940, submitted his concerns to my predecessor Lischka, or presented, after elaboration, an ordinance inspired by the Gestapo. After 1940 he came to me with all the issues;

they were either approved or discarded. If it was necessary I naturally had to have the other interested central authorities, that were also involved take part. If the proposal was approved it was a legal ordinance and binding for all Jews who came under the Nuremberg Laws.

The "Emigration Fee Ordinance" of the Reich Union was issued before my time. Like the Israelite Religious Community in Vienna, the "Reich Union" also had to carry out this ordinance. The determinations were administered rather more formally and strictly in the Old Reich than in Austria, where Löwenherz presented his submission and I then approved his directives in a short procedure. In the Old Reich, Eppstein had first to travel with the prepared sketch to the Stapo, where the officials studied it in detail. After days and weeks Eppstein received his proposal back and had normally to change it in some points – it was even more bureaucratic, whereas in the Eastern Realm[62] the responsible Jewish chiefs could freely proceed according to their own discretion because they were in all cases covered by the supervisory authority. Only the financial budgetary aspect, thus the emigration expense, was established according to guidelines, and there one could not make rough estimates.

Emigration and its Obstruction in the World

The "Central Office for Jewish Emigration"' which I established in Vienna gave the best evidence of the fact that the German government was serious in solving the Jewish question through emigration, even forced emigration. Although considerable emigration figures were reached, it must be said that already at that time the insufficient readiness of foreign nations and even of the Jews abroad to accept Jews obstructed the efforts of the German government. When, after 1939, those Jewish organisations which had demonstrated the highest performance in the field of emigration saw their activity limited or even stopped, the organisational work of emigration ran into all sorts of difficulties. Insofar as individual Jews had personal connections with foreign European or overseas countries, they made a certain, but in no way brisk, use of these in the years 1933 to 1937. After Hitler came to power there prevailed in Jewish circles a wait-and-see attitude with regard to emigration; for some had assumed the Hitler regime would anyway be only of short duration. This false hope was for propaganda purposes nourished by enemy circles, especially in foreign countries.

---

62   Eastern Realm was the name for Austria during the Third Reich

Now when, at the end of 1936, the final exclusion of Jews from the public life of the German nation was brought into effect, the individual Jew – to a certain degree in an atmosphere of panic – tried to make every arrangement to be able to emigrate. But there existed a sharp foreign currency restriction which made it practically impossible to obtain foreign exchange. Besides, the Jewish emigrants did not know the individual problems of innumerable German offices. However, most important was the fact that now suddenly there were increasingly sharp restrictive measures abroad which opposed these Jewish emigration efforts. Many countries suddenly demanded an increase in the "token funds" for the emigrants which always had to be paid in the particular local currency or in US dollars. Even the requirements to qualify for emigration were in general tightened. Already before my time in Vienna I tried, together with the Jewish political functionaries, everything possible to loosen these obstructions – within the scope of my security police responsibility.

Adolf Böhm's descriptions in his book *Der Judenstaat* prompted me to arrange permission from my superiors to activate the two Jewish "national funds" within the "Zionist Union for Germany" once again. According to their entire aim the Zionist organisations had, since their founding, facilitated the idea of emigration – of course, with Palestine in mind. The British Mandate authority at that time in Palestine had established yearly emigration levels for these Jewish homes anchored in the Balfour Declaration,[63] but these were absolutely insufficient to accept the full stream of those now willing to emigrate. The efforts of the Jewish political leaders in the Old Reich and later in Austria to alleviate the distress of the Jews through illegal emigration were – with regard to Palestine – tolerated, doubtless with the knowledge of the Arab offices responsible for this. In the subsequent period no obstacles were placed in the way of the Zionist organisations. They had permission to meet together, could work freely and travel abroad for the organisation and collection of foreign exchange; they could continue their retraining efforts especially in agricultural professions, and also the orthodox part of the Jews living in the Reich was not prevented by us insofar as it was occupied with emigration efforts.

---

63   Balfour Declaration. The name is related to James Earl of Balfour, 1902-05 English Prime Minister, 1915 First Lord of the Admiralty, 1916 Foreign Minister, made a declaration named after him, on 2 November 1917, about the establishment of a Jewish homeland in Palestine.

During my entire activities I never heard of an emigration plan that the Reich Bank President Dr. Schacht[64] is said to have set up although just the position of its initiator at that time would have made this "plan" uncommonly interesting.

It remains a bitter fact that "Jewish persecution", became a powerful propaganda issue against the Third Reich, but no country in the world extended its hand to accept significant numbers of the Jewish population. Many Jewish as well as non-Jewish authorities hoped that emigration on a grand scale would bring about a quick resolution of the problem. Both sides were disappointed. At that time the Jewish leaders were very critical with regard to many foreign governments which, through a continual tightening of the emigration conditions, allowed only a modest level of Jewish emigration. But to be fair it must be stated that even the German red tape worked extremely slowly and, besides, the foreign exchange control acted as a brake. In this way up to 1938, out of the 500,000 religious Jews present in Germany in 1933, including the Jews in the sense of the Nuremberg Laws, no more than around 130,000 were able to emigrate. In this connection the creation of a "Central Office for Jewish Emigration" in Vienna was now a really great achievement. Obergruppenführer Heydrich had suggested to me that I carry out the emigration from Austria as quickly as possible; and I believe that I fulfilled this order in the best possible way for both sides.

Dr. Richard Löwenherz as office director of the Religious Community, Dr. Rothenberg as chief of the Palestine Office and the two leaders of the Jewish orthodox institutions, whose names unfortunately escape me, worked with us on a proper objective basis. Passport offices, Gestapo, the upper financial steering committee, Ministry of Economics and the Jewish organisations themselves were represented by expert managers in the "Central Office". The Jew who wished to emigrate could have his passport issued within a few hours, more quickly than the German citizen.

I had the instruction to also solve the problem of the "acquisition of foreign exchange", for which I received a concrete Jewish proposal and sent Jewish political functionaries abroad. In this were involved especially Löwenherz, Rothenberg, commercial councillor Storfer and the leaders of the "Aguda Israel" who wished to raise money from the

---

64   Dr. Hjalmar Schacht, Reich Bank president, Reich Minister from 1933 to 20 January 1939, acquitted by the IMT in Nuremberg on 20 September 1946.

foreign Jewish aid organisations. They returned to Vienna with modest results. The foreign exchange thus obtained was first "offered" to the Reichsbank according to the legal regulations. In our case it meant that it was checked by the foreign exchange control office in Vienna, for I had already previously obtained the permission to simply have the deposited foreign exchange amounts placed at the disposal of the emigrating Jews by the Israelite Religious Community – under the supervision of the Control Office in Vienna – in order to add this to the demanded "token funds".

The exchange rate of the foreign currency that was placed at the disposal of the emigrating Jews was determined from case to case by the Religious Community itself. The exchange rate was established according to the financial situation of the individual Jew; the "token funds" were in this manner placed practically free of charge at the disposal of Jews who were almost without any property, whereas the propertied or indeed rich Jew had to pay a twenty-fold higher exchange rate. The "profits" obtained in this way served the defrayal of the budget of the Israelite Religious Community with its five hundred officials. From it was also paid the welfare of the needy Jews; for the exclusion of Jews from the various social fields of the German nation resulted in the fact that a social insurance had to be organised, otherwise a certain percentage of the Jews – beyond the normal – would have fallen victim to criminality.

The Jews had to receive at least as much support as to be able to eat and buy themselves boots or trousers that they needed. For that I had to scrape up funds and therefore I enabled the Jewish functionaries leave the country so that they could conduct their foreign exchange collection tours to England.

Now I did not have a single non-Jewish lawyer sitting in the "Central Office" who would have known the entire foreign exchange legislative documents as such. I knew nothing of the existence of a law for "foreign exchange aid". What laws were passed in the meantime in Berlin were also not known to me. I was interested in the emigration. I did not worry about the foreign exchange laws, but just single-mindedly went my own way. In the foreign exchange office in Vienna there sat a Reichsbank councillor Wolf, an approachable, unbureaucratic gentleman. I described my needs to this man. I related to him how I had in the "Central Office" all the responsible officials together with the Jewish functionaries on a sort of conveyor belt in order to make possible a quick handling of the red tape in matters of emigration. Now it transpired that the emigration offices constantly raised the token funds and really did not omit any effort to get at the throats of the Jews.

On our side we made all efforts to bring them as quickly as possible to emigration, wherein the Jews themselves helped the authorities. In this way we supported the Jews and they us, mutually. But a large amount of foreign exchange was necessary, and when, for example, the USA demanded token funds of two hundred and fifty dollars per head, other countries placed, compared to this, even higher demands. I explained to him further the necessity of the financing of the work of the Jewish Religious Community, the financing of insurance, its medical aid and everything else; for the Jews were allocated no money by the state. So I asked this banker to grant permission for the Religious Community to sell their dollars at the highest exchange rate. I dictated my endorsement and was therewith covered. Then I could say gleefully to my friend Löwenherz: "Now you can flog your foreign exchange, deliver it to Wolf, there it will only be deposited, but you have it at your disposal, you can thus go ahead. If you have ten families and every family needs five hundred or a thousand dollars of token funds, then you get this sum from Wolf and need only to produce the proof that you have exchanged 10,000 dollars not for 30,000 marks but for 300,000 and in some cases even for 600,000." Then, one day, Löwenherz came to me and related the case of a Jew who still had money at his disposal and was ready to pay twenty marks for every dollar of token funds. As usual I approved that and waited for everything to proceed in order as usual.

Inexplicably this case was apprehended and caused a huge racket. The Reich Ministry of Economics had taken the view that "Eichmann in Vienna is undercutting the value of the mark abroad". A big commotion began which went up to the SS Reichsführer, but I received not a single criticism from my superior and I know how Heydrich laughed heartily over this escapade and encouraged me to ruthlessly clear the hurdles of these obstacles. Then this "trouble" was smoothed out by my superior.

Once the finance was raised, the Jews in concentration camps went free immediately once a concrete emigration possibility was given, for which my office worked in cooperation with the Jewish organisations. In this respect Dr. Löwenherz was extraordinarily active in exhausting all the possibilities. In spite of the great work and the continual strain on the part of the Jewish organisations, as on the part of my office, the emigration possibilities acquired by us, despite our strenuous work, was not anywhere near enough.

I would like to emphasise that in the years 1938-1939, had the other countries at that time been more willing to accept the Jews, then hardly a single Jew would have still been left in a concentration camp. The ordinance of the SS Reichsführer expressly stated that the Jews in the concentration camps must be immediately released if an emigration possibility for them could be shown. An emigration possibility naturally depended on whether there was a possibility of immigration. So in spite of the attainment of impressive figures, we were only relatively successful because of the reluctance of foreign countries to accept Jews. At this time, and until the beginning of the war with the Soviet Union, the SS Reichsführer and therefore the entire Gestapo and the SD, considered the Jewish question as a question that could only be resolved politically. Acts of arson in synagogues, smashing of shop-windows, looting of shops, and other such things were rejected most severely by me and by my immediate superiors and my comrades.

The Central Offices For Jewish Emigration

After the establishment of the Protectorate of Bohemia and Moravia I received from Heydrich an order to establish a "Central Office for Jewish Emigration" in Prague and around the same time a "Central Office" in Berlin. In broad terms, each of these "Central Offices" worked according to the same system as the Vienna office.

The emigrating Jews could take their entire furniture with them, which was stored in large overseas crates. These crates often had the size of a small furniture van. Shortly afterwards "Administrative and Clearance Offices" were created, for the collection and administration of Jewish assets. Mainly real estate. These departments worked meticulously and were regularly subject to checks by the German Audit Office. It is because of this that many Jews, could, immediately after their arrival in the country of immigration, continue their lives in financial security. The SS Reichsführer often intervened personally in the smallest detail, with regard to the Jewish assets, applying the strictest administrative requirements which were then further processed by lawyers.

The "justification" of the economic measures against the Jews that was valid for us at that time gives at the same time a comprehensive explanation of why, in general, measures were taken against the Jews. I would like to comment on that in the following manner: In the case of the economic measures taken against the Jews, it was a matter of excluding the enemy from the economic life of the nation. The Jew had not only assumed an enormous share of the economy of his host nation but also held key positions, and to such an extent that it did not stand in proportion to his relatively small share in the population.

The commercial exploitation of the German people by the Jews in the harshest of economic conditions created in increasing measure the resentment and wrath of the host people, so that when the NSDAP took up the issue of opposing the Jews in its party programme, it obtained from the start an extraordinarily strong resonance among the German people because there was already present a general trend against this Jewish economic exploitation. It was not a matter of whether ten Jews possessed more than a hundred Germans, but of the fact that the Jews with their extraordinarily sharp understanding of the commercial issues had exploited the German nation's period of distress after Versailles. If the Jew had made an effort in those years of constraint, the NSDAP would never had found such success in the German nation. This battle gained for the NSDAP votes that it would otherwise have never received.

If the exclusion of the Jews from the German economy is considered from this standpoint, then it becomes immediately clear that many Jews themselves were to blame for that. The Jews have also complained that they had to atone for their racial comrades who themselves had brought forth this frightful dilemma. In particular the assimilated Jews were ashamed of their own racial comrades and steered clear if they ever just saw a new immigrant Jew; they themselves referred to them as "scroungers" with whom they did not wish to have anything in common because they felt themselves disgraced by them. The assimilated Jews were aware of the danger of shameless exploitation and wished to prevent difficulties from developing.

For the administration of the Jewish assets it was the principal intention of the SS Reichsführer to secure, within the scope of the then existing laws of the Reich or the Protectorate government, the assets of the Jews and to remove them from the grasp of unauthorized people. The SS Reichsführer ordered that a public-legal body was to handle the assests, and to this end he had the agreement of the other central authorities. I cannot state anything about the detailed work or the very high value of assets that were dealt with in these administrative offices; for I was not responsible for these offices. If I still remember correctly, the supervising authority was the chief of the Sipo and the SD.

In Vienna the Jews at that time had, when they were ready for emigration, ordered their crates and packed their three or four-room flats into them. Then there was nothing further to "collect" apart from "financial assets", for which however only the Chief Comptroller in cooperation with the other offices involved in it, such as the Ministry of Economics, foreign exchange offices, etc. was responsible. But in Prague the Administrative and Processing Office was necessary; for at that time the emigrating Jews could no longer take everything with them as a year earlier in Vienna.

Some experts helped me in the establishment of this administrative and processing office, insofar as it had to do with accounting matters, whereas the legislative part was directed through the crown lawyer of the commanding officer of the Sipo and SD in Prague, an old senior councillor named Maurer[65] from Austria. For Bohemia and Moravia everything was now forced through the Reich Protectorate channel and, after a few weeks, this entity arose. With that my task was fulfilled; for I was not a businessman and the further commercial course of things did not belong to my area of responsibility. Roughly twice a year the Reich audit court sent a controller there who then crouched for weeks behind the books and finally either issued an approval to the supervising authorities or caught them when some issuances were made that he refused. Hundreds of millions of marks were administered, and everybody was glad when everything tallied and no differences emerged. Later there was established also in Vienna such an administrative and processing office on the recommendation of the senior comptroller, but the high-point of the emigration had already been passed.

In Vienna, the supervising authority was the inspector of the Sipo and SD. Both the commanding officer of the Sipo and SD in Prague and the inspector of the Sipo and SD in Vienna carried out special checks. They had head-office SS leaders in the "central offices" as civil employees; for

---

65   Gerhard Maurer, SS Oberführer in the Economic Administration Head
      Office of the SS, departmental leader.

they were not direct government offices, but also not private offices, but offices of a corporate body under public law. These civil employees were in turn checked by some head-office SD members, whereby they were subject to the immediate control of the heads of the "central offices" in Prague and Vienna, Sturmbannführer Gunther and Hauptsturmführer Brunner.[66] For his part the chief of the Sipo and SD had not only to carry out the audits according to the government regulations, because it was a matter of public bodies, but in addition a special departmental head of the administrative head-office of the SD, Sturmbannführer Broecker, was commissioned who carried out the entire annual audits in the administrative offices within the higher sections of the SD.

Personal enrichment from Jewish wealth was, in my opinion, forbidden. How the control measures in the Generalgouvernement were handled I do not know because there the Gestapo Office was in general not responsible for this. However I know one story which is characteristic in itself. An SS Gruppenführer[67] and Lieutenant General of the Police[68] had been an inspector of the Sipo and SD in Munich. One day he was imprisoned, and likewise his chauffeur and several other persons. It emerged from the proceedings before the SS and Police Court that he had appropriated a number of furs for his wife. The outcome was that the General was demoted to an SS man and sent to the front. Nobody wanted to have him in Dirlewanger's probation battalion; I saw him again years later somewhere as an SS Captain. He was promoted many times on account of "bravery before the enemy" and clambered up the entire promotion ladder again. That was a typical example of the punishment of illegal appropriation of foreign wealth. There was nothing like that among my men, but certainly there were more of such incidents which were severely prosecuted and punished.

In Prague, the work went quickly; for I had the good fortune there that the commanding officer of the Sipo and SD was Dr. Stahlecker, who had in the meantime been transferred to Prague. During my

---

66   Anton Aloys Brunner was active in the Jewish question in Vienna, Berlin, Thessaloniki, Paris and Preßburg. He was a SS Sturmbannführer. His work in the mentioned cities consisted of, among other things, participation in the Jewish deportations. In the Austrian capital he was sentenced by a so-called People's Court to death and killed on 10 May 1946.

67   SS Major General

68   The case occurred. Eichmann's description contains several deficient statements in order to avoid mentioning the name of the person concerned who was still living.

absence from Vienna the office was directed by a brother of my regular representative Günther. In Prague, the emigration movement began to operate quickly and the Jews stood in queues. Dr. Edelstein[69] and Weiman were appointed by me as the leaders of the Jewish organisations; I also engaged the leaders of the orthodoxy. In Prague we could spare ourselves much effort and work because we had gone through the entire incubation period in Vienna. In all of the Bohemian-Moravian area there were around 100,000 Jews whom I wished to lead to emigration in a record time.

Dr. Edelstein and the other functionaries had, exactly like Löwenherz, to exhaust all possibilities to promote the emigration of Jews. They too could depend broadly on the experiences gathered by Löwenherz that had to do with the acquisition of immigration approvals and everything related to them. The whole thing was naturally not a deportation but an emigration. Any threats against the Jewish leaders of concentration camps in case they did not fulfil the emigration quotas belong fully to the realm of fantasy, just as also the version – as it has now been indicated to me – that the poor Jews of the Jewish Religious Community were led to emigration whereas the rich Jews normally dealt with the Gestapo. On the contrary: not only in Bohemia and Moravia but also in Austria and in the Old Reich it was my principle to let the rich Jews raise the finances for the emigration of the poor Jews. That seemed to me to be no more than right and economical, and at that time the Jewish leaders felt that it produced among the Jews a sense of social responsibility and a feeling of belonging together; for they told me that this was previously unknown among the Jews. Only on rare occasions did I become involved with visas for individual Jews, for it was the task of the Jewish organisations to get hold of these visas. I only promised the Jewish political functionaries that, should the visas cost money, I would devalue the corresponding Reichsmarks.

On the basis of my experiences in Vienna, I believed that I would be able to arrange the emigration of as many Jews in the Protectorate. Basically it was easier in Prague because I could use the experiences gained by the Religious Community in Vienna. For this reason I often ordered the visit of Dr. Löwenherz to Prague so that he could convey his experiences to the Jewish leaders there. Later I had Löwenherz come to Berlin as well. Basically it was indeed not so pleasant for him to have to drag the fruits of his efforts and experiences everywhere

---

69   Jakob Edelstein (1903-44) was a Zionist who served as a Jewish Elder in Theresienstadt.

and, on the other hand, it was not so fair to Dr. Eppstein in Berlin, for example, to suddenly have to tolerate Löwenherz now as an adviser.

At that time I was fully committed to this task of emigration, and it infuriates me when I now read that I threatened Dr. Kaffka, a Jewish functionary in Prague: "... that I would seize three hundred Jews and send them to Dachau and Merkelsgrün ..." To that I can only say that when Dr. Kaffka pointed out difficulties to me of such a sort that I did, as always, everything thinkable to loosen the block somehow and to acquire other financial prerequisites for Jewish organisational life; thereby – as I should like to repeat here – first, criminality was stopped, secondly, the actual administrative apparatus was financed, and, thirdly, the emigration was financially secured.

Catching Jews street by street and bringing them to emigration was a matter of the Jewish administration, which was granted the greatest freedom of action by me. At that time it was not in any way a matter of deportations, which were not even imagined, but of forced emigration. In cooperation with the Jewish leaders I had the Jews from the interior brought to Prague and thus filled the vacuum arisen through the Jews who had in the meantime succeeded in emigrating. If, for example, there were previously in Prague 50,000 Jews and 20,000 emigrated, then I had place for 20,000 Jews from the provinces, which gradually became free of Jews in this way.

In Prague both the Jews and I had the great advantage that there they were under the control of the Jewish functionaries; these enjoyed my unrestricted trust. The Jews were in this way financially provided for, did not fall victim to criminality so easily and get immersed in an atmosphere of emigration psychosis. Many wrote from Prague to their acquaintances and relatives abroad and emigrated not through their organisations but of their own accord. In the interior they perhaps still had many Czech friends and did not take so quickly to ideas of emigration.

I have since learnt that in October 1938 – almost a year before the war – the Polish government issued a regulation according to which some 60,000 Jews of Polish citizenship would become stateless in Germany, if they did not get a special stamp in their passport that was obtainable only in Poland.[70] These measures of the Polish government could not

---

70   Eichmann refers to the Polish ordinance of 6 October 1938 through which the passes of those citizens who lived outside Poland were declared to be invalid

have been known to me at that time because I was not active in an executive position in 1938, but at that time I directed the "Central Office for Jewish Emigration" in Vienna. In any case these measures of the Polish government demonstrate how, even long before the war, in the so-called democratic countries, such measures were taken against the Jews.

The Difficulties for the Jews to Emigrate

If it is maintained that the acceptance of the Jewish emigrants abroad did not succeed because their papers had been falsified or were not complete, this does not in any way correspond to the truth. The emigrating Jews obtained normal passports, as they would have been issued to any one of us. These Jewish passports had on the first page a rather large "J", in order to comply with a legal requirement. *The addition of the "J" was to comply with a Swiss recommendation* which was conveyed in the normal way through Swiss diplomatic representation to the Reich Foreign Office. The German police had nothing to do with this. The Swiss initiator of this proposal, Dr. Rothmund, was some high police chief who was not known to me. The Jewish desire to emigrate was so strong that many Jews went over the border illegally – and on account of these illegal emigrants difficulties were made for our Foreign Office by the different foreign representatives in Berlin because inquiries had to be made and investigations undertaken.

Because of the confusion created by propaganda regarding my responsibilities, and that of my office, and the individual relationship between the individual offices at least up to the founding of the RSHA which must seem to be very confusing to the outsider, I wish here to try to describe this relationship for my period in Vienna and Prague.

Neither in Vienna nor in Prague did I belong to a "head office" that was endowed with executive authority. I worked for Office VII which had no executive authority. The "Central Office" in Vienna stood

---

if they were not provided with a stamp that was obtainable only in Poland after the presentation of appropriate documents. The Polish government set as deadline for this the end of October 1938. In the case of a non-compliance with this condition on the part of Jews, the latter were to be declared stateless. The German ambassador in Warsaw, von Moltke, demanded in the name of the Reich government that the deadline be extended. Through this Polish measure, 17,000 Jews in Germany became stateless who then fell into difficulties connected with deportation.

directly under my leadership, and indeed I had, as the divisional head of the inspector of the Sipo and SD, received, at my suggestion, the order to create a "Central Office for Jewish Emigration". The inspector of the Sipo and SD for his part had previously asked for authorisation from the Reich Commissioner for the Reunification of Austria with the German Reich. He had received an authorisation decree from the latter although the state police control office in Vienna would have been responsible by law. The chief authority of the "Central Office" on behalf of the Reich Commissioner of the inspectors of the Sipo and SD was Dr. Stahlecker. I was the immediate superior of the Jewish Religious Community in Vienna, but as the office director of the "Central Office for Jewish Emigration" I was not responsible for executive measures. So at that time I was not responsible for taking a Jew into custody, for I had no sort of executive authority to do so.

When I was transferred back to Vienna I was paid as the Jewish expert and divisional head of the Senior Division of the Vienna SD by the Senior Division of the Danube SD. I retained my capacity as divisional head in the SDHA although I did not work there any longer, for my task in the SD lay now completely in the "Central Office for Jewish Emigration". Thereby I was also the office director for the Reich Commissioner for the Reunification, but at the same time still divisional head of the Senior Division of the Danube SD. This personnel combination did not last long. In the Senior Division of the Vienna SD, the former Obersturmführer[71] Germann was the expert for the Jewish question, because I did not have any more time for that. As the office director and as divisional head I had, in all administrative matters, insofar as they could promote emigration, an unrestricted authority which could in no way be removed from me by the state police head office in Vienna. The inspector of the Sipo and SD had supplied the state police head office with the relevant instruction that they could issue no orders to me and that, before state police measures against the agents of the Religious Community or other Jews could be taken that had anything to do with emigration, my clearance had to be first obtained.

All individual measures relating to the state police in Austria lay fully within the domain of the state police, and there I in turn had no right of objection. In practice however I got in touch with the responsible official of the state police head office in Vienna, Dr. Ebener if I had any wishes. The "Central Office for Jewish Emigration" in Vienna was

---

71   SS First Lieutenant

thus an office subject to the inspector of the Sipo and SD. However, even the Reich Commissioner for the Reunification could have a decisive say, for there were present in the "Central Office" not only persons subordinate to the inspector of the Sipo and SD but also the officials of the Jewish Religious Community, officials of the Gestapo, the Ministry of Economics, the foreign exchange office, the Ministry of Finance, all of whom offered their service working alongside one another and along with the Jewish officials. When Dr. Stahlecker inspected this office, he greeted the Jewish officials with a handshake, and even Heydrich naturally responded this way, only he said "Good morning", not "Heil Hitler" to the Jewish officials.

In Prague the inspector of the Sipo and SD who was transferred there, Dr. Stahlecker, managed to transfer me from the Senior Division of the Danube SD to the commanding officer of the Sipo and SD in Prague. I was therefore immediately under the commanding officer of the Sipo and SD in Prague. I received from him the commission to set up a Jewish "Central Office" on the Viennese model, and he obtained the necessary authorisations through the Reich Protector.[72] The latter signed his order in a simple procedure and placed it before the commanding officer of the Sipo and SD. Later, all that became still simpler because Heydrich became the representative Reich Protector. The Reich Protector for his part gave to the Protectorate government a memorandum or instruction that it had to make available official personnel corresponding to the "Central Office" for work at an assembly-line for all the formalities of the emigration.

In terms of personnel and supervision I stood under the commanding officer of the Sipo and SD in Prague, but had nothing to do with any Senior Division of the SD or anything similar. Like the office of the Reich Commissioner for the Reunification, the office of the Reich Protector in the Protectorate had a right of objection. But use was not made of that; when later Heydrich was named deputy Reich Protector, he was anyway my chief, from whom I had to take orders. Heydrich's orders were to be carried out without delay whereas the orders given to me by the Reich Protector von Neurath could be carried out only if I had received the approval for it from my superior.

The elaboration of these cases assumed such a scope that I had to create a special division for it within the "Central Office". The numerical summary of

---

72   Upon the annexation of Czechoslovakia in March 1939, Hitler appointed
      former Foreign Minister, Konstantin von Neurath, as Reichsprotector.

the Jews succeeding in emigrating through the "Central Offices" in Vienna and Prague has remained very sharply in my memory. Since the founding of the "Central Office in Vienna" in less than a year 100,000 Jews emigrated.

In the summer of 1938, the work of the "Central Office" was only warming up, but nevertheless in spring 1939 we accomplished the first 100,000 emigrants. The emigration was continued up until after the beginning of the war with the Soviet Union in summer 1941; in this way over 200,000 Jews emigrated. From Prague there emigrated far more than 100,000, although a few months after the establishment of the "Central Office in Prague" the war broke out. I remember quite precisely the figure of 94,000, whereby naturally it is to be considered that, before the invasion of Czechoslovakia, a certain number of Jews fled from Germany and Austria normally and over the green borders who were included partly or entirely in the total emigration figure. After Heydrich's visit to Vienna, I received an order from him by telegram to report to Berlin with my regular representative. In the meantime the Reich Security Head Office was established as a combination of security service, state police and criminal police.

Instead of our old armband "SDHA" we received a new one with "RSHA". At this time the party, and state sectors were merged with the Reich Security Head Office. That is why the letterheads ran "Reich Security Head Office, The Chief of the Sipo and SD". I do not know how the budget was ordered and how far the state gave grants to the party coffers – or vice versa. I never had anything to do with that, and it seems insignificant to me. In any case I know that up to 1945 the Reich Treasurer of the party, Schwarz had a say in it. Likewise I can testify that *the relation between the SS Reichsführer and the Reich leader Bormann*[73] *was always excellent.* Bormann was Schwarz's chief and, after Rudolf Heß'[74] flight to England, chief of the party chancellery, the first man after Hitler. The letters that I had to write for my superiors to Bormann were written always without any subservience and were in a friendly and comradely tone.

---

73   Martin Bormann, Reich Leader of the NSDAP, at first Secretary to the Führer and Reich Chancellor Adolf Hitler; after the flight of Rudolf Hess in 1941 to England he stepped into his place without receiving the titles "Reich Minister" and "Deputy of the Führer". The International Military Court in Nuremberg sentenced him on 30 September 1946 in absentia to death. His fate is uncertain. There are witness statements that report that he fell on 30 April 1945 to a Soviet grenade in Berlin.

74   Rudolf Hess, Deputy of the Führer, sentenced by the IMT to life imprisonment. Hess allegedly took his own life in Spandau Prison, West Berlin in 1987 at the age of 93.

SS Gruppenführer Reinhard Heydrich in 1940.

When we arrived in Berlin, the office chief of Gestapo Office IV of the Secret State Police, Gruppenführer Müller, informed us that I should be transferred to his office in Berlin. I had my doubts on account of the "Central Office" in Prague; besides, neither my regular representative nor I were eager to be enlisted in the executive. We were oriented to the SD and had our experience in it, whereas the task in the executive was new to us. I was able to return to Prague, and we thought we had already won, but some weeks later came a telegram that we had to report again to Berlin. I went along with the Gestapo Office chief Müller to Heydrich. Heydrich informed me that I had to conduct my work henceforth as divisional head under Gruppenführer Müller in department IV-B4 and moreover in cooperation with the "National Association for Jews" and now had to establish a "Central Office for Jewish Emigration" also in Berlin on the model of Vienna and Prague. However, in Berlin the "Central Office" did not function well.

Although I had made Dr. Eppstein the chief of the Central Office and this excellent lawyer who had some definitely Prussian characteristics was a valuable personality, I discovered however that I had managed matters in Vienna and Prague in a bureaucratic manner that turned out to be impossible in Berlin. Central authorities like the Reichsbank, the Ministry of Economics, Ministry of Finance, etc. denied me for a long time the centralising of their responsibility within the "Central Office". On the other hand, the most sophisticated secret work abroad could not open up any more possibilities of acceptance. The countries increasingly closed their borders, and instead of reducing the token funds to permit Jewish emigration, the foreign countries raised them and made difficulties wherever possible. After the outbreak of the war, a general prohibition of travel abroad was then imposed by the SS Reichsführer. Doubtless the entire conduct and agitation of the Jews on the international level significantly contributed to it. But it is also certain that the SS Reichsführer could issue the prohibition of travel abroad only with the agreement of Hitler; for Himmler could not simply go around the order of Göring, who had ordered the forced emigration.

As Jewish Divisional Head at the Gestapo

In 1940 I was transferred to the Gestapo, with responsibility for dealing with the Jewish question. I dealt with this matter not in a robotic manner, but on the contrary, I was pleased to do so. It thrilled me to be able to work on these matters, especially since I obtained, under a chief like Heydrich, the opportunity to occupy myself with the study of theological matters. I was able to conduct this study for two years; my chief even sent me to the Near East to improve my knowledge. In my enthusiasm I even learnt Hebrew ..., albeit not perfectly. But I could in any case read entire Yiddish newspapers effortlessly. It was for me very appealing to be able to help in the solution of a problem that aggrieved both my own people and the Jews themselves. I took up my work in such a way that I repeatedly emphasised to my own comrades and leading Jews that, corresponding to my entire predisposition as a nationalist, I would be the most enthusiastic Zionist that one could imagine if I were a Jew. That is why it infuriates me when it is written that I, for example, carried out mass shootings in Poland; for *I never carried out or authorised, either in Poland or anywhere else in Europe, the killing of even a single Jew.*

Again I emphasise that my task only consisted in capturing through the police those who were "enemies" of the Reich after the Jews had in 1933 declared, over Radio London, war against the German nation through their spokesman, Dr. Chaim Weizmann.[75]

---

75   Dr. Chaim Weizmann, the first president of Israel. At the 25th Zionist Congress (Geneva, August 1939) he called for war against National Socialist Germany.

The Step to the Security Service

In my function as head of department at Office IV of the Gestapo in Berlin I received *a much broader field of duties*. Whereas up till then I was never occupied with legislative activity or executive ordinances, it now transpired that, through the bureaucratic course, new executive ordinances originating from some central authorities reached my office. Mostly these ordinances were first sent to "law and administration" and from there on to me; I had to sign my receipt of them. That was my entire participation in these matters.

Around 1940, on the basis of several new laws, ordinances and decrees, the simplification of all the individual clauses in the legislation relating to the Jews was already accomplished; now it took only a few messages from the Stapo and the Stapo control offices. Practically the course of things was then somewhat as follows: a Stapo or Stapo control office informed, for example, that a German serving maid had been appointed at the Jew X's, although in the Jewish family in question there was a young man of over eighteen years. Then the Jew was, according to the law "For the protection of German blood and German honour" arrested. Instructions were requested if he, according to the decree of the SS Reichsführer, should be conveyed to a concentration camp. In my office then it was received by either the government bailiff or the police chief inspector, depending on what initial letters accompanied the Jew's name Then it was considered what ordinance was at hand for such a case, and decided accordingly. Thereupon the instructions were given to the responsible Stapo control office with wording such as: "It is indicated that the Jew X according to the decree of the SS Reichsführer no. ... according to the law ... is to be committed to the ... concentration camp." The imprisonment order was then sent also to the head of the preventive custody department for acknowledgement or submission for review. The case could be reviewed every three months. I never had anything to do with ordinances relating to the obligatory registration of Jewish assets or the requirement of identification cards, since they took place before my time.

I remember the ordinances on the implementation of changes in Jewish family and first names, it was submitted to me at that time in Office VII by the SDHA. I do not know who established the list of names, but I wondered very much at that time at the really exhaustive choice of names, which were partly dug up from the earliest period of the Jewish kings. I suppose that the Chancellery Office of the Führer was involved in this. Likewise Streicher seems to have striven and hurried to report names to Berlin, and doubtless the Jewish associations too were commanded to suggest names. I think I vaguely remember that the Sturmbannführer Lischka, my predecessor as advisor for Jewish affairs in the Gestapo, showed me this list. I had no involvement with the Jewish reparation[76] for the murder of the German diplomat von Rath or with the other consequences of the Night of Broken Glass.

The ordinances that Jews were excluded from participation in cinema and theatre representations and public concerts also had little to do with me. I think these ordinances were issued by the Reich Cultural Administrator Hinckel[77] on his own authority. I got to know Hinckel personally during the time when I led the "Central Office" in Vienna. He always introduced himself as "Party Number 9"[78] He had written the book *Einer unter Hunderttausend*.[79] He visited the Gestapo "Central Office" and was enthusiastic about our work. In the course of time I developed an extraordinarily warm relationship with him. He was a man who was "firm" in his field and did not answer to anybody but Goebbels. He esteemed the SS Reichsführer and was a distinguished SS Major General. I think that he was the first to have an SS evening tailcoat made for him. At that time in Vienna he had arranged the film ball in the area of the Hofburg to which I was also invited. Immediately after the film ball I drove through the night with some Slovak officers to a place called Engerau, where a minor uprising had started. I think it was at the time when Slovakia became independent and had left the state of Czechoslovakia.

In March 1939 *an ordinance on the Law of the Hitler Youth* (Hitlerjugend) was issued wherein the acceptance of Jews in the HJ was forbidden but granted to partial Jews. The partial Jew was supported by us because *the half-Jew of today is the quarter-Jew of tomorrow and the full-blooded German of the day after.* The partial Jews represented a considerable number; we could not indeed preserve the interests of German blood by "throwing out the baby with the bath water". *We needed the partial Jews,* even the half-Jews, if they were not Jews in the

---

76 In the *Reich Law Gazette* I, pp.1579-81 and p.1676 of 1938 was announced: The ordinances on the exclusion of German Jews from the German economic life, on the payment of a contribution ("reparation") of 1 million marks, further on the reparation of the damage caused by the riots on 9 November 1938.

77 Hans Hinkel (1901-60) was, from 1942, also head of the film department of the Ministry for National Information and Propaganda.

78 That is, he was the ninth person to join the NSDAP

79 *One In A Hundred Thousand.* The book was published in 1938.

Members of the Hitler Youth in 1939. Many of them were to die in battle by 1945.

sense of the legislation, that is, if they were not circumcised and did not belong to any Jewish religious community. Naturally, partial Jews in the HJ outraged many party comrades and seemed intolerable to them. We had however a firm rule to which we adhered. Besides, there were many partial Jews in the army, some were even commissioned officers. To undertake something against partial Jews would have meant opening a can of worms.

After the war some people like to represent things as if the legislation against the Jews had been prepared well in advance. This was not the case - on the contrary, it came in gradually as things developed. The Jew was proclaimed as an enemy of the state by the legitimate national government. The government must have had its reasons to remove this enemy as a matter of urgency. After this order had been given, it had also to be carried out. It was not our task to question what reasons the government had for regarding this enemy as a danger to the people and the state. As the police we only had to act in accordance with the law.

The ordinances were often directed through the "Reich Association for Jews", as, for example, the ordinance on the *Use of Public Transport* by Jews. Such an ordinance arose normally through the fact that someone from the Transport Ministry pointed to the overcrowding of public transport and then made his comment on it to the ministry. The police as the servant for the state then had to instruct the "Reich Association" to publish this ordinance in their bulletin. Even the ordinance relating to the *"Transfer of delinquent Jews to a concentration camp to serve their sentence"* had nothing to do with my executive treatment of the Reich's enemies. This ordinance represented a purely formal legal arrangement between the Reich Justice Minister and the crown lawyer of the Chief of the Sipo and SD. If such an ordinance was issued, the justice authorities were guided in a given case by it, and neither my department IV-B4 nor another department of the RSHA needed to be involved.

Now, whether the Jews in question were directed to concentration camps was not my affair; I did not think about it at all; for I simply had to think about my obligations. I was neither responsible for all the disgraceful actions nor for all the good deeds with regard to the Jews. At first I was exclusively responsible for Jewish emigration; only later was I then gradually involved in individual cases. These cases were however generally regulated by the ministry, that is, by law, decree and ordinance, and there my responsibility ceased. These things were only reported to me for acknowledgement.

The police ordinance for the *identification of the Jews* was issued in autumn 1941, at a time when I was already head of department in the Reich Security Head Office. In this matter I was not once asked for my opinion. Out of bureaucratic considerations I, as the responsible head of department for the Jewish question within the Gestapo, which was under the chief of the German Police and therewith under the Ministry of the Interior, had simply to give my signature to it.

One day there arrived at my department a yellow roll of cloth with stars and the German word "Jude".[80] stamped upon it. I do not know who designed this, or where the idea arose. It may have been the deputy Führer's chancellery through the Senior Councillor Dr. Reischauer[81] or the Propaganda Ministry relying on *Stürmer* methods or another office that developed this idea. In any case, I received the roll of cloth and had to hand it over to the Jewish central organisations. The initiative for *the wearing of a star* came from a higher office and was naturally reported to the Ministry of the Interior, which then asked the Sipo for a corresponding police ordinance. When I think more carefully I remember, however, that the introduction of the Jewish star was above all driven by psychological considerations. It

---

80 Jew

81 Herbert Reischauer (1909-45) Took part in the two conferences that followed the Wannsee conference, in March and October 1942, in Berlin.

is typical of the German mentality to always attend to another when he sees him oppressed. The Reich wished to see that Germans refrain from and, to a certain degree, feel embarrassed about sympathising and communicating further with the Jews. I think I can remember that the initiative came from the Propaganda Ministry. In any case, Streicher got much pleasure when *Der Stürmer* dedicated an entire issue to this matter.

There is strong evidence that Canaris may have suggested the Jewish star, but I remember that a Jewish lawyer in Vienna, Dr. Löwenherz once said to me: "Mr. Sturmbannführer, I wear this star with pride". I said to Dr. Löwenherz: "If ever I should be in a country where the German is ostracised and is distinguished in such a special way, then I would be proud to be able to wear something like "German". Certainly you will be molested only by idiots. But take care that you increase the number of emigrants, organise foreign exchange, and then, when your people are settled, you will live as a nation". The man impressed me, he was an idealist; I then let him also emigrate soon afterwards.

The checking of the compulsory registration lay with the ordinance police, that is, with the responsible local captain, in Austria with the responsible commissioner's office. In the case of violations, the imprisonment was also carried out by them, that is, in the cities by the local captains and in the country by the country policemen.

With things like "Establishment of hostility to the nation and state", "Withdrawal of German citizenship", "Confiscation of assets" and such matters I had something to do, within my department IV-B4 (sub-division IV-B4a), led by councillor Suhr[82] and after his departure by councillor Hünsche.[83] That is, the state police control office X placed a request to the Reich Security Head Office, according to an implementation ordinance related to the law "For the protection of people and state", to carry out the determination of the hostility of the Jews to the nation and the state. Once this happened, then there followed the withdrawal of the German citizenship, and, if all the preconditions were in agreement, the confiscation of assets was automatically added. The person concerned may have long left the concentration camp or the national borders or fallen into the custody of the police if he were still

---

82   Friedrich Suhr, Government councillor and SS Sturmbannführer, jurist specialist in IV of the Reich Security Head Office.

83   Otto Hünsche, SS Hauptsturmführer, successor of government councillor Suhr. After 1945 sentenced to imprisonment by a German high court.

in the territory of the Reich. The state police control office explained now in detail why it was placing this request for the determination of the hostility of the Jews to the nation and the state in the case of Jew X. Normally the text of a questionnaire was added to this request, or the interrogation was fully copied out in a letter. Here legal experts worked who had at their disposal cadre personnel, and indeed always a councillor and an assessor. This routine work was soon completed. Then the case was worked on by the responsible police chief inspector within my department on the basis of office records. These were presented to the assessor or the councillor.

The determinations of "hostility to the nation and the state" were collected and published every fortnight. The lists ran through me and were directed to the Gestapo Office IV Chief with a request for his signature. Then they followed their path to the state printer's and were published, according to the law, in the "Reich Gazette". At the same time, a letter was sent to the Reich Finance Minister with the request that the Chief Financial President may arrange for the collection of the confiscated assets. Simultaneously a letter was sent to the Foreign Office with the regular request that the person concerned had lost his German citizenship so that in case of a meeting with the authorities no passport may be issued any more and also no other documents from which his former German citizenship may be detected. That was all routine; the texts could be copied repeatedly, only the names were different, otherwise nothing else.

IV-B4 occupied itself only with the legal, never with the material acquisition of Jewish property. It was thus determined that the assets of the Jew, as a result of this or that violation according to the law and statute, were to be considered as forfeit. The acquisition of the material property was carried out by the responsible chief financial officer. But he in turn could do that only if the executive body, in this case IV-B4, had "confiscated" the values for the Reich. That was not a confiscation with a furniture van but only a formal confiscation, for the effective confiscation was the task of the chief financial president. How he did it was his business. But it could transpire that in cases of doubt the regional state police office had authorised some treasury or something similar to ascertain the values. The object could be sealed in the knowledge that it was already confiscated. If it was confiscated, then the Sipo had nothing more to do with it, as it became the responsibility of the Finance Ministry. With the exception of important documents that had to be worked on or archive materials, the state police could not annex anything. That was the expert field of IV-B4a.

The Step to the Security Service

After this description of the administrative procedures it should now be explained in what form the "field services" brought such matters to the Office. I should indeed declare that the *Führer's decree on confiscating the assets of "enemies of the state"* came as a surprise to me, because I was not involved in any way in its draft. Naturally we could not determine in Berlin who had made himself guilty in Munich, Stuttgart or elsewhere of activities hostile to the state. That was the matter of the responsible higher division of the Sipo and SD. They determined that the emergency ordinance of the Reich President "For the protection of the state", along with the different implementation conditions and the additional laws, was to be brought to bear on a certain person under their jurisdiction. Thereupon they compiled a comprehensive file. If the man was still in the territory of the Reich – a rare case –, he was summoned; if not, all efforts were made to obtain validity. All that was sent in summary to Berlin, with the request for the withdrawal of the German citizenship on account of "hostility to the nation and state" and with the request to have the assets appropriated by the Chief Financial Officer.

We in department IV-B4 did not have to examine personal things; for that the Stapo or Stapo Control was responsible as the final authority, unless an appeal were made against it. In my department it was merely determined if the legal basis was present in the concerned case. For the central authority the person was not important, only the matter. The publications of the "Reich Gazette" bore in all cases the file number of my department IV-B4. Decrees, ordinances, laws and such which concerned Jews are very often to be traced back to the initiative of individual police offices, party offices or administrative offices. They confirm that in the Jewish question there was no central control system. Even if nobody today can believe that the Jewish issue was not centrally controlled I must nevertheless declare that there was no central control. Naturally the post-war literature has striven to awaken in everybody the image of a "Pope for the Jews" who was in touch with everything and provided relevant documents on everything, and ordinances and orders, which he perhaps received directly from his immediate superior, whereas he directed everything else in a central manner like a spider in its web. And this spider must naturally have been me. This belief is widespread; for the German people think that, the former soldier thinks that, and the former official thinks that, the enemy thinks that and the world too, exactly as the majority of people who discuss the Jewish problem firmly believed that international Jewry is directed at least as strictly as the Jewish policy in the Third Reich and that international Jewry is also centrally controlled and directed by an office which likewise sits like a spider in its web. One "spider" is as great a nonsense as the other "spider".

Administrative Confusion in the Jewish Policy

In the Third Reich every central authority issued some "Jewish ordinance" of its own. Sometimes that went very far: If Adolf Hitler had held a talk in which he, as generally after 1939, denounced Jewry as being responsible for the war and therefore threatened it with sanctions, then it could be expected that a week later some central authorities or party authorities would issue a new supplementary ordinance against the Jews.

Already earlier I mentioned that the Reich citizenship laws were issued in 1935, but nevertheless years later it could occur to somebody: "Stop, we have forgotten here to legally establish that the entry into the Hitler Youth is forbidden to the Jews" or something similar. And so there was issued years later a new implementation ordinance to the Nuremberg Laws. Thus was it everywhere. Two or three ministers spoke with one another or a minister with a Gauleiter or some Reich Leader with another authority of the Reich, whereby in the course of the conversation they decided that the Jews should be excluded also from this or that sector or that this or that Jewish matter should be classified under the field of responsibility of the concerned person. That was then discussed over a glass of cognac and determined; then followed a correspondence in which this arrangement was confirmed. A typical example of this was the arrangement between the SS Reichsführer and the Reich Justice Minister that the transfer of the Jews from the penal system to the custody of the concentration camps must occur through the WVHA.[84] Exactly as in the field of legislation laws, ordinances and decrees arose mostly in the decentralised manner described, so there existed a similar decentralising in the executive work.

A real expert will never be able to maintain that the Gestapo, Gruppenführer Müller, or I had the Jewish question in our hands in a centralised way. How would it otherwise have been possible that I was never responsible for it in the occupied Soviet territories, in the Generalgouvernement,[85] in Lithuania, in Estonia, etc. and had nothing to do with it officially? I had nothing to do with the executive procedures even in Hungary and also not in the several other countries because these were taken care of locally, in Hungary thus by Hungarian executive departments.

---

84 SS Wirtschaftsverwaltungshauptamt, the Economic Administration Head Office of the SS.

85 German-occupied Poland.

The Step to the Security Service

I understand that it is hard to believe but there are a number of examples to support this. Even the Reich Security Head Office was not always the directing office in the Jewish question. We were perhaps the "servant for everything". Where, on the basis of an ordinance, an instruction or an order of much higher superiors, the Jewish matter was taken from our hands, we just had to see how we would accomplish it. Naturally that did not mean that in the Generalgouvernement and in the occupied Soviet territories the forces of the Sipo and SD were not operative in general in the solution of the Jewish question – other units too had to deal with it on occasion. But the Reich Security Head Office and its department IV-B4 had nothing to do in those territories. There other, local or higher commands were appointed by the SS Reichsführer and received orders directly from him without any obligation to report to the Reich Security Head Office or IV-B4. Naturally the senior SS and Police chiefs reported to the SS Reichsführer. He occasionally instructed the Chief of the Security Police, whereby I was acquainted with files on many things, but I could never influence them. These local higher commands were also in no way provided with guidelines by the RSHA. They received these in the form of direct orders from the SS Reichsführer.

As the consultant of IV-B4 *I could never give an order*! That would have contradicted the principles of a police central authority. I could only provide the local offices of the Gestapo with "directives", but never with orders; for one cannot "order" an official, one can only direct or instruct. The Einsatz Command in the occupied Soviet territories had a military character. They had to take orders. In the Generalgouvernement it was a mixed arrangement.

Especially after the war it has been attempted in all possible and impossible ways to make me the central figure of the Jewish matters in the Third Reich, a "Pope for the Jews" equipped with all authority and unrestricted ordering power. Basically this idea was suggested even before the war.

From 1935 to 1945, for ten years I conducted, not only in the Old Reich but in Austria, in the Protectorate of Bohemia and Moravia and in many countries in which we exerted our influence, thousands of discussions with Jewish and non-Jewish offices. Thus I stuck out like "a sore thumb" and had to worry about certain details as well as basic matters. Jewry had simply got used to seeing me as a central figure. At the beginning of the war an instructor named Wurm, who worked under Streicher, placed on my table an entire collection of foreign newspapers from which it appeared already at that time that Jewish matters in the Reich – insofar as they did not deal with "Streicher stories" were my affair; I think that it was the *Pariser Tageblatt* that in Spring 1940 brought out a story on me on the first page, in which it described me as the "Tsar of the Jews". It said there that I was "hunting" the Jews in Bohemia and Moravia after I had operated and ruled in the Old Reich and in Austria.

If only these Parisian hacks, instead of instigating, investigated how precisely through my activity in the "central offices" in Vienna and Prague so much blood was preserved among the Jews, then they would never have written the article. This article was as bungling as any random article from the *Stürmer*.

A Jewish State in Poland

The quick defeat of Poland on the one hand and, on the other hand, the growing difficulties to provide *emigration possibilities for the Jews* prompted in me the idea of making an attempt to form a sort of "Jewish state" on Polish territory. Around this time I had practically nothing to do with Berlin, but was under the commanding officer of the Sipo and SD, Dr. Stahlecker. In him I found a superior who was extraordinarily energetic and active, perhaps also somewhat ambitious, but always on the quest for creative ideas. In this sense he was not in the least bureaucratic, where everything was done according to "the book" bureaucrats are transferred or remain in the same place until they become pensionable or die. New ideas are not born among bureaucrats; if one dares to put forward political solutions of a new sort of structure, the bureaucrat is in general unapproachable. Stahlecker was not like that, and so I could immediately carry out through him the plan to achieve a "central office for Jewish emigration." As always I was, even in the case of the "Jewish state in Poland", inspired by Adolf Böhm's book *Der Judenstaat*. It inspired me to find a solution of the problem through which a homeland could be given to the Jews, and at the same time the German nation could become "free of Jews". "Homeland" was indeed also the familiar term of the "Balfour Declaration".

Stahlecker accepted my idea with enthusiasm, to carve out from the great number of square kilometres in Poland a territory of the size of a German district, in order to establish there a sort of Jewish state. There we would settle all the Jews; they would have their own administration and their own schools; the Chief of the Sipo and SD would only be a supervisory authority. Doubtless Stahlecker informed Gruppenführer Heydrich of it; I received the approval to start my plan. Obviously Stahlecker could act so much more convincingly with Heydrich since he knew that I saw possibilities for the realisation of such a plan. Stahlecker was in no way a petty pedant who wished to know everything to the last detail already in advance. He liked to be present everywhere but, on the other hand, hovered over the things and tried to direct them from a higher control position. Heydrich resembled him in that. He and Stahlecker could have been brothers. Stahlecker had faith in my plans and in my work, because I had proven through the "Central Office" in Vienna that I did not just "talk" about things. Besides the "Jewish state in Poland" signified a *political solution* that had always been much striven after.

When I had obtained the approval, I went about looking for a suitable place within the Polish territory. I came to the San, saw a blown up railway bridge and an extended landscape, endlessly large, from horizon to horizon, almost a plain. The river San was a powerful water-bearer; as a support-point for the first days there was at my disposal Nisko, a rather large village close to the demarcation line.[86] The area seemed to me to be ideal. I drove back and made for Stahlecker sketches and descriptions of the area. In his enthusiasm he decided to drive with me there to see everything himself. That may have been in the middle of October 1939, two to three weeks after the Polish cease-fire. We drove to the German-Soviet demarcation line and conversed with a GPU[87] commissioner. I still see before me the tall, broad-shouldered man with his brown leather jacket as uniform. He directed as it were the control post at the entrance to the corridor. He accompanied us a short while and stood on the footboard of the vehicle until we reached a control post of a Siberian regiment stationed along the demarcation line. There he let us know that we could pass freely and unhindered. Some soldiers accompanied us through the Soviet corridor so that we might be spared of any unpleasantness, for we drove in full uniform.

The corridor was perhaps twenty kilometres long. Even Dr. Stahlecker was excited when he looked at the area chosen by me; I obtained the

---

86 Nisko, a locality west of the San in Galicia, ard on the German-Soviet demarcation line of 1939.

87 Gosudarstvennoye Politicheskoye Upravlenie, State Political Directorate, the secret service of the Russian Soviet Federative Socialist Republic.

approval to start immediately with the practical work. My intention was to organise the matter immediately on a large scale and to realise it in the shortest possible time. For that I reckoned around 2,000 Jewish workmen and corresponding supervisory personnel would be needed. I had frequently delegated administrative work to the rabbi Dr. Murmelstein;[88] so I gave him responsibility for the formation of the work-groups. The best workmen from Moravian Ostrau and the best experts and workers from Prague and Vienna were picked out from Theresienstadt, where we had many barracks, and I also arranged collection of the initial necessary material. In addition I obtained some trains for the 2,000 persons and the material to be dispatched. Among the personnel was a veterinary doctor who asked for permission to take his son with him as an assistant. I granted that.

The Jews did not work under our direction, but under the leadership of the different Jewish consultants and experts. Naturally I had told Dr. Murmelstein how I conceived of the settlement. I drove with him through the area and gave him my explanations. The village of Nisko should be the first outpost in this district which I hoped to obtain fully for my plan. Numerous transport trains should bring men and materials there to carry out the settlement of the Nisko outpost. The San was the border of the Jewish territory. One must imagine this land in its borderless breadth. Perhaps within a radius of fifty kilometres from Nisko there was nothing. Farther away lay the city of Radom in the district of Lublin. I wished to have this entire district and make the city of Radom the first capital of the Jewish state. But practically I reckoned with Nisko on the San first, for at the moment, I could only think in vague terms of Radom because there greater administrative ordinances would be required to resettle the local Polish population. I preferred to begin the matter on a small scale and pushed forward first to a region where I had to fear no decree or ordinance. The winter had already broken out, and there was much snow. Nevertheless the building works were energetically expedited, and took only a few weeks.

Murmelstein was also excited, and even the other Jews understood that in Nisko there was a small Jewish state in the making. There was available in the beginning a neutral zone of 10 square kilometres which I had easily taken for myself. There were horses there also. I said to Murmelstein: "Rabbi, here you must learn to ride too and not

---

88   Benjamin Murmelstein (1905-89) was an Austrian rabbi who the last of the
      Jewish Elders in Theresienstadt.

just sit at the writing desk". There Murmelstein crept onto a horse for the first time and sat, but clearly without much enthusiasm. There were very few cars, but because the territory was so large, horses were indispensible.

It was a small beginning which I believed would grow into *an autonomous Jewish state* in the district of Lublin under the protectorate of the German Reich. Naturally I also wondered how this state could be viable, if it concerned only Jews. That was not to be achieved overnight, and I could not all at once transport two million, one million or even 500,000 Jews there. There they would have died off like flies. For the danger of epidemics is in such cases great. For that reason I first brought the specialists there. They should build barracks, build up Nisko into an outpost and cause the necessary industry to arise there. Apart from the experts, labourers too would have been necessary – all that was possible, for even our concentration camps had grown, in a place where earlier nothing had existed, into large concentration camps with 100,000 and more inmates. Only here there should arise not a concentration camp but an autonomous Jewish state.

At this time I was, naturally, often at the demarcation line. It did not represent any hermetically closed barrier. At the chief crossing points there were control posts, but only for 10 or 20 km. There was nothing to be seen either of the Soviets or of us. Already during the war negotiations many Jews had moved from Poland in an easterly direction. From the end of September 1941 thousands of Jews had moved over this border because within Poland it was becoming a matter of concentration and ghettoising. In the "worst of times", and when a Soviet post arose, the "emigration" cost at most a wristwatch, as Murmelstein once related to me. The number of the Polish Jews who had moved at that time to the east I could only guess that it possibly amounted to a quarter million, for they crossed over the entire length of the demarcation line – and we had no control over it. When the Jewish measures were begun in the Generalgouvernement, they naturally came in still greater numbers into the Soviet territory. At that time I estimated it to be a quarter million of these "emigrants". I even think that we entered it into our statistics, however, as 100,000 – because we wished to be quite sure. When now at the beginning of 1940 the 2,000 Jewish experts under Murmelstein's leadership were in Nisko and the pressure against the Jews became stronger, the "emigration" increased once again. So I cannot state exactly how many Jews moved over the border.

At this time I naturally went on many inspection drives to Nisko on the San. When one day I spent the night at Krakow, the commanding officer of the Sipo and SD, Streckenbach[89] informed me – he considered it as a joke – that the Reich minister for Poland Hans Frank[90] had given an order to the Senior SS and Police Chief in Poland, Friedrich Krüger,[91] that I should be arrested on entering Poland. The "Jewish state" was starting up well after overcoming the initial difficulties, when this order of Generalgouverneur[92] Frank put a spoke in our wheel. On the next morning I drove back to Prague and made a report related to this. It appeared that Generalgouverneur Frank had protested against my "Jewish state" to Göring or somewhere else and had succeeded in his protest. Never again did I receive an order to travel to Nisko on the San, but I had to have the camp there dismantled around the end of the year and conduct the Jews back again to their place of origin or to Theresienstadt.

Unlike Konrad Heinlein[93] in Bohemia and Moravia, who was an extraordinarily humble man, "Polish Frank" was extremely arrogant. He was loud and always sought the limelight. Streckenbach, once related to me that when "Polish Frank" drove from his office to his home, he was accompanied by a large contingent of police vehicles with sirens wailing, as if he was an oriental prince going on a journey. Frank apparently saw me as a competitor and he wanted to take all initiatives himself. For the sake of the truth I must state most sharply; If "Polish Frank" had allowed the RSHA to operate and administer from the end of 1939 to 1941 in the district Nisko on the San, and if he had not prevented my plan, for which I had the approval of my superiors, then he would never have had anything to do with the annihilation of the Jews, and then the entire question would have been resolved in the Generalgouvernement *in a totally bloodless way*. He

---

89 Bruno Streckenbach, SS Gruppenführer, Commanding Officer of the Security Police, later director of the Personnel Department of the Reich Security Head Office.

90 Dr. Hans Frank, Reich Minister, Generalgouverneur in Poland 1939-1945, sentenced to death by the IMT in Nuremberg on 30 September 1946, hanged in the Nuremberg detention centre on 16 October 1946.

91 Friedrich Krüger, SS Obergruppenführer, from 1939-1945 Senior SS and Police chief in Poland (Krakow), took his own life on 9 May 1945 in Liebau/Silesia.

92 Governer General

93 Konrad Henlein, leader of the Sudeten German Party, after the annexation of the Sudetenland, Gauleiter there in Reichenberg Liberec.

needed only to hand over the district of Lublin to me; for I wanted to work up from Nisko to Radom and, further, to Lublin.

The "Jewish state in Poland" was to be a *final solution of the Jewish question*, a political, and a bloodless solution; for me it was a "last gathering together of total decisiveness", penetrating power and creative force. I was not yet bound to the police, nor had I taken any police oath, I was still free. I was a member of the SS, and as such had been able to make my superior, the commanding officer of the SD, Stahlecker, interested in my idea, I could still have my own thoughts, and still step forward as an initiator, I could still be creative in my attempt to find a solution. Later it was excluded, I could not do that anymore because it did not lie within my capability, but I would have encroached with it on other responsibilities and the whole world would have fallen on my head because I would have been considered a maniac ... It is a paradox that as the leader of the "Central Office for Jewish Emigration" in Vienna I had a much greater power than later as departmental head and division leader in the Reich Security Head Office.

Even my "Jewish state in Poland" was disturbed by some forces and made impossible – and I fell into a web from which I could no longer extricate myself. But I cannot absolve Generalgouverneur Frank of being the co-initiator of the enormous Jewish destruction in the Generalgouvernement because he, perhaps from short-sightedness, perhaps from anxiety about his competence, had made a bloodless solution to the Jewish question in the form of an autonomous "Jewish state" impossible. For me this development was a bitter disappointment. Nevertheless I continued my efforts for a political solution of the Jewish problem and *somewhat later I produced the Madagascar Plan*, to which I shall come back to later.

With regard to the 2,000 Jewish workmen and tradesmen of Nisko on the San, obviously they cannot in any way be considered as having been "deported". They were a work force in the truest sense of the term. *I did not have anything to do at that time with deportation*, since I was transferred to IV-B4 only in 1940. Naturally, after the overthrow of Poland, even Polish offices received the order to remove the Jews, in the Warthegau for example, and to transfer them to the Generalgouvernement, in order to settle Wolhynian, Bessarabian and other ethnic Germans from the east. That was the work of Hermann Krumey, who belonged to the Settlement Head Office until 1944. If one maintains now that out of that workforce of Jewish workers and manual labourers in Nisko on the San there were only a "few survivors" that is a complete lie.

The Privileged Jews

In the case of the Jewish legislation there existed a great number of exceptions which were carried out under the blanket term of "privileged Jews". In the first place were considered as such the partners in mixed marriages, then the owners of bravery distinctions and the wounded from the first World War who could prove this, then Jews who rendered services in national matters, to which in some cases also Jewish economists belonged. The arbitrariness of some offices sometimes broke through the limits here, but the matter was later straightened out. The "exceptions" were never abolished, only these Jews were later for the most part sent to Theresienstadt, which served as a privileged camp. Thus, for example, the Austrian general, Sommer, a Jew, was taken there, where he was given so-called "prominent accommodation". He lived here undisturbed in his little house and to my knowledge, he survived the war. The public offices adhered strictly to these "exceptions", which is not to say that there were not occasionally infringements. We were under martial law and were all trained to confront life bravely; we were especially trained to have respect for those who had fought and bled for the German Reich. So we could not make any exception in the case of the Jews and therefore respected among them the soldiers of the first World War.

Our attitude was highlighted quite clearly in the case of the fifty or so SS men with Jewish blood who had fought for the NSDAP in the political meeting brawls and whose origin was established only by genealogical research. In other party organisations there were many hundreds of members with Jewish blood, among them also "old fighters".

Around 1937/1938 one began to conduct genealogical research again in the Old Reich and in Austria, wherein the mentioned cases of the SS men with Jewish blood or even SS men who were full-blooded Jews were brought to light. We did not strike these people on the head but prepared the way for a proper life: they could emigrate freely abroad, but also remain here; the majority preferred emigration, though in not a single case did it come to light that they, as it were through bitterness or other reasons, had worked against the Reich. A small number of them, mostly former officers, shot themselves. I had also a first sergeant in whose particular case it emerged that he was a full Jew. In general I did not bother with such individual cases, but I let this man come to me to speak of his future plans; I was glad that he was not depressed but only said: "Hard luck, Sturmbannführer! It was a fine time, but it is now so, and one can do nothing". After some time he visited me once again and informed me that he wished to go to Switzerland in order to found as a musician a music ensemble there. He had money himself, or else we would have given it to him; he obtained a passport, the border crossing offices were instructed by me to let him through and therewith everything seemed to be in order. But when he came to the Swiss border, he must have become somewhat mistrustful and sought to go over the green line. He was called back, but did not stop, the border guard shot and killed him according to his orders. I saw to it that everything would be accurately recorded and investigated. It emerged that the border offices were not to blame. These SS men with Jewish blood were and remained our friends; among them their Jewishness receded and the comradeship, often also from former political meeting brawls, stood in the foreground.

Among the Jews there were many who were freed from the wearing of the Jewish star, as there were also Jews who were never arrested and remained at home. I know no individual cases but the "privileged" represented a collective term; they came under a certain police ordinance which indicated which Jews were to be excluded from any measures. There were thousands of them. Naturally there were certain districts whose Gauleiters proceeded in an especially harsh manner and autocratically ordered the transfer of even privileged Jews to the camps; this was then again revoked; the "privileged" were in general transferred to Theresienstadt and only then towards the end of the war.

Schellenberg ordered hundreds of Jewish representatives – it may have been thousands in all – whom he then appointed as agents in the occupied territory, and also abroad. Many of the Jews from Germany went to Lisbon, which I know for sure because I had to certify their harmlessness before they obtained a passport. I know that some of them conducted espionage for the German western campaign.

From the outset the Jewish question was subject to many interventions. Reichsmarschall Göring intervened on behalf of individual Jews on many occasions, and effected exception clauses for them because he needed these Jews in his capacity as Commissioner for the Four-Year Plan. The Churches of both denominations, especially the Protestant, likewise intervened continually. The present provost of Berlin, pastor Krüger, was especially tenacious and had to be warned repeatedly by the state police. I conveyed different warnings to him, of course in a friendly, but very definite manner. But he did not desist from his activity. After the third warning I had to inform him that another intervention could result in a transfer to a concentration camp. He did not allow himself to be intimidated, and he was sent to a concentration camp, where he remained until the end of the war on the orders of the SS Reichsführer. His wife pestered me very much and even succeeded once, through a trick, in getting me personally on the phone. I had however to give her a negative response, but let her apply to the SS Reichsführer. Krüger's hobby horse was the care of non-Aryan Christians. These occupied in the legislation a special place and, if pastor Krüger had left it at that, all would have been well. But he took issue with the relations of these non-Aryan Christians also, thus with a group of persons who were not privileged according to the law. In his ignorance of the facts of the matter, the increasingly repeated warnings to Krüger could almost be construed as forbearance.

The Catholic bishop Münch, at that time the permanent director of the Fulda bishops' conference,[94] came once or twice every month to my office in Berlin. His chancellery arranged with my outer office the hour of meeting; almost always I could send a Second Lieutenant to him who escorted him from the guardhouse to my office. Münch had noted on a piece of paper his wishes, which I was able to satisfy or not. In many cases I promised to make inquiries into whether, and to what extent, in any particular case, something could be done. Then these questions were deferred to the next meeting. In fact it is not correct to say that Münch intervened, as he rather collected enquiries partly also on the commission of several cardinals which he, as the director of the bishops' conference, was to a certain extent delegated to do.

The Interventions

There were interventions at the "assembly line": the SS Reichsführer himself led the way with his example; for he liked to immerse himself in individual details in individual cases. Now, if the SS Reichsführer intervened, and likewise Göring, generals of the Waffen-SS, and bishops and provosts, then I could not refuse interventions to other people, although it was in itself generally forbidden to intervene. Naturally I did not dare to deal with Göring; he also did not in any way turn to me, even his office did not call mine but Göring discussed such a matter directly with the SS Reichsführer; the latter then

---

94 The Fulda Bishops' Conference is the episcopal conference of the bishops of the Roman Catholic Church in Germany.

sometimes came up with things which stood exactly in contradiction to the orders that he had issued just a short while before.

After the annexation of Austria, the lawyers swarmed into Vienna to represent the Jews before the authorities or on the basis of their contacts to try to obtain provisions of exception for their Jewish clients, for which they naturally demanded to be highly paid. Since thereby the guidelines established by the SS Reichsführer could no longer be applied in all cases, a considerable confusion arose, and there remained nothing else for me but to warn these solicitors about their actions. But even this did not achieve any results; the consequence was that both the experts at the Gestapo central office in Vienna and my experts too at the "Central Office for Jewish Emigration" finally no longer knew according to what guidelines to proceed in individual cases.

After I had discussed the matter with Dr. Stahlecker and he doubtless had sought corresponding instructions in Berlin, I had the chief of the NS solicitors' league come to Vienna and announced to him that from now on – on instructions from Berlin – every solicitor who intervened on behalf of Jews in future is to be immediately taken into custody. With that the interventions ceased suddenly, but I drew upon myself the enmity of almost all the Viennese solicitors. I heard that as "reprisals" they screened my curriculum vitae most carefully from my birth to the day of the prohibition of interventions in the hope of finding somewhere a "dark spot" in order to have me thrown out of Vienna. But they did not succeed – and I was at that time very amused! Later everything was sorted out; for I had no enmity against any of them personally.

Even Gruppenführer Wolff,[95] Chief Adjutant of the SS Reichsführer intervened in individual cases. I clashed with him once very harshly on the telephone when I tried to explain that I had in a certain case acted exactly according to the ordinances of the SS Reichsführer; Wolff wanted to obtain an exception for the Jew in question, but this was impossible because there was not present a single point to justify reclassifying this case as an exception. Wolff became very indignant, but my decision was not sustained by the SS Reichsführer. As far as possible I complied personally; for the individual case did not play any role in the case of the large majority of Jews. However I naturally had to

---

95 Karl Wolff, SS Oberstgruppenführer, Himmler's liaison officer to the Führer headquarters, Himmler's adjutant, from 1943 highest SS and Police chief in Italy, sentenced to 15 years by the high court in Munich, released from prison on health grounds.

keep my composure in front of my own lawyers, who had to supervise these regulations. I acted similarly before my officers in the Foreign Service, who were in the same situation. If the central authority had, on the basis of expedience, made an exception which was not provided for in the implementation regulations of the SS Reichsführer, such a wrong decision could have had disastrous consequences. Many German offices were waiting as it were to intervene on a larger scale, naturally supported therein by the efforts of Jewry. A wrong decision of the central authority would within the shortest time have caused complete confusion in which nobody would have known what to do with the result that conversely even Jews who, according to the general rules, should not at all have been deported would however have been deported, which would have led to an enormous number of difficulties, to foreign political complications and disgrace for the central authorities of the Reich.

When later the demands of the war were increasingly more palpable, and, on the other hand, the SS Führer's order arrived to comb the individual districts for Jews who came under consideration for deportation, there was another sort of intervention. Around this time the Sipo and SD partly conducted very hard battles against the offices of the armaments industry which employed Jews in large numbers in their factories and wanted indispensability certificates. Stapo and Stapo control offices had then to bring forward the evidence with painstaking work – often on account of a single Jew a large correspondence was conducted by the control offices of the RSHA, from there to the armaments industry or to Minister Speer and from there back. In Dresden there was a stubborn director in an armaments plant; but Gauleiter Mutschmann[96] wanted his district to be free of Jews – as so often the initiative did not come from the Stapo and the Stapo control offices, but rather from a party office, in this case from the district leadership. There was a similar contest as in the case of the factories, which could not quickly enough announce to the German Labour Front that the plant belonged hundred percent to the Labour Front. In his battle with the armaments director, Mutschmann resorted to an extraordinary means; he had that director arrested, had a piece of paper hung around his neck and made him go through the city in the company of a constable; on the paper it said: "I am the greatest protector of Jews in Dresden". Thereupon Mutschmann succeeded very quickly in making Dresden free of Jews. At that time many Jews who were declared to be indispensable in the armaments

---

96   Martin Mutschmann, Gauleiter of Saxony.

industry could be apprehended only in individual cases, although the WVHA had affiliated armaments industries to individual concentration camps.

Theresienstadt : A Model of Ghetto Formation

Theresienstadt actually arose on the basis of a proposal that I made. I was once summoned to Heydrich in the presence of State Secretary Frank,[97] shortly after his appointment as Deputy Protector of Bohemia and Moravia. He said to me: "I promised that the Protectorate of Bohemia and Moravia will be free of Jews in a few weeks; the press people have published that in the newspaper ... What do we do now? Something must happen. Make a proposal!" I was not previously informed of what it was about, and therefore came unprepared to my most senior chief, where I now had to make a proposal. The choice seemed to me to be very big. So I said: "Obergruppenführer, *give me a big city with the necessary country around it! Then we shall take all the Jews of the Protectorate to it as into a ghetto*". At that Heydrich turned to Frank and asked: "What city comes under consideration? Propose!" Frank then named Theresienstadt[98] and therewith my idea found its first concrete manifestation. Only now have I learnt that Heydrich is supposed to have been the great enemy of the ghetto idea. To that I can only say I myself did not observe or hear any of that; in our initial discussions he himself said "the Jewish ghetto Theresienstadt". This is his own expression. Only later did the SS Reichsführer no longer want the designation " Theresienstadt Jewish ghetto" but changed it to "Theresienstadt old-age home".

Theresienstadt was a small garrison city where some thousand Czech labourers and tradesmen had settled, as it was customary in this area for garrison cities. Heydrich decided to relocate the garrison and to resettle the local population with full recompense; the Czech Protectorate government managed the technical matters without any loud complaints becoming evident. IV-B4 took over the

---

97 Karl Hermann Frank, SS Gruppenführer. German minister of state in the Protectorate, Deputy Reich Protector of Bohemia and Moravia, sentenced to death in May 1946 in Prague, hanged on 16 October 1946 in the detention centre in Nuremberg.

98 Theresienstadt lies in the district of Litoměřice/north Bohemia on the Eger near its confluence with the Elbe. Fortress from 1780-1892. In the thirties Theresienstadt had over 7,000 inhabitants. It became a Jewish ghetto during the war which was also exhibited to the International Red Cross.

different functions from army administrative officers, and therewith Theresienstadt was free for our ghettoising plans. For the first time a ghetto was formed on the territory of the Reich. When we marched to Poland in 1939 Heydrich was not yet the Deputy Protector. In Poland there were ghettos which had been maintained by the Jews themselves; now more inhabitants entered it, both Jews who had up to then not lived in a ghetto and also those who previously lived isolated in the country. The ghettos in Poland were watched and sealed off, partly with barbed wire, for example, with walls or even in other ways.

The orthodox Jew has always advocated ghettoising, especially in the east, because throughout history he had to tolerate regular pogroms. In Germany in the Middle Ages there were similarly ghettos of orthodox Jews. Zionism did not exist at all at that time, but perhaps individual Jews tending to assimilation, money-changers and later mainly financiers who interacted with the princes. Both sides had always seen advantages in ghettoising: the princes and city governments found it better for supervision, and the Jews received greater security. The Jew tending to assimilation however did not by preference live in the ghetto and was unhappy when he was forced to do so. In our age ghettoising agreed with the orthodox and Zionist sections of Jewry: they felt the life in the ghetto as a wonderful opportunity to accustom themselves to the communal life, which is why we did not hear a single complaint from this group against the ghettoising. On the contrary, Dr. Eppstein from Berlin said to me once that Jewry was thankful to me because, through the cohabitation in the Theresienstadt ghetto, it was becoming acquainted with the real community; this was a great school for the future life of these men in the state of Israel. I repeat: only the assimilationist Jew felt the ghettoising as an "exclusion from the community" and a degradation, and likewise did the non-Jew who could not in general sympathise with the Jewish mentality and therefore perceived in ghettoising a brutal coercive measure. I think even today that the unity of orthodox Jewry through the centuries is due to the ghetto idea.

Theresienstadt was in no way a concentration camp, but was exclusively under a Jewish leadership, starting with the Chief Rabbi Baeck to Murmelstein. It was sealed off by the Czech gendarmerie but only to a certain border, because the Berlin-Prague highway ran through the centre of Theresienstadt. Every week or fortnight we supplied to the camp the provisions in cargo trains and often had difficulties with the Gauleiter of Saxony, Mutschmann, and many regional group leaders because it was sometimes actually better for the Jews in Theresienstadt

A football match at the Theresienstadt gheto 1943.

in terms of provisions than for the German civil population. The Jews worked for the armaments industry and were paid by their employer[99] exactly the same rate as our own workers.

In his impulsive manner Heydrich had "made a promise" and I could now see how it was to be fulfilled; it was fulfilled with the full support of the leading Jewish personalities. At that time I was in Berlin and only occasionally visited Prague while the building work in Theresienstadt was in full swing. There I learnt that the commanding officer of the Sipo and SD in Bohemia and Moravia[100] had ordered the hanging of three or four Jews in the middle of the ghetto under construction. Today I can no longer describe the circumstance precisely: Günther, my chief Sturmführer and the then chief of the "Central Office for Jewish Emigration" in Prague, who was in charge of the implementation and development matters of Theresienstadt, had determined that some Jews had schemed or wanted to scheme something forbidden; this he had reported to the commanding

---

99   Jews were employed in the mica works.

100   According to Jewish reports, Theresienstadt received the first transports on 20,23 and 26 January 1943. In August 1943 a delegation of the Danish Red Cross under Dr. Juel Henigsen visited Theresienstadt.

officer of the Sipo and SD as the responsible supervising authority of Theresienstadt. The public hanging of the culprits was then ordered by the latter, that is, the commanding officer of the Sipo and SD, as a deterrent.

The mood of panic of the Jews already present in the ghetto was palpable, since we had naturally explained to them, as indeed it was also planned, that they could build their own territory in Theresienstadt. When I went there the Jewish functionaries gave me hell, but, I had to stand by the measure of the commanding officer of the Sipo and SD and therefore explained to them that I could do nothing against legal violations on the part of the Jews and their punishment by the local commanding officer. On the other hand, I assured them, and this assurance was fulfilled, that in future here in the camp no more hangings would take place, but that I expected as a counter-assurance that the council of elders would prevent a repetition of such offences.

To this end I granted the Jews their own police, who rose in numbers to a strength of 150 men; they were distinguished by an armband. Soon the commanding officer of the Sipo and SD reported his doubts about this to Berlin, because this regular Jewish police began to train and conduct military exercises in the camp area. However the police were retained, but I had an age limit established: only Jews from fifty to fifty five could from now on be policemen. I hoped therewith to have forestalled the possibility of any military efforts by the Jews.

To come back to that public hanging, I must mention also that I lodged a protest with the concerned office and explained that one could not, on the one hand, promise the Jews that they could build up their own administration in Theresienstadt, if, on the other hand, we alienated them from the beginning with such a measure. The punishable Jews could indeed have been sent to a concentration camp, as this was also the customary method of punishment. In the case of this protest they fully agreed with me. The new commanding officer of the Sipo and SD had apparently ordered this through ignorance of the circumstances; the order of the SS Reichsführer stated that punishable Jews were to be sent to a concentration camp. Theresienstadt was however not a concentration camp. Basically the Jews in the Protectorate were legally under the Protectorate government; the latter had made an arrangement with the Reich Protector according to which the Czech population of Theresienstadt, as mentioned, was moved and fully recompensed, for which the Czech Protectorate government placed all Jews within the domain of their administration under the responsibility of the protector; the transfer to Theresienstadt was assured to them. However, as there were not enough admission possibilities, the Protector ordered that a certain percentage of the Protectorate Jews be sent to eastern concentration camps.

In Theresienstadt the Jews, from the moment of their arrival in the camp were under the responsible supervising authority, that is, the commanding officer of the Sipo and SD. He had there a regular command of five to six men from the ranks of his office members, while the external watch was conducted by some fifteen to twenty Czech constables, which meant practically one man for every two kilometres. The supervision of Theresienstadt was also to a certain extent under the RSHA, since I had founded and established it, but was transferred to Berlin and the detail work was now directed by Günther, who for his part was under the commanding officer of the Sipo and SD. There were no more executions or other punishments from the German side in Theresienstadt, and it remained in accordance with what I had said to the Jews: "Punishments will no longer be meted out by German government bodies and offices – punish them yourselves!"

After the war I read that one of my people – I think it was Seidel – was sentenced by some court to death and presented exclusively Jews as witnesses for the defence. All of them spoke in his favour and I have myself read that the Theresienstadt Jews did not understand how Seidel and the other chiefs of Theresienstadt were sentenced to death and hanged. That was not justice at all, but an absolute wilfulness, comparable in some ways to the three or four Jews hanged in Theresienstadt at the start.

The SS Reichsführer always listened sympathetically to things that had to do with Theresienstadt. For example, when I once pointed out that it was advisable for the Jews in Theresienstadt to create their own theatre, a kindergarten and other cultural institutions, that was immediately approved; for Theresienstadt was not to be a concentration camp but a ghetto or a sort of old age home. A brutal person would never have granted members of a race that had declared war against his own people such favours – only a man of the stature of the SS Reichsführer could grant this concession.

On the basis of the assessments now conveyed to me from the hostile post-war literature, I wish to explain once again in summary on Theresienstadt: after my chief Heydrich had been named the Deputy Protector of Bohemia and Moravia and had assured the press that in a matter of months the Protectorate would be free of Jews, I received the commission to fulfil his press declaration. I no longer remember how many months Heydrich had mentioned, but I still know that it was an astonishingly short time which made a solution through emigration fully impossible, for from whence should I obtain in such a short time the required immigration possibilities? Heydrich also realised that, but something had to happen since the press had already been informed that the Protectorate would be free of Jews.

As so often in all my talks I now developed once again the idea – for the umpteenth time – that the entire Jewish problem of the world was rooted in the homelessness of this people. For that reason I proposed to Heydrich – as already mentioned – granting a territory within his Protectorate with a city in its centre, where the Jews of the Protectorate were to live under self-administration insofar as it was possible in terms of numbers. State Secretary K.H. Frank proposed the city of Theresienstadt. Indeed, what could I do with a city in which hardly ten thousand men could be accommodated? It was therefore no solution, hardly an intermediary solution. I still envisaged a far larger territory where, for example, even food could be produced independently in sufficient measure. But something of this size was not available. The few hectares of land which surrounded the city were in no way sufficient. According to the instruction of the chief of the Sipo and SD in Bohemia and Moravia, Heydrich, or according to the ordinance of the Deputy Reich Protector Heydrich, the transfer work to Theresienstadt was set in motion through the regional offices. A Jewish "council of elders" installed in Theresienstadt worked on the details of order in the city. The supervising authority was the commanding officer of the Sipo and SD, under whom stood, the "Central Office for Jewish Emigration" in Prague.

Gradually, under Himmler's order, Theresienstadt became a home for prominent people, both old and young. The Jews of Theresienstadt administered themselves, they had their own money, their own stamps, issued by the postal administration of the Protectorate, their own police, kindergartens, schools, a theatre, a hospital and coffee houses as well as their own crematorium under Jewish administration. The food came by and large through the commanding officer of the Sipo and SD to the "council of elders", which distributed and also administered it.

There were only a few Czech police who guarded Theresienstadt, and they were at the boundaries of the city as well as at the Dresden-Prague

Jewish children at Theresienstadt during an inspection by the Red Cross 1944.

highway running through the middle of Theresienstadt. Further there was, as mentioned, a small SS contingent of six to at most ten men with the task of taking care of the food provision, the control of the different sanitary arrangements as well as the continual reporting on the Jewish life in the city to the commanding officer of the Sipo and SD in Prague.

Jewish functionaries confirmed to me repeatedly that they were grateful for Theresienstadt, because they possessed here in relation to their Palestine plans a good training possibility, especially relating to the education on communal life. Most of the Jews, I was told, became acquainted with a communal life for the first time here and were encouraged to communal work.

From the "expert" post-war literature, so rich in errors, I may mention another gross mistake, since it concerns Theresienstadt. There for example it says: "... like Theresienstadt, Belsen was "politically" administered by IV-A4b, Eichmann's office .." It seems as if such "expert" authors need only to see a number of capital and small letters, Roman and Arabic numerals, to confuse everything: my office belonged to IV B; IV A was a rather completely separate and different one from that – the difference between IV A and IV B was rather as great as between the southern and northern hemispheres.

I dare to close the chapter on "Theresienstadt" with the remark that one may just ask the around 10,000 Jewish inhabitants of Theresienstadt who were discovered there by the Allies after the end of the war, what their experiences in the ghetto, old-age home or camp for prominent people of Theresienstadt were – always taking into consideration the fact that there was a war; the answers cannot appear anything but positive. There was, so far as I have been informed about the last days, never anything ordered by Berlin that could afterwards be counted as "war-crimes or crimes against humanity".

If I may add this for the sake of thoroughness, there were constant transfers to Theresienstadt on the orders of the SS Reichsführer, which at first led to overcrowding. In order to prevent epidemic outbreaks, the SS Reichsführer ordered two or three transports of many thousand Jews to be transferred to Auschwitz.[101] Therewith they were removed from the field of responsibility of the chief of the Sipo and SD and transferred to that of another head office, the Economic and Administrative Head Office (WVHA), which stood in this capacity under the SS Reichsführer.

Eichmann Describes His Tasks

With the stalling of the war against the Soviet Union, Hitler ordered the *physical annihilation of the Jews,* and their *emigration was then forbidden.* On the former I shall go into detail in another section of these explanations.

The prohibition of emigration resulted in the fact that Gestapo Office IV-B4 from now on had to deport the Jews according to orders to certain destination stations, always near the concentration camps. In the meanwhile, my department IV-B4 had dealt with many Jewish measures. In order to give a clearer idea of the tasks and responsibility of my department I wish to describe how ordinances, orders and decrees were dealt with by it. As an example I take the obligation of the identification of the Jews. On closer recollection I do not think that the legal, that is the ordinance-technical side arose from my department. This took place in another office, even though my department was involved in it, and through one of my legal administrators. The office

---

101 Auschwitz (Pol. Oswiecim), city in the Krakow voivodeship, lies on the Sola, fell to Austria in 1773. In the second World War concentration camps and armaments factories were established outside the city. When it was handed over to the Soviets in 1945 the camp held 32,000 Jews.

that was in charge of this invited all the central authorities concerned to relevant discussions. In other cases I could naturally be occupied with the processing of the implementational conditions of any ordinances, so that the police would be placed in a position to observe and check their application. In such a case I received from my chief, Gruppenführer Müller, or directly from the chief of the Sipo and SD, Heydrich, the commission to submit the regulation through decree or police ordinance, under the respective code word, by a target date. Such a commission I then discussed in concrete cases on account of their legal character not only with my government magistrate, and my police inspector but also with a government councillor or government assessor. Then followed the determination of who was to be considered as such. For that the Nuremberg laws were referred to; then the border cases were determined and finally the penalty in case of noncompliance.

The implementational outline contained the guidelines of such things as on what side of the clothing the identification is to be attached, how big, in what colour, whether to be worn on the street or at home, and how the offices had to act if a Jew were encountered on the street without any identification. A structural outline was always formed quickly, but implementation of the law had to be discussed for a long time; for there always emerged new questions and new proposals that had to be considered. If I had prepared such an outline in my work discussions, which I, the government councillor representing me or my regular representative, had to personally preside over, then I had this structural outline signed by all the delegates participating in the discussion, completed it and sent it as an enclosure to my letter to the chief of the Sipo and SD or to the chief of the German Police. Thereupon the outline was signed by the SS Reichsführer or the chief of the Sipo and SD and came back to me. Afterwards it was sent to all the offices and published as a police ordinance. Such a matter had an external fallout which could not be hidden at home or abroad, and for that a considerable apparatus was set in motion.

But there were also police ordinances which arose in a quicker way which however did not have such a fundamental importance. An example: An office outside reported to me difficulties in some aspect of the "treatment of enemies"; this could affect one of my advisers or some state police control office. This office now reported to me that there were ambiguities or that difficulties occurred in practice, and a uniform operation could not yet be achieved; therefore it was requested to clarify the matter generally. Then I called my responsible expert, went through the matter with him and ordered him to work on it and to present all the instructions and decrees that were already present in this field. At the same time he should examine how far the entire matter could be regulated by a decree or whether a police ordinance was necessary. After he had studied the facts, he informed me that in this case, for example, a circular to all the police offices would be sufficient. This circular had to be published for notification to the inspectors of the Sipo and SD, to the commanding officers of Sipo and SD and also to the higher SS and police chiefs. If I was in agreement or if I thought that further difficulties or ambiguities could arise, then the entire matter returned to my consultation folder for another consultation with my office chief. But if he did not consider it so important that the chief of the Sipo and SD or indeed the SS Reichsführer was to be brought in here, then it was decided to clarify the matter in a circular. This circular was drafted by my expert and signed by me. The expert placed his seal under the sign IV-B4 and I placed mine to the right of it, then the circular went to the Office Chief of IV for his signature, then afterwards to the Chief of the Sipo and SD, who likewise signed or just placed his seal, and finally to the SS Reichsführer. Then I composed, on the basis of this chancellery outline, the final circular for all police and police control offices. If it was a small matter which could be regulated within one's own field of responsibility, I signed it with my name, or Müller of Heydrich signed. As divisional head I could never issue a police decree without involving the apparatus of the authorities, even if it were very minor.

Only in the rarest cases did a divisional head in the Gestapo office bear the intellectual authorship in the case of decrees and ordinances. In the police system it is always the case that practical cases are brought from subordinate offices to the superior authorities and therefore the "intellectual authorship" is to be sought below. If it is a matter of more significant cases or of cases of a fundamental sort, then decrees, ordinances, etc., come down and are imposed from above. A divisional head in the Gestapo office was less creative than, for example, a divisional head in Office VII. In Gestapo Office IV it was not the task of a division head to be active in a creative manner; he had rather to preside over the operational apparatus. Active in a creative way were Office VII, Office III, the Propaganda Ministry, the Chancellery of the deputy of the Führer.[102] The divisional head in the

---

102 The Party Chancellery (Parteikanzlei), was the headquarters of the NSDAP led first by Hitler's deputy, Rudolf Hess, and from May 1941 by Hess' successor, Martin Bormann.

Gestapo Office was the chairman of his bureaucratic machine which had to revise what came down from above according to the issued instructions and orders. If no instructions and orders had yet been issued, he provided these on the basis of consultations.

It could happen that one of my officers from abroad came to me and, for example, said: "I have a great difficulty here; I think we cannot go on with this. I think, Obersturmbannführer,[103] that we must undertake something for the laws in this country are of such a sort that a transfer of the Jews with this citizenship is impossible, so long as a special legislation is not present here or an implementation possibility is worked out in a legal way." I listened to him, had the responsible expert come, in this case it was a lawyer. He was either aware of the difficulty in the concerned country or not. He thought, for example, that the matter was in itself very simple; for we needed only to propose to the Foreign Office, through its ambassador in the responsible office abroad, to see to it that a supplementary ordinance be added to a certain law in this or that sense so that one might have a lever and be able to operate. Then I decided either that the matter should be presented in this sense or that I would undertake further consultations relating to it. On the next occasion I then submitted this proposal to Müller; if he found it good a letter was prepared for the Foreign Office. Such a letter was never signed by me but by the office chief. Only when it was a quite simple matter, which went from the hands of the legation councillor von Thadden[104] to the Foreign Office, did I sign the letter myself. In the first mentioned letters to the Foreign Office, signed by the office chief, attention was drawn to the concerned circumstances and it was requested to investigate and explore to what extent and under what conditions the order of the SS Reichsführer in question could be implemented in the concerned country.

It was always a very protracted process with the Foreign Office; one had to keep drilling ... or the matter died out and was placed in the files. Ordinances which were inspired and developed by me also exist, however only in relation to insignificant matters. Heydrich, for example, never allowed his authority to be taken out of his hands. In the case of Kaltenbrunner it was simpler. If it later emerged that the control was really a matter of the Foreign Office or the Reich

---

103   SS Lieutenant Colonel

104   Eberhard von Thadden, government councillor, was from May 1943 Jewish adviser in the Germany section of the Foreign Office. He was sentenced by the high court in Frankfurt to 8 years.

Economics Ministry, then Kaltenbrunner never raised an objection, whereas Heydrich thundered when a matter was taken out of his hands.

A Few Words on the Madagascar Plan

In the "Madagascar Plan", the initiative came from me; and there I was involved in a "creative" way – if one wishes to call it that, but again not alone, for even the Jew Herzl himself had taken up the idea because he had little success in Palestine. But such cases were quite rare; for it was not the task of the divisional head to ponder what was to be done here. In general that did not happen; for precisely in the case of the "treatment of enemies" there was such an abundance of influences outside the department, thus from the external police offices, from the party, from influential persons, that such a matter could only be developed in a police-technical manner, that is, with the involvement of the entire police apparatus. It was my task as departmental head to take care to avoid any outline of a decree that would have meant an extraordinary overburdening for the subordinate executive offices. There was such an abundance of suggestions that had to be screened accurately; a department head did not at all need to fabricate something on his own. It worked in this way not only in my case as head of department of IV-B4 but also in that of all the other heads of departments.

Concentration Camps, Laws and I

In this context it should, in my opinion, be clearly explained what I as divisional head of department IV-B4 of the Gestapo Office in general had to do with the concentration camps. Thereby a distinction must be made between the time in which the Gestapo Office had to decide on individual cases, thus until around 1941, and the time in which the *Führer order "for the physical annihilation"* was issued. The concentration camps arose in the first period; those who were later "big people" were still small. Already at that time some guidelines were established which were partly elaborated on, or even removed later. There arose an entire list of measures which were to be taken when a Jew had become known on account of a race-damaging relationship or on account of smuggling foreign currency, when it was a matter of an offence against the most basic aspects of life of the German people.

Ordinances were issued which were repeatedly supplemented, elaborated, or even revoked by the SS Reichsführer. In a few areas where dealing with the enemy still had to be worked out, the highest chief, the SS Reichsführer took a personal interest in the details. It was sufficient if Ley, a Gauleiter or somebody else, on some occasion – be it at a meal together – approached the SS Reichsführer on a certain matter, to cause him to issue ordinances personally; these even stood in many ways in contradiction to that which was valid previously. On the other hand, other matters were regulated legally. The Gestapo or the police central office wrote, for example, to the Gestapo Office: "The Jew X has begun this or that illegal activity. It is proposed to send him to the concentration camp; I (the chief of the Stapo control office) request instructions'. This matter then came to IV-B4; my government magistrate or my police inspector worked on the case by checking if the conditions were present to admit the concerned Jew into a concentration camp. If the case was clear, it said in the reply to the Gestapo or Police central office: "Admission to the concentration camp according to the decree of the SS Reichsführer". This letter did not go from IV-B4 or from the office chief to the state police central office – for example, Munich – but as an outline to the detention department in Gestapo Office IV. A government or criminal councillor presided over this department; he either signed himself or the office chief signed it and then passed on the necessary instructions. Later such inquiries to subordinate or superior offices were regulated to the Gestapo Office through the central registrar's office of Gestapo Office IV in such a way that the detention department first received and handled such inquiries in the way my expert too would have handled them; I myself or my regular representative had only to sign the clearance. But the detention department could not decide in the matter; it was only an "extended registrar's office"; therefore it was not directed by a government councillor but by a government criminal councillor who did not belong to a "higher echelon".

Naturally I was responsible in the first place and had to have my expert examine under what considerations a certain Jew could or could not be admitted. Later, for simplification, it was arranged in such a way that we in IV-B4 needed only to sign, for there were dozens of such cases.

Such an inquiry had roughly the following form:

"State police central office (Munich)

File number ...

The Eichmann Tapes

To the Gestapo Office

Attn. Gruppenführer Müller

Ref. Jew X (Lemberg)

born ... residing at ...

Ref. Circular decree of the SS Reichsführer of ...

The above-mentioned Jew was sent by the foreign currency investigation office of the local   office because he sold currency illegally. With reference to the above-mentioned circular decree I request for approval to transfer the Jew X to the concentration camp (Dachau). I request instructions.

signed. ... "

The reply could then run as follows:

"According to the recent inquiry of ... the Jew X is, according to the circular decree of ..., to be taken into custody.

Date of detention review: ½ year.

signed. ... "

This letter first went to the detention department where the dates of detention review were determined; then it went again to the concerned state police central office, which subsequently transferred the Jew X to the concentration camp. I did not have anything further to do with the concentration camp or the detainee. Only in relation to the date of detention review did the state police central office once again make inquiries. This was then either newly determined or the possibility may have arisen in the meanwhile to grant to the Jew emigration to country Y. Then the state police central office further informed that the Jew X was imprisoned on account of foreign exchange smuggling, and inquired if an emigration could be granted since there was an order of the SS Reichsführer relating to this according to which release was to be immediately granted to the Jews imprisoned in concentration camps if an immigration approval could be shown. Everything was checked precisely, decided in a positive or negative manner, according to the existing decrees.

There was an abundance of individual cases; my people had to work day and night to deal with all of them, for in every individual case it had to be checked if the concerned person was, according to law, decree and ordinance, a Jew or a non-Jew, if he had committed a serious offence, to which of the concerned offences the penalty that was proposed applied, and finally if now the entire matter stood actually in accordance with the laws or the police ordinances.

Everything had to go according to the law. IV-B4 could not say one thing at one time and another at another. If it was not conducted precisely according to a certain procedure and a wrong instruction had been given, the admonishment from above would perhaps not have been so bad. It would have been worse if the police official were able to say: "Yes, earlier laws were applied, but today one apparently does not know the legal situation". That would have been frightful and therefore we could not give any wrong instructions.

Special Treatment in the Concentration Camps

There was *special treatment*, but not only in the case of Jews. If at that time a Jew had acted against the Nuremberg Laws, for example, through proven sexual intercourse with a person of German blood and he could be found, he was taken to a state police office. Then this office wrote exactly as in other cases: "The Jew Y was admitted because he was found on …. in race-damaging activities. According to the decree it is inquired if special treatment should be carried out." My expert examined the case; the facts of the case did not concern me; on the basis of a special agreement between Himmler and the Justice Minister these cases were no longer brought to the courts. In Jewish matters only essential cases of special significance were transferred to the justice, but here the SS Führer had to be in agreement that the responsibility of the justice was restricted.

If the examination of my expert showed that everything was clear, the decision went once again back to the concerned police office, and the Jew X could be directed to special treatment. *This special treatment consisted of shootings or hangings*, according to the regulations of the Reichsführer relating to this. In matters of punishment the Reichsführer was very fastidious. So, for example, he allowed flogging in the concentration camps and specified precisely the number and manner of the blows to be administered.[105] Flogging could be administered only in the presence of a doctor and buckets of water had to be ready. On 12 blows only the office chief could decide. 25 blows only the chief of the Sipo and SD could decide, and 50 blows was a punishment where only the SS Reichsführer himself could decide. A divisional head could not order a single blow.

Visits to Concentration Camps

After the order of the Führer for physical annihilation, I travelled often to the concentration camps, thus to Auschwitz, near Lublin and to Oranienburg. My visits to the concentration camp near Lublin I shall describe in detail in another section. I went to the Oranienburg concentration camp in connection with the Grynszpan affair; it was a single case. I was repeatedly with Höß[106] in Auschwitz; for I had to have contact with the concentration camps that my deportation trains had to deliver to. This is easily explained: Let us take as an example that Wisliceny from Slovakia had put together a transport for (X number) of Jews, or that Dannecker in France planned eight transport trains with altogether ten thousand Jews. Before the travel plan conference with the Reich Transport Ministry, a discussion took place with the responsible persons of the WVHA. For the inspector of the concentration camp system had to inform me where these transports were to go.

The chief of the WVHA, Pohl, had the basic instruction from the SS Reichsführer to pick up all Jews; where he took them was his business. If Auschwitz was determined, then, for example, the Reich border between Hungary and Austria was made out to be the departure station or in other cases Auschwitz the destination station. Then the deportations rolled, but the WVHA had given me a maximum number to which I had to adhere to the regulations of the chief of the WVHA that the Jews should be transferred in an unobjectionable condition of health. So long as everything went ahead in an unobjectionable way the transports rolled and nobody worried about anybody else. But practice is sometimes different than theory. So, for example, I frequently requested the State Secretary

---

105 Often practically meted out.

106 Rudolf Franz Höß, last rank SS Standartenführer. Commandant of the Auschwitz concentration camp up to November 1943, then representative of Richard Glücks as Inspector of the concentration camps.

Endre[107] in the case of Hungary that the Jews should be fit for work on their arrival. Nevertheless the Hungarian gendarmerie beat the Jews in some cases into the wagons because a wild Hungarian gendarmerie constable, for example, did not "wish to waste too much time". Sometimes the food and provisions were insufficient, and although it became better on German soil, the Jews arrived in a bad condition. That may have occurred not only in the case of the Hungarian transports but also in others; for there were difficulties everywhere. So there came to me a representative from Höß or even he personally, or I received a telegraph from Müller, that I should go without delay to Auschwitz to discuss and ascertain difficulties which might arise. He requested me in addition to come to Berlin to make a report. So I had to travel to Auschwitz perhaps three or four times in all during my stay in Hungary.

At the height of the Hungarian deportations, the limit was exceeded once; for there were numerous difficulties. At that time there were five to six, or even ten deportation trains per day. On certain days transport trains did not come through on account of a bomb attack and lay standing, or something else happened in between. The next transport rolled immediately after, and so it happened that once ten or twelve or sixteen transport trains arrived at the same time in Auschwitz. Thereupon Höß became "furious" and desperate. I was summoned to Pohl, who clearly could not control himself and shouted at me in an immoderate manner; I had not been responsible for it at all. I learnt of the difficulties from Höß. In war times higher force ruled and a scapegoat had to be found. For the clarification of such cases I therefore visited the concentration camp, in no way out of "personal curiosity" but as result of an invitation of the commandant, who perhaps incidentally gave himself pleasure in showing a "desk-jockey" the conditions which were expected of a concentration camp commandant. Something like that was of course never said to me but I felt it in that way. Perhaps I too would have reacted in this way.

This was the reason why I had something to do with a concentration camp at some stage. Exactly as little as a departmental head in a police office needs to be creatively active, as little does he have to do with a concentration camp; he was the chairman of his bureaucratic

---

107   Dr. Lászlo Endre, Vice-Gespan a Hungarian administrative title, chief of Budapest province, then 2nd state secretary in the Hungarian Ministry of the Interior, killed by the Soviet Union.

apparatus as in every office with executive authority. In Office VII or in Office III, that office which had no executive authority, the departmental head was not just the chairman of his bureaucratic apparatus. However, the departmental head in the Reich Criminal Office or the Office of the regular police, or the Gestapo Office was just the chairman of his bureaucratic apparatus. The SS Reichsführer had distributed the responsibilities clearly and was very well advised on it; he never let his police act and administer according to their discretion but had them firmly in his grasp so that they fulfilled their duties systematically insofar as it was a matter of executive issues. In other things however the SS Reichsführer was exactly the opposite; I think that to him nothing was more detestable than "going by the book" among people from whom he expected independent vision and thought.

Our strength in the executive lay not in creative action, but in our complete supervision. We had to supervise the matters and strive to work out a matter within the context of the Reich as quickly and as comprehensively as possible without bringing the Gestapo into difficult situations with other central authorities, without creating cases which could bring the chief of the Sipo and SD or the SS Reichsführer into unpleasant situations. Moreover, as the representative appointed by the state, as the divisional head of IV-B4, I had to see that no half-heartedness of service crept in. Fulfilling this task meant such a full measure of work that the divisional head no longer managed to think elaborately about his own matters, which anyway lay by the dozen in files, as suggestions from below or even from superior offices, and were dealt with routinely anyway.

The Jewish enemy must today know the technique described here and the actual connections better, because he has indeed his own secret police in the state of Israel. That is why he certainly knows today how things like that are done. Moreover I am convinced that no eastern security police, neither the Soviet police nor the Hungarian nor the Czech works any differently. Any other method of working is not imaginable. I cannot believe that a Soviet or Hungarian commissioner can act freely according to his own judgement. That does not happen anywhere in the world, not even in the "West". A head of department only works on that which is brought to his attention from above and from below. We did not at all need to be creative because every phase of a procedure was already considered and thought through by other minds.

Where I had Commanding Authority

It has become customary to point to my "unrestricted power". In reality my commanding authority was narrowly circumscribed. I had a commanding authority with regard to my subordinates. These were

- a government councillor,

- a government assessor,

- my regular representative,

- a government magistrate,

- many senior police inspectors and police inspectors,

- some police and crime secretaries,

- many crime assistants,

- many police employees,

- many chiefs of the SD, occasionally an Obersturmbannführer of the SD,

- many subordinate officers and men of the SD who functioned as police employees.

That was my department in Berlin, to which, as an extended arm, belonged the "advisers on the Jewish question" in the German missions and among the commanding officers of the Sipo and SD. Here however my commanding authority was subject to a limitation, for these "advisers" stood in the first place under the ambassador, or the envoy, or the commanding officer of the Sipo and SD. In case these "advisers" could not follow some functional order that they had received they were free to come to me. That was different from the situation among the officials placed immediately under an ambassador or commanding officer. The "advisers" could then explain to me why they could not carry out the concerned order, perhaps because it was in contradiction to an instruction received from the department; then they could ask for a clarification. When this was given, they returned again to their office.

Herewith I have outlined precisely the field of my direct commanding authority. A circular to all state police control offices could have as its letterhead "The chief of the Sipo and SD" and my department number and also be signed by me; that was then an instruction and not an order. From this one can reason that I had unrestricted "instructing authority" over all the subordinate offices of the Chief of the Sipo and SD. But first it was up to the leaders of the Stapo (control) offices to expresses any doubts. Only after the removal of these possible doubts did the instruction naturally enter into force. If the doubts were well-grounded, then one proceeded differently. Basically however a letter was sent out to all the state police offices and Gestapo central offices with an instruction in the form of a telegram. These telegrams however existed in the files. Such a file looked as follows:

I Memorandum: Here everything was factually brought together, developed, worked out and explained.

II Such an instruction was sent out to the State Police offices, especially if it was issued to many State Police offices, and quite especially if it was a matter of a circular to all State Police and control offices. In addition, under II, the matter was presented to the Chief of Gestapo Office IV through the official route with the request for acknowledgement, approval and signature. This meant that an instruction to more than one office had as a rule to be signed by Gestapo Office IV.

III If it was a matter of a circular to all the State Police control offices, as a rule the signature of the Chief of the Sipo and SD was added.

In exceptional cases, the chief of the office signed. Only in quite exceptional cases if, for example, neither the chief of the office nor the Chief of the Sipo and SD were present was I able to sign such a circular, but then I had to mark it as point III: "Since nobody was to be found and there existed a danger of delay". But afterwards I had to vouch for the fact that I had myself signed and ordered a circular. If my reason was found to be insufficient I had to accept an official admonition. But such a case never occurred, for the office chief Müller indeed had his representative, for a short while Schellenberg and later regularly Huppenkothen.

In the case of a "special treatment", the office chief had to decide and endorse it with his signature. I could sign only routine matters to State Police control offices; the letter was incidental. What was important was the letterhead; for, even in routine procedures, a memorandum had to be drawn up in which the expert had to give the reason for granting a request, or why it had to be handled negatively. Under point II he then prepared the draft of the letter

Heinrich Himmler, Ernst Kaltenbrunner, and other SS officials visit the Mauthausen concentration camp in 1941.

and under III I decided if this letter draft would be signed by me or if I had to present it to the office chief for signing. But even all this can from a legal perspective be picked to pieces: If, for example, doubts came to the Chief of the State Police control offices about carrying out a certain instruction, he had to draw up a memorandum; for naturally he could not ignore the instruction. In his memorandum he had to express his doubt and thereby grant himself a delay in the implementation. His memorandum had to clarify his supposition that this certain instruction was of essential importance and that he wished to have further discussion with the chief of Gestapo Office IV before the ordering of this measure. In such a case the letter went once again on its way; that was necessary for the chief of a police control office. But if through this delay harm would arise to the Reich, then he was responsible for it, if an unequivocal, clear instruction from the RSHA, in this case from the Gestapo Office, was present. For, in that case, he did not have to question any further if this instruction was legitimate or not. He would then have had to carry it out in an exact way, independently of his personal interpretation. If it was a matter of human life or of the deprivation of freedom, these matters, although in themselves sensitive, were always handled with the greatest caution.

Marriages Between Jews and Non-Jews

One of the problems that were handled during the war in my department in a bureaucratic way was the matter of people of mixed race, its solution and the question of compulsory sterilisation. Many proposals were made regarding this issue but in practice it never came to any implementation.

The Party Chancellery was always obsessed with the problem of people of mixed race. I was superficially acquainted with the Nuremberg legislation and did not know the law of people of mixed race by heart. I therefore admired my expert, who immediately recognised the legal condition for every case. I was not capable of that and always had to check up and did not notice all the conditions. Senior Councillor Dr. Reischauer mastered this complex of questions completely. I always wondered that it was precisely the Party Chancellery that was concerned about these relations of people of mixed race with such impatience. I was always of the view – and I considered the view of the SS Reichsführer to be similar – that this problem decreased in intensity with each generation because the legislation prevented further mixture with pure Jewish blood so that the share of German blood of the people of mixed race would consequently become increasingly higher. Up to then I had always been opposed to the entire legislation regarding people of mixed race.

I still recall that Dr. Reischauer was always stuck in this, to me, vexatious groove. In spite of endless discussions, a practical implementation was not reached, although the Party Chancellery pushed for one. Nevertheless the people of mixed race all remained in the Reich, the entire matter was long-winded and brought nothing but difficulties with it.

A Favourite Subject: Responsibilities

The responsibilities and powers were circumscribed painfully precisely in Gestapo Office IV. A small anecdote may serve to substantiate this opinion. My department was responsible for the identification of those who were hostile to the people and the state along with an authorisation of confiscation of their assets, as has already been described in another section. This matter was worked on only by lawyers after "hostility to the state" had been established on the basis of some decree. It was examined if the conditions applied and, if this was the case, the claim was allowed. According to the police ordinance the confiscation and sequestration of the assets was requested; thereupon followed the publication in the "Reich Gazette" so that all the offices concerned with it may be informed. Above this official information stood, I think, "the Reich Minister of the Interior" and below "by order of … (signature)".

Gruppenführer Müller was at one time not available. In my file of signatures there were several of these publications, and I consulted these and signed the draft, which was written in a clean copy and went to the printers. In the publication therefore it said "sig., Eichmann". When Gruppenführer Müller came back, I received from him a sharp reprimand. He drew to my attention that I had overstepped my competence and forbade such interventions in future. I should have left the matter standing or presented it to his regular representative for signature.

Even the colours of the ink in the RSHA were fixed! Thus the SS Reichsführer wrote in green, the Chief of the Sipo and SD in blue, Gruppenführer Müller in orange and I myself in violet.

On the Reinhard Operation

A report has only now come into my possession on the so-called "Reinhard Operation"[108] according to which rags and clothes were itemised, as well as the incredible figure of "thousands of kilos of women's hair", it is hardly an original report. I know that, on account of the danger of lice-infection, every concentration camp inmate, man or woman, was shaved, but I consider "thousands of kilos of women's hair" and "train-loads of bed springs" however as very improbable.

Liebenschel or Glücks once said to me that in every concentration camp all hair was shaved and the inmates were rubbed with a certain solution in order to kill the lice. The women received a head-scarf. That is nothing special; for, in all the eastern countries all the hair of inmates are cut because the louse there transmits typhus. Throughout the east one does not have a greater fear of any animal than of the louse; for, in contrast to the merely unpleasant crablouse, the body louse can

---

108 "Reinhard Operation", a liquidation operation led by SS Gruppenführer Globocnik against Polish Jews. Globocnik was SS and Police chief of Lublin, later in Trieste. He died at Weißensee in Carinthia in 1945.

cause death. Many inmates of the concentration camps, especially in the east, fell victim to typhus epidemics. Then very urgent measures had to be taken, and I remember that I once went with Globocnik through the sequestered barracks of a typhus camp. There the sick lay on upholstered straw mattresses. They were minor cases, seriously ill people and those who had already died or were dying.

Sometimes a decision may also have been taken to kill these sick people in order to prevent the danger of a spread of the epidemic. A copy of a letter presented to me just yesterday, written by the Reich Governor in the Warthegau,[109] authorises the killing of Poles who suffered from open tuberculosis in case their incurability was established and certified. The SS Reichsführer had been requested to provide the means for the killing of the incurably ill. How it transpired I cannot say, and even less if the proposal was authorised. I can only say I was not responsible for it, or for the treatment of the Jews in the Warthegau.

The Infamous Gas-Vans à la Grafeneck[110]

The gas vans for the terminally ill were prepared in Berlin, but I had no idea of it in the RSHA, because we received no information about it. Müller knew about it, but I did not occupy myself with it. So also nothing further was known to me about the matter of the open tuberculosis. But the letter of Greiser to the SS Reichsführer is again a clear confirmation of my often repeated declaration that department IV-B4 was not always involved in such initiatives.

Some Reich Leaders[111] or chiefs would meet at official conferences, lectures, official travels or even during a meal together, and arranged such things directly among themselves. The SS Reichsführer then decided either negatively or, if in agreement, ordered everything within his area of responsibility autocratically.... Everything that he considered practical and opportune within the scope of his responsibilities was then made ready for the implementation of his orders.

---

109   The Warthe district in Poland.

110   The National Socialist Grafeneck Euthanasia Centre was based in Grafeneck Castle in Baden-Württemberg.

111   National leaders of the National Socialist party.

Responsibilities for the Deportation

In the territory of the Reich my department was responsible for the rounding up and the transportation. Abroad generally the rounding up of Jews was carried out by the respective regional police; my department was only responsible for the transportation. Even in this matter I do not shy away from fully accepting the responsibility I had, but I categorically deny any responsibility for events for which I was in no way responsible.

If I received an order to carry out a deportation from a certain country, the transport trains had to be first secured from the Reich Transport Ministry. For that a travel-plan conference was arranged which took place in the Reich Transport Ministry, which a travel-plan expert of the railway administration from the area where the embarkation should take place attended; also in attendance were the responsible officials of the Reich railway administration from the area of the destination station, as well as my transport adviser, Hauptsturmführer Nowak.[112] Such travel-plan conferences were always very long-winded and tedious; even two deportation trains could not roll without a travel-plan conference having taken place earlier; for the deportation trains had to be incorporated into an enormous transport network in order to harmonise with the normal trains. To set up a travel plan is a science in itself which I cannot outline.

I was never responsible in the Generalgouvernement, so I did not have anything to do with the setting up of transport trains there. For that even the Reich Transport Ministry was not involved; for in Krakow there existed a Reich railway administration and so long as such transports ran within the Generalgouvernement, Krakow would work out the travel-plan by itself; the Reich Transport Ministry were only involved if these trains travelled in its own territory. Thus even in Serbia, in the Protectorate and in the eastern territories the travel-plans were made independently. The travel-plan conference determined, for example, how many closed wagons had to be made available. These wagons were naturally not taken from a wagon yard in some place in Germany but from the normal transport. Thus, for example, goods trains went to a certain place, were then unloaded and redirected. Then the trains were assembled and had to arrive according to the travel-plan on a target date at the destination station.

---

112 Franz Nowak, Hauptsturmführer, Eichmann's travel-plan adviser, imprisoned in Vienna in January 1946.

The travel-plan conferences were a source of lasting anxiety. Throughout the year I grappled with the Transport Ministry and my expert for transports complained to me incessantly about the difficulties of getting transport trains. On the one hand, my superiors pressured me and demanded the evacuation transport urgently, the regional offices of the Sipo as well as of the police authorities did not leave me in peace; sometimes they pointed a pistol at my chest and when I had arranged everything at full speed the Reich Transport Ministry then said: "We have no trains" or "The railway line has been bombed". Then we had to had to set up a travel-plan meeting once again.

Very often the Transport Ministry would call for other orders or total stoppages. If IV-B4 generally "kicked" or pestered long enough, a couple of trains could be obtained as a fraction of the actual requirement; but in times of general stoppage all such efforts were hopeless. On occasion there were train stoppages of four to eight weeks, and even of three or four months. Every start of an offensive meant naturally a total stoppage. Only later, when the trains with food supplies, munitions and soldiers had gone out and came back empty, did I have the opportunity to obtain an allocation of transport on a limited scale. I remember that I did not obtain anything for a while and said to myself in resignation: "Then Heydrich must do it himself".

After the number of trains available was determined at the travel-plan conference, it was then arranged to which camp the Jews were to be transported. The chief of the WVHA gave these instructions but sometimes it was the SS Reichsführer. It would have been much more advantageous for administration purposes to have always followed the rule, that is, to entrust Gestapo Office IV through the Chief of the Sipo and SD with the direct acquisition of the instructions for the transport to a certain camp. Naturally only in rare cases and only in those of the larger operations such as, for example, Hungary, was Pohl the commanding authority in person, otherwise however the inspector of the concentration camps, Brigadeführer Glücks, and in the case of minor matters Glücks' expert, Obersturmbannführer Liebehenschel.[113] If there were any questions to be resolved by Glücks I had to do this. If it were matters that could be discussed with

---

113 Arthur Liebehenschel (1901-48) succeeded Rudolf Höss as commandant of the Auschwitz concentration camp in December 1943, a post he held until May 1944, when Höss returned to Auschwitz. Liebehenschel was at that time made commandant of the Maidanek camp. He was arrested at the end of the war and was sentenced to death in the Auschwitz Trial in Krakow.

Liebehenschel, my regular representative normally went. Only the WVHA or, as mentioned, the SS Reichsführer decided which camp the Jews were to be taken to. It was not up to IV-B4 either to propose a death camp as the destination, or to determine the numbers since indeed the intake capacity of the individual concentration camps was never intimated to us.

The considerations of the WVHA were based on the given intake possibilities as well as the production plans. It was a question of what new factories had arisen, how many mines had to be operated, what other production important for the war had been installed in the area of the concentration camps, what number of workers was needed, how many female and how many male workers, how many office personnel and many other things like that. The commandants' offices of the individual concentration camps intimated their requirement of personnel to the WVHA. And even afterwards the transports were categorised. *The SS Reichsführer could doubtless have personally given Pohl the "liquidation order" and the latter may have supplied, through Glücks, to the commandant of the concentration camp* the guidelines according to which a certain part of the prisoners were to be sent to their death, another to be brought to work at the production. This division between those "fit for work" and those "unfit for work" did not in any case concern the concentration camp commandant himself but there were doctors of the WVHA for that. According to the instructions to the individual commandants, the people were picked out after their disembarkation by the doctors' commissions – at those times when the annihilation order was valid. The Gestapo Office had in general no influence on this, did not have any knowledge of the detailed circumstances and was also not interested in them. These were exclusively the responsibility of the WVHA.

After the political solution, had failed, we were also naturally incorporated into implementing the further phase of the "final solution", but only for transports and in some cases in the rounding up, everything else did not concern us; our work was completed when we, together with the Reich Transport Ministry, set up the travel-plans and were given the names of the receiving station. The rounding-up was *basically* not carried out by IV-B4 - for that I would have had to have in my department at least 2,000 male personnel, which was demonstrably not the case.

The Confusion of the Political Authorities

From the relevant post-war literature individual photocopies and other writings have now been presented to me for assessment, of which one part is forged and another may raise a question about its genuineness. In any case it has become clear to me that an uncanny number of these "documents" bear my department sign IV-B4; this circumstance prompts me to explain the relations in greater detail. Much to our cost, the SS Reichsführer involved himself in the smallest details, gave orders which overruled his own existing orders and thereby sometimes caused chaos. I have often stressed that neither I personally nor my department IV-B4 had anything to do with the occurrences in the Generalgouvernement and in the Soviet Union. The chiefs of the Einsatz Command, the chiefs of the Einsatz Groups[114] never drew their instructions from departments but always from direct orders of the SS Reichsführer.

It seems to me today certain that individual offices, commanding officers of the Sipo from the eastern territories may have been able, as much as any other office, to request the Gestapo for instructions in cases of ambiguity. Obviously my department either approved or refused these instructions according to the circumstances – taking into consideration the restrictions and the methods of origination already mentioned previously. Even here the pertinent laws formed the criterion for a positive or negative decision. That was true also of police ordinances, orders and instructions of the SS Reichsführer or the Chief of the Sipo and SD. Only on the basis of these could the expert in general "decide". There were – and I think there is – no government magistrate, no senior police inspector, no government assessor and no government councillor who would have ever made a decision in a central authority office and presented it to his department for a signature or authorisation with a request to relay it through the official channels, that is, for authorisation by the office chief, if it was a matter of an essential sort, or to forward it through the office chief to the Chief of the Sipo and SD or, if it was a question of high-ranking matters, with a request to forward it to the SS Reichsführer for the purpose of authorisation.

There has not existed a member of a German central authority office who can decide on any matter without such a paper-trail of

---

114 Einsatz group, One of the commands of the Security Police set up for security reasons in the rear army area (security in the greater Russian territory).

instructions and without the presence of ordinances and instructions. This was the official route to subordinate offices. These ordinances arose either on the basis of the decisions of the legislative bodies or on the basis of direct orders of superiors. But they could also arise through the fact the departmental head wrote on his own accord to his superiors through the official channels, informed them about the circumstances in a memorandum and put forward a request for acknowledgement and instruction. In such a case the departmental head "encouraged", to a certain extent, his superior of his own accord to comment on a certain subject and to decide how the departmental head was to proceed in future.

In this way naturally there came to be also letters with the file number IV-B4 to offices with which I had nothing to do, to whom I could convey no instructions at all. Thus, when the responsible expert of a commanding officer of the Sipo and SD from somewhere in the east turned to IV-B4 to obtain an instruction or explanation, that was obviously given to him in response, and his inquiry was noted clearly in the right corner beneath the letterhead under the concerned file number, insofar as it dealt with the responsibility of IV-B4. Then there followed a file number with a stroke, finally there followed the two last numbers of the year. The Einsatz Groups from the east had to write nothing; with them there was in general no correspondence.[115] They conducted a brief operation in this region and had to carry out a general order without any questions. They had no "guidelines" to observe, there neither the consideration for "old infirm persons" nor guidelines regarding bearers of orders and distinctions from the first World War, and because there were no guidelines, they proceeded according to a summary order; there was therefore no need of correspondence.

When letters went from IV-B4, they were not always signed by the departmental head but often by his regular representative. If the scope of responsibility of the department no longer sufficed, then the letter went to the chief of Gestapo Office IV, and if he no longer had responsibility, to the Chief of the Sipo and SD.

In every bureaucratic central authority office, no matter to what ministry it belonged, a certain procedure according to a certain plan was customary which no man could impede. It is, besides, the same procedure that is encountered, with small organisational differences, in almost all civilised countries of the world.

---

115   Eichmann is wrong. There was correspondence.

Matters of extraordinary significance – like the letter I took to Globocnik – went out not through the normal channels but had to be handed over personally with the instruction to burn this letter after a report of completion of the task. In my public registry, I had 200,000 of them, in my secret registry 30,000-40,000 files. This relatively small percentage of the secret registry is to be explained by the fact that, on the basis of existing orders, all measures connected to the deportation were automatically treated as "secret state information" so that the enemy could not be informed in advance. A superior office could send out letters referring to IV-B4, and as a rule this happened as well. If the letter pointed to legal regulations or existing orders, this did not necessarily have to be the case. If, for example, there was a case in which the Nuremberg Laws applied then I could simply sign on the basis of this.

One day I received an order to summon the leader of the Israelite Religious Community in Vienna, Dr. Richard Löwenherz, as well as the two leaders of the Religious Community in Prague, Dr. Weiman and Edelstein, to Berlin, and to receive, besides Eppstein in Berlin, some other gentlemen on a certain day in my office.

When they all appeared, I informed Gruppenführer Müller of their presence, who then came to my office. I stood a little to the side of the group of Jewish functionaries, some steps away from Müller. Müller issued a declaration to the effect that since it had been determined that Jews were involved in the acts of sabotage at the "Red Paradise" exhibition, I have by order of the SS Reichsführer summoned you here to make the announcement that (4 or 6) functionaries of the Jewish Religious Community in Berlin have been sentenced to death. The State Police central office in Berlin has in the meantime arrested these Jews and taken them into custody.

So far as I can remember they were Jews who had already attracted the attention of the State Police. They were then taken to the concentration camp in Oranienburg and there killed according to orders. In this case, it was not my task to even inform the Jews of the order of the SS Reichsführer who had ordered the enforcement of a death sentence. That would have exceeded the scope of the department.

I Was Neither A Mass-Murderer Nor A Murderer

The post-war propagander describes me as a murderer, indeed as a mass-murderer, and I repeat my statement that neither I nor anyone from my department killed a single Jew, or killed anybody in general, or even issued an order to other offices to kill Jews. Only towards the end of the war and in my absence was an order for the killing of individual Jews given by a member of my department; I shall come to this in greater detail later. These false reports are based partly on the emblem of IV-B4 which appears on different documents. I often received the order to draft and write out letters which were then signed by the Chief of the Sipo and SD or by the SS Reichsführer. I do not in any way think that Heydrich had any intention to use my department sign in the case of very serious letters; for it was unthinkable that the Chief of the Sipo and SD could have written all the letters himself. Precisely for Heydrich I had to draft many letters, to all the ministers of the Reich, to all the persons of equal rank as his, insofar as it dealt with my field of duties. In that case I was summoned to him; in short, choppy phrases he gave me the outline of the concerned letter; at first I used to make short notes at lightning speed, later I did not need that any more, for a year of working with a chief makes one familiar with his entire milieu so that there is a spontaneous feeling of how the individual ministers are to be addressed. Müller was very undemanding in his correspondence; his letters only had to be factually and professionally correct, without any personal feeling. But Heydrich was much more demanding, he was a master.

My department had two subdivisions: IV-B4a and IV-B4b. IV-B4a was under Councillor Suhr and, after his departure, Councillor Hunsche; IV-B4b was led by Günther, combined with that he was my regular representative. IV-B4a reviewed, as already described, the determination of "hostility to the people and state" and other legal matters. The other subject field was under me and was led by Günther. At the end of 1944, Günther and Hunsche were called "departmental heads", whereby I became the chief of the department, thus at such a late stage that practically this was no longer in effect; for no more trains rolled, and we trudged from one makeshift arrangement to another; as the State Police control offices were more or less battered, and increasingly advisers and departments in my office were brought together, there remained hardly any place for me anymore.

The travel-plan department of the Hauptsturmführer Novak belonged to Günther's department; the registry, the public and the secret, led by

The Eichmann Tapes

Untersturmführer Martin with a small apparatus of police officials and SD employees, was directly under the chief of the department. Then there was also the "business room" under the leadership of Obersturmführer Jänisch, who controlled also the vehicles and, further, a technical field under the leadership of a Untersturmführer, under whom were all the house matters, buildings, air-raid shelters, etc. Later a telegraph office was built where the individual branch offices could communicate with Berlin. Underground there was a large telephone exchange.

I have always had a love of architectural drafts and so I drafted in my free time a special shelter against air-raids. There was an electric powered hose ready, and in the yard was a pond. As soon as air-raids with fire bombs occurred, I kept all the men on their toes and so for a long time it was the only building in the surrounding area that remained intact. I had the walls protected with sand-bags, for this work I had during the entire war a detachment of Jews whom I simply made "privileged Jews" because they partly lived in mixed marriages anyway. Such a small matter, which stood directly under me and took place in my immediate vicinity or in the immediate vicinity of the office, I could accomplish myself.

In the evenings these Jews hid their Jewish stars, went home and returned in the morning. Actually they had to wear their stars, but they received from us a certificate that they had permission to move freely and not to be punished with police measures. During the entire war I had an old, very efficient construction foreman whom we provided many times with a "certificate of indispensability" since he would have otherwise landed in the "death camps". He got by with almost nothing and obtained, along with his unit, the necessary materials from the rubble areas of Berlin. I explain this technical section somewhat in detail so that one does not get the idea that I had had this department for the planning or building of gas chambers and things of that sort. Not at all, for *not a single line was drawn by me for the building of gas chambers, concentration camp installations and the like*, but the technical department had only one task: the protection of the office from the air battle and other provision for the air battle such as, for example, the construction of air-raid bunkers.

When I came in 1940 to Gestapo Office IV we created a sort of organisation to protect the roof over our files from bombs and fire. When it was not burning in the neighbourhood, we performed fire-brigade service until the normal fire-brigade relieved us. Our air-raid bunker installations were so large that the entire neighbourhood got permission to use it during an air-raid alarm. They only had to pass through the guard and, when returning, return a pass which allowed them to go along a certain path to the bunker installations. Thereby it was avoided that anybody could remain in the building. This general bunker for the civil population stood under the command of an Untersturmführer and was far better than the bunker for the office employees. It had, besides, an alarm system attached to the office bunker to provide help in cases of emergency. Kaltenbrunner visited this annex once, and I said to him: "Beleaguered people seeking protection under the wings of the wicked Gestapo". As soon as there was an air-raid alarm I moved everybody from the office to the attic – and naturally I myself went first to set an example – in order to deal with the fire-bombs; in this way my office survived after the others had already been burnt down.

Not Responsible for Poland and the USSR

Neither in Poland nor the Soviet Union was there ever a "Jewish adviser" from IV-B4. The offices there received their instructions from higher offices than my department. The commanders there were in the position of Einsatz commanders, who received their orders from the Einsatz Group chief and not from Berlin; the Einsatz Group chief received his orders directly from Himmler. Naturally the Einsatz Group chief had a departmental head in connection with this in his staff, but he was in no way connected to IV-B4.

Not once did an order or instruction go from me to the East. By "East" I mean the Generalgouvernement and the occupied Soviet Union areas. To that I also include Lemberg; I managed to travel there once. A commander of the Sipo showed me a hilly terrain and remarked that here 6,000 Jews had been shot. I never once gave this commander any orders, he received neither "orders" nor "advice" from me, but from a higher control position, from where also Globocnik received his orders, that is, from the Chief of the Sipo on the orders of the SS Reichsführer, but never from a department of IV-B4, not even from the chief of Gestapo Office IV. *With the exception of the letter to Globocnik, I know of no written order for killing which would have referred to my department IV-B4.*

Eichmann as a Recipient of Orders

If I had been in a position of real authority where I could freely decide our Jewish policy, international public opinion would have necessarily interested me. But since I did not prefer to have such a post, and in the truest sense of the word – especially after the outbreak of the war with the Soviet Union – where I was only a recipient of orders, I did not have to ask what consequences arose abroad.

How far would we have advanced if every recipient of orders had asked himself if the order received by him was meaningful and to what extent it could work for or against the interests of Germany? We would not have been able to withstand the enemy for five years but after one or two years would have had to surrender.

Until the end of 1941 I "thought" not silently but aloud. I thought aloud to Müller and my colleagues and expressed my opinion that I considered the solution of the Jewish question to be a non-violent solution, a non-violent separation through a legal ordinance that leads to a division between the guests and the host peoples. That was my entire aim – and from this opinion there arose in me the idea of the "Central Office for Jewish Emigration", the idea of a "Jewish state" in Poland, of the self-administered "Theresienstadt" camp, of the settlement in Madagascar. In order to be able to realise these ideas I fought and *struggled shoulder to shoulder with the Jewish leaders.* In this way the relationship between these Jews and myself became blurred; we proceeded together on the common task in such a way that finally one could no longer ask: Is that a Jew or an SS chief?

At that time I was obsessed with my goal, at that time I still "thought", at that time I could still develop certain initiatives and actually put ideas into practice. But when the events of the war assumed such a dramatic scale that these "civilised methods" could no longer be adhered to, things were decided differently at a higher level. From this moment on I only received orders which – whether I agreed with them or not – were to be carried out according to my oath of office. If I had considered the entire matter at first in its details, especially those things for which the central authority and IV-B4 were not at all responsible, perhaps other "thoughts" would have come to me through purely humane considerations.

The Step to the Security Service

I only took care of the transports and the legal support in the individual countries under our influence so that they would deliver their Jews to us. Everything else I did not wish to see, and did not wish to have anything to do with. In the case of the transportations, the only "consolation" was that I did not even know who would die and who not die. The fact that I was not responsible for it was my only support, that I did not even know what happened and to what men.

I mention at this point how I discussed with Wisliceny in the thirties my view that National Socialism and the Reich would never last a thousand years, but that it would collapse at the latest after the death of Adolf Hitler to the military interests, as every great empire of history collapses after the death of its founder.

When, after 1941, I was burdened with unfavourable tasks, I sought many times to extract their significance: Why this degree of harshness against the Jews, if nothing lasts forever? Perhaps there spoke in me still a vestige of my Christian education from my youth? And no order was more welcome to me than the one that stated "avoidable harshness was to be avoided". Perhaps a dozen times I dictated this order and clamped down everywhere where I encountered such excesses even from a distance.

What effects the orders of our highest leadership had and could have for the German people was not something I had to be interested in. As a pessimist I said to myself already from the start: For us everything is hopeless; we want to try to build our house strong and firm for our children so that they will not have it as hard as we. We cannot do more, and the more generations come after us the more peaceful and better it will be.

If I am not inclined to take upon myself the responsibility for everything that was described and decided as an action of department IV-B4, this is in no way a shaking off of any responsibility. The reality is that everybody was involved in the "final solution", because everybody believed that he had to contribute to the aims of the higher leadership. Many scrambled to this task, but today naturally they do not wish to know anything about it. Today there remains only my department IV-B4, the Gestapo Office IV, which the hostile media describe as a "spider in a bloody web".

The Limits of My Power to Issue Instructions

The commanding officers of the Sipo and SD often had to go to Berlin for reporting and receiving orders. They therefore never came to me. On special matters the commanding officer could also be summoned to the SS Reichsführer.

In practice there developed from this chain of command, where the commanding officer received orders from the Chief of the Sipo and SD and from the office chiefs generally, while the implementation of the orders were left to the individual departments. For the latter therefore the commanding officers had to contact the departmental heads. Considered in this way, there were two possibilities. Just as I had a way downwards, the commanding officers had one from the bottom to the top. When I ponder this precisely, there is hidden therein a diabolical possibility that the executive could justify itself in an administrative legal way before foreign governments. Heydrich must have wanted this double possibility – such "Jesuit characteristics" point to only one person: Heydrich. All the people in the RSHA and outside had to be coordinated and adjusted according to desire and mood. I could work on the bottom level exactly as the commanding officers could on the top. There was no divisional head in the RSHA who had, along with the BDS[116] – the Chief of the Sipo and SD – another immediate office-bearer in the concerned country apart from the divisional head of IV-B4, thus, me. So I could, for example, go to Müller and say: "Now the representative of the BDS in Paris, Knochen, is coming. Please tell him that this and that matter must be taken care of. Müller did that or not; it was in any case a way which stood open to me and because I possessed no direct powers I had to use back-doors. My back-door was thus my own office chief.[117] I could give Knochen no orders or demand anything of him. But the office chief could use Knochen's personal report discussions to carry out this or that. I was sent out repeatedly to the different countries because there were difficulties, but even then I could not "instruct"; I could only enforce the desire and/or the will of the SS Reichsführer, of Heydrich, Kaltenbrunner or the chief of office IV who was most feared, more than the SS Reichsführer among the commanding officers.

If I "threatened" a BDS with the chief of office IV, then he yielded

---

116 Befehlshaber der Sicherheitspolizei und des SD, Commanding Officer of the Security Police and SD

117 Heinrich Müller

and promised to do everything possible as soon as possible. Such a thing happened directly, in the form of direct missions, but was never derived from any "authorisations to issue instructions"

More on the Birth of the Madagascar Plan

My work in department IV-B4 made me a "living filing cabinet". I had to deal according to orders, but I thought for myself too, otherwise I would have indeed been only an unskilled labourer, without a mind – dead. When emigration stagnated, and the attempt at the Jewish state in Poland had collapsed and Theresienstadt could, because of its capacity, only be a drop in the ocean, I pondered how the emigration of Jews was to be stimulated again. The western campaign was over, France had fallen. In Böhm's book I had read how Herzl in his tenacious attempt to create for the Jews their own homeland, had approached the Sultan, and wished to deal with Kaiser Wilhelm. In his frustration Herzl had then proposed Madagascar as a solution. Herzl separated himself from the right-leaning orthodox Jews who all wished to hear only of the Holy Land, of Erez Israel. The first World War however brought the Balfour Declaration and therewith offered the Jews the possibility of a homeland in Palestine, at which point all the other plans such as the Madagascar project had become irrelevant.

During these days of our victory in the west the Madagascar Plan emerged again. It was of course older and did not originate from any German initiative. I had recognised that the territory of the scale of the district of Lublin, fraught with many deficiencies, had anyway already become too small. I turned my attention most energetically to the newly budding possibility of Madagascar. I wished to clinch the matter quickly before it would become too late. The victory parade of the German troops in Paris was over. The forces of the national opposition within the Reich, on the one hand, and the bombastic confidence of victory that led here and there already to a slackening activity, the lack of a military consequence of Dunkirk and other small details to which I thought I could attribute symptomatic significance made me become increasingly pensive and gave ever wider room to my pessimistic attitude with regard to a victorious outcome of the war. Therefore I wished to carry out the Madagascar Plan, in itself old and already developed by Jews themselves decades ago, in a way favourable to both sides, both in the interests of the Jews and in those of the Reich.

As the divisional head of IV-B4 I presented the "Madagascar" idea to Gruppenführer Müller, and afterwards to the Chief of the Sipo and SD, Heydrich. I received the approval to get everything necessary under way. As a non-military and non-political person, I could not judge to what extent Madagascar stood at our free disposal. There were a number of meetings of departmental heads which the departmental heads from all central authorities took part in. The Foreign Office had a speaker in Mr. von Thadden, the chancellery of the Führer in chief government councillor Dr. Reischauer, who was appointed as the regular liaison officer between the chancellery representative of the Führer and department IV-B4, and even all the other central offices were involved in this project, even if they were only marginally involved. Every central authority saw to it that its significance was in no way to be overlooked.

I think that at least fifteen to twenty large meetings took place in my office on the "Madagascar Project" in which things were intensively worked out with the participation of 20-25 people. Through the lawyers who were at my disposal I had a regular bill issued for the resettlement and settlement of the Jews in Madagascar, which should be declared a Jewish territory where the Jews, obviously under the protectorate of the Greater German Reich, should live freely and under self-administration. Therewith a final solution would have been found for all Jews, not only from Germany, but from the entire European territory, a final solution within our sphere of influence. In the Reich Ministry of the Interior there existed already from the end of the previous century a "Reich Office for Emigration", which, as is well known, had been created to advise German emigrants on climatic conditions and other matters worth knowing. From the chief of this office I had documents and figures given on the conditions in Madagascar and the acceptance capacity of the country which were extraordinarily satisfying. I know even today that Madagascar was to be divided to a certain extent into two zones, a northern and a southern, of which one possessed very favourable climatic conditions. Details arising therefrom were not our task but that of the Jewish self-administration, of the Jewish Madagascar government. A collection of clauses of over hundred chapters was drafted; partially even implementation regulations were worked out. The bureaucratic hurdles were dealt with and, already after a few months, the "Madagascar Project" was "ripe for the ministers" and could be presented through the State Secretary to the individual ministers for signing.

A large amount of work was performed therewith. Contact was established with the Vichy government;[118] legation councillor von Thadden was present at every meeting, and every draft had to be signed by the Foreign Office. We proceeded step by step; in some cardinal points it was the matter of the Foreign Office to certify the clearance, wherewith the question of the agreement with the Vichy government was solved for me as a member of the Gestapo. Naturally it would have contradicted all the customs of a central authority if the Foreign Office had of its own mandated a territory like Madagascar without dealing with the relevant government. I thought that I did not have to worry about that at all; for me the signature of the Foreign Office was binding. Legation councillor von Thadden, who could naturally not express himself in a binding way, because he had a far too modest office for that, represented the Foreign Office as a middle-man to its regular representatives in Vichy; he may have reported what Laval[119] said about the Madagascar project.

For the transportation of the Jews to Madagascar somebody had already calculated the necessary tonnage. Safe conduct of the English fleet was of course not available. The transfer should take place in a proper way; for the Jews should arrive in Madagascar fit for work. Madagascar should become neither a ghetto nor a concentration camp but have a regular Protectorate government. That was also the reason why everything was worked out to the last detail and through all the responsible central authorities. The "Madagascar Project" was a solution legally developed with the approval of all the central authorities, which were also to regulate the fate of the inhabitants of this island in a responsible manner.

As evidence of the thoroughness with which I drafted the "Madagascar Project" I state further that I similarly worked out everything to the last detail in Hamburg in the Institute for Tropical Hygiene. For the ship voyage I had an expert available and received, through the ministerial councillor, who was in charge of the emigration advisory office of the Reich Ministry of the Interior, likewise experts who however derived their viewpoints from the laws of the previous century. For the embarkation different European ports were to be available.

---

118 Vichy government, seat of the government of Pétain in occupied France.

119 Pierre Laval, well-known French politician. During the German occupation of France he was, from April 1942 to September 1944, French Prime Minister in Vichy. He was killed in the Frèsne prison in Paris on 15 October 1945.

Heydrich never let his control of the "Madagascar Project" be taken from his hands. He had a very receptive head for things which concerned the priority of the Sipo. In the "Madagascar Project" he saw, after the "central offices" in Vienna and Prague, a second opportunity to extend his powers. He spoke directly to Göring and gave himself general powers for "the final solution of the Jewish question" in the form of a decree. After the project was signed by all the authorised heads of department of the central authority and it was ready for the ministers, it was then forwarded through the Chief of the Sipo and SD, to first Heydrich, naturally, then to Reich Marshal Göring. Since Heydrich had general powers, no central authority could sway him in the Jewish question, or make any suggestions or reproaches.

When the "Madagascar Project" sank and other directives were issued from the highest control post, Heydrich and even Himmler certainly extracted from this decree the right to do, and have done, everything further according to their own discretion, for Heydrich's power was not limited to the "Madagascar Project". Rather more was this project for Heydrich the occasion to create for himself a wide-ranging licence and authority. The seriousness with which the many difficulties that emerged in this project were overcome, as well as the circumstance that the "Madagascar Project" could represent a reasonable solution, made it for me unthinkable that there was space here for anything devious. Not only did it represent a favourable solution for the German Reich government but also to the Jews, who pledged their cooperation, especially since the conservatively disposed Jews were already familiar with the "Madagascar" concept and it seemed to them to be a duty to cooperate with the plan. When Heydrich was appointed by Göring to implement the "final solution" of the Jewish question in Europe, the term "final solution" was never understood to mean "physical annihilation".

The "Madagascar Project" encompassed, finally, a complete collection of laws with a number of basic clauses and an abundance of implementational regulations, as a result of weeks-long cooperation of our own lawyers with the legal experts of the most important central authorities, who to a certain extent gave me their backing and help, such as, for example, Dr. Reischauer from the Chancellery of the Deputy of the Führer, the responsible man from the Foreign Office and the representative of the Propaganda Ministry. Therewith I had obtained from the start the three most important central authorities for my project; for one represented the party, the other the Foreign Office, and the third the Propaganda Ministry, a powerful structure if I had had it working against me. So I had the heavy artillery on my side. I have already spoken about the involvement of the Ministry of the Interior, who, although they had considerable reservations, did not have any effect on the plan. After the "Madagascar Project" had been presented to all the ministers, additional meetings were deemed to be necessary; they were held in the form of ministerial discussions with Himmler, whereby Heydrich also was involved. I was called upon only insofar as I had to draft the correspondence for Heydrich or the SS Reichsführer with individual central authorities for clarification of any problems. This lasted longer than the fundamental work. It cost effort and patience to overcome one obstacle after the other in the administrative jungle of the central authorities. But with tenacity and skill we succeeded.

The scales of war did not tip in our favour. I think that there was some attempt by de Gaulle to seize Dakar.[120] In any case we had to resign ourselves to some setbacks when Madagascar became inaccessible to us. At that time I was totally preoccupied with the Madagascar plan, but the project had to be dropped, which to this day I still regret. My dream, which I shared with the Jewish pioneer Herzl was over. And it marked the end also of the search for a solution that would have served the interests of both sides, the interests of the Jewish and the non-Jewish camps.

---

120   The Battle of Dakar in September 1940 was an unsuccessful attempt by the Allied Forces to wrest Dakar in French West Africa from the Vichy government and to install Free French forces there under General de Gaulle.

II

A New Wind Blows

War with the USSR -
Its Consequences for the Jews

Our own land hardly sufficed for the German people, and on the territories occupied by the German troops there was no available territory of the desired size. The efforts for the creation of a "Jewish state in Poland" had collapsed because of a lack of understanding by people whose agreement was necessary, among them, in the first place, "Polish Frank". The efforts to find a solution in an overseas territory were then overtaken by the military situation.

The campaign against the Soviet Union had begun. The security police had often left no stone unturned in order to solve the Jewish problem in a humane manner, and even without the co-operation of foreign countries which had not been forthcoming. This humane solution had been, in the first stage, "emigration". In the second stage, we strove to find land for the Jews in some territory accessible to us. I swear that this corresponded to the wishes of a large part of the Reich government in National Socialist Germany.

From the beginning of the Russian war another solution was pursued which set us – me and my immediate subordinates of my department in the Secret Police Office of the Reich Security Head Office – in a secondary place in matters of the "final solution of the Jewish question". What now loomed was shifted to other entities and the WVHA, which was under Himmler. I shall come back in another section to this tragic chain of events and the fateful sins of omission of foreign countries – including the lack of support from international Jewry – with regard to the Jews in our sphere of power.

A War of Excess

Until the beginning of the hostilities against the Soviet Union the situation seemed relatively harmless, but now the entire world broke loose upon us few Germans. Our state leadership was not able to advance step by step but allowed ourselves to be partially or fully through our own fault encircled on all sides. There were relatively few experts in any field; in every sector the volume of work became increasingly greater, so that every expert had to oversee wide fields. Naturally he was not able to do that. Regional offices emerged that were no longer directed by the regulations but by the events.

I can also imagine that anyone who had experienced that some close relative had been massacred or fallen under enemy action would now direct his thoughts and efforts to the destruction of the enemy. Finally he could no longer differentiate whether and which ethical measures were to be observed or whether everything should not be allowed, as long as it served victory.

If now such elements had to carry out certain tasks in the Generalgouvernement or in the occupied Soviet territories, then every Einsatz Group chief, every leader and every non-commissioned officer had a very wide leeway there. In this way did it come occasionally to unimaginable things; for those responsible were too far removed from the central control which would normally have tightly controlled them.

The Liquidation of the Jews
and the Kaufman Plan

I am aware that the events that led to the Jews being subjected to physical annihilation are historically of the most far-reaching significance. I shall strive here also for the full truth as known to me, influenced or pressured by nobody. But at the outset I wish to say the following:

I, with my subordinate officers, junior officers, men and district officials, were not in any way responsible for the liquidation of the Jews. My office could not in the least intervene in a corrective way either in the general development of the war or in the origination of the liquidation orders; for it was too small within the regime. Neither I nor my subordinates killed men, nor could we influence such actions.

The Eichmann Tapes

If I add something more precise about this, I do that with a good conscience, without wishing in any way to cast blame onto others. The trial of the chief of our Administrative Head Office was conducted before the American military tribunal in Nuremberg. Thus the whole matter is anyway on file.

Somewhere around the end of the year 1941 early 1942, the Chief of the Sipo and SD, Heydrich, *informed me verbally that the Führer had ordered the physical liquidation of the Jewish enemy.* What reasons may have caused Hitler to suddenly issue this order I did not and do not know. Today, as then, I can only suppose that because Hitler had often publicly announced that the war that Jewry itself had unleashed against the Third Reich, however it may fare, would prove Jewry to be the losers. The whole world was aware of this declaration.

At the end of 1941, it was clear that the Russian campaign did not proceed so rapidly as expected. There was now a two-front war, which was for Germany dangerous, nay, devastating. Already for a long time the leaders of international Jewry had declared war against the German Reich. The last possible obstacles had now clearly disappeared. These are my conjectures; they could be right, but they *do not have to be.* For *I have never myself seen the liquidation decree from Hitler.*[1]

The declaration of war by the United States was quite generally felt to be the result of Jewish efforts. Even before the entry of America into the war we received a detailed description of the so-called "Kaufman Plan".[2] Kaufman was a confidant of Roosevelt's who would certainly not have published his plan without the support from leading Jewish circles. The primary goal of this plan was the complete annihilation of seventy or eighty million Germans; it was explained in detail how the German army should be sterilised division by division, as only men above 70 years and women above 50 years should be excluded otherwise the entire German nation including the children and babies should be sterilised. *Kaufman intended the complete extermination of our people by means of a programme of total sterilisation.*

---

1   Eichmann refers to the subject of the "Führer's order for the liquidation of Jewry".

2   Published immediately before the campaign against the USSR. The editor has seen a reference to the Kaufman Plan in a IC report of a security division of the Central Army group in the Military Archive of Freiburg im Breisgau. Hitler was aware of the plan, and well as the Propaganda Ministry.

Germany
Must Perish

BY THEODORE N. KAUFMAN

ARGYLE PRESS, NEWARK, NEW JERSEY

Title page of "Germany Must Perish," published in 1941 by Theodore N. Kaufman the Jewish adviser to US President Roosevelt.

Today I think that the Kaufman Plan was possibly thought out only as a means of provocation, in order to achieve from Germany a violent annihilation policy against the Jews, in order to obtain a Jewish state with international guarantees. If the Kaufman plan was meant as a provocation, then one can only say that the Jews have achieved their goal. It is perhaps to be supposed that awareness of the Kaufman Plan in our *highest* leadership circles became a *triggering factor* for their own annihilation measures.

The Eichmann Tapes

At the end of 1941 - early 1942, the Chief of the Sipo and SD, Heydrich, informed me of, that as well as the order for the "physical annihilation" of the Jews, *the SS Reichsführer* had also instructed that *the prohibition of Jewish emigration was to be strictly observed from now on*; the order had already been issued at the beginning of the war, but since then there had been a considerable number of exceptions granted.

All Jews in the sense of the Nuremberg legislation, with the exception of the Jewish part of a privileged mixed marriage, as well as the wounded and bearers of bravery distinctions of the last World War, were, according to it, to be committed to the Chief of the SS WVHA to a place named by him – mostly concentration camp railway stations. The SS Reichsführer reserved a few exceptions for himself. In addition, Heydrich informed me that while the Security Police had nothing to do with physical liquidation, its task remained restricted to purely the rounding up.

When Heydrich said to me: "I come from the SS Reichsführer; the Führer has now ordered the physical annihilation of the Jews", the words were so pregnant that I could not assess them even in an approximate manner then; because there was a lack of any precedent, it was only later that I could assess their enormously weighty burden; I knew Heydrich – the manner in which he conveyed this information to me I could see in his face that even he had not reckoned with such a development.

In the first moment I wanted to clarify what "physical liquidation" now really meant, and Heydrich must also have noticed that. He informed me further that the SS Reichsführer had commissioned the SS and Police leader Globocnik in Lublin to use the Soviet anti-tank ditches for the mass liquidation of the Jews. I myself should go there and give a report to Heydrich of the progress of the operations. After the receipt of this weighty order I reported to my office chief, Gruppenführer Müller. Obviously he knew about it already; for I could recognise it steadily in his wordless nodding combined with a dull smile around his sharp lips. He remained in the Prinz Albert Street office thereafter and did not budge from his writing table. But he knew everything that happened within the German Reich and in the territories occupied and influenced by us.

I travelled towards Lublin; I do not remember what the place was called, a Hauptsturmführer accompanied me; there I met a captain of the regular police; I was not a little surprised that *he had built little houses, hermetically closed*, and he said to me: "The Jews are gassed here now". I was still thinking of the Jews being shot in anti-tank ditches, but he explained to me how well he had sealed everything so that really nothing could get through from outside. I was fully consternated.

In connection with this first order of annihilation, which was given to me as Heydrich's mail carrier to Globocnik, I consider it appropriate to deny here that Heydrich had years before the war devised a plan down to the last details for the so-called solution of the Jewish question. If such a plan had existed I would have known about it. If however it is meant that Heydrich made a continuous efforts towards finding a solution of the Jewish question, then I must of course fully affirm this. To these efforts belonged the solution of emigration, the desperate attempt to develop a Jewish territory in the district of Lublin, and the later attempt with the "Madagascar Project", efforts which were all wrecked. Then arose the large-scale concentrations, which ended with the deportation of the Jews to the concentration camps. But a "general staff plan" was never decided on, rather, the moment directed these decisions.

Eichmann and the Einsatz Groups

What I felt then in relation to the first orders for liquidation is hard for me to describe. I abstain from it. Up to then I had indeed heard of orders for shootings, which the SS Reichsführer had issued directly to individual chiefs of Einsatz Groups of the Sipo and SD positioned in the east. But those orders stood independent of the present order from the Führer. Nevertheless, I must declare that even now the entire matter did not assume the forms that one had originally imagined. All Jews fit for work were to be set to work and therefore survived. In the Generalgouvernement and in the Soviet Union, the local offices of the Sipo and SD arranged transport trains, whereas, in some other countries controlled by Germany at that time, this happened through the police or gendarmerie units of the concerned countries.

The first time I was ordered to Globocnik, my mission was purely for information purposes; after I had seen the remarkable little houses and their goal was explained to me, I returned to Berlin and informed my superiors accordingly. In purely human terms my seeing Globocnik again was gladdening; for I had a very warm relationship with him from the early days of our party's struggle. I knew him from our days in Vienna and my efforts towards the establishment of the

"Central Office for Jewish Emigration". Globocnik was the Gauleiter of Vienna, when I discussed my notes with him. He pressed every conceivable button to help me. Then I went to Berlin, where I did not see or hear of Globocnik until this commission from Himmler to travel to the Generalgouvernement and determine how far Globocnik had progressed with the preparations for the implementation of the order. I reported to Heydrich what I had seen and was summoned to him again soon afterwards. On this occasion he informed me that, on the order of the SS Reichsführer – or just "on order", *250,000 Jews were to be sent for liquidation*. I do not know any more today whether I received the letter in relation to this or whether Heydrich ordered my office to prepare this letter. If I had issued this letter, it must have routinely borne the file number IV-B4 and the entry number. *In any case this letter would have been signed by Heydrich as the Chief of the Sipo and SD*. So I was ordered to courier this letter and to hand it over personally to Globocnik.

When I arrived at the Lublin camp, I did not recognise it, for a fine police station, a guest-house, office rooms and large drawing rooms had been built. Globocnik led me through his technical department and related to me how he had received from Himmler a special commission and that was the construction of the models according to which in future the SS and Police bases in the east should be constructed. He had different models partially drafted, partly modelled in miniature in wood. The drafts were architecturally complete. In the technical office there worked not only Poles compelled to work but also Jewish architects, mathematicians, technicians and experts of the woodwork industry. Globocnik showed me an enormous joinery room in which Jews worked, who prepared the most beautiful things according to specifications. Thus the furniture of the SS and Police base in Lublin did not in general give the impression that one was in an abandoned eastern corner of the Generalgouvernement but in a well-equipped area of the capital.

Globocnik showed me his room, where he had also set up his bed. There I gave him the letter. He took it and read. Because it was marked "Secret Reich matter" he had to give me confirmation of receipt with a special number, which I accepted. Behind or near a picture a small safe had been built in; he opened it and secured the letter inside. Then he said to me: "See, comrade Eichmann, one must always have everything in black and white". This expression "in black and white" was a common phrase among us. One did nothing without an instruction or order.

Perhaps half a year later I visited Globocnik for a third time. I had to hand over to him a similar letter. This second letter was different from the first in two points: one, in the word *"further"* *250,000* Jews and then in the signature; it was that of Müller *representing the Chief of the Sipo and SD*; I think that, at around this time, Kaltenbrunner was already effectively the Chief. During this visit I ascertained how far Globocnik had taken the work forward; for, at the exit from Lublin, was a camp which had previously looked really pitiful, but now, during my last visit, had already assumed really large dimensions.

Globocnik must have burnt the two letters mentioned; for the order obliged him as the bearer of a "secret matter of the Reich" to do so. One was obliged to protect secret matters of the Reich from seizure, even with the sacrifice of one's own life.

The house staff of Globocnik consisted of female Polish personnel and a number of SS orderlies, the mostly seriously wounded persons who were unfit for the front. In front of the fireplace stood a small tiled table which had extraordinarily beautiful designs. Both in the service and privately Globocnik was quite informal. He was not bound to any strict times; he would have got along well with Himmler. He had been the combative, tenacious corrupt Gauleiter of Austria[3] and had then caused few difficulties as Gauleiter of Vienna, when he was thrown out to make place for a German governor, Reich commissioner Bürckel. Globocnik placed work before people – and that was obviously not forgotten, because the SS Reichsführer appointed him as SS and Police Chief. Later he became a senior SS and Police Chief in Trieste and had regained the same rank that he had given up without complaint. So it is understandable that Globocnik played a completely different role than the other SS and Police chiefs. Even the Generalgouverneur Frank could not ride roughshod over Globocnik, for Globocnik wrote personally to the SS Reichsführer, which, in the case of the others, would have meant a circumvention of the official channels. Thus the SS Reichsführer had commissioned him to design the so-called police colonies or base-colonies – a very large task, for these SS and Police stations were conceived as fortified regions. They were to provide shopping for the German settlers of the surrounding areas, provide doctors and hospitals, and things like that. Such a post would stand in constant contact with the small outposts. This network was planned

---

3   Globocnik was appointed Gauleiter of Vienna in May 1938 but stripped
     of his office in 1939 when it was discovered that he had engaged in illegal
     foreign currency speculation.

for the entire east, so that the police would have their secure quarters and could be quickly shunted round the entire country. In cases of emergency even the entire population, no matter whether German or non-German, could immediately find shelter here. That is why Globocnik had so many workshops in operation in which he accepted the Jews, even the "council of elders", to whom he had promised favours in exchange for their cooperation.

Where, And How, Did Liquidations Take Place?

In the Generalgouvernement, the Jews were rounded up by German, Lithuanian, Ukrainian and Estonian agencies and sent to concentration camps. Globocnik had mainly Latvian units which carried out these tasks in the district of Lublin. These men were hard, for they had passed through a frightful school. Once I travelled overland with Globocnik on a bitterly cold winter's day, and we met some Latvians or Lithuanians. Globocnik pointed to one of them; the man in question told us that he had sworn revenge, for his wife, his parents, and his brothers who had all been murdered by the Bolshevik Jews. The German police units had in such hard-tested men harsh daredevils who generally did not tolerate any resistance; apart from Warsaw, there was in fact not the least resistance. Personally I know only a single exception, and this was when once on a journey from the east to the west I came upon a camp where Globocnik had carried out killings around that time. It was in the eastern district of Lublin, in Treblinka or Maidanek or in another nearby camp, in any case a small one, for an Obersturmführer was the camp chief. How they killed the Jews I do not know; but I do not think it was with gas.

This Obersturmführer had a tracked armoured reconnaissance car, a very low vehicle which I used to tour the immediate camp area. It took me an hour before I could steer the thing well, and this is why I have retained this camp firmly in my memory. When I returned to Lublin again, a close colleague of Globocnik, Hauptsturmführer Höfle related to me a story about this camp. An SS member of the camp was having a uniform made for him in the camp's tailor-shop. During one of the trial fittings, the SS man took off his belt and pistol and laid it to one side, when a Jew suddenly burst out from behind the uniforms and shot this SS man with his own pistol. Thereupon, as if by command, the towers of the guard-posts were stormed and the guards killed, and with them some other SS members. The Jews then seized their weapons. They even started the armoured reconnaissance car and shot the guards with the machine-gun. Afterwards a large number of these imprisoned Jews managed to escape, whereby some fell victim to the mines. After a large search campaign most of the Jews, with a few exceptions, were recaptured within a few hours.

Apart from these visits as "letter-courier" or for the purpose of an inspection, I had nothing to do with Poland. After the Nisko project had failed, and thanks to the efforts of Frank, there came about an order for my arrest. I did not in general worry any more about Poland, not even in matters like ghetto development, the Jewish councils of elders, etc. Frank could see to all that from where he was. I think that Frank later regretted all this, for he was now forced into a situation that he did not at all want. Frank wanted the Generalgouvernement to be free of Jews – I had wanted him to fill just one district full of Jews, but he threw me out; now he had to take the Jews camp by camp; and later the task of the "final solution" which including the "physical liquidation". Whether this task was pleasant for him I do not know. In any case he was in charge of the entire story of the final solution.

Everything would have occurred differently if my Nisko project had not been "torpedoed". Whether Frank ordered it himself or whether it came from a higher position I do not know. Frank had a big battle with both Heydrich and Himmler and also against me, because I was involved in it in a small way. In any case, I managed to remain outside all the stories of the Generalgouvernement.

If I myself had received the appropriate order, then I would of course have had to obey, but I did not. Perhaps they wanted to let Frank "stew in his own juices", for even his requests to the Reich Minister Rosenberg for the Occupied Eastern Territories[4] to take the Jews away from him produced no results.

Throughout the entire Generalgouvernement Gestapo Office IV had no responsibilities. Globocnik had a special commission not only in his district, but also in all the remaining districts, although he was only "SS and Police Chief of the district of Lublin". His powers extended over the entire Generalgouvernement, and even the higher SS and Police chiefs had to support him.

---

4   Alfred Rosenberg (1893-1946), who occupied this office from 1941 to 1945. Rosenberg was executed in October 1946.

The Order For "Physical Annihilation"

In conclusion and, at the same time, in contradiction of other opinions that have now been presented to me, I wish to summarise once again the origin and process of the "physical annihilation":

It is completely wrong to think that, with the beginning of the Russian campaign Himmler, Heydrich, Müller and myself had decided on a policy for the "extermination of Jewry". Rather, Heydrich, as the chief of the Sipo and SD, had received the order for it. In my opinion, it was not in the least his idea. I still remember precisely the moment when Heydrich said to me: "The Führer has ordered the physical annihilation of the Jews". I heard the term "physical annihilation" for the first time in my life and so it has remained in my mind. I may have forgotten many things, but this moment I shall never forget. Neither Müller nor Heydrich nor I nor anybody else from the RSHA were involved in the decision, but rather *the decision was taken by the Führer and the SS Reichsführer.* Thereupon the SS Reichsführer gave this order to the Chief of the WVHA.

Perhaps Heydrich and Müller, who were in charge of the individual Einsatz chiefs in the Soviet Union, were the first to mention in this context the use of "anti-tank ditches". When I was summoned to Heydrich I received from him an already worked-out plan whose preparation by Globocnik I had to inspect and on which I had to report. Heydrich informed me that Globocnik had already received the order directly from the SS Reichsführer to undertake the preparations and to make use of the Russian tank-ditches, by which he meant to shoot the Jews in the tank-ditches and then to level the graves. I was ordered to travel to Lublin and report back to Heydrich how far the work had progressed.

Today I can no longer say if the phrase "final solution of the Jewish question" was coined by me or if it originated from Müller. When I read that about Theodor Herzl in Böhm's book *Der Judenstaat*, I encountered the phrase "solution of the Jewish question" for the first time. When in 1935 I received the Zionist association as my field of expertise in the SDHA, I began already at that time to use the phrase in the files. After the annexation of Austria, the concept of the "final solution" was crystallised. "Final solution" had nothing at that time with the end of a physical person, but the term was used increasingly widely. Nobody thought then *that this concept would include the killing of Jews.* When later, at the end of 1941, or early

Identity photograph of unknown Jewish girl in Auschwitz.

1942 physical annihilation was ordered, we allowed the term "final solution" to be retained also for that. Nevertheless, the concept "final solution" retained also in these times its original meaning, for, even the emigration through Kastner[5] in Hungary or the ghettoization had nothing to do with annihilation. "Final solution" was thus a blanket term, a bureaucratic concept which became unclear.

Heydrich was a very cold man, very self-controlled, but I am convinced that even he inwardly shuddered before the expression "physical annihilation", for he spoke on the matter in a manner in which he never did. He was in himself brusque and energetic, whereas however in this case he used a sort of "loose colloquial speech", in any case no commanding tone, so that one had to suppose that he was astonished. For we all still imagined that we could take the Jews out of the country, and even during the war, as mentioned clearly, a series of attempts were made in this direction. Apart from the deficient cooperation with foreign countries, it may well be that the victory disappeared into an ever greater distance and Adolf Hitler hardened himself increasingly in every speech.

---

5   Dr. Rezsö (Rudolf) Kastner, journalist and jurist, leader of the illegal Aid-
     and Rescue Commission in Budapest, fell victim to an assassination attempt
     on 4 March 1957 in an internal Jewish conflict. In 1958 he was cleared by the
     Israeli supreme court.

Therefore he could have given the order for physical annihilation one day. This order he doubtless gave to the SS Reichsführer. The latter must then have communicated it to the Chief of the Sipo and SD. The other instructions in relation to the concentration camps the chief of the WVHA, Pohl, will have received personally from the SS Reichsführer.

Hitler himself neither worried personally about the final solution nor got involved or gave instructions directly. *Naturally I do not know what he communicated to the SS Reichsführer.* Himmler set to work immediately and went over camps like Auschwitz. Hitler, on the other hand, never. If he had ever done that I would have known it precisely because it would have gone round like wildfire.

I do not know if Himmler had considered other camps than Auschwitz, even though I know that he was personally friends with Globocnik. I never spoke to the Führer himself. I was never introduced to him. In the bureaucratic hierarchy I occupied the office of a departmental head, above me I had an immediate superior, an office chief, and beyond that a head office chief, then came the Reich leader, the SS Reichsführer, and then the Führer.

In every speech the Führer dealt with this problem sometimes more, sometimes less thoroughly and clearly. Therefore all occupied themselves intensively with this problem as with no other. The SS Reichsführer, Heydrich, later Kaltenbrunner and even my immediate chief, Müller all took pains regarding this issue over all other tasks. This also created difficulty for my office, for where my comrades from other departments dealt only clearly according to laws, ordinances and decrees, I always had to look left and right to see if any of the superiors, for example, Heydrich, created a precedent through some individual decision that I had to observe and prevent this decision from being overruled by another. Now, to the extent that my superiors attended to the Jewish matter in detail, I had obviously no more possibility of even being presented to the Führer; for details could be presented to the Führer only by my superiors. On Jewish matters the SS Reichsführer, Heydrich and later Kaltenbrunner went to the Führer. Gruppenführer Müller was not presented to the Führer either in these matters or in other matters; for among us it was no longer as it was in the early days of the party when a comradely contact existed. For us the Führer was inaccessible.

Even Heydrich was very seldom with the Führer – I remember only one single time. So long as Müller was still in Munich with the Police, he was doubtless presented to the Führer. Müller never mentioned a word about it. He was a very hardworking, industrious "filing cabinet". As his subordinate I was also that. Duty, oath, and order made me immune to unhealthy ambition. We fulfilled our duty quietly and humbly as soldiers of the Third Reich.

Not Involved in Murders, but Deportations

As to a version conveyed to me, according to which at some time I received an order signed by the SS Reichsführer for the physical annihilation of the Jews, I must explain that this is an outright lie. The truth is that Himmler never set down a line in writing. I know that he also always dealt orally with, for example, Pohl of the WVHA. Neither in writing nor orally did I ever receive an order of this sort from the SS Reichsführer.

As I have already stressed, Heydrich said to me personally that the Führer had given the order and that the SS Reichsführer had commissioned Globocnik with the implementation, but this matter would in future be handled not by the police but by a special head office of the SS Reichsführer.

I personally was, in the beginning, responsible for the emigration and later for the police round-up when it was a question of large deportations, and indeed in the entire area where these were carried out, with the exception of the Generalgouvernement, the Soviet Union and Romania, as I was not responsible for these areas.

The deportations had destination stations which were suggested to me by the Chief of the Sipo and SD. His instructions were received from the WVHA, which was alone responsible for the concentration camps. With the physical annihilation, not only I and my subordinates but also the entire Sipo and SD had nothing to do with it, unless on the basis of individual special orders of the SS Reichsführer to the Einsatz commandos in the east, which had to carry out the killing measures as their own responsibility. But the Secret State Police Office, especially department IV-B4, had nothing to do with it.

A Small Man's Attempts at Reconstruction

If I were to reconstruct today the situation and were asked *where the initiator of the first order for physical annihilation is to be found*, I am clear about the fact that the responsibility for this question is of great significance. For it was not the commissariat decree, of which I hear for the first time here and now, which envisaged the killing of Soviet commissioners and Jews but the first order to Globocnik within the authoritarian state that had initiated annihilation as a means of war.

Without doubt the SS Reichsführer gave the Globocnik order to Heydrich; the initiator of this plan however was, *I feel*, neither Himmler nor the Chief of the Sipo and SD, Heydrich. *But I know there is not the least bit of evidence that the Führer's order existed in writing.*

It is right that Heydrich was cold by nature and Himmler likewise; when it was a matter of our people both acted without feeling. But both had to reckon not only with the SS members but with their officials, and therefore I do not think that an order of annihilation could come from them. In my opinion, the initiative must have come from the political sector, the sector of Goebbels-Bormann.[6] After the Führer had determined that everything had become muddled in the Jewish question, after even Goebbels and Bormann, who were indeed present at the discussions on the "Madagascar Project", knew about the collapse of a political solution, and around that time the Führer listened increasingly more to these advisers. He hardly listened to Himmler, for the latter had always been the second authority until he became, after 20 July 1944, the commander of the substitute army and Reich Minister of the Interior.

The SS Reichsführer was of course at first Reich leader, but not a minister, he was a state secretary, but also Stuckart was a state secretary, even first state secretary – and thereby Himmler's superior. When the Führer had made the decision regarding the Globocnik order, he obviously called up the SS Reichsführer in order to commission him with it and to inform him of the opinion of his advisers. The SS Reichsführer may have said something about it: "It is the only solution, my Führer; we have attempted everything else without success." Himmler knew through me – he summoned me to him many times – and through

---

6   Ohlendorf represented the view that the chief initiator of the liquidation measures against the Jews was Martin Bormann. This view has gained in plausibility.

the circulating reports of the difficulties and the exhaustion of the political possibilities. Even through his office chiefs, perhaps also through the other people of the German central authorities, he was in the know about the constant efforts and failures in solving the Jewish question in a political way. That is why Heydrich could tell me: "The SS Reichsführer has informed me that the Führer has ordered physical annihilation".

As deputy Reich protector Heydrich was directly under the Führer and was thereby in close contact with him; but I nevertheless do not think that Heydrich was the initiator. That is my opinion, not because I was his subordinate – he is dead, and my statement cannot either harm or benefit him anymore. Based on the state of affairs and the knowledge of my highest superiors, I am convinced that neither Heydrich nor Himmler were the initiators of the plan; so then it must have been Hitler. Heydrich was no actor, he spoke always openly, never concealed anything from me, and I got along very well with him. If he had been the initiator he would perhaps have told me: "Finally the time has come, Eichmann, now we have done it ...now we have eliminated all the fools at the ministry and can finally have free rein". But no, he did not say that. Precisely these circumstances that surrounded the order of annihilation and the Globocnik commission make it, in my view, a complete absurdity to wish to maintain that "the order of annihilation was no secret in higher party circles in March 1941". In March 1941 there were no "liquidations"; when Heydrich announced to me the order for annihilation, the word "Russian anti-tank-ditches" was used, thus it must have been after the beginning of the Russian campaign.

But it is complete nonsense to maintain that a month before the eastern campaign "the Eichmann office directed a circular to all consulates wherein it was informed that Göring had forbidden the voluntary emigration of Jews from France and Belgium, because thereby a similar emigration from the Reich would be prevented and especially that *the final solution of the Jewish question was doubtless quite imminent.*" How could I have had the audacity to issue a circular to all the consulates? Not only that, the Foreign Office would have – rightly – pounced on me, and Müller or even Heydrich would have sent me to the next concentration camp if I had written such a thing. The author who claims this has either interpreted the matter completely wrongly or it is a barefaced lie. Not even an office chief of the SD, or even the Chief of the Sipo and SD, could write to the consulates, let alone then that I was able to drop such a circular into the post-boxes. When the same author maintains further that I made a proposal "to construct the first gassing installations near Riga and Minsk", that is already – in short – the third great, perhaps intentional lie with which he throws all his other opinions open to question. Never did I, either orally or in writing, make a proposal to construct any liquidation centre, quite simply because it was not my responsibility.

If I had received the order to construct something of the sort, I would have certainly done it, but in this matter I did not receive any such order, for I had nothing to do with gassing and killings. Against such an opinion I must moreover declare that even the hostile post-war literature ascertained several times that IV-B4 had nothing to do with anything like that and certainly not with the related measures in the Generalgouvernement or the Soviet Union.

Eichmann's Jewish Advisers

My department IV-B4 despatched during the war so-called "advisers" into the foreign lands occupied or influenced by us, for example, Dieter Wisliceny to Preßburg, Dannecker to Berlin, Burger[7] to Athens, Abromeit[8] to Zagreb, Zöpf[9] to the Hague. They received the most precise guidelines; as advisers for the Jewish question they were subordinate in the concerned countries either to the German Embassy, like Wisliceny in Preßburg, or commandeered to the commanding officer of the Sipo and SD, like Dannecker in Paris. It was their task to carry out the orders and wishes established in general by the SS Reichsführer and the special orders and wishes of the Chief of the Sipo and SD, which had been developed in detail by me as a responsible departmental head. While one adviser had difficulties with the concerned government another could carry out his tasks smoothly.

---

7   Anton Burger (1911-1991) worked with Eichmann in Vienna in the Eichmann Special Einsatz Command. In 1942 he was ordered by Eichmann to Brussels to supervise the deportations of Jews from Belgium, Holland and France. He served as commandant of Theresienstadt from July 1943 to February 1944. In February 1944 he was sent by Eichmann to Athens to replace Wisliceny.

8   Franz Abromeit (1907-64?) was Jewish adviser in Croatia from 1942 and worked with Eichmann again in 1944 in supervising the deportation of Jews from Hungary.

9   Wilhelm Zoepf, SS Sturmbannführer, Departmental head with the Commanding Officer of the Security Police in the Netherlands. Sentenced to jail time by a German high court in Munich.

Rudolf Höss commandant of Auschwitz concentration camp.

In principle the concentration of Jews had been accomplished in all countries, but to evacuate them was harder. In many cases the governments were at first reluctant because the laws of the land were against it and new legislation had to be introduced. For the entire treatment of the Jewish question the precondition was that the individual governments introduce new legislation. Only in this way was it possible in terms of international and state law, that the concerned country could transfer the Jews of their own citizenship to a "foreign power" like Germany. It likewise belonged to the tasks of the "adviser" to present through his superiors in the region the introduction of new laws as being urgently desirable with a view to the final goal of making possible the deportation of the Jews. That was what the order of the SS Reichsführer to the Chief of the Sipo and SD said and the one from the latter to me. The difficulties were in general great, and only a fraction of the settled Jews were actually evacuated at any time from the countries to the Reich territory.

The "advisers" were under me, and since I was responsible for their success, I ordered them to report to me at intervals that seemed opportune to me, or I travelled to them myself. If I recognised difficulties of a foreign political sort, if I observed that consciously or unconsciously, deliberately or not, if a resistance on the part of the German embassy or mission in any country was noticeable, I had this recorded by the concerned "adviser" in a note, in order to discuss the problem with the current legation councillor of the Foreign Office who was responsible for the Jewish question. The Under-Secretary in the Foreign Office was Luther,[10] the legation councillors were von Thadden and Rademacher. Under-Secretary Luther and I had obviously worked together intensively, but only in writing. It did not come to a personal meeting, and so I cannot even remember his face.

Gruppenführer Müller always dealt directly with Luther, whereas I dealt with Rademacher or von Thadden. I know that Müller and Luther met very often. If it was a question of minor matters, I could have a meeting with the concerned legation councillor. The concerned ambassador was then instructed through a note from the Foreign Office to implement this or that, with a reminder to complete it by a certain date. Therewith the matter went into the files. If it was a matter of fundamental things, for example, the lack of legislative support for an order to the security authorities for the concentration of the Jews and their transfer to the German authorities, then a completely different route had to be taken. After a working conference in connection with this, the legation councillor directed a report to his superiors and through the latter to the State Secretary of the Foreign Office. This was, after consultation with the Reich Foreign Minister, either discarded or acknowledged. If an adverse decision of the minister threatened, it was my task to inform the Chief of the Sipo and SD through Gruppenführer Müller. The most difficult task perhaps was to arrange new legislation in the concerned country. For that, it first had to be presented to the Foreign Office; then it was the task of the responsible officials of the Foreign Service to exert a corresponding pressure on the foreign government. Not political, but rather more economic pressure was exerted to enforce an order of the Führer. As a rule it succeeded.

In individual countries like, for example, Romania, the government officials were politically weak or sat on the fence. So they thrust thousands of bureaucratic difficulties into the foreground even though these could have been removed with a stroke of the pen. It was the art and the skill of the "advisers" to influence the ambassadors in such a way that they for their part would "barrage" the protocol

---

10   Martin Luther, Under Secretary of State in the Foreign Office from May 1940-April 1943. Chief of the German department in the Reich Foreign Office, from April 1943 in the Sachsenhausen concentration camp, from which he was released during the end of the war. He died after the capitulation in a Berlin hospital.

officials of the concerned countries in order to go up to the Foreign Minister and present the Jewish question to him in the desired form. Thus much depended on the personality and vigour of the envoys. Ludin[11] in Preßburg was massive and robust, whereas a von Killinger[12] in Bucharest proceeded in a finer and more elegant manner.

In general, the "advisers" enjoyed in all countries the greatest esteem, for they were considered as the extended arm of the SS Reichsführer. That was true also of the ambassadors. For a little word from the SS Reichsführer would have sufficed to remove them from their post. I hardly think that the "advisers" had a warm relationship with the different ambassadors, but instead in an objectively professional relationship serving the tasks of the moment. Only partly did my "advisers" recognise this necessity; I personally recognised it very early, just as Gruppenführer Müller did.

None of the "advisors" had a higher rank than that of Hauptsturmführer, and each had to fulfil their mission. If however difficulties of a fundamental sort were present, then I was sent in. The "advisers" had at most three of four orderlies and one or two typists. They did not possess executive powers and could neither give any ordinances to their own police nor to the local police in an occupied or allied country. Thus they had, for example, no powers to carry out house searches or the like, for that obviously falls under executive authority. So any "enrichment" in this way, as is claimed in the post-war literature, did not come into question. I am today glad and happy that I sent abroad from my department only such people whom I would vouch for even today.

During my entire time in office I have not heard on a single occasion even the smallest complaint in this connection, whereby it must be borne in mind that my colleagues stood too much in the public limelight for any false move on their part not to be registered immediately and sooner or later communicated to me or to one of my thirty fellow departmental heads. They were thorough and modest, respectable and unassuming, orderly and correct in terms of their world-view and – I think with the exception of Wisliceny – all married. Because indeed they did not have any executive powers they were called "advisers". If they were with me in my department they obviously had executive powers within the Reich territory.

---

11   Hans Erhard Ludin, German Envoy in Slovakia.

12   Manfred Killinger, SA Obergruppenführer, from 1941-44 Envoy in Bucharest, committed suicide on 3 September 1944.

Apart from Ludin in Preßburg and Veesenmayer[13] in Hungary there were no representatives of the Foreign Office abroad with whom I had contact directly, either orally or in writing.

As Jewish post-war authors maintain, it is right that the Foreign Office acted as the initiator of deportations but only in decidedly individual cases, possibly in Slovakia and in Romania. There were no such initiatives issued from the RSHA but from the offices of the Foreign Office. Thereby I expressly declare that in no way do I – in this case as well as in others – seek to deny my own responsibility or to cover up actions that were begun. But I must speak for my department IV-B4 and its members and even for the Sipo, where the Security Police cannot be made responsible in terms of initiative, I do not need to take upon myself any responsibility. On the other hand, I prefer that my insignificant person remain bogged down in an affair rather than let the impression arise that I am trying to save myself like a rat. If I received orders to carry out the deportation from a country with speed, then the initiative clearly came from me. If it emerges from documents that in Slovakia and Romania the Foreign Office was the initiator, then that is exactly just as clear.

By and large the work in the occupied or allied foreign countries went ahead normally. Only occasionally were there difficulties. As a rule it was only of short duration; for, through personnel change or personnel exchange, everything was soon put on the normal track once again. Only the sensitivity of the states that were founded in our times, like Slovakia and Croatia, caused headaches because they insisted in demonstrating their sovereignty.

With the exception of Hungary and Denmark, I experienced that everywhere the separation of the Jews from the different spheres of life of the concerned nations was open to free debate and not in even a single case did it cause us difficulties in advance. And it made no difference if the emissary went there from the Chief of the Sipo and SD, the Foreign Office or from a party office. The offer of the Reich to take the Jews was regarded as a salvation, so that I often had to consider just how the necessary transport space was to be found in order to carry out everything as quickly as was demanded in the different countries. It even came to the point that the Chief of the Sipo

---

13   Edmund Veesenmayer, active as Reich Plenipotentiary in Budapest during the second World War. Sentenced in the Nuremberg Wilhelmstraße Trial to 20 years. Released in 1952 from imprisonment in Landsberg/Lech.

and even Müller said to me: "In a month or so things start there and there, see that you obtain enough transport materials; we have already spoken with Pohl. The Jews go there and there". I then always arranged with the Reich ministry the travel-plans for the transports which then often had to be cancelled, for doubts had arisen in the concerned countries because the first transports had mobilised certain hostile forces, whereupon some functionary who had regulated everything was dismissed or transferred or was suddenly no longer there and as a consequence the remaining trains had to be cancelled. This was true of all countries that were "free", apart from Denmark, where from the beginning people raged against the deportations. Difficulties existed also in Slovakia and even in France, though things ran smoothly there in the beginning. Even in Holland the transports went smoothly in the beginning but then difficulties later arose.

In the beginning there were no difficulties anywhere, but hardly had the first transports departed than the matter dragged on until another transport could be carried out. Almost everywhere in the beginning around ten thousand persons were evacuated, then there was a pause until again a contingent of ten or fifteen thousand or even only five or four, three or even only two thousand were placed at our disposal. Only in the case of Hungary was it different, because there the Jews were given away to us like sour beer; it was the only country for which we could not in general work fast enough. Only in Hungary was I under constant pressure and could not at all, in spite of my efforts, find the necessary transport material. Even the receiving stations in Auschwitz had difficulties with accommodation. This tempo was initiated by the Hungarian government itself. On the other hand, in Denmark, difficulties were actualized from the first day, something that was not observed in any other country. These two countries, Denmark and Hungary, represent the only, and contrary, exceptions in comparison with all the other countries of Europe.

I cannot give exhaustive information on which countries urged the transfer of the Jews, but only on those where I myself conducted negotiations. How Hungary gave its Jews to us I have already clearly expressed, Slovakia did so in exactly the same way. In France, Laval not only presented no difficulties for us in the beginning but it appeared as if we would be able to get all the Jews of France without any difficulty. But as soon as it was a question of Jews with French citizenship, there was, practically, nothing more to be done. In Holland, in the beginning, train after train departed and the expert, a commanding officer of the Sipo, had his hands full, so that I sent him my Hauptsturmführer Burger as support, and for a period even Brunner. I do not know who conducted negotiations. In Belgium, some transports departed immediately, and then came to a complete stop. But in a way the example of the Hungarian gendarmerie commander who said to me: "We give you the hide without having the authority for it, in the name of the people" is symptomatic. He then explained to me further that a monument to me in Budapest was certain if I would succeed in eliminating the most frightful enemy of Magyardom; but a couple of days later the same man was on the opposite side. It was the same everywhere: in the beginning bright enthusiasm and a couple of weeks later everything subsided like straw fire because the concerned official was no longer as keen as in the beginning or because he was no longer there.

It was even often maintained that the Jews were killed or gassed. This version of the Jewish annihilation emerged from the end of 1942/ beginning of 1943. If I was asked, I never said to the government people of these countries: "No, they are not killed". As a rule I gave an evasive reply. I said to the people: "What is happening is happening. The Führer has also more than once said on the radio in his speeches: "Jewry will be annihilated". If I was told: The Jews are being liquidated in this or that place, then I always replied something to the effect that "I do not know. For the moment your contingents are at the destination station, they are under the WVHA, which deploys the Jews for work, either in the concentration camp itself or in the enterprises which were attached to the concentration camps. What happens to those unfit for work is not known to me. Perhaps they are liquidated, but the Sipo is not responsible for that. So ask the SS Reichsführer." I said the thing to Dr. Kastner, likewise in Slovakia and in Amsterdam. There I was invited to an "Indonesian atjar"[14] and I spoke with a Dutch functionary, whose name I no longer remember, about the possibilities of liquidation. Even in the St. Jude Hotel in the Hague where I regularly spent the night I spoke once with a Dutch functionary about it. These Dutchmen were not uninformed. I do not know if they were members of Mussert's movement.[15] Perhaps they were employed by my people because they were so-called "anti-Semites".

---

14   An Indonesian sweet and sour salad.

15   Anton Mussert (1894-1946) was one of the founders of the National Socialist Movement in the Netherlands. He was sentenced to death in November 1945 and executed near the Hague in May 1946.

Camp Inspection in Theresienstadt

The attempts to carry out inspections and the "explanations" that followed thereafter on the possible liquidation of Jews were always dealt with orally. Only the International Red Cross in Geneva requested permission for inspection in writing. In the other countries these requests were expressed during discussions and negotiations and registered by us in file notes.

Obviously the term "gassed" was not used in the file notes, but "sent for special treatment" or simply "for work deployment in the east" or "as part of the final solution of the Jewish question". The term "gassed" was registered in the file notes only when the negotiation partner of the other side needed it. The file notes on all discussions were routine with me, for I had to repeat everything and obtain instructions or permissions for an inspection. In almost all countries my people reported to me that this or that person had again requested to visit the Jewish camps. It was always pointed out that it was not possible at the moment. Even Richter,[16] my adviser for Romania, mentioned to me the names of Romanian government members who wanted to visit Germany and demanded entry to the concentration camps.

Involvement of Foreign Countries in the Deportations

I am not aware of a single case where some country really worried about the deported Jews, and providing them, for example, with food and clothing. On the contrary, the Jews were handed over to me like "poor church mice". I think that the commandant of Auschwitz, Höß, would have been happy if the trains had been somewhat better supplied because even the food supply, which was still good in the first transports, became increasingly more meagre. In no case was there a question posed by any country for the support of the deported Jews, not even from Slovakia. The different countries and governments were concerned to retain as much of the Jewish property as possible. If, for example, at first a second coat, a third blanket, private possessions, food, were allowed to the Jews, all this was in many cases later ruthlessly snatched away. Former members of the WVHA could give detailed information about this insofar as they had something to do with it.

---

16   Gustav Richter, SS Hauptsturmführer from 1941-44, Jewish adviser in Bucharest.

The Jews were sent from the individual countries practically without personal papers. The transfer rules did not declare that they were to be handed over to us either with or without personal papers. The concerned countries could deal with that as they considered it right. In the beginning, naturally, lists of names were issued, demanded by the transport drivers and handed over to the receiving offices of the WVHA. What individual documents the individual Jew had with him I cannot remember; that was the concern of the Jews or of the offices that rounded them up. In any case, there was not a general police measure to transport the Jews without personal papers in order to prevent escape attempts in this way.

In some transport to the east – perhaps from France, but possibly from Holland – a young woman was brought in who declared that she was not a Jew. The concerned transport was destined for Auschwitz; my adviser was informed by the WVHA of her explanations; investigations revealed that she had probably spoken the truth, for which reason I had this woman taken immediately to Theresienstadt and had interrogations arranged. In Theresienstadt she received accommodation in the "prominent persons' quarter". Dr Eppstein from the council of elders in Theresienstadt pestered me very much on this account because he clearly did not want to tolerate non-Jews being sent to his community. It was a counterpart of the later "reparations" for the Jews, where the Jews also did not wish that others "travelled along" on their account. Precisely because the Jewish council of elders had cautioned me often, I have the case of this woman still clearly in my memory. Yet no sort of office from her homeland supported this woman. When one day I learnt of the clarification of this case, she was again transferred to her homeland, as far as I remember.

The rounding up of Jews and the transfer to the German authorities happened in most countries through the local agencies, as, for example, in Slovakia and Hungary. The transport escort commando always consisted of Germans. In Holland, German agencies carried out the rounding up with the assistance of the Dutch police, who performed the herding service. In France, the French police assisted. My adviser there could count on the help of a French commissioner. Naturally, I am not convinced that, for example, in France, or elsewhere, the local police proceeded always in a very humane way in the rounding up and concentration. How it was managed in Belgium I do not know. In Denmark, the German police had the rounding up solely in their hands, perhaps with the help of some army units, but I cannot say precisely. In *the other countries,* we ourselves did not carry out any rounding up, because this encroached on their sovereignty rights; there were thus not too many countries where we could act on our own accord.

The transports were not carried out by the central office but by the individual Stapo control offices. The central offices only issued the guidelines, on the basis of an order of the Chief of the SS and Police, Himmler. I received instructions, but then also not always; for even Gauleiters and other party offices could call up their Stapo control offices and give them a commission that a certain area should be free of Jews by a certain date. Naturally, transport trains were requested from us; for that we were responsible. We then had to request the train material, in every case, from the Reich Transport Ministry. I had to issue the guidelines according to which the deportations occurred in the Reich territory, according to the instructions of the Chief of the Sipo and SD. These guidelines were not signed by me, for neither I nor any other divisonal head could act so independently. The deportation trains were controlled by local guard teams who were provided to me and could not be chosen by me.

The Sudden Reluctance Of Others

Stalingrad signified a decisive turning point in the eagerness of the different countries for the solution of the Jewish question. After Stalingrad I had the greatest difficulties in all countries that had to be dealt with.

There were no difficulties which were caused on the basis of "humaneness", only for the purpose of reassurance. The people in charge of decisions could not stop requesting me, as a small departmental head, to attend ministerial discussions and inviting me to off-duty entertainments or private meals. Because, after Stalingrad, the scales of the course of war tipped very much against the Axis powers, these personalities were concerned to exploit the situation to their advantage. The Jewish question was a welcome occasion to conduct a "resistance" and to deploy the entire force of their personal power to saving the remaining Jews that were left to save. These personalities had ministerial agents at their disposal and a correspondingly broader field of influence. I wondered generally that they had allowed it to go so far. Up to the end, the round-ups, concentrations and deportations of the Jews were carried out by the local police in each country.

Guidelines for Deportations

The guidelines which were used in the Reich in the case of the deportation of Jews were valid also for the foreign countries. These guidelines were developed through the course of the years. They began with the demand of the SS Reichsführer that we allow the Jews to take with them what was permitted to the Germans at that time in France, that is, up to a total weight of 50 kg. Before the deportations began, the Jews could take with them while emigrating complete four and five-room houses; often they conducted an exchange with expatriate Germans who were returning to Germany.

The "guidelines for deportations" encompassed roughly one and a half pages of typed text. It is impossible for me today to repeat them fully but I think that I can still summarise them in a way. In regions where no partisan formation was to be feared, there was a sort of age limit which was determined, not according to years, but according to transportability, that is, only transportable people could acquire embarkation. Insofar as it was a matter of the Reich territory and the Protectorate, nobody could be evacuated whose spouse belonged to a Christian religious community or was a non-Jew in the sense of the Nuremberg Laws, that is, lived within the concept of privileged mixed marriages. Baptised Jews could not be evacuated anywhere. Possessors of bravery distinctions or the injured from the first World War could not be evacuated. Epidemic carriers could not be evacuated.

On the Baptised and "Privileged" Jews

When it is maintained in the hostile post-war literature that the International Red Cross could not even prevent "baptised Jewish children" from being sent to Auschwitz, that is a regrettable lie, for something like that never happened. Jews who had converted to a Christian religion were excluded from the deportations. In Slovakia, where a priest[17] was the president, he came to me personally and said: "Leave the Catholics in peace to me". Even in other countries this was also true, where the so-called "non-Aryan Christians" had their own association and were not at all affected. Had we dared deport any baptised Jews, we would have burnt our fingers on it.

---

17   Msgr. Josef Tiso, from 1939-1945 President of the Slovak Republic, killed on 18 April 1947 in Preßburg after being sentenced to death.

159

We were likewise powerless if the Jews contracted a pseudo-marriage, travelled abroad and got divorced. The legislation standing at our disposal prevented any such intervention, and we could only look on. This occurred often, and I estimate that these cases ran to ten thousands. Neither the Nuremberg legislation nor the Jewish legislation in the other countries made it possible to undertake anything against this. Local interventions obviously occurred and therefore Bishop Münch, the permanent representative of the Fulda Bishops' conference, came regularly with his lists of wishes. That is why I had all the cases where State Police officers had exercised some intervention brought into order, through telegrams. Naturally, we were struck by these many pseudo-marriages between Jewish and Christian partners but we could not intervene against that. After these gaps in the Nuremberg legislation were recognised, a non-Jewish German citizen could, for example, marry a Jewess at the registrar's office. Perhaps she paid her German partner 20,000 Reichsmarks, perhaps also nothing at all because it was a love-marriage. Only in the last years of the war was the non-German part taken into custody. But if the German or French Jewess or Jew married a Jew or a Jewess of foreign citizenship, we could not undertake anything, for the Nuremberg Laws provided no obstacle to that. I cannot give a precise figure of these cases, but this must also have been tens of thousands.

On the Course of the Deportations

For the transport itself it was ordered that the embarkations take place in a normal form and all avoidable hardships be avoided. The transport trains had to be equipped with the necessary food and drinking water supplies, and the necessary latrines. Every wagon had a Jewish transport steward who was identified by an armband. It was ordered to replenish the drinking water supplies and empty the latrines at the junctions where a long halt was scheduled. How many people could be loaded into the wagons, was specified as 48 persons. This determination of a maximum of 48 was implemented on the basis of a very old law, from a time when the individual soldier had copious baggage which took up much space. During the last war the field-kit of the solider was significantly smaller in size and weight, so as a rule the covered railway carriages also contained more than 48 soldiers. In the case of evacuations, fifty or sixty persons went in, but hardly more. The duration of the deportation journey as well as the climate and season, even the sex of the evacuees had to be taken into consideration and was also considered in the

Reich territory. The partial non-observance of these points by the Hungarian gendarmerie was the cause of many difficulties between German and Hungarian offices. After the wagons were loaded, they were not locked. But there was no rule about that in any case, for the transport escort commando of thirty men with an officer was sufficient for security. The Jewish transport steward could leave the wagon at any time during the stop in order to report incidents and difficulties to the transport driver. I can no longer say today how the food supply took place and what was specifically contained in it. Food was supplied wagon by wagon, but there were no cooking facilities. Bread belonged to the rations probably also sausage or cheese and margarine, for the transports at most lasted three days in transit.

In the course of the war, rations and allowed baggage naturally became smaller. The rations especially were adjusted according to the duration of travel. Naturally, the camps were concentration camps, but even here there was an orderly ration, which consisted of morning coffee, afternoon meal and evening meal and for the workers in addition so-called "snacks" in the morning and partially also afternoons. That remained this way until the last months of the war, when the entire transport system was bombed by the Allies and therewith the food supply of the German population was also much endangered; the fighting troops received coffee or warm food three times a day, but I know even today that the prisoners in Dachau ate five times a day.

The guidelines were humane. One who maintains today that the evacuation transports of the Jews were carried out with the most brutal harshness speaks a falsehood. Naturally there occurred local deficiencies everywhere. Orders can be supervised but again only by men and only according to their will and ability. Nowhere is there a complete elimination of every hardship. My deportation colleagues on the Russian, Slovak, Czech, Polish or the Israeli side today can certainly confirm this from their practical experience. After the war the deportations of Germans and other ethnic citizens ran into the millions. They were certainly not organised with the same Prussian-German precision in the field of victualling and the quick implementation in terms of transport engineering as it occurred in our times, although we stood against almost the entire world in the war and could obtain the food as well as covered wagons for the transports only with the greatest difficulties.

Jews were never deported in open wagons, but always in covered railway carriages and always in the quickest way and in the fastest possible trains. Nevertheless there occurred, especially in harsh winter times through sudden temperature changes, difficulties during the transport, even difficulties with fatal consequences. During the war, the latter did not disturb me insofar as they were unavoidable, because I was not allowed to be upset anyway that the dropping of bombs on German cities demanded mortal sacrifices among children and women. Therein perhaps lay my entire attitude to the orders that I received.

The Highs and Lows in the Deportations

From almost all states whose Jews we evacuated there came requests for inspections, even the International Red Cross requested such a permission. In my reporting to my superiors in relation to this I constantly requested clarification on the measures that I had to officially implement. The states that had previously given away their Jews to us like "sour beer" suddenly showed themselves to be worried and wanted to be sure of gentle treatment. These worries emerged every time that the transports ran at full speed. These things proceeded in waves and every evacuation had its own "wave", strong in its rise but falling after its peak. The moment that the peak had been passed, the different governments appeared before the German government in order to inquire after the welfare of their deported Jews and to propose inspection commissions.

It is clear that I, on account of the different receiving stations and the different travel-plan schedules, was not in the position to accurately follow some thousands of Jews on their way to some district, especially since these transports to foreign countries were often consigned without personal papers. These prevalent requests of the individual governments for the sending of commissions could finally be stopped when I proposed to the SS Reichsführer through my superior, Gruppenführer Müller, to let a commission of the International Red Cross come to Theresienstadt. Gruppenführer Müller and I would receive them and, after crossing the border between Saxony and the Protectorate, actually leave them complete freedom to deal with all the Jewish offices of the Theresienstadt camp and to speak to whoever they wished, even in private. I had proposed Theresienstadt because it was the only camp of the German Police. The different governments finally requested from the SS Reichsführer such an inspection; the

SS Reichsführer found a "Jesuit" solution in that he forwarded this entire file complex of requests to his police, to the Gestapo, which was responsible only for the Theresienstadt camp. If he had forwarded this entire file complex to the WVHA, then an inspection in Auschwitz for example would perhaps have been unavoidable. To this extent the countries had made a mistake in their request, even though, naturally, nobody abroad could have imagined that a distant head office like the WVHA had to deal with the receiving of the deportees and were exclusively responsible for that.

So it came about that only the International Red Cross sent a commission to Theresienstadt thrice. During the first visit Gruppenführer Müller and I received this commission and led them to the Jewish council of elders, whereas the second and third time I had, by order, to receive them alone and, after the welcome, hand them over to the Jews with whom they could speak and deal as they wished without my presence. One of the commission leaders from the Red Cross was called Dr. Dinar or something like that. He asked me if the Jews could smoke. I said: "No, it is officially prohibited, but they smoke nonetheless." The relatively good Swiss report on these visits was rather weakened because it was maintained *a priori* that Theresienstadt was only an "outward show". But whatever may have been maintained was irrelevant to the German Police, for there was no other camp under their responsibility anyway.

On the Separation of the Jews

When the post-war Jewish literature relates that, in November 1941, 25,000 Jews were expected but in reality only six or seven thousand arrived who were then partly taken back to Theresienstadt, this proves how one always operated in very large numbers. If discussions were held at a high level, the Gauleiters and other offices mentioned huge figures in order to emphasise the urgency of their case; but in reality the local police never rounded up such high number of Jews. Often I did not obtain the necessary trains too – the "cattle wagons" as they were always nicely called, even though there were only "goods trains" in which not only Jews but also soldiers and even the wounded were transported. Even entire ambulance trains were constituted of these.

If I am questioned today I cannot at all say how many ghettos there were. What does "ghetto" mean anyway? We took names and ideas from the Jews and collected them together in an area which may have

German troops escorting Jews from the Warsaw Ghetto Uprising 1943.

seemed more or less like a ghetto. The intention was to isolate the Jews in order to put a stop to the partisan and gang units, especially since we suffered constantly from a lack of personnel and could through concentration hold large masses of men under control with a rather small investment of personnel. Allied governments did this likewise, for example, the Hungarian, the Croatian, Slovak, Romanian and Bulgarian governments. In the individual ghettos it may have looked partly better, partly worse. That was dependent on the intelligence and the organisational capacities of the respective supervisory authorities. So the maintenance was better in one ghetto, worse in another. If it was worse, possible local frictions of no significance occurred there. Warsaw formed an exception; for the Warsaw ghetto leadership stood in closest contact with the first Polish underground army, led by General Bor.[18] A colleague of mine in the concerned department of the RSHA dealt with Bor and took him to Berlin, where he declared that he was ready to cooperate with the Germans. Unfortunately the Jewish council of elders in the Warsaw ghetto had allowed itself to be deceived into trusting the victory fanfares of the Polish underground army, opened attack prematurely and had to be killed – it was indeed war. If the Jewish council of elders maintained their nerve, waited and opened attack at a time that was strategically better, then this would have been very successful for the militant leadership of the ghetto.

---

18   Count Tadeusz Bór-Komorowski, Senior Commanding Officer of the Polish underground army.

The Consequences of the Warsaw Uprising

That the uprising in the Warsaw ghetto in spring 1943 had as a consequence sharpened measures against the Jews in the entire German domain is incontestable. One day I received in the department through the official channels a photo album, which Himmler had already looked at, as was apparent from the accompanying letter. It was signed "H.H.". This album contained many dozens of pictures in which the phases of the battle in the Warsaw ghetto were represented. Even today I know that the units which had to put down the uprising were surprised at the harshness of the battle and the heavy arming of the enemy. The SS and even units of the army had disproportionately high losses. I do not know any more whether Müller or Kaltenbrunner informed me that Himmler had said: "If we had clamped down at the right time, sharply and thoroughly, valuable blood would have been spared."

Personally I could not at all imagine that ghettoised Jews could fight in this way. When the blood losses increased, even our battle tactic was forced into a ruthless attack, and indeed as ruthless as probably any other unit in any other country too would have adopted in a similar battle. The harshness of these measures could be nowadays compared to the procedure of the French in the Arab quarter of Algiers, whereby it is to be borne in mind that perhaps the same harshness was not necessary because there such large masses of men were not packed together in a relatively small area as in the Warsaw ghetto. Nevertheless, the Arab ghettos with their small alleys offer a parallel to the Warsaw ghetto conditions.

As a consequence of this uprising and the related losses of the German army, Himmler gave the order to the responsible offices of the Generalgouvernement to comb the last alleys ruthlessly for Jews. I think that happened too, so that sometime after the Warsaw uprising there was no more Jewish question in the Generalgouvernement.

One of the most important measures concerned Globocnik on account of the fear that in his numerous factory-like concentrations, where indeed thousands of Jews worked, something similar could occur; on the basis of the sharpened orders where he carried out liquidations. These Jews would otherwise have survived the war rather like the thousands who were employed in the Heinkel aircraft works and in other concentration camps in the Reich. These constituted no danger because they did not live in the ghetto, where their activity

Polish Jews pulled from a bunker by German troops Warsaw Ghetto Uprising 1943.

was uncontrollable. In the affiliate works the activity of the Jews was controlled on an hourly basis; they stood under strict supervision. The Jewish work troops with Globocnik, on the other hand, stood under a very light control, because he did not have the necessary number of guards, so that the Jews were herded together in a sort of ghetto manner. Doubtlessly the SS Reichsführer had allowed himself to be led by ideas which arose from the Warsaw uprising when he personally ordered me to the work. It was his intention to scour Hungary with a huge strike force even before the Jews could organise any resistance. Our measures were preventive and were therefore more than justified. If these preventive measures had been taken in Poland it would certainly not have come to this bloody uprising. That would have been an advantage for the respective units of the army as well as an advantage for the Jews.

I do not know whether leading German officials were called to account on the basis of the Warsaw uprising, for the uprising was a matter of the Generalgouvernement insofar as it concerned officials. SS men were, as far as I know, not punished. If local punishments occurred I do not know. It would be completely possible that one or another was, on the basis of his negligence, called to account; for that was indeed customary; perhaps even the responsible persons were caught.

I myself was sent to Warsaw to survey the ghetto after the uprising. That was, in Müller's language: "My dear Eichmann, go there and see how bad it can get". In the ghetto they showed me the resistance nests, which could be dug up only with explosive charges, and I also saw the areas where the battle had been severe. I have never seen such a place destroyed in battle as the Warsaw ghetto. These pictures also remained in my mind when I was in Hungary and so Budapest constantly caused me a very great worry, which I repeatedly indicated even to my subordinates. But more frightful than an uprising in Budapest would have been a partisan area behind the front in Hungary which would have destroyed our lines of contact. After I had seen Warsaw, I would have been guilty of the death penalty if I had, especially in eastern Hungary, allowed any leniency in punishment and not clamped down where necessary.

In the countries where "Jewish advisers" worked, they were, after the uprising, instructed to set everything in motion to have the remaining sections of the Jews still present there transferred. It used to take a long time, the beacon of the Warsaw ghetto uprising made the fear of similar events become so great that the responsible government offices, for example, also in Slovakia, declared that they were ready to deport the remaining Jews in the quickest method, insofar as they could still be rounded up. The uprising of the Warsaw ghetto occasioned a sharpened rounding up of the Hungarian contingents, precisely in order to avoid a second Warsaw. After the uprising, the interventionist attempts had died down even in the Reich. The entire armaments industry, the directors of the large works, the Speer office and even the "commissioners of the Four-Year Plan" had constantly intervened. All that ceased abruptly if we just asked: "Will you take the responsibility that there will not be another Warsaw uprising?"

The photo album on the Warsaw uprising[19] was not given so that Stroop could shine in his "heroic" acts, but to show the Reich government what the consequences of a too lax treatment of the Jewish question were like. Hitler intended to give his chiefs a clear warning with this album. There had also, in fact, been a mistake in setting up large ghettos as

---

19   Jürgen Stroop was the SS officer who destroyed the Warsaw ghetto and was then made SS and Police leader in Warsaw. Stroop was sentenced to death in July 1951 and hanged in March 1952.

in Warsaw. I was not the initiator of the ghetto idea in Poland; rather, ghettos were already present in the Generalgouvernement which we took over because they meant a great economy of personnel in relation to their supervision. The Jewish ghettos consisted altogether of 30,000, 40,000 or even up to 50,000 Jews. For the first time a large ghetto was developed in Litzmannstadt which comprised about a third of Litzmannstadt and was populated by around 200,000 Jews.

The uprising in the Warsaw ghetto was for the Jews, and for the Germans, a catastrophe.

III

The Deportations From Abroad

Deportations from Slovakia

Hinkel's film ball in Vienna must have taken place in autumn 1939. I remember that because I was invited to attend, and we wore our so-called "society cords" on our uniforms for the first time. The same night I travelled to Preßburg with certain Slovaks who later became government members.

Before Slovakia had declared its independence[1] no deportations took place. In Preßburg the envoy was Ludin; my representative Dieter Wisliceny was assigned to him as "Adviser for Jewish problem" at the German Embassy in Preßburg. Wisliceny had got this appointment for himself. He gloated about it because he had succeeded in receiving, as a sort of attaché, a diplomatic pass. But this was Wisliceny's only function. He was never assigned to the "Jewish Central Office" founded by the Slovak government. My official routine in Slovakia was therefore to meet first with Wisliceny's chief, the envoy Ludin. The Slovak Minister of the Interior, Mach[2] took personal responsibility for the solution of the Jewish question in an energetic manner, and there existed a very good working relationship between Wisliceny and Mach so that the latter perhaps received professional technical advice from Wisliceny for the "Jewish Central Office". But in his official mission Wisliceny was never attached to any Slovak authorities, only to the German envoy. The Slovak leadership offices consisted of old Hlinka

---

1   On 14 March 1939.

2   Alexander Mach, Minister of the Interior of Slovakia from 1939-1945, sentenced to 20 years' imprisonment in 1947 in Preßburg.

169

guards[3] and keenly watched over the Slovak sovereign rights and their inviolability.

As a result of his corpulence Wisliceny had a certain calmness of temperament, but he was an excellent negotiator and it pleased him that he did not have to apply much workforce in Slovakia because the envoy Ludin constantly smoothed out any problems with the Slovak offices. I myself visited Ludin two or three times, and I had to describe to him most precisely the guidelines that we had from Himmler. When I got to know Mach he was not yet a minister; on the occasion of this first visit to Mach I had a consultation with the president, Monsignor Tiso.

Around this time the transport trains were already running, and Envoy Ludin informed me that Tiso wished to speak to me. During the conversation with Tiso it emerged that he was not exactly pleased with having to hand over the Jews of Slovak citizenship to the Reich. He made his view clear that these measures were of course necessary, but he requested that they be carried out in a humane way. He also inquired about the conditions of these transports. It became clear to me that Tiso was an anti-Semite, but not a politician who wished to solve the Jewish question systematically, but was only ruled by an aversion to Jews. He especially wanted a binding commitment from me that Jews baptised as Catholics remain untouched. I still remember how I wondered at that time at his readiness to place the other Jews at our disposal; for Tiso was wearing his priest's cassock, and I thought to myself that he was indeed more of a politician than a priest. This discussion must have taken place at the beginning of 1942, and the deportations were under way. I remember having come into difficulties with the Reich Transport Ministry on account of the travel-plan.

The deportations from Slovakia were not carried out as quickly as they were later in Hungary, but presented delays which often lasted many weeks. The only person in the government who caused no great direct difficulties but made complaints of a formal sort was Tuka. In the beginning the Slovak government would have been happy if we had taken all the Jews from it in one night. But when a man like Tuka[4]

---

3   Hlinka Guards, named after Msgr. Andrej Hlinka, the Chairman of the Catholic People's Party of Slovakia, who died on 16 August 1938. The successor of Hlinka was Msgr. Dr. Josef Tiso, President of the Slovak state from 1939-45, killed in Preßburg on 18 April 1947.

4   Dr. Vojtech Tuka, Prime Minister of Slovakia from 1939-45, killed in

direct from the party's battle-time was placed at a desk and came into the ministerial service he naturally developed doubts because he heard many protests and perhaps feared disadvantages of an economic sort for Slovakia. Tiso, on the other hand, never interposed any veto. He also did not put forth any difficulties like, for example, Horthy[5] in Hungary. The Minister of the Interior, Mach, saw no need to operate in a difficult manner with the Jewish problem, especially since he, on account of his political position and opinions, wished to have the Jewish question solved today rather than tomorrow.

The Slovak government made a mistake in its removal of Jews in that it at first proceeded in the city of Preßburg without consideration of the Jewish partisan movement. The Preßburg Jews had to construct residential areas and went into camps where they had to work for the Slovak government; therefore the government preferred to keep the work camps on Slovak territory. Only later was a legal status established which authorised the Slovak government to hand over their own state citizens to a foreign state, the Reich. Such a legislative task always consumed a lot of time until it had finally passed through all the concerned central authorities.

After the legal status had been obtained, the transportations proceeded regularly. It may be that the destination station was Auschwitz but I do not know if transports also went to the Generalgouvernement. I do not wish to deny the latter especially since I did not have to determine it, as this was solely the responsibilty of the Chief of the WVHA, Pohl, or his inspector of the concentration camp system, Brigadeführer Glücks.[6] The trains were always directed in the way the WVHA wanted, not as we wished them, for we indeed had no ability to receive trains; only Pohl had this ability. The selection of the groups of persons who were deported from Slovakia was a matter of the Slovak authorities; according to what guidelines the rounding up was carried out was likewise left to Slovakia. The rounding up itself was conducted by police agencies. So there is absolutely the possibility that

---

Preßburg in August 1946.

5   Miklos Horthy von Nagybania, Regent of Hungary from 1 March 1920. In 1944 the Germans arrested him because he wished to remove Hungary from the alliance with the Axis powers. Horthy went to a concentration camp.

6   Richard Glücks (1889-1945) was, from 1939 to 1945, the head of Office 4 (devoted to the concentration camp system) of the WVHA and the chief concentration camp inspector in Germany. He committed suicide in May 1945.

even children were evacuated, because even this was left to the Slovak government. In Slovakia, exactly as in other countries, the German government had already declared its readiness to accept all Jews.

If the Slovak government had requested the German government to send some family member on to an already deported male Jew, then it is unimaginable that even a single office of the Reich government would have placed a veto, and I certainly would have been the last to do so.

The development in Slovakia can be represented in the following manner: there was an offer of the Slovak government to deport the Jews. We had to proceed carefully not to damage the Slovak sovereign rights. The "Jewish adviser" Wisliceny was active only within the work sphere of the German envoy. This does not mean that his reports to the office of the Secret State Police were definitely to be sealed or signed by the envoy. His first task was to see to it, through the envoy, that the Slovak government approached the Germans with a request to accept the Jews with Slovak and other citizenships, insofar as it fell within the scope of the ordinances of the SS Reichsführer. So long as such a request was not present, nothing could happen from the German side. In addition, it happened that we could not appoint the personnel for the rounding up but Slovak police agencies had to collect the Jews and carry out their embarkation. If the transport was loaded, it was accompanied by a transport command of the German regular police in groups of 30 or 25 men. This commando accompanied the train up to the destination station, which was indicated to me by the WVHA. Before such transports went, not only did the request of the foreign government have to be obtained but also the agreement of the Foreign Office and of the SS Reichsführer. The Minister of the Interior Mach was instructed by Monsignor Tiso never to send baptised Jews or those from mixed marriages with a Catholic partner for embarkation. We did not offer any resistance to that especially since it was also Himmler's intention not to endanger the whole exercise on account of some individual groups. The offer of the Slovak government to place the Jews at our disposal for deportation did not come about, in my opinion, under pressure.

I had to deal with the Slovak Ministry of the Interior twice and both times I had the impression of the great willingness to proceed extraordinarily quickly in order to make Slovakia free of Jews as quickly as possible. Even considering the efforts of the Ministry of the Interior itself one can hardly speak of "pressure", as the rapidity with which the large contingents were transferred indeed suggests. There were for a while great difficulties in putting together further transports, but not because the Slovak government did not show any readiness any longer but because local doubts were present which perhaps arose from a wish for guarantees or a doubt regarding their own daring.

On the day of the assassination attempt on Heydrich I was with the Slovak Minister of the Interior, Mach. It was a courtesy call. We were at skittles after dinner when an orderly of the Ministry of the Interior delivered the message. Mach gave instructions to his representative in Prague to send reports every half hour and so I learnt of the details. I interrupted my travel trip and travelled that night to Prague, but I was not to see Heydrich any more. As a consequence of his death, in spring 1942, we had difficulties with the deportation which continued for quite a long period. That caused Gruppenführer Müller to send me to Preßburg; before I spoke with the Minister of the Interior Mach I visited the German envoy and "held the knife to his throat" saying to him: "The SS Reichsführer wishes immediately and without delay all efforts to deport the last Jews from the Slovak territory." I said the same, on orders, with rather unembellished words, to the Slovak Minister of the Interior also, with whom I could speak in a quite different way than with the official German envoy, because I knew him from a time before he was Minister of the Interior.

I remember that, at the end of 1942, attempts were made to raise support for the members of the soldiers of the 8th and 22nd divisions camped in the Batschka from the Jews in payment of some emigration fees, but I do not know any more from whom or when the stimulus for it was given. If it is now suggested to me that Wisliceny had himself been paid fifty thousand pounds at the end of 1942 in order to organise the deportations from Slovakia, there are only two possible explanations: either the cited source is lying or – what strikes me as very difficult to believe – Wisliceny had become disloyal.[7]

In addition, I must anyway ask what a man in our situation at that time should do with such a horrendous amount of 50,000 pounds. It is a mystery to me. And finally I must add that nothing is known to me about the receipt of this sum or about an order to obtain 50,000 pounds. I had nothing to do with the production of counterfeit

---

7   At the time of this record Eichmann does not yet know the statements of Wisliceny and others (Editor).

pound notes, but I know that later millions and millions of pound notes were printed in Germany. Therefore I cannot suppose that some office wished to collect a paltry 50,000 pounds in order to "sell" a fundamental right, for such a thing would have been talked about, and the Jewish question would have then been dealt with in the individual European countries only on the basis of money and therewith become practically unworkable. When I hear such a nonsensical sentence as: "Wisliceny showed that he could not be trifled with and sent three thousand men to the gas chambers", I can only say that the source cited to me lies shamelessly – or Wisliceny had at that time bluffed incredibly, which I would not like to believe of him.

I had no right, no commanding authority to send even a single Jew to a gas chamber, even to shoot down with a pistol, to beat down with a truncheon, to hang, or do anything similar to a single Jew – how much less would therefore a captain subordinate to me have had this right! If it is further explained to me here that the hostile post-war literature maintains that Wisliceny tried, on the basis of a payment of two million dollars, to discontinue the deportations in the whole of Europe apart from Germany and Poland, and the Jews had in desperation sought for the money but could not raise it, I do not in general wish to hear this nonsense any more for that is objectively and certainly also subjectively untrue.

But let us just take the case that one of my captains had demanded two million dollars in order to discontinue the deportations; let us further suppose that the German Reich office issuing the commission for that had put up with the enormous loss of prestige among our allies at that time, then Jewry would certainly have been able to raise these two million dollars and would have gladly raised it in order to preserve so many Jews from a deportation, especially since later, under Standartenführer Becher[8] in Hungary, it was a question of quite different sums. Around that time Wisliceny possessed neither the right nor the ability to do any such sort of business. Standartenführer Becher managed to see to it through the SS Reichsführer that something similar occurred later - there it was a matter not of money but of ten thousand cargo wagons which were determined for the eastern front. Wisliceny, on the other hand, had neither the right nor the order for that. I have never heard of this matter, and it certainly would not have remained hidden from me. I

---

8   Kurt Becher, SS Standartenführer, Chief of the Economic Staff of the Waffen SS in Budapest.

supervised my men, as far as possible, constantly in order to ensure that they held the straight course and I know that I was likewise constantly checked by Müller. That was to me quite right. Anybody who is proper can allow himself to be supervised. I am only annoyed about this primitive hotchpotch of lies and wonder how something like that can be presented to the public.

Similarly absurd is the story that Wisliceny visited me in Berlin and conveyed the desire of the Slovak authorities for an inspection regarding the destination of the Slovak Jews, to which I am supposed to have said: "The Jews are being killed there slowly as a result of the secret order of Himmler". That is a typical statement under torture; for if I had ever said something like that then certainly I would not have said "the Jews are being *killed there slowly* ..." It is possible that Wisliceny had explained to me that the papal nuncio had intervened even though this also seems improbable to me. For I did not receive any massive representations in any form from the Catholic Church. What is maintained and placed in my mouth does not quite simply correspond to my way of speaking. It is simply impossible that such a conversation could have taken place. It would have exceeded the official limits and is for me a mendacious nonsense.

After a pause of around two years the deportations were resumed in summer 1944. I know nothing about a visit of the SS Reichsführer at that time to Preßburg. Around that time I was in Hungary, but I remember that Wisliceny returned to Slovakia when the deportations in Hungary stopped. The Jews of Slovakia were then rounded up, and we proceeded from east to west because partisan groups were already active. In this way did the deportations began anew.

In 1942 it worked in reverse, and the area was scoured from west to east, but we were not responsible for that. The Slovak government first wished to have their capital free of Jews and to use the now available living space for the Slovak authorities who were thrown out of the government offices in Prague by the Czechs. Therefore the Slovaks gave away the first Jewish transports to us like "sour beer". The partisan groups mainly consisted of Jews, and were in 1944, at work in eastern Slovakia. Even this time the rounding up was not effected with German personnel but through the "Central Jewish Office" of Slovakia. It is certain in any case that these Jews were in no way sent for liquidation, for at that time Himmler's order stopping the annihilation already existed. Besides, in October 1944, certainly no more Jews were deported because around this time no more Jews were being deported anywhere. It may be that local offices of the Sipo and SD evacuated of their own accord some small groups of Jews which could not have been in the least of importance numerically, especially in areas plagued by partisans. If partisan uprisings were suppressed, that had nothing more to do with deportations but was instead matter of "combating the partisan gangs". My task was of a preventive sort. To prevent partisan groups from being able to form after the sad experiences in Warsaw. If Jews were flushed out in the course of the partisan attacks they were all treated the same way, not because they were Jews but because they were partisans. But that was not my task.

If the post-war literature maintains that I had "forcibly deported" Jews at the time when negotiations between the SS Reichsführer and the Jews were being conducted, then that is also fully false. If I had ever dared to ignore an order of the SS Reichsführer, then Himmler would have dealt with me in a frightful way. Only a fool can believe that an Obersturmbannführer could dare to reverse an order of the SS Reichsführer directly or indirectly into its opposite. Ever since Himmler had set up the measures for an exchange of 1,000 cargo wagons for a million Jews in May 1944, deportations to Auschwitz was no longer a goal. The Slovak Jews were distributed to other camps according to the accommodation possibilities announced by the WVHA. Wisliceny got Brunner as support for the last deportations from Slovakia, but doubtless there the partisan activity of the Jews worked as a triggering factor.

How far the Haganah was involved in the uprising in Slovakia I do not know. I only know that I pointed out this danger with the constancy of a Cato in the Roman senate. Moreover, I am of the opinion that the Haganah should have been watched more sharply. The Haganah was finally the reason for the fact that I at that time sought the friendship of that man from Palestine and the reason for Heydrich's allowing me to accept the invitation to the Near East. As long as I was occupied with Zionism I was also occupied with the Haganah. At that time Mussolini was our ally and also "the sword of Islam", reason enough to avoid difficulties. The Haganah belonged to the groups that interested us and with which we had a close contact. It would not surprise me if the Haganah had rushed to the help of the Slovak partisans at the last moment when there was nothing more to fear.

When I discussed economic questions with the Minister of Economics in 1942 – probably in the week of the conversation with

Tiso – the possibility was mentioned of sending family members on to already deported Jews. When I departed from Berlin to Preßburg, I naturally already knew what questions the Slovak authorities would pose to me. Either my representative Wisliceny had conveyed the different points to me after Ambassador Ludin had discussed them with him, or the latter had given them directly to Wisliceny as my adviser. Obviously the Jews in question were alive at that time – this is a further proof for the fact that deportations at that stage were not the equivalent to death by gassing, as so many Jewish hacks now state, but signified deployment for work. It seems to me that the Jews deported from Slovakia were in general not sent to concentration camps but to eastern ghettos. Whereas Auschwitz was a concentration camp with an enormous number of workplaces including a mine, in the eastern ghettos there were also workplaces of smaller size. I do not wish to say thereby that Slovak Jews could not have been sent to Auschwitz, but that these transports, even when they were directed to Lublin, were not taken control of by Globocnik but directly assigned to the workplaces. Otherwise I could indeed not at all have assured the two Slovak ministers that there was a possibility of uniting family members.

If it is claimed that I had shown Wisliceny a secret order according to which the entire Jewish race was to be exterminated, then that is a nonsense extracted forcibly from Wisliceny, or a clumsy attempt to distance himself from this matter.[9] It is a stupid and clumsy attempt because it is a question of someone who himself strove most keenly to enter this area of work and to thrust himself upon me even though I had once earlier been his subordinate. Perhaps he hoped to be able to oust me in the course of time and to set himself in my place.

Finally, about the number of the deportations of Slovak Jews I can only suggest that I think I remember a figure of 40,000-50,000 Jews were deported from Slovakia, a figure which includes the last deportations of 1944. A very substantial part of these deported people must have survived the war especially since, during the last operations, it had been ordered to discontinue their physical liquidation.

---

9   These and the following explanations of Eichmann's followed when he knew Wisliceny's explanations completely as reproduced by Reitlinger and Poliakov.

Deportations From Serbia

I never had an "adviser" in Belgrade and also did not carry out any deportations. If such took place in this area, they were not a matter of IV-B4 and I was therefore not responsible. I do not know anything about the deportations of the Jews from the Batschka and their subsequent ghettoization in Belgrade. I must explain the same thing about a supposed letter of the German envoy in Belgrade, Benzler, who is supposed to have requested me to deport Jews from the Belgrade ghetto to Poland and the Soviet Union. I am supposed to have explained that there was no place in the mentioned countries and I therefore could only propose to summarily shoot them. Not a single word of that is right. I could never have made such a proposal, for I was responsible for evacuation, but not for liquidation. Such a proposal was not made by either the IV-B4 office nor by my department even in a single case. At this time the liaison officer between the Foreign Office and my office was the Legation Councillor Rademacher. If there were any difficulties for the offices of the Foreign Office abroad that concerned the Jewish question, he came with his notes to me in order to discuss such matters. If the envoy Benzler had wished to get some decision with reference to the Jews in the Belgrade ghetto, Legation Councillor Rademacher would certainly have informed me of it. But I could never say to a Legation Councillor, a member of the Foreign Office: "I advise you to have the Jews shot". Such an advice I could at most have given to a member of the Sipo and SD, but I did not do that, for around that time, people were not "liquidated so freely". The Einsatz Groups in the east dealt directly on the instruction and order of the SS Reichsführer, perhaps also occasionally on the order of the Chief of the Sipo and SD, but even here Gestapo Office IV-B4 was fully excluded. Such a sort of "advice to shoot" would have gone fully beyond the scope of my responsibility.

It is, in any case, characteristic that the sources presented to me now point to the fact that this entire matter has once again been raised in connection with the "Wannsee conference" which was many months after my supposed "advice" to shoot the Jews summarily. This is therewith to be dismissed entirely. Besides, the expression "no place in Poland and Russia" is obviously nonsense extracted forcibly, exactly as is the opinion that three transport trains from Serbia, which went to eastern Poland, "disappeared on the way". That must have sprung from a fantasising brain; for three fully occupied transport trains cannot simply "disappear" without anybody knowing how that came about. Even the Jews themselves have registered in the most accurate manner numerically smaller cases of twenty or thirty persons. One should, however, have known where the transport trains were to be directed. Even a single transport train which departed from a place was recorded with its departure and destination railway stations. Besides, I could not order overnight any three transport trains just like that "with the telephone receiver in my hand"! That is absurd – and then these three trains are supposed to have simply "got lost"!

I admit to all that I have done in regards to carrying out my orders, but I am not ready to let everything simply fall on the department, such as, for example the callous "order": "I do not know where to send them – so shoot them!"

In terms of transport technicalities, my department did not have anything to do with those Jews who lived in Poland, in the Soviet Union, or in the Serbian territory. Three trains from Belgrade to eastern Poland means a route through Croatia and Austria to the Generalgouvernement for which naturally a travel-plan conference would have been necessary which someone today must still know something of.

Deportations from Romania

In Romania the SA Obergruppenführer von Killinger was the German envoy. On the demand of the Foreign Office, my Hauptsturmführer Richter went to Bucharest as "adviser for the Jewish question" and was attached to the Sipo. His task was to make clear to the envoy the guidelines that were valid in other countries as a result of the order of the SS Reichsführer. We generally did not take any Jews from Romania; for the Jewish question was solved there exclusively by the Romanians, under Romanian sovereignty and without the support of German offices. Richter was the "adviser" of the German envoy; it depended on the discretion of the envoy if and to what extent he should bring Richter in contact with the Romanian authorities. Richter received almost every four months an order to report to Berlin. As far as I can remember he repeatedly pointed out that he had an excellent relationship with the envoy von Killinger, but that the latter conducted all negotiations himself with the Romanian offices. Whereas Wisliceny in Preßburg accompanied the envoy Ludin to all possible offices or the Slovak government, von Killinger in Bucharest kept all this to himself personally and always negotiated by himself. Thus Richter's sole task lay in advising the envoy.

Richter often pointed out to me that Killinger practically placed a muzzle on him, which is why he came personally to me since he could not report in writing. Richter was clever and, in my opinion, combined the pleasant with the useful. I had indeed given him instruction to always, when he could not deal with matters, get on the plane or the highway to report to me personally when it was a question of anything essential. Von Killinger apparently wished to operate in Bucharest in an authoritative manner and got on very well with Richter so long as the latter was subordinate to him. When Marshal Antonescu[10] conceived the plan of "evacuating" Jews from Romania to the territories occupied by us, I naturally resisted it, for my task was to make the territories under our control free of Jews.

Obviously I was also, in this respect, not at all responsible for the eastern territories, but had nevertheless to prevent Jews being sent there. The world is large enough. The Romanian Jews did not need to come into the territories that we controlled. In this matter I was asked for advice by Legation Councillor Rademacher. He was a rather "casual man" who never particularly asserted himself. If the hostile post-war literature now represents it as if I had allowed Romanian Jews to be deported to "ethnic German settlements" in order to liquidate them there, that is also nonsense. It would have been unthinkable that I had given even the smallest order with respect to Romanian Jews under Romanian jurisdiction. The chauvinism of the Romanians would never have allowed that. It was for me very right that the Romanians solved their own Jewish question, and I knew from Richter that they actually did this. I had no authority at my disposal to issue a liquidation order even for a single Jew, let alone that I had the authority to "deal with" the Jewish question in Romania, not to mention at all "liquidating".

I can also not remember a single transport from Romania and I also do not think that one train departed from there. If this had been the case, that is, if the Romanian government handed over some Jews to the German authorities, then the Chief of the WVHA would have perhaps named Auschwitz as the receiving station. But I repeat that I do not know anything of deportations from Romania and that the SS Reichsführer never had the intention of deporting the Romanian Jews to the Lublin area. I do not think that the SS Reichsführer made such a suggestion; for the WVHA could still place a veto because the receiving town was determined exclusively by this head office. If the

10   Ion Antonescu, Romanian chief of state, imprisoned on 18 September 1944, killed in Fort Jilava on 1 June 1946 .

SS Reichsführer ordered Lublin as the destination town and there was a place, then his order was naturally to be carried out; but if the Head Office had no admission possibility then the transports went to Auschwitz or to another camp. In this case it would have been the task of the Obergruppenführer Pohl to correct the original instruction of the SS Reichsführer. The impulsive ordinances of the SS Reichsführer could in practice be carried out only with difficulty or sometimes not at all when it encountered actual obstacles.

Even if the hostile post-war literature cites expressions such as "State Secretary Luther sent a communication to Eichmann", that is a complete misinterpretation of the situation. Obviously I stood in good contact with Luther personally without having a personal connection to him, but State Secretary Luther never sent "a communication to Eichmann"; for that would have been improper and would have exceeded the professional limits. That we knew each other from some meetings does not in any way mean that I was subsequently justified in writing personal letters to him, or that he addressed official letters to me. He and I had to keep to the official channels; if he had to convey a communication to me this was directed to the Chief of the Sipo and SD and only in special exceptional cases to the office chief Müller, my superior in Gestapo Office IV. Only thereafter did I receive this communication with the corresponding instruction of my chief.

I can no longer remember if the plans emerged as an idea or instruction from the SS Reichsführer, from the Foreign Office or from another central authority, but I can remember to a certain degree that I once wished to exchange a large number of Germans of military service age for a number of Jews. Among them there could have been also five thousand children, but it is certain that this operation failed.

If it is maintained now that I urged quick implementation since the time was not far off "when the emigration of five thousand children from the east can no longer be technically effected", I have no recollection of that. Therewith I do not wish to deny that at all; for I considered it as uncommonly interesting to trade Jews for Germans. Perhaps I actually said, like a trader who advertises his wares: "If you do not do it today, it may perhaps become more expensive tomorrow ... " It was indeed war. If this proposal dates from 1944, it is also possible that I could secure transport possibilities only through a quick implementation or that the choice between those fit for work and those unfit for work in the camps was available to me only within a short period of time.

Photograph allegedly showing dead Jews on overcrowded train from Iasi, in 1944.

That the World Jewish Congress made "ransom money" available for the emigration of 70,000 Romanian and French Jews and that the English allowed this "trade" is not known to me. I know only that the hostile foreign countries undertook practically nothing for a bloodless solution of the Jewish question. The illegal emigration of the Jews from Romania must have been very great; for practically all "illegal" emigrations of Jews from Hungary approved by me passed through Romania.

It is also known to me that the Romanian commissioner for Jews, Lecca[11] was in Berlin, perhaps together with Richter. However, he did not visit me but perhaps I got to know him at some meeting or meal – the name is somehow familiar to me. If he had visited my office this would have gone beyond the scope of the normal daily work and would have certainly remained in my memory, especially since it was my custom to invite such gentlemen to lunch or dinner even privately.

The operations carried out in the late summer of 1944 by IV-B4 in the Hungarian-Romanian border area, were undertaken solely with the intention of extracting the ethnic Germans settled there from the

---

11   Radu Lecca, "Jewish commissioner" of the Romanian government, killed in Fort Jilava on 1 June 1946.

Soviet attack. I did not have anything to do with Jews in this area, I did not see or speak even once to a single one of them. Nobody from my command had anything to do with Jews there.

In conclusion let it be stated in regards to Romania: Although Richter was sent there as the "adviser" of department IV-B4, he played only a supernumerary role. Not a single deportation train was handed over to the German authorities and I myself was never once in Bucharest.

Deportations from Bulgaria

It seems improbable to me that Hauptsturmführer Dannecker would have been present in Bulgaria in spring 1943. In 1943 Dannecker was in Paris, where I myself often was in those years. So I think that Dannecker was probably in Bulgaria, in 1944.[12] Dannecker in general played no role for my office. If it is said to me: "Deportations took place", with the classic addition: "They went to Auschwitz and were gassed there", then I only ask myself how it could be possible that one later met all these Bulgarian Jews …

I had sent Dannecker to Bulgaria, where he was subordinate to the German consulate. If Bulgaria had had a Jewish commissioner,[13] Dannecker must, with the clearance certificate of the German ambassador, have supported him with advice and action or assisted the envoy within his field of service with the concerned Bulgarian office in the Ministry of the Interior.

His work was in no way successful, because no Jew of Bulgarian citizenship was handed over to us for evacuation. It may be that some transport trains departed with Jews from areas which at that time had been ceded to Bulgaria; these were then sent to my department as Serbian or Greek Jews.

Deportations from Greece

That the Jews in Greece were forcibly collected for work and that this duty was abrogated on monetary payment I cannot at all remember.

---

12   Eichmann seems to err here; Dannecker was actually in Sofia at the beginning of 1943.

13   A. Beleff, Jewish commissioner of the Bulgarian government in Sofia.

If the post-war literature says that a man called Wulf was sent as an emissary of the Eichmann office to Greece, and that I myself went there later, I must declare that firstly I had neither an "adviser" nor an SS chief with the name Wulf in my office. Secondly, I myself entered Greek territory for the first and only time in 1937, and that was during my visit to the Near East. Such statements by these different post-war authors in general permit unequivocal conclusions regarding their veracity ...

I do not know if we had a state police office in Greece and if a commanding officer of the Sipo operated there. If the latter was the case, there could have been an adviser called Wulf in his office. If this was the case, then he was naturally not under me. He can only have obtained instructions through his superior offices in the Reich Security Head Office. Obviously I do not know what all those people were called as I had nothing to do with them personally. Hereby I must further declare that such "Jewish advisers" of a commanding officer of the Sipo could indeed prepare for their chief a letter to the RSHA but could not themselves sign. For that only the commanding officer had the authority.

The expert from IV-B4 in Greece was Alois Brunner, whom I gave to assist Wisliceny. At no time did they have at their disposal orderlies or anybody else. That is why we also did not carry out the rounding up and loading of Jews who were actually deported there. I do not remember any more who did that. Greece was far away, and apart from the mentioned "adviser", my office had no further personnel there. In what way and with whom the "adviser" operated was solely his task. I only know that some transports departed from Greece.

The name of the rabbi Koretz[14] is vaguely in my memory. If it is pointed out now that this rabbi stood in our "services" and described to the Greek Jews the advantages of a settlement in the "Jewish state in Poland", I do not believe the first at all, and of the other is to be said that my efforts for a "Jewish state in Poland" lay significantly earlier. It may be that the offices which carried out the rounding up and loading operated with this instruction in order to facilitate the work.

---

14   Zvi Koretz, Chairman of the Jewish council in Thessaloniki from October 1942, a rabbi who was earlier in Berlin-Charlottenburg. Apparently he was killed in the Belsen concentration camp.

If I am now asked what I know of a Jewish transport in August 1944 which departed from Rhodes, I cannot say much about it. From March to Christmas 1944, I was in Hungary continuously and appeared only occasionally in Berlin in order to solve questions related to Hungary. But I could not thereby interfere in the matter of my adviser. For that I would have had to first get acquainted with the matter. Even as a divisional head, though at that time commandeered, I could not sit down at my writing desk during the few hours of my stay in Berlin and take over the leadership of the department again. For that I would have to first study the files in order to have a view of current cases. My regular representative made a report during these visits in 1944 on the events of the past week, because it was also in his own interest to make sure of my intention. But I was too far from the central authority to remember something like the deportation of the Jewish population of the island of Rhodes.

I remember that once it was attempted in Greece to prevent some deportation on the pretext of an epidemic. I had the case investigated and the deportation carried out since there was no epidemic. If I had not done this we would suddenly have had "epidemics" in all the other countries. Not a single case of typhus was reported from the camps to which these supposed infected transports were directed. Against this it cannot also be countered that, in the case of illness, these Jews were immediately sent to liquidation. For there were Jews of all possible citizenships who remained alive, knew nothing of typhus and were not threatened with physical liquidation.

It is right that in Greece numerous Italian officers married rich Greek Jewesses in order to take them to Italy. After all, why should it have been different in Greece than in the other countries? Such fake marriages for payment of horrendous sums were commonplace. They were then mostly immediately divorced in the "safe foreign countries". These cases were, moreover, not so numerous that they would have had a fundamental significance. All possible things took place on the back of the Jews: economic interests, among others also of the Italians, secret official efforts of every imaginable sort, uprising and partisan efforts. The fake marriages in any case did not disturb our larger measures; if the marriage was perfect, we could do nothing against it. The individual "advisers" would certainly have written complaining reports if they had glimpsed a danger in these fake marriages. The fact that Wisliceny went to Greece to support Brunner proves that the Jewish deportation from Greece stood under a special pressure from above, from the government. Even in Holland I was constantly pressured and sent either Brunner of Burger to support Zöpf. So I can still remember having commandeered many of my men to Greece.

A number of Greek Jews went to Theresienstadt, which has remained accurately in my memory because they were somehow conspicuous there – perhaps because they were much more cunning traders than the others. The council of elders of Theresienstadt was unhappy to have to accept these Greek Jews, so they later went to Auschwitz. The procedure was not the task of these offices, which must therefore have been interested in the deportation. It is also possible that the army approached the SS Reichsführer, who could have then ordered a "lighting operation" in his impulsive way. Thereafter, I presumably commandeered my best people, Wisliceny for the negotiations, Brunner and Burger for the technical side of the operation. Whether the deportations from Greece actually coincided with the retreat of the army I cannot comment on since I was in Hungary from March to Christmas 1944.

Deportations from the Baltic Countries

I never had anything to do with the Baltic countries; that means the Jewish question was solved locally. There the hatred of the Jews was very great, especially since many inhabitants had been verifiably abducted and murdered during the Soviet occupation mostly by Jews. Dr. Stahlecker, together with whom I had attempted to implement the "Jewish state in Poland", was later chief of the Einsatz group in the Baltic countries; I had nothing to do with him in this capacity and also did not meet him anymore.

It is certain that some transports were sent from the Reich to Riga; on the other hand, which could possibly have occurred on the direct orders of Heydrich. The chiefs of the Einsatz groups were certainly ordered from time to time to Berlin for reporting, on which occasion they were possibly informed that certain transports were planned. Indeed, I did not have to determine the destination stations; no chief of an Einsatz Group or concentration camp commandant would have been pleased that a departmental head simply sent him thousands of men, though it is possible that I received instructions to direct some transport trains to Riga.

Deportations from Croatia

In Croatia, IV-B4 had an "adviser", my Hauptsturmführer Abromeit. His task was to try to influence the Croatian government in such a way that it would request the German government to take over Jews of Croatian citizenship. Abromeit had to report to me constantly on his efforts; I still remember how he described to me that the Ustaša[15] likewise sometimes sent Jews on its own responsibility for liquidation. In general, Abromeit's activity had very little success; he did not succeed in extracting substantial contingents of Jews from Croatia. The opposition from the Croatian government however did not arise so much from the demand to protect the Jews present there as rather from the pressure to preserve their sovereignty at all costs; therefore they preferred to solve the Jewish problem on their own. Very few transports departed from Croatia; I do not think even one of them was directed to the Generalgouvernement.

That the Poglavnik Pavelić[16] opposed our deportation plans is completely possible, but that then corresponded exclusively to his wish to demonstrate his own sovereignty to the outside world. Pavelić himself I did not see or speak to, either then or later. But I do not know that he changed his attitude "fundamentally" from 1944 and, among other things, issued permission to the International Red Cross to visit his Jewish work camps. Indeed, why should Pavelić have acted differently in his territory than the SS Reichsführer did in his domain of sovereignty? Indeed, Himmler did the same as he had negotiations carried out through Bernadotte[17] and thereby had Jews from the concentration camps loaded into white Swedish buses and handed over to Sweden. In that regard it was, for the SS Reichsführer, not a matter of placing himself in a milder light, and I assume as little in the case of Pavelić that he wished to assume a better position through milder regulations or actions. These concessions were in his opinion nothing but the attempt to create a dialogue with the enemy, something similar to the "exchange of 10,000 cargo wagons for a million Jews".

---

15 The Croatian nationalist movement which persecuted Serbs, Jews and gypsies during the second World War.

16 Ante Pavelić, from 1941-45 Poglanik, that is, Führer, as well as chief of state of Croatia.

17 Count Folke Bernadotte, Swedish politician, with whom Heinrich Himmler made contact on 19 February 1945 for a separate peace.

I recall that Abromeit wrote in one of his reports that Italians Jews had been concentrated on an island. Abromeit was a rather "clever man", perhaps a Danziger. He was able to penetrate areas where he could get authentic information. Thus he always described the current situation very well to me. However, I hardly think that Abromeit approached the German Police attaché in Zagreb on the matter of the deportations, unless he allied himself professionally in some way with him, which indeed was left to his responsibility, since the task of the "commissioner for the Jewish question" consisted in making contact with all possible German as well as Croatian offices, though always with the agreement of his German superior in any particular field of work.

The number of the Jews deported from the whole of Yugoslavia I can only estimate. Ustaša and Chetniks[18] took care of the Jewish question on their own responsibility and the majority of the Jews fled to the partisan territories anyway. At the most perhaps two or three trains departed.

Deportations from Italy

Everywhere where the Italians entered as occupying powers they tried more or less to protect the Jews. That 15,000 Jews were deported from Italy seems to me most unlikely. I cannot remember any interventions from Weizsäcker in favour of the Jews. It may be that, after the return of Mussolini, some deportation trains departed. By and large I must consider Italy as a "bagatelle", and as such it was certainly taken away from me by my regular representative, so I cannot remember anything. I myself was never in Italy during the war. Only in 1937 did I travel through Italy when I went to Egypt. I visited Italy at Easter of 1939 privately and only visited again in 1950.

That Jewish transports from Italy had to return because they could not pass the Brenner due to the Allied bombing, I am hearing this now for the first time. In 1944, I hardly operated in Berlin anyway and my regular representative was not compelled to report everything to me because I was for the major part of the year in Hungary and he would not have required any decisions from me anyway.

---

18   Chetniks were Serb nationalists who were fundamentally opposed to the Axis powers although they collaborated with them during the war for their own ends.

Abromeit once described in his reports how the Italian Jews were concentrated on an island and how the Jews, after the Mussolini story and our corresponding occupation of the Italian zones, fled either to the Yugoslav partisans or in the direction of southern Italy to Bari. Only a small part could be seized by us. In Italy the actions against the Jews failed exactly as they had in Belgium and in the Nordic states.

Deportations from Finland

My department IV-B4 never had anything to do with Finland. I did not know that many senior officers in the Finnish army were Jews nor of the allegation that soldiers and officers of Jewish origin in the Finnish army generally fought on the German side. In general we did not worry about the Jews in Finland for they were very small in number. As far as I know, not a single demand for the delivery of Finnish Jews was made – and in no way from my department.

Deportations from Norway

I cannot understand even today that we were involved in the regulation of the Jewish question at all in the Scandinavian countries. The Jewish population there were not high; there was no "Jewish problem" as such. There were hardly a thousand Jews in Norway.

That requests from the *Swedish* government with regard to the acceptance of Jews through Mr. von Weizsäcker,[19] State Secretary in the Foreign Office, were refused is completely due to the course of the official hierarchy of the Foreign Office; some years previously, when I was searching desperately all over the world for immigration possibilities for Jews, such an offer from Sweden would have been most welcome; if 30,000 or 40,000 Jews had been accepted at that time we would have gladly paid for it.

When we had the contract to make Norway free of Jews it would have been extremely right for us to be able to send the evacuees, as well as Jewish children who were to be accommodated, to neutral Sweden. If at that time people worked against that, it must have

---

19   Ernst, Freiherr von Weizsäcker, State Secretary in the Reich Foreign Ministry until April 1943, then Envoy at the Holy See. In April 1949 sentenced by the US Military Tribunal in Nuremberg to 7 years imprisonment. The penalty was reduced to 5 years. On 6 August 1971 Weizsäcker died in Lindau.

been purely with the intention of causing further difficulties for us. People like Weizsäcker were perhaps laughing up their sleeve; for, in the Scandinavian countries, there was never a Jewish question as had existed in Germany.

I remember Reich Commissioner Terboven[20] in connection with the letters which I had to draft for the Chief of the Sipo and SD. During the unfortunate affair in Denmark I flew in a four-engine plane from Copenhagen to Berlin and saw Reich Commissioner Terboven at the Copenhagen airport, where he was being seen off officially by the military commander. However, I never spoke to him; around this time I felt no pleasure at all in talking to anybody; for I had to consider how I could clear away the bad "stench" cooked up by others. Numerically the Jews evacuated from Norway were not significant.

Deportations from Denmark

Who the father of the unfortunate idea of deporting Jews from Denmark was I do not know. There was no Jewish question in Denmark and the one who set the "flea" in the SS Reichsführer's ear of "making it free of Jews" must have been a bad adviser. Only with a magnifying glass could a couple of Jews be found in Denmark. They caused the German government and my office more headaches and bother than the deportation of 300,000 Jews from Hungary. My department had in general no interest in Denmark – the "adviser" of the SS Reichsführer in this matter brought Denmark into play either through stupidity or malevolence. Perhaps Himmler thought of it himself, even though there were in Denmark, as mentioned, only a couple of thousand Jews.

Department IV-B4 however did not take the slightest initiative. If it had been different, either the chief of Gestapo Office IV or the Chief of the Sipo or even the SS Reichsführer would, on account of the enormous complications of the entire matter, have given me a juicy reprimand because I was of the lowest service rank on whom one could most conveniently put the "entire blame". But that did not happen, because it was not possible; from this it is clear that I was in no way the initiator in this matter.

After the order for the evacuation of the Jews from Denmark had

---

20   Josef Terboven, at first Gauleiter in Essen, then Reich Commissioner in Norway. Took his own life in May 1945.

been given, IV-B4 had naturally to step in, and indeed quickly. If the hostile post-war literature mentions Rademacher[21] in this connection being a "spy for the SS in the diplomatic corps" that is not at all right. Rademacher himself came from the diplomatic track and was, I think, a legation councillor of the first rank. It is also totally new to me that the SS Reichsführer is supposed to have ordered Gruppenführer Müller to include Jews in a list of Communist and other Danish resistance leaders in order to arrest them in this way. I never heard anything of it nor did I occupy myself with it.

After much toing and froing a small group of Jews from Denmark was finally shipped to Germany; on the voyage some jumped into the water and committed suicide. In the case of deportations there were only a few cases of suicide. I do not think this is characteristic of the Jew. I had to follow up those suicide cases of Danish Jews and went to see the commanding officer of the Sipo and SD, Dr Rudolf Mildner;[22] it was to be clarified at the same time if elderly Jews had been in the transport as the inevitable complaints had suggested this. The whole thing annoyed me immeasurably because here I had to deal with the smallest details of individual cases, something that had never belonged to my duties. I found Mildner depressed. He was glad to finally have with him a departmental head from the central authority to whom he could, to a certain extent, hand over everything. I perhaps visited Best along with Mildner and think I can remember that the first proposal on the return of the Jews to Denmark came from Best.[23] Even in my opinion this was the only way out that remained after too much nonsense had already been created. At first a return seemed to me like something monstrous since there had never been such a measure. I had the couple of Danish Jews brought in a very orderly manner to Theresienstadt so that they were retained by me and stood under my control, though their accommodation there occurred very much to the sorrow of Dr. Eppstein, and I myself did not at all understand how such old Jews had been sent on the journey. Perhaps all the others had been brought to safety? I hardly think that a man of my department was responsible for the choice of the old Jews; I would certainly have

---

21 Reitlinger's opinion is not demonstrable. Reitlinger wrongly described the person mentioned as a "spy".

22 Dr. Josef Mildner, SS Standartenführer, Chief of the Secret State Police in Upper Silesia, later Commanding Officer of the Security Police in Denmark (Copenhagen).

23 Dr. Karl Werner Best, Reich Plenipotentiary in Copenhagen. Sentenced to death there in 1946. Later his sentence was reduced to 5 years.

"rapped him on his knuckles"; so I would have surely been able to remember it.

In the matter of the return of the Danish Jews, Best in any case was able to have his way after he had kicked up a terrible rumpus in Berlin. Basically we laughed a bit about the powerful exertion of force that was necessary to evacuate a handful of Jews from Denmark and then, on top of it, to have to send them back there. My department in any case did nothing else in the entire matter than arrange transport. An order is an order, deportation as much as sending back. In Denmark we disgraced ourselves and annoyed the Danes, and the whole episode was not worth it.

If I had been responsible in some way for the Denmark affair I would have naturally been aware of it, as I would like once again to emphasise in conclusion: my immediate superior Müller was only too prompt to issue service reprimands; if one of his departmental heads had arranged such a brainless thing without the agreement of the other central authorities, he would have proceeded wickedly in this case! In any case I did not receive the slightest service reprimand.

Deportations from the Netherlands

In the Hague there operated a commanding officer of the Sipo and SD; it was determined at a high level that councillor Zöpf had to work on the Jewish problem, and had for this reason to get in touch with the concerned divisional head of the Reich Security Head Office – thus IV-B4. I do not remember any more how I got to know Zöpf; it may be that he came to the RSHA and presented himself as the commissioned Jewish departmental head in the occupied Dutch territories; in any case, he got his guidelines from my department. Zöpf had another colleague, whose name comes to my mind having already mentioned him, Aus der Fünten. He was, I think, Zöpf's representative.

Since the commanding officer of the Sipo and SD in the Hague was fully absorbed in his "radio game" with England and could also give proof of the success of his work through a number of captured enemy parachute agents, he had personally no time to take care of the solution of the Jewish question in Holland. Therefore Zöpf generally had a free hand; I know that he, for example, visited the Reich Commissioner Seyß-Inquart as well as the Minister of Economics, Zöpf. But Zöpf also had Dutch agencies on hand which were endowed with executive powers. He was an extraordinarily gentle man who was distinguished by official zeal, official punctuality and official loyalty. He planned things by himself and he had to deal with many difficulties; for example, transport contingents on the scale of twenty to fifty thousand were planned, but frequently less than ten percent of that was achieved. I myself had to travel five or six times to the Hague to strengthen Zöpf's position as well as to take care of the legislative support and the required executive ordinances. For the above mentioned reasons, the evacuation of even a couple of thousand Jews took a long time.

In order to be able to work against the constant interventions in Holland I often had to devour "Indonesian atjars" and spend many hours in conferences in the old, dusty but otherwise quite orderly and middle-class Hoted Des Indes. Occasionally I travelled to Amsterdam, where Zöpf had a departmental head, a Hauptsturm or Sturmbannführer from the staff of the Commander of the Sipo. He was, in my eyes, at that time the right man who effected the right police measures at the right time and was thereby successful. In Amsterdam, he was based in the centre of Jewish life in Holland; he was criminal commissioner or criminal councillor and was called, I think, Lages.[24] With Zöpf's characteristics the legal consolidation of the deportations could be achieved only through the normal channels with many difficulties; once this occurred, Zöpf was no longer the suitable man for further work because he lacked the necessary experience for it, and so I sent him a number of available "advisers" who were under the commanding officer of the Sipo.

One day Gruppenführer Müller informed me that I should place Ferdinand Aus der Fünten too with Zöpf; he did a "crash course" with me then he was sent as assistant to Zöpf. When these advisers worked in Holland everything was regulated in such a way that Zöpf only had to smooth the way for the completion of matters, that is, through the commanding officer of the Sipo to the individual experts of the Reich commissariat and to the senior SS and Police chief Rauter.

There were many difficulties in Holland, and mostly from the Dutch side. Once, if not twice, I had to give a sort of lecture to Rauter, on the orders of the Chief of the Sipo and SD, that the patience of the RSHA was now nearing its end; we had done everything and, in

---

24 Wilhelm Lages, Commander of the Security Police in Amsterdam. In 1949 sentenced to death by a special court in the Hague; in 1952 reprieved to life-imprisoned.

terms of personnel technicalities, everything was now arranged for the implementation of the solution of the Jewish question in the occupied Dutch territories in a forceful way. I probably had a "special programme" for Rauter in which everything was ordered according to points so that he could issue the pertinent ordinances and under certain circumstances provide missing authorisations on the spot. Rauter was a very orderly, pleasant man with whom I got on well. He was at that time an adviser to Dr. Friene,[25] the founder of the "Homeland Security"[26] whose chiefs were drawn from the SS. This explained why we understood each other so well: I came from Linz and could converse with the Styrian Rauter in the local dialect. Our good relationship also had positive results in the work conferences.

When I finished my negotiations in the Hague, I travelled back to Berlin and waited for the things that were to come. From the Hague I had been given figures which I now presented to my transport expert; it was then his task to draw up the appropriate travel-plan within the agreed time and to obtain the necessary trains. The transports went ahead until they had to be interrupted if, once again, too many obstacles came up. Then the travel-plan was once again upset, much to the sorrow of the Transport Ministry, and as a consequence the entire travel-plan order, which included not only our transports, had to be prepared anew. That was very often the case in the Dutch deportations. Rauter himself always had certain doubts about our evacuation programme that I sought to dispel; it was very complicated to seize Jews with Dutch citizenship; for the Dutch knew of no "Jew with Dutch citizenship". He knows of only the Dutch and the non-Dutch. So he baulked at the evacuation of any "Dutch citizen".

I know that a Jewish ghetto was created in Holland following the eastern European model. Zöpf had arranged everything for that: the Jews were rounded up in the ghetto of Amsterdam. It may also be that the Jewish "council of elders" set up peat camps, just as the "Reich association" in Germany did, following an idea of the "council of elders", which founded different work camps in Theresienstadt. But I do not think that the security police spent any time on peat camps. Of local measures such as, for example, a razzia in the historical Jewish quarter of Amsterdam I know as little as the railway strike which is now mentioned in connection with it. I am also not aware that, after

---

25   Dr. Friene belonged to the large German wing of the Homeland Security, a counterpart of Prince Starhemberg.

26   Heimatschutz

some incidents, once 400 Jews were arrested as hostages on the orders of the SS Reichsführer. My department was not responsible for that. We had to repeat over and over again that we undertook only the transports. There were other departments that dealt with sabotage, assassination or strike matters. All persons that other departments had seized were taken separately to the Reich. If, however, it was not a matter of Jews within the scope of the solution of the Jewish question, then I did not have anything to do with transports, for the concerned department was responsible for all related questions. For those involved in sabotage, assassinations, hostages, etc. it was a matter of indifference to me if they were Jews or non-Jews.

Today it is maintained that in June 1942 I wrote to the legation councillor Rademacher that from the middle of June 40,000 Jews should be transported from the Netherlands and an equal number from occupied France. To that I must state that it was just a sort of plan; the reality was quite different: after personal consultations I received in Holland the target of a contingent of 40,000, but the difficulties were too great to obtain this number, especially since so many Jews were protected. So it was frequently the case that a planned transport of 40,000, in the end only 5,000 or 8,000 was achieved. This number of 40,000 followed me through all the countries and turns up even now. It seems to me almost as if my advisers had agreed on this figure during their meetings in order to transmit it to me. Naturally I already knew from experience that the mentioned contingents were never fulfilled and had no travel-plan made up for transports of 40,000, but only at most for 10,000 persons. If the number happened to be higher, a travel-plan for a continuous operation could easily be developed since it was possible to incorporate a new one into the already existing one.

The associates of the Reich Commissariat for the Occupied Netherlands were ready to do everything that was required, but they also had to fulfil other tasks, for example, with regard to the economy, and therefore demanded a large number of exemptions which had to be permitted in order not to let any gear in this large machine malfunction and let the machine itself finally run dry. These offices were, besides, compelled to incorporate slowly, step by step, our demands into their economic programme; the same was true of the political sector. The Sipo was impatient, since it stood under the order of the SS Reichsführer. To control this impatience without thereby "losing face" before the SS Reichsführer was the task of Seyß-Inquart and his people. I never dealt with him personally, nor with his most senior colleagues.

Emigrating Dutch Jews leaving Amsterdam in 1941.

To characterise Rauter as particularly "stupid" is, in my opinion, particularly foolish. He was nothing but a recipient of orders and indeed the immediate orders of the SS Reichsführer, which he always acknowledged unconditionally and for whose implementation he was ready to tackle the obstacles of the doubts of the Reich commissariat at full gallop.

If it is maintained in the post-war literature about Holland that, at first, considering the psychological effects, only 25,000 Jews and refugees were to be deported, and it is added: "... while Zöpf and Aus der Fünten arrested everybody that they could", I must remark that Zöpf followed the "guidelines" strictly; I did not invent the latter. Rather, they were born in the course of time through orders of the SS Reichsführer, supplementary ordinances and practical doctrines. The practical experiences of the departments were our own participation in the "guidelines", whose basis naturally was formed by the orders of the SS Reichsführer; supplementary orders were added to that, even the Chief of the Sipo often had something to contribute, the chancellery of the deputy of the Führer came forward with certain things – all wished to have said something, and so the "guidelines" proliferated like a cancerous ulcer.

Originally it was planned to create in Holland a "Central Office for Jewish Emigration"; I think also that such a thing functioned for a while, but nothing came of it, since I always found anxious faces among the central authorities and nobody dared to undertake anything. What we had achieved in Vienna immediately and with great momentum could be repeated once again in Prague because Heydrich was behind it; but already in Berlin this did not happen anymore – the central authorities refused to transfer the necessary personnel and especially the required police powers. At that time in Vienna perhaps nobody calculated what the practical consequences of such a transfer of powers would look like; nobody expected that the police would deploy their own power. Only when I once "sold" dollars collected for the emigrating Jews at an exchange rate of 20 Reichsmarks to the director of the foreign exchange trade office did the realisation set in; if my superiors had not covered me at that time, I would have faced difficulties. In Berlin and the Hague. I could not register success with the "central offices" because the necessary powers were not present.

It is possible that the Amsterdam Jewish council had more than 14,000 employees who were then "reduced" by the Gestapo to 13,000. Indeed, in Amsterdam every second person was a "Jewish official"! Finally, the release of workers into the peat camps along with their relatives is evidence of how tolerant the Sipo were.

Among the numerous "privileged Jews" in Holland there were also diamond grinders; in reality they were not "privileged", rather "exempted" and were considered according to the law as "indispensable". Today I can no longer remember if Zöpf demonstrated in his report entitled "The dejudaisation of the Netherlands" that 71,000 Jews possessed certifications according to which the measures directed against the Jews did not affect them …" But I know that in Holland very many Jews were "privileged" or "exempted"; for, even in Holland the Commissioner for the Four-Year Plan[27] had his emissaries "sweep through", and jewel traders, antiquity traders and art traders immediately received their protective pass. If the Reich Marshal pursued such a passion it is not a wonder that Tom, Dick and Harry were concerned to exempt Jews from the measures directed against them either for personal or professional reasons. In the case of the diamond grinders it was a matter of an elite

---

27   In October 1936, Göring was appointed Commissioner for the Four-Year Plan of the National Socialist government.

group of experts who had ground some famous stone whose name I no longer remember. In general the SS Reichsführer respected all ordinances of the Commissioner for the Four-Year Plan. In the case of these numerous exceptions it is to be considered that councillor Zöpf worked with the commanding officer of the Sipo and SD in the Hague who, from the start, manifested a great amount of tolerance; Zöpf was friendly with him, but was sent to Berlin when differences appeared – exactly like Dannecker.

That the Warsaw ghetto uprising called forth sharpened measures even in Holland corresponded to the general course. No circular or anything similar had to be issued by IV-B4, but the responsible SS and Police chiefs did what was necessary, because they were indeed responsible for the security in their territory.

Whether the Jews deported from Holland were necessary for the Buna works in Auschwitz I do not know. In Auschwitz there was a Heinkel works as well as a Buna works; but where the WVHA took the Jews to was not in any file and did not concern me; for I only had to supply the transports to the destination places given to me. That Dutch Jews were taken to Sobibor is not known to me.

A small Sephardic community was exempted from the deportation; that was a single case for which I was not responsible. Obviously such a case was not mentioned in the "guidelines". It is possible that the commander of the Sipo in Holland had exempted those Sephardic Jews from the deportation at his own discretion.

Deportations from Belgium

In general, in Belgium we had no success with deportations. When it is quoted that in Belgium there were 85,000 Jews but only 42,000 remained at the end of the war, this circumstance is explained to a large extent by their flight. Neither the Belgium military nor the civil governor had any interest in supporting our measures. I remember that on Heydrich's instructions I had to draw up draft letters for both of them. Heydrich attempted to clarify the questions propounded by the regional Sipo offices in Belgium in some form and to advance the Sipo matters.

I also remember that I opposed the taking of further non-Belgian Jews from Belgium since even the Jews of certain foreign citizenship were exempted from the deportation according to the "guidelines": I could only consider stateless Jews as eligible for deportation, or those with a citizenship related to the countries occupied by us. My order said that Belgium was to be made free of Jews according to the issued guidelines; thus Falkenhausen's procedure quite contradicted the order of the SS Reichsführer. I had to proceed against it and I persuaded the Foreign Office, which then intervened in Belgium. This development and course of events I do not wish to deny.

With regard to some opinions in the Jewish post-war literature, I would like to expressly stress here: there could never have been a commission to the concentration camp commandant's office that Belgian, Dutch or Hungarian Jews were to be liquidated. There was nothing like that, but exclusively an order of the SS Reichsführer which was from time to time changed; it said: "Jews fit for work are to be taken to work deployment, *those unfit for work to liquidation*". Neither Pohl nor Zierach nor Höss could determine the fitness for work or the unfitness for work, but *only the doctors' commission in the individual concentration camps*. If, in Amsterdam, a certain number of Jews were seized because these had shot German or Dutch soldiers, measures of the SS Reichsführer against this group were naturally possible. But it is completely incorrect to maintain that the liquidation were undertaken according to nationalities!

Although I cannot remember individual cases any more, I can remember that the Belgian population stood strongly on the side of the Jews. Practically considered, we therefore achieved very little in Belgium; that may well have been the reason for the fact that I had to repeatedly prepare letter drafts for Heydrich and Kaltenbrunner to the SS Reichsführer. I would strongly doubt that altogether more than 80,000 Jews were deported from the territory of Netherlands and Belgium; a large number of Jews must have survived the war without being evacuated.

The Return of 367 Spanish Jews

It appears that in December 1943, the return of 367 Spanish Jews from the Bergen-Belsen camp to Spain was negotiated between Mr. von Thadden of the Foreign Office and the Spanish diplomat Diaz. If it is said to me now that these were "released from the concentration camp", this does not in any way mean that I, as divisional head of IV-B4, had to be informed of it. Around that time there existed a fundamental order of the SS Reichsführer not to release Jews any more until the end of the war, in contrast to those earlier in concentration camps; from this time on, the order for commitment to concentration camps was no longer presented to the divisional head in the detention department. It would therefore be completely conceivable that legation councillor von Thadden approached the SS Reichsführer through the Foreign Office and that the latter thereupon instructed the Chief of the Sipo and SD to release the Jews of Spanish citizenship from the concentration camps. If this was the case, the SS Reichsführer issued this instruction also to Pohl, and the Chief of the Sipo must have forwarded it through the official channels to the chief of Gestapo Office IV. Then the latter gave an instruction related to this to his detention divisional head which was also forwarded to the WVHA. It said that this specific category of Jewish inmates were to be handed over on a certain date to certain offices.

For a better understanding I must at this point elaborate further: A fundamental difference is to be made between the commitment to the concentration camps before the war, in the first years after, and the summary transfer to a concentration camp at a time when the war had reached its high point. If people – Jews and non-Jews – were sent to the concentration camp through the State Police office on the basis of an activity against existing laws or ordinances, it was decided at regular detention reviews if an individual person had to remain in the concentration camp, could be released, or be "re-educated" successfully or not.

Later, on the basis of an order of the SS Reichsführer, the Jews especially were sent automatically to the concentration camps and no filing cards compiled on the individuals; in line with this the date for detention review was discontinued. It was then left to the WVHA to decide if they were to be deployed in the aircraft works or the other industrial enterprises which had been affiliated, or not. That did not concern either the detention departmental heads or the other departmental heads in Gestapo Office IV.

Previously, that is, so long as the emigration was still permitted, I was actually in charge of such releases from the concentration camp, since the order of the SS Reichsführer to obtain emigration possibilities for the Jews extended also to Jews who were incarcerated in concentration camps. These cases, that is, the acquisition of emigration possibilities for Jews in the concentration camp, were so frequent that I created a special department for it in the "Central Office" in Vienna. When the SS Reichsführer later prohibited the emigration, I generally had nothing more to do with people who were in the concentration camp.

For this reason the matter of the Spanish Jews was a question which was to be clarified between the Foreign Office and the SS Reichsführer. For the implementation of the release measures naturally the WVHA and the RSHA were also brought in. It may be that the Spanish ambassador, after a reception or on some other suitable occasion, spoke to the SS Reichsführer on this matter. Then there came about a decision of Himmler's which overturned one of his own earlier orders.

On the entire matter I can only declare that, basically, no Jews with foreign citizenship were seized, because this contradicted the binding "guidelines". Even in France, to give an example, Jews of neutral or allied countries could in no way be evacuated *en bloc* in a summary process, if the responsible governments were not agreeable to it. It was, for example, impossible to transfer even a single Jew with English citizenship to Auschwitz or to another concentration camp; for this a special treatment[28] was provided.

Perhaps the Spanish Jews in question went to the concentration camp by mistake; for my department in any case the guidelines were binding and fully valid. But I am convinced that in the Generalgouvernement, where IV-B4, it must be repeated here, had no say, finally no difference was made any longer between stateless Jews and those of Polish or other citizenship; naturally, I do not know this exactly; but it could explain the presence of the Spanish Jews in a concentration camp.

If it is correct that these Jews were released from Bergen-Belsen in February 1944, it is also understandable that I knew nothing of it; for, from January to March 1944, I had to set up a small village in a wood some 100 km. from Berlin in which the offices of the bombed State Police were to be accommodated. When Gruppenführer Müller visited this barrack city which I had built up there, he informed me already of the order of the SS Reichsführer according to which I had to prepare with immediate effect a deployment in Hungary; an absolute oath of silence was placed on me so that I could not even put my regular deputy in the picture. So I can emphasise once again that I knew very little of the matter of the Spanish Jews; it was for us an incidental case, since department IV-B4, had nothing to do with

---

28   The term "special treatment" is indeed not to be understood here in the sense of liquidation.

it. Even if I had been in Berlin, my regular representative would have dealt with it, not I, since I had to deal only with cases which concerned my department directly and which were of fundamental importance.

Deportations from France

A number of Gauleiters in the south-west of the Reich had gone wild and had organised, independently, a deportation of Jews after the defeat of France. I dealt with it at great speed and remember that it was indeed a matter of five or six railway trains. Without a travel-plan conference I then had these directed through occupied France and conducted them personally from the last occupied station to the first unoccupied, and precisely this small stretch entailed the most work. I hear now for the first time that during these deportations a number of deaths had occurred.

My commission was only to obtain the necessary wagons from the Transport Ministry and to take the Jews to the unoccupied territory. It was difficult to conduct trains from the occupied to the unoccupied territory, especially because the Jews were not wanted there also. It may be that I took one of my officers as an escort; I do not remember any more. I remember well that I had to lead the French railway officials by the nose, declaring the trains to be "army transports", and in this regard the railway chairman from the unoccupied territory was helpful to me. I took care that the preparation took place quickly and, after the trains had left the occupied territory, the track was blocked by the French railway officials. My worry was that the Jews would be sent back; so even the transit offices were instructed not to allow any more Jews back into occupied France. I do not believe a word of the cited dead on these trains; for, when 6,000 men are loaded into six trains, nobody can say that they were "jammed" in. Besides, there would have been great complications if these trains of all things had been "corpse trains". I believe, on the contrary, that they were provided for in every respect, so that only small difficulties arose; for, in unoccupied France, we were to a certain extent in foreign, albeit controlled, territory. If I had been the "sadist" that I am given out to be, I would have been able to propose in this case that these six trains should be sent to a concentration camp; therewith I would have spared myself much work and annoyance.

If it is maintained now that it was Heydrich's intention to use unoccupied France as a reservoir for the unwanted Jews of Germany and that he thereby deviated from Hitler's line, that is in my view outright nonsense; for Heydrich always did exactly what Hitler demanded.[29]

It may be that the Foreign Office tried to set up a "Central Office" following the model of Prague and Vienna. This attempt will then have had the executive authority in the Foreign Office; for indeed in France I had, working with the commanding officer of the Sipo and SD, an "adviser for the Jewish question" who stood under the Jewish commissioner of the French government.

It is to be stated that hardly any country fought so much for the Jews of their citizenship as France did. Even the French officials who sought a solution of the Jewish question resisted handing over the Jews born in France or Jews with French citizenship to us. In itself it was bad that a "Jewish adviser" in France was subordinated to the commanding officer of the Sipo and SD. For that reason alone the "adviser" had to come immediately into conflict with all French officials, no matter how good colleagues they otherwise were: the French saw in him an adviser of the commanding officer of the Sipo and SD in "their" France. Everything that the "adviser" did or spoke was already from the start refused by these nationalistically disposed French, even though they did not perhaps originally like the Jews. In addition, the "adviser" Dannecker was perhaps not the right man; for he was as plain as he was clumsy; so he reached the rank only of Hauptsturmführer in the SD; a loyal, orderly file-worker. He had never learnt a real profession; from 1935 or 1936 he had dealt with the "assimilated Jews" sector. In that he became an expert, and because the large part of the Jews of France were assimilated, Dannecker was delegated to France as expert. For good reasons I agreed to it, because I myself had no better man available. Even a skilled person would, as an expert of the commanding officer of the Sipo and SD, have come to grief in Paris. We should have installed one man in the Vichy government or the Foreign Office. But that did not happen because we were instructed to accommodate even the Jewish adviser within the apparatus of the Sipo now set up in France. Therein lay the reason for the failure of the capture of the Jewish enemy in France.

The "Union générale israélite de France" occupied a middle position between our "Reich Association for Jews in Germany" and the

---

29   It is to be considered if these deportations to unoccupied France are not connected with the Madagascar plan.

"Israelite Religious Community" in Vienna or Prague. This was a contrast to the Jewish councils in the Polish districts. The Jews of the "Union générale" were not "yes-men", but were more like Dr. Eppstein from the Reich Association or a Dr. Löwenherz in Vienna; these people negotiated and were not recipients of my orders.

The Jewish problem in France was characterised by the fact that the French government fought doggedly for its Jews, Dannecker was weak, the commanding officer Knochen likewise and the senior SS and Police chief Oberg had a rather small assertive power. That is why I went to France three to five times in spite of my constant lack of time, in order to check things. But if one went there only seldom, one was besieged with every possible report and the difficulties were represented as extreme; so I finally had to be content if I accomplished anything at all.

At the beginning even the councillor and Sturmbannführer Lischka, my predecessor in the Gestapo Office as divisional head of IV-B4, was active in France on Jewish matters. Lischka suited Dannecker worthily. When he was still departmental head in Gestapo Office IV, he developed no initiative but did only that which the law obliged him to do. He did not even check if the law was implemented. Therein I was fundamentally different from my predecessor; for, to be sure, I did not do anything but apply the law, but I took more trouble to see that the wishes of the legislators were carried out. So I was for my colleagues not always a comfortable superior. With Lischka I often had professional tensions, when I was a divisional head in the Security Service Head Office without full powers, Lischka handled the same field as divisional head in the Gestapo Office, but with executive powers. Therefore it came to a never expressed but present aversion on both sides; for I felt that I was an idealist National Socialist; Lischka was only a salary earner. When I heard for the first time that Lischka was the representative of Hellmuth Knochen,[30] I was very surprised. Knochen came from the same division of the SD as I, only I dealt more or less with the press. Lischka was a weakling and complemented Dannecker.

France was for me a problem child; for the slow process of things in France was not hidden from my superiors. They heard long before me

---

30   Helmuth Knochen, SS Standartenführer, Commanding Officer of the Security Police in Paris, sentenced to death on 9 October 1944; pardoned by de Gaulle and released from jail.

from their political informers, through their correspondence with the public authorities of the party and in other ways of the situation on account of which I was often ordered to Paris. In general, I had to act forcefully in order to attain just a few successes in Paris. Dannecker loved the good life and later married the secretary of his office. As a result of that he was "tied" to Paris; I threatened him many times with immediate transfer back to Gestapo Office IV if he could not carry through certain matters. Only in this way were a few modest successes to be recorded. I say this because it is the truth, especially since I never concealed the muddled situation from Gruppenführer Müller.

In France I had to fight with a "super bureaucratic state", tackle and overcome a hundred obstacles of legal clauses and a hundred authorities in order to extract even a single transport. The German administrative apparatus was, as regards the Sipo, completely muddled in France.

I do not know that an SS Obersturmführer Sommer had made an attempt to blow up two Paris synagogues so that he caused difficulties between Field Marshal Keitel and Heydrich. I am unaware of this entire incident. Indeed, Sommer was Dannecker's representative, to which post he had been appointed by Knochen, but there is a remarkable coincidence of circumstances in this connection. Around that time I was summoned by Heydrich to a lunch at the Prague Castle, at which only Heydrich, the senior SS and Police chiefs in France, Thomas,[31] Heydrich's adjutant and I myself were present. I cannot understand what reason Heydrich had in inviting me to a lunch with Thomas. No word was spoken about France. Did Heydrich wish to demonstrate to Thomas that his colleagues must unconditionally carry out orders received? Only in this way would this coincidence have had a meaning. Around that time, power struggles may have taken place in France and shortly thereafter Oberg was placed in Thomas' place. *In October 1941 the Chief of the Sipo and SD was commissioned by Göring with the final solution of the European Jewish question.*

In regards to the French I have no documents from Secretary of State Weizsäcker at hand, but I do know that Gruppenführer Müller had a good relationship with the secretary of state; I myself drafted a dozen letters which dealt with cardinal problems and were sent by Gruppenführer Müller to Weizsäcker. Even if it can no longer be stated

---

31   Dr. Max Thomas, SS Gruppenführer, from July 1940 to September 1941
      Senior SS and Police chief in Paris, then transferred as Senior SS and Police
      Chief to Kiev, Ukraine.

Jews in Paris are forced to register with the French police.

what their contents were, I do know however that I had to exert the greatest precision and professionalism in composing these letters in an unobjectionable manner. That was the opposite of the letters which went to Luther and were often dictated quickly. In the correspondence between Gruppenführer Müller and Weizsäcker it was a matter of basic things; Gruppenführer Müller apparently had a great influence on Weizsäcker which must have worked to Müller's satisfaction; if it were the contrary I would have noticed it.

I remember very well that one day it was debated whether to extend the requirement for French Jews to wear the Jewish star. Who issued this instruction to me I do not remember any more - I do not deny it, but I'm unable to give the exact date. Thereafter the Jews in the occupied part of France were required to wear the Jewish star. That the French Jewish commissioner of the Vichy government resigned on the basis of the introduction of this regulation is possible, just as also that I perhaps "enforced" it successfully for a long time through Dannecker and Knochen.

When we arrived in France, our lack of good intelligence on French Jewry became apparent very quickly; therein lies another reason for the failure of our operation. On our arrival almost nothing was done regarding the Freemasons; for they had become uninteresting to us, even in the Reich. The necessary Jewish archive material had in any case to be secured. I remember that the "Alliance israélite universelle" had published a newspaper which found a considerable readership in Germany. We therefore believed that the "Alliance" represented a significant group. When now the men of the commanding officer of the Sipo and SD arrived in France, the offices of the "Alliance" were also searched; I remember how Dannecker related to me that our people had been surprised at the small, unimpressive apparatus of this organisation. It seemed to be a corner business of the first rank where nothing at all was discovered. If I say "nothing at all" I mean that from the viewpoint of the executive agency, not from a member of Office VII who was interested in the library of this organisation. The Gestapo proclaimed the confiscation of such libraries and archives; Office VII secured it. So the "Alliance" held no interest for me, but that does not mean that this group was insignificant in an ideological sense – and that alone interested Office VII.

Near Fehrbelliner Platz in Berlin was the large archive of Office VII; in the basement lay hundreds of thousands of books and volumes which were categorised by a librarian. This work however he could not complete; when the war came, the importance of Office VII was strongly reduced, especially in terms of personnel. Such a confiscation in France naturally took place with the agreement of the French police. While in France we needed the agreement of the French authorities, I think that this was not necessary in Holland.

The material found by us in France on our invasion was paltry; even our information service and our representatives had little in their hands, for we understood the "Alliance" to be something quite different, perhaps because this organisation had been made into an especially big issue by certain quarters. If we had set out on our task with only our documents in France, without the preparation for the registration and capture of Jewish persons performed by the French police already before the invasion, we would not have accomplished anything at all. Near Paris there was a large detention camp where the French police sent the Jews; from there they were evacuated. For that a French commissioner, whom I was introduced to, was responsible.

The French police needed no instructions; they had refused these, for they were much more anxious about their sovereignty than, for example, the Hungarian gendarmerie. In France, the government supervised everything more strictly. The Drancy detention camp was made available to us completely and filled without big negotiations with

Jewish youths in the Drancy concentration camp, 3rd Dec 1942

the commissioner. For the rest it was clear that the "deuxième bureau" cooperated with the corresponding army offices, and the "securité" with the Security Police. I cannot give exact descriptions but I know that Dannecker entered into a "large bureaucratic institution" and I did not need to offer any advice to the man. The Dutch police rather properly watched over the Jewish emigrants before our invasion, similar indications are lacking to me for France.

I remember how great the difficulties in France were for I was sent to Vichy. There the RSHA or the SS Reichsführer, perhaps also the Foreign Office, had some man whom I had to visit in order to support him. Vichy created more and more difficulties. Even the role of Laval became steadily more opaque. Knochen said to me that Laval wished to examine the naturalisation of the Jews, but it never led to practical results.

The post-war literature mentions that I had insisted that the possible legal basis should be created which would make it possible to consider the Jews transferred to the destination stations as stateless on entry into the Reich territory, and if one did not take steps in this field great difficulties would have to be expected in national political terms which must in any case be avoided in the implementation of the SS Reichsführer's order. I remember how we once had great difficulties with Jews of French citizenship.

During my Paris visit no individual subjects were discussed; for that the regional offices of the Sipo were responsible. In Paris I did not have to deal with rounding up the Jews or with other details; only the fundamental things interested me: that France offer the Jews to us. I travelled there in order to achieve this legal regulation. In case of emergency a senior SS and Police chief could have carried this out even though this was not his duty; for even he had to worry about fundamental things and indeed to be able to assert himself, along with the German ambassador, before Laval.

After Dannecker had shown practically no successes, I deployed Röthke to Paris with the aim of gradually replacing Dannecker. Dannecker was a thick-skull, and somewhat clumsy. In France we needed a more nimble man who "left the mallet at home". In no way is it right that Dannecker ran nightclubs or similar things. But he was rather listless and not equal to the difficulties in France, especially since he possessed not the least legal training.

The story now made known to me of 4,000 French children who had supposedly been driven together without appropriate supplies into a Paris sports stadium I did not hear of at the time. Their capture was a matter for the French police, and I cannot take any responsibility in this, and according to the reports, it is a very sad case. In addition, it is to be mentioned that in these reports it is maintained that I gave instructions from Berlin by telephone for these children. That I never did; we did not at all work through telephone calls. The saying that "the enemy is eavesdropping" was observed. Such matters certainly came under "secret information of the Reich" and I would never have arranged anything by telephone. If at all, through telegrams. Apart from that, I would be able to remember such a incident of 4,000 children. Such an accommodation and transport as is described in these reports contradicts the "guidelines" in every point. If the offices in France charged with that did not adhere to the "guidelines", then I must say that a service supervisory authority cannot do any more than issue "guidelines"; every member of the Sipo and SD stood under an oath of service and had therefore to follow their instructions, ordinances and guidelines. As the departmental head of the central office it could not be my duty to visit every individual transport train personally.

In Germany, I was present at embarkations only once, but abroad never. It is obviously the task of the subordinate office which has to adhere to the instructions of the superior. From Gestapo Office IV everything proceeded in a purely bureaucratic manner and according to the present ordinances. Based on my knowledge, reports on high casualties in the deportation trains before their arrival at the destination stations should be relegated to the realm of atrocity stories.

Let it be repeated: I cannot remember a transport of 4,000 children; and the described terror in this sports stadium and collection camp must be exaggerated. Whatever the case may have been, IV-B4 was not responsible for local deficiencies. If things were not conducted according to the guidelines, that was the fault of the local offices or the agencies that carried out the rounding up. If I say that I cannot remember the children's transport, one should believe me: I have not been reticent about anything and I state what I know. I would confess everything even in this case without faltering if I could remember it. It is only certain that I had Dannecker removed because we were not satisfied with his work. The claim that I strove to obtain Jews from North Africa is absolutely ridiculous! Our entire effort was to remove the Jews from Europe – how then should I have taken over Jews from outside Europe!

Deportations from Hungary

At the end of 1943, the Allies massed their bomb attacks on Berlin. Under these rather heavy bombardments even the office of the Gestapo suffered very much. Only the greatest damages could be remedied so that the office work could continue, but after every heavy bombing it was put out, even if only for some hours. So my chief Gruppenführer Müller gave me either in the last days of December 1943 or in the very first days of January 1944 the order to set up a second office of Gestapo Office IV, thus of the Gestapo, some 80-100 km from Berlin. I was the only one amongst his 30 or so departmental heads who had some technical experience; thus I received this order. I looked over the area and then drafted a letter to the commanding officer of the Sipo and SD in the Protectorate of Bohemia and Moravia, Dr. Weinmann; therein I requested around a dozen and a half barracks which were redundant in Theresienstadt to be given over to Gestapo Office IV on loan and to have them ready along with a group of Jewish manual labourers and Jewish builders. Gruppenführer Müller signed this letter. Some time later I travelled to Theresienstadt. I organised the classification and loading of the material into two cargo trains in such a way that the pieces that I needed first would be unloaded first so that the small railway station would not be blocked for too long.

The Jewish commando from Theresienstadt worked very well, and some weeks later the barracks were set up. One day, it must have been at the beginning of March 1944, Gruppenführer Müller inspected my work. On this occasion he explained to me that, on the SS Reichsführer's orders, I had to prepare for deployment to Hungary. Müller wished me good luck on it. I had to maintain silence with regard to everybody, even my regular deputy. Some time remained for me to hand over the work on the new village that I was building for the Gestapo and put my professional matters in Berlin in order.

Around a week before 19 March 1944 I was sent to the Mauthausen concentration camp. I had a free hand in the choice of the persons under my command and I took the most capable persons of my department with me. In Mauthausen, we were to a certain extent isolated in an outer block from the outside world and we could not leave the camp. There numerous vehicles arrived, knapsacks, combat packs and many other materials. As a precaution the higher leadership had reckoned with the possibility of a certain resistance on the part of the Magyars. We spent the free time as well as we could, with chess or card-games. I often visited a Hauptsturmführer of the Mauthausen camp administration whom I had befriended there. He was a passionate hunter, and I gladly conversed with him in his hunting room. He had, for eleven years, the same orderly, a German Communist called Otto, who had been interned in various concentration camps. Otto offered in a friendly way to pack my knapsack in a way that I myself could certainly not do, for he had been a junior officer in the first World War. When I asked him how he could cope with the fact that he had been robbed of so many years of his freedom, he replied to me, to my great astonishment: "Well, Obersturmbannführer, I cannot really complain ... you see, I wear the blue arm-band, I work till six with the Hauptsturmführer, enjoy his trust and work for nobody else in the camp. At exactly six o'clock I scoot, go to Mauthausen, sit in the pub, drink my beer and go back to the camp at ten o'clock. I don't escape, for they will get me back anyway".

We saw next to nothing of Mauthausen, for there was a sort of enmity between the camp personnel of the concentration camp and the Sipo in this week of our forced life together in Mauthausen. Even the personnel of the concentration camp had in the meanwhile become "parlour officers" who competed in their mess with the affectations of Prussian Guards officers. Between these officers and us national officers of the Sipo there was a gap; apart from the SD people, there were with us also criminal secretaries, criminal councillors, police inspectors, senior police inspectors, all of a rank above Untersturmführer, who looked down on those "parlour officers" of the concentration camp exactly as the latter looked down on us. I got on more or less well with the aforementioned Hauptsturmführer in Mauthausen only, otherwise we were avoided like the plague. Moreover I did not have the highest rank. In Mauthausen I had other things to do than go over the concentration camp area; in addition, I was glad to finish my work of organisational preparation, so there remained to me no opportunity at all to occupy myself more closely with the Mauthausen concentration camp.

The day of departure to Hungary was nearing. As the most senior officer of the commando, the entire marching block of the Sipo and the regular police was placed under me. There were around 150 or 180 lorries and two tank wagons. From this vehicle park I took out 40 fast cars and placed them under the order of Sturmbannführer Krumey.[32] Even Sturmbannführer Wisliceny was in this group; he was not chosen for Hungary himself, but requested me to take him with me, for he was especially interested in this work. The group of 40 vehicles departed 24 hours earlier from the camp area to Hungary; I followed with the bulk. In the night of 18 to 19 March my motorcycle infantrymen stopped, doubtless on the instruction of some of my captains, and the column stood at a standstill. The chiefs under me came to my vehicle and flooded me with a flask of Austrian rum, for it was actually my birthday, which is the reason I can remember this date very vividly. We journeyed further; the regular police formed the rear of this vehicular column. On the way we had air-raid alarms some times and refuelled twice. On the Sunday after, we crossed the Hungarian border in the afternoon in radiantly beautiful weather. We were treated with wine, white bread, meat and cigarettes by the jubilant Hungarian village population. Afterwards we tended to our hand guns and oiled them again; for there was hardly any thought of resistance. The army representative anounced the marching order; I travelled with my group attached to the 1st Panzer Lehr Division.[33]

---

32   Hermann Krumey, SS Sturmbannführer in the RSHA, Eichmann's deputy in Hungary.

33   The Panzer Lehr Division (tank training division) was an elite armoured division of the German army formed in 1943 and composed of elite training

Already in Mauthausen I had given Krumey the first orders for action in Hungary. So he had to immediately collect the Jewish political functionaries around him and moreover take care that they did not come to harm in the enthusiastic commotion of a possible popular uprising of right-wing elements. Due to past experience I intended working together with these people.

In the afternoon of this Sunday I arrived in Budapest. Some rooms in one of the big hotels were provided as quarters for me, where I worked almost the whole night and set up something like a small office. I issued the first ordinances with the aim of holding the next day the first conferences with the Jewish political functionaries. I lived in this hotel for some days, then through the senior SS and Police chief I obtained a villa as private accommodation and, as an official, the Majestic Hotel on the Schwabenberg. There were many hotels there, in one the commanding officer of the Sipo and SD worked, in the next hotel was his Secret State Police and in another hotel the Hungarian Secret State Police. So the Schwabenberg was both from the German and also from the Hungarian side, the centre of the police offices and the political police. I commissioned Hauptsturmführer Wisliceny, my most skilled and talented colleague, to make contact with the Hungarian offices, and indeed through the Hungarian experts of the Gestapo. These Hungarians were under the Chief of the Gestapo office of Budapest, Dr. Geschke.[34] After some time Wisliceny reported to me that he had succeeded in making contact with the Deputy Prefect of the county of Budapest province, a certain Dr. László Endre.

This Dr. Endre had begun his career as a magistrate and finally became the deputy chief of the county of Budapest province. Many years ago he had published a book which dealt with the solution of the Jewish question. He was deeply imbued with the idea of making Hungary free of – as he said "the Jewish plague". Wisliceny informed me that Dr. Endre was eager to make contact with me; I therefore had my visit to him announced; and lacking time we agreed on a meeting on one of the next days in the county hall of a Budapest province.

---

troops.

34   Dr. Hans Geschke, Commanding Officer of the Security Police in Budapest.

Dr. Endre gave a small dinner; a uniformed orderly stood always at his side. Apart from the host two or three administrative officials took part as well as my Hauptsturmführer Wisliceny and perhaps also Krumey. On this first evening I explained to Endre my programme and I saw that he was enthusiastic, at which I was very surprised since I had braced myself for battles and difficulties. I did not need to speak any more, but could devote the rest of the evening to the testing of different Tokay wines.

This evening determined the fate of the Jews in Hungary. When I got to know Dr. Endre and observed his energy, I felt immediately his fervent desire to serve his Hungarian fatherland. I discussed these difficulties immediately with the senior SS and police chief in Hungary, General Winkelmann,[35] to initiate an attempt with the Hungarian government to incorporate Dr. Endre directly into the Hungarian Ministry of the Interior. Naturally, such a transfer is not implementable overnight in the state sector of any country, so it took some weeks in this case. I got acquainted with the Jewish life in Hungary and had enough to do listening to all the possible ideas of the Jewish functionaries, because rash measures had been taken on the Hungarian side and the Jews now came to a certain extent for help to the German authorities.

In the mean time I directed my office. One of the first police officials whom Gruppenführer Müller gave over to me from some other department that also dealt with the Jewish question was police inspector Mös. He worked very conscientiously; I soon effected his promotion to senior police inspector, and he became "associate Hauptsturmführer". He distinguished himself also by the fact that I never knew if he was looking at me or at the corner for he squinted terribly. I had Mös come to Hungary because he gave me the guarantee of an exact bureaucratic course of things. Actually it had been my mistake to appoint Krumey as deputy; for he had until March 1944 been used to directing offices himself in the SS Race and Settlement Head Office. So he was too independent for state police activities; for, in the state police, things cannot be ordered or instructed in a rough way. In order to set up a bureaucratic brake here I had old Mös come, whom I had had with me since 1940 as a "living rule-book". Where Mös sat nothing was arranged in a free manner any more but executed in a bureaucratically precise manner. In such matters I trusted neither Wisliceny nor Brunner nor Burger. I could not have

---

35   Otto Winkelmann, SS Obergruppenführer, Senior SS and Police Chief in Budapest.

them constantly under my eyes just to see that things were effected; they often did stupid things and referred to instructions which had not at all been issued. So my bureaucratic matters were conducted in my office only by my officials, on whom I could fully rely. Mös was such a good old official, who had fulfilled this function already in the Weimar Republic. After his arrival in Budapest the usual bureaucratic order prevailed in my office.

Baky[36] became the First Secretary of State and my new friend Dr. Endre Second Secretary of State in the Hungarian Ministry of the Interior. The executive, thus the police and the special Hungarian gendarmerie, stood under Baky. The legislative part was placed under Endre. Herewith the preconditions for the command that I had received for Hungary were formed, namely, to remove the Jews from Hungary at lightning speed. Indeed my Hungarian task was motivated by the anxiety of higher offices that the Jew in Hungary might enter the developing resistance movements, strengthen them or could organise quite new ones. The Red Army were at our heels and so I received the instruction to scour Hungary from east to west. The frightful occurrence in the Warsaw ghetto obsessed our highest leadership and also us; its repetition on Hungarian soil had to be avoided at any cost.

It is possible that Kaltenbrunner was in Budapest on 22 March 1944; but I neither saw him nor spoke to him there. In any case I think it is quite exaggerated to suggest that we had manoeuvred Baky and Endre into a "Hungarian Jewish commissariat". That was not at all necessary from the German side and, if so, it was not the duty of the Chief of the Sipo and SD to create such a thing in Hungary but the task of General Winkelmann. Thus I still remember very precisely having once participated in a discussion with Winkelmann when somehow the wish for a change in the list of ministers was expressed. At that I said to myself: Look, Winkelmann rules here like the late Metternich, naturally on a smaller scale. The moving of the figures on the "chessboard" here and there were taken care of by Winkelmann insofar as he could indeed do it, not Veesenmayer. The latter naturally acted in a more solid manner but Winkelmann sought to push in this chess game those figures in whom the SS Reichsführer and the Chief of the Sipo could have an interest, and in this way Baky and Endre

---

36   Lászlo Baky, First State Secretary in the Hungarian Ministry of the Interior; after the collapse of the Arrow Cross regime in Budapest sentenced to death and executed.

were able to enter into the game. But the initiator and the decisive organiser was quite definitely not to be found on the German side.

It was clear to me that I, as a German, could demand no Jews from the Hungarians for deportation. Other offices operated something similar once in Copenhagen with all the success of a great fiasco. I left that to the Hungarian authorities themselves. Dr. Endre was a capable man. It can be credited to Endre and Baky that Hungary was almost the only country where we generally experienced no difficulties of an administrative or any other sort in the solution of the Jewish question. These two secretaries of state simply ruled or ordered, and the Hungarian Minister of the Interior signed because he had to sign. Endre issued the appropriate laws and ordinances, and Baky made the Hungarian gendarmerie available. In Hungary I had only to take care to obtain the necessary trains from the Reich Transport Ministry and to find out the destination stations for the transports from my superiors in Berlin. Berlin instructed me to direct all the transports to the Auschwitz railway station. Hauptsturmführer Novak had an order from me to have the necessary transport trains made available by the Reich Transport Ministry and to hold travel-plan meetings which were practically carried out in the Transport Ministry by office chief Stange.

Even in this case I conveyed to the two secretaries of state the orders for the rounding up and the loading which we were accustomed to use. As elsewhere I requested that, as in the case of the German police, there would appear the remark that *"all avoidable hardships are to be avoided"* in the orders of the Hungarian executive.

In the beginning I heard no complaints on the part of my Jewish functionaries that the Hungarian gendarmerie were marked by rather brutal acts. Even the Hungarian gendarmerie worked together with the Jewish functionaries extensively in the counties. It is a riddle to me even today how political functionaries could allow themselves to be collaborators, to work together with their enemies and in this way make their work easier for them. Every county stood under the supervision of the Hungarian lieutenant-colonel Ferenczy and the rounding up and loading operation took place under his immediate direction, I sometimes placed one of my colleagues at his disposal as an adviser. In Hungary I had nothing to do with either the police rounding up or with the loading. The transports rolled smoothly.

The Eichmann Tapes

The post-war literature maintains that on 31 March 1944, the Jewish council of Budapest had a discussion with me in which I said "Do you not know who I am? I am a bloodhound!" Perhaps I actually said that, but only through a mixture of humour and sarcasm. Just as I said a couple of times to Jewish functionaries: "Well, you know where you are? You are with the "Tsar of the Jews", have you not read the *Pariser Tageblatt*?" With such expressions I wished to indicate that the concerned Jewish chiefs did not in general need to have any doubts, worries or anxiety in talking to me, for they could themselves ascertain that I was not at all "the bloodhound" even though I was described and decried as.

In the course of time the representatives of the different Jewish organisations reported to me; as did, one day, Dr. Rudolf Kastner. Dr. Kastner was a fanatical Zionist; he often appeared in the company of his wife, who joined in the negotiations. From that I inferred that she was widely familiar with the Jewish work. Dr. Kastner's efforts in fact had only one goal - to get valuable sections of the Jewish people in Hungary freed and to make emigration to Palestine possible for them. In the meantime the Arrow Cross (the Hungarian National Socialist Movement) had become increasingly stronger and had their representatives sit in the individual counties as administrative officials or inspectors who often had extensive influence on all the proceedings and also on the work of the Hungarian gendarmerie. They were bigoted and knew no exceptions, no consideration. This explains the fact that the Jewish functionaries preferred to present their wishes in relation to individual cases, or their complaints, to the German authorities. They recognised that they had to deal with people who were informed about Jewish matters in great detail through years of activity. The large majority of the Hungarian functionaries had indeed dealt with the Jewish question only for a few weeks. They became impatient too quickly because they thought they glimpsed Jewish excuses or lies everywhere. They could not get an overview of the matter since they had not been absorbed in it.

Dr. Kastner assured me at the outset that he would cause me no difficulties in the rounding up operations; he said to me frankly that he had *no interest at all in assimilated Jewry*; he discussed repeatedly the biological aspect of the problem and demanded from me that I give him biologically valuable, thus productive, human material, likewise only Jews fit for work. He explained to me plainly that *he had very little interest in old people*; he wanted only young Jews. Because Kastner promised me his cooperation for my task, I for my part *explained that*

The Deportations From Abroad

I was ready to close both eyes and allow some thousand young Jews and Jewesses to emigrate to Palestine illegally. Such an emigration had to be concealed from the Hungarian authorities as far as possible just as the illegal emigration of the Jews to Palestine from the English Mandate authorities. From the beginning there arose a regular relationship of trust between me and Dr. Kastner. The meetings piled up and his demands became constantly heavier, but it still remained at some hundred or thousand Jews. So that these Jews would not be bothered by Hungarian authorities they were concentrated and "supervised" by soldiers of the Waffen SS. In this way they held themselves ready for Dr. Kastner's call to emigration through Romania to Palestine.

Today one will believe these discussions with Dr. Kastner after I learnt from newspaper reviews that Joel Brand[37] published a book and has referred to these connections. Previously one would certainly never have believed me. The effort of the German Reich government to get the Jews outside the German Reich, outside the German sphere of power runs like a red thread through the history of my activity; for the German government wanted a solution – and the entire world knew that it had also established this intention legislatively. But nobody, no office in the entire world wanted to accept these Jews! *Even international Jewry with the Jewish World Congress at its head gave only paltry help.* Witnesses to these immense difficulties are not only Dr. Richard Löwenherz and Dr. Rothenberg from Vienna, whom I allowed to emigrate to Palestine, but also numerous Jewish political functionaries who worked with me and were my partners in many hundreds of conferences and meetings. They all gave up, they all clearly had expected a generous support and help from international Jewry. *The last witness was Dr. Kastner, but doubtless Kastner had to die, exactly like the Swedish Bernadotte; for both clearly knew too much about the useless efforts of the Jewish political functionaries to send the Jews in significant numbers somewhere in the world with the help of international Jewry or the supposedly pro-Jewish governments.* They all knew too much of the negative result of our efforts and had therefore apparently become too uncomfortable to the Jewish power-holders of the time or to those interested in Jewish political events. *The Jew Joel Brand travelled over half the world to find accommodation for a million Jews, that is all Hungarian Jews and the rest from Germany, Austria and other countries,* wherever their own Jewish organisations wanted

---

37   Joel Brand, who left for Syria during the Eichmann-Kastner negotiations, was to return in 14 days, which did not happen. Joel Brand may have gone to Syria by land.

them to be taken. To find these million Jews had indeed been the task of the Jewish functionaries; they would have been able to find young Jews fit for work without any difficulty. Joel Brand describes in his book what resistance he encountered in his efforts. *We had demanded in exchange for these million Jews nothing but 10,000 winterised cargo lorries with trailers*; without doubt I could honestly ensure, on the basis of the instruction of the SS Reichsführer, that these cargo lorries would be deployed without exception on the eastern front.

I have not read Joel Brand's book, since it was not easily available, as it was published a few months ago. But through a series of discussions in different newspapers the events of that time have become vivid again in my memory. I shall come back to them later. Dr. Kastner spoke the same language as I, as did Dr. Löwenherz too, with whom I extensively discussed the aims of the Zionists, their plans in Palestine, their inward connection to this country and their ideas of life in Palestine. I spoke also with Dr. Rothenberg on this, even if less often. Now I encountered in Dr. Kastner a certain intellectual bond; for, even within the SS, we indeed strove for attachment to the soil, loyalty to the blood. The Zionists did not wish anything else, they planned nothing else in Palestine, which they wished to make "their country" once again after two thousand years, and the Jewish construction fund, the Jewish national fund, did not wish anything else. They bought land in Palestine which was in no way resalable. In all the countries of the world they collected money in the construction funds in order to obtain Jewish national land and to exploit it appropriately. The Jewish pioneers of the Chaluzim were inspired by that, exactly as we by the idea of "blood and soil". The peasants behind the plough with the weapons on their shoulders, the tractor drivers who had their weapons standing next to the steering wheel of their tractors, ready to fire. These are the peasant population of both sexes who are rooted in hard work and ensure that it bears fruit year after year and nourishes the people.

For the Zionist Jews there was the same ideal feeling as for us in the Schutz-Staffel[38] when we heard of the work ethic, at first among the young people of the HJ, then among the Reich compulsory labour service, or when we heard about the farmhouse legislation, the support and help which our National Socialist German Reich government granted to every farmer, for he was indeed the favourite son of our people because he ploughed and worked the German soil. On account

---

38 SS

of these parallels I said to Dr. Löwenherz and repeated it also to Kastner that, if I had not been a German and a National Socialist but a Jew, I would certainly have been the most ardent Zionist.

It was clear to me from the beginning that the idealistic Zionist leaders like Kastner stood at that time in the final battle for the end of the war exactly as we did; for even we knew that their matter, their dream would be decided after the end of the war. They worked towards that, as the post-war events have proven, already during the war.

Everywhere I had the good fortune to be able to work with people of real quality among the Jewish functionaries who served my task, but at the same time also their own plans, that is, to collapse the Mandate government of Palestine through infiltration. Naturally there were also among them different characters; Dr. Löwenherz, for example, conducted himself in the first years, with extraordinary servility with regard to me, which I would never have done with regard to my enemies. Dr. Kastner, on the other hand, never conducted himself in a servile way with regard to me, he was energetic, flexible, in full possession of his physical powers, a relatively young man, rather of my age, whereas Dr. Löwenherz was an old gentleman who was appointed by me as office director of the Israelite Religious Community in Vienna. He had only one modest wish - he had relatives in London, I think even married children and, when the matter was settled, could I make an emigration to London possible for him. If I would promise him that, he would be fully pacified; for he believed my word, I had always kept it. Thereupon I assured him: "Mr. Löwenherz, you can depend on it that I will have you brought to London elegantly". Dr. Kastner aimed still higher with his requests, but the price of 15,000-20,000 young Jews for illegal emigration to Palestine did not seem too high to me; for that was to a certain degree the payment for his guaranteeing peace and order within the Jewish camps. Kastner was for me a Jewish "privy councillor for peace"; he took care that I, along with my German agencies, did not need to intervene but could allow the Hungarian authorities to operate.

The transports rolled – Kastner was the key to the secret of quick, even lightning-like evacuation of a relatively high number of Jews in a relatively short time. Thereby it should not be forgotten that precisely at that time the fulfilment of the technical preconditions for it became increasingly more difficult: railway stations such as, for example, Györ, and many others on the way to the west were struck by Allied aircraft. If nevertheless in such a short time actual successes could be pointed to, I owe this, on the one hand, to the good cooperation between the two often mentioned Hungarian secretaries of state and, on the other hand, to the peace and order in the Jewish camps which Dr. Kastner guaranteed to me.

All border crossings were instructed by me to let Dr. Kastner pass at any time; thus he could travel when and how he wished, to Slovakia, to Romania or Poland; only for travel to Austria or into neutral foreign countries did he have to check with me. Kastner did all the work: Kastner handed over the Hungarian Jews to me without a single shot being fired, without the least demonstration, without having to deploy even a single man apart from my Jewish advisers. If such a man made my work easier and spared me much care, it would have been ingratitude to restrict his freedom of movement even in the least. Dr. Kastner brought Pohl to outbursts of rage and caused Höss to travel repeatedly to Hungary and to expressly demand fewer transports and better supplies. Thereby there remained for me relatively easy writing-desk work in the office in the Schwanenberg; thus nobody need wonder that such a Jewish confidant could also claim gratitude, which I could grant only to personal generosity.

If I am asked if Kastner ever appeared anxious – not to mention cowardly with regard to me or as an arrogant intellectual without inner connection to the simple man, I must answer "no". Kastner was not cowardly, only extremely cautious; he would have been a good official of Gestapo Office IV, the Gestapo Office. He was ice-cold, sober, a logically thinking mind, almost predestined to be a future envoy or ambassador of the state of Israel. He was not an arrogant intellectual, but stood in the service of the Jewish blood-and-soil ideas. So he explained to me that old and assimilated Jews did not interest him; for they were not usable for the new state; he said to me frankly and repeatedly, for which reason I also repeat it, that *he must have young people, productive Jews.* He was a hard negotiation partner, not a groveller; he possessed much personal ambition. He could be characterised as a callous intellectual only insofar as he would thoughtlessly sacrifice thousands or hundreds of thousands of his blood in order to achieve his political goal, and his political goal was EREZ ISRAEL! For that he needed valuable human material, and for that he bargained hard with me. They were to a certain degree Jewish SA or SS men for Israel who moved into Palestine illegally, thus against the will of the High Commissioner, through Romania, and developed the resistance organisation of the Haganah and other associations that finally contributed their part to creating Israel.

If I try today once again to penetrate into the Kastner matter, if I think through Kastner's attitude without considering it so positively from the National Socialist and especially from the "blood and soil" idea, I must say that I can somehow understand how there were a group of men in EREZ ISRAEL who were ready to shoot Dr. Rudi Kastner – as an extremist in Palestine I would perhaps have done it too. Kastner's standpoint was: Everything that benefits EREZ ISRAEL will be undertaken; old Jews and those in favour of assimilation do not benefit EREZ ISRAEL or not much, we therefore do not need them. Jews in Palestine of the category of the "champions of Zion" and religious fanatics see Kastner's attitude from another perspective; for them another standard is indeed necessary. The SS Reichsführer and his people had another view of the means and ways to the creation and strengthening of the German Reich than Niemöller.[39]

Dr. Kastner cooperated with me; the Israeli lawyer said in the course of the trial, which Kastner with iron logic had requested against himself, that not the fact of having worked with me, but of having allowed himself to get too deeply involved with me was punishable. Kastner was an ice-cold lawyer, a politician, a man of the Mapai.[40] The present-day Israel is led by the Leftist party,[41] whether it is now the Foreign Minister Golda Meir or Ben Gurion, they all come from the Mapai, from the same group as Kastner. Theoretically considered, Kastner naturally "betrayed" Jewish blood, for he supported our special command in Hungary in its task of scouring the country from east to west – practically without its own manpower – in order to prevent similar uprisings as in Warsaw. The Hungarian executive helped thereby not only according to the standard of a provincial government, but handed over to the German Reich half a million Jews *en bloc* and legally corroborated. I had to take them over and to grapple with the problem of being able to generally obtain the necessary transport material from the Reich Transport Ministry. Now Kastner acted there as Dr. Löwenherz in Vienna, for example, never did. Löwenherz was a Zionist, but above all a man who would have helped,

---

39   Friedrich Martin Niemöller (1892-1984) was a Lutheran pastor who opposed the National Socialists' control of the churches and was imprisoned in concentration camps from 1937 to 1945.

40   Mapai, acronym for Mifleget Poalai Erez Israel, that is, Workers' Party of Palestine, or Israel, essentially social-democratic; before the foundation of Israel, it directed the Jewish Agency. Ben Gurion and Golda Meir belonged to it.

41   Eichmann writes this in the 1950's.

and did help, every Jew, no matter of what political complexion. Dr. Kastner, on the other hand, was hundred and fifty percent committed to his own goal, finally to have land under one's feet, finally to be a free Jew, no matter what it cost. A goal, thus, that sanctified every means. So Kastner is, on the one hand, a betrayer of his own blood; for he said to me – let it be repeated here once again: "Old Jews and those in favour of assimilation do not interest me; their fate I find regretful – but one cannot do anything about it." On the other hand, as a warrior he was again right in the establishment of EREZ ISRAEL, for only the establishment of the state of Israel could indeed guarantee a real protection of their blood, a real defence against periodically erupting, provoked or unprovoked, anti-Jewish actions throughout the world. This goal demanded sacrifice like any great aim that was to guarantee security throughout the future.

The complicated nature of the Kastner case comes from the fact that, on the one hand, a Jewish organisation sent their people to kill this man but a few hours later the Israeli government, the Mapai and thousands of members of other Israeli organisations gave the murdered man a cortège of honour to his last resting place. In truth he was thus somehow recognised, only the hardness of his battle was not understood. It is possible that Kastner is, with the exception of the older leaders, rejected in present-day Israel and will be understood only in a hundred or more years.

Just so are idealistic National Socialists judged even today, ten, twelve years after the end of the war. Certainly, in a hundred or more years, laurels will be handed even to National Socialism. If today it is maintained that I am a sort of Caligula, that sprang from the perverse brain of some man to whom nature accidentally lent a pointed pen but who never in the least penetrated the actions and intentions of the National Socialist Reich government, such a man has clearly not taken the trouble which I have taken here, that is, to penetrate into the mind of the enemy. I hardly think that any other man can better understand Kastner's psyche than I. The new Israeli state has forced itself through violence and robbery into possession of the country, but I must acknowledge that the Israeli government clearly knows what an invaluable mind they had in Kastner; I allow myself to exercise a criticism of that group which calls itself the "champions of Zion" and is clearly constituted of half or fully crazed orthodox elements who demanded the life of Kastner as a price for the appeasement of their orthodox religious conscience.

If I said previously that I too could perhaps have ventured for Kastner's murder, I meant thereby that I, as a small "Israeli Untersturmführer", would have been ready for it because then I would have failed to recognise that Kastner had "betrayed" Jewish blood in order to reach a higher goal that I did not know of then.

Dr. Rudolf Kastner has a claim to my seeking to characterise him more closely. Of course, it seems that he has only maligned me. Unfortunately or, rather, also thankfully – for in principle it is the same to me – I am not in the position to malign him, because I see in him an idealist, a fanatic, such as I have always been. For the creation of his state and therewith, in the final analysis, for the final security of his people he did not shy away from being a "betrayer" of his own blood. The battle for freedom, for one's own state always costs blood. The average person may not recognise what a great mind foresees – just as little as a junior officer may recognise the measures of his general and even criticises them even though the general wishes only the best with his decisions; perhaps not the best for his junior officer himself, but for his family, for posterity. With this example of the "junior officer and the general" I would like to explain the situation between the critics and Dr. Kastner.

Already at that time in Budapest Kastner occasionally had difficulties with different Jewish offices. But he proceeded very cautiously for he knew that I would immediately remove difficulties from the Jewish side in order to help him, my most important colleague in the Hungarian territory. Kastner and I together mastered the situation in the Hungarian territory in a sovereign way – one may forgive me this hated term in explanation. Perhaps Kastner came to me in the beginning with mistrust, but as soon as we had become somewhat closer I was for him no longer the feared great Gestapo: He came to me for discussions, smoked one cigarette after the other, often brought his wife with him; if one reads all this psychologically correctly one recognises that we were enemies who dealt with each other fearlessly, it was a purely political issue.

Not only with Kastner but also with the other Jewish functionaries I had a correct, professional relationship, if it was now Dr. Löwenherz, the office director of the Israelite Religious Community in Vienna, the umbrella organisation of all the Jewish associations working at that time in Austria, or Dr. Kastner in Budapest or Dr. Eppstein in Berlin and many others. I had very open discussions repeatedly with them and said more than once that I had no racial hatred and rejected so-called "hotspur methods". None of the Jewish political functionaries can complain that in the innumerable conferences and discussions of those years they ever encountered in me a raging, sadistic "murderer". My superiors allowed me to conduct these negotiations with open visor. "Open visor" is a common term with me, which I first used in 1938 with Löwenherz and Rotternburg. At the beginning of our cooperation I warned my Jewish negotiation partners roughly in the following manner: "I speak honestly with you, you can take my word for what it is without twisting and turning it. I do not want to be deceived, betrayed or cheated by you. If we speak the truth to each other, we will come to an understanding quickly and spare time and energy. If you lie to me, it is bad for you; if you lie to yourselves, you will cheat and betray me, so I demand the truth." In this sense did I work with my Jewish colleagues the whole year long and proceeded well thereby, for the word got around. In order not to fall into the suspicion that I wish to present myself today in a milder light than befits me, I stress that I had the approval of my superiors as well.

Dr. Eppstein, commercial councillor Storfer from Vienna and, I think, also Dr. Weiman and Edelstein from Prague were in 1944, during my absence, transferred from the Reich territory without my knowledge to a concentration camp, where they died. I had to some extent worked together professionally with these Jewish functionaries for years, in a way that was correct on both sides. When I learnt later that they had been taken to the concentration camp, I did not conceal my regret and lack of understanding, neither from the Jews nor from my superior Müller and my regular representative. I had once promised Dr. Rothenburg, the director of the Palestine Office in Vienna, to let him emigrate to Palestine on the first suitable occasion; I kept my word. Even to the commercial councillor Storfer I had made this promise, which I could not now realise. I had Dr. Bach and Dr. Murmelstein appointed to the directorship of Theresienstadt. Naturally, the relations in Theresienstadt were also conditioned by the war, but it would be a falsehood to maintain that it went badly for them and the other inhabitants of this Jewish city.

One day – it may have been May or June 1944 – a quite different Kastner came to me in my office. The otherwise so determined and ice-cold smooth Jewish politician with characteristics and manners that would have honoured any diplomat, now showed the deepest resignation, and was almost tearful. Sorely oppressed, he opened up to me: "Obersturmbannführer, we are being sacrificed here and get no help, either from the Jewish nor from the non-Jewish side; now they have deported my wife as well. It is hard to be a Jew." I invited him to sit down and offered him a cigarette. He always had more cigarettes than I. They were good-smelling cigarettes which he kept in a beautiful silver cigarette case and always lit with a small silver lighter. I explained to him that I could ensure that no harm would come to his wife from any German office, for I would like to meet the person who would dare to remove a negotiating partner from me. It could certainly have been only Jewish or Hungarian offices. Kastner assured me that Jewish offices were out of the question, so there remained only the Hungarian. I consoled him as well as I could and promised to talk immediately after our meeting to the two secretaries of state Baky and Endre to track his wife somehow. Then I said to Kastner: "You said that it is hard to be a Jew and that you have been abandoned by all, by the Jewish side as well as by the non-Jewish. I repeat to you: If I had not been a German and a National Socialist but a Jew, I would have been a fanatic Zionist. But you see, no goal is reached without sacrifice. Even we National Socialists have had to offer our blood sacrifices until we gained power." Kastner explained to me that it was for the Jews especially tragic that I of all people, with my organisational capacities, had been sent to Hungary for I would here deprive them of the eastern human material especially valuable for Jewry which they need most urgently for EREZ ISRAEL. Then he added: "American Jewry does not help us, and in Palestine there are only relatively few brave people who fight against the Mandate Power through the promotion of illegal immigration." I then said to him that it seemed to me as if Wall Street was consciously sacrificing European Jewry in order to achieve its political and economic goals. Kastner closed his eyes for a moment and looked tired and harrowed and said in a short while: "Help me! Give me my wife back!" This conversation confirmed to me that Dr. Kastner was desperate regarding the battle which he had to conduct in Hungary alone and abandoned.

Apart from this day and under the pressure of this personal incident he never expressed himself privately in this manner; he was an ice-cold calculating person who seemed to me to be without any feelings. Perhaps he should never have spoken to me in this way; he indeed dealt me a certain trump card for free with respect to our negotiations, because I now obtained a glimpse into his inner life which he had hidden from me before. Here he showed himself soft and I could have exploited that. But I did not need to do it, and moreover I tolerated it when the Jewish functionaries sometimes formulated the truth to me in such a way that they would have actually made themselves punishable; I said to myself that, in the heat of the negotiation battles, one should not lay everything on the scales; it was a question of each side reaching its goal. So I also did not see that I was entitled to exploit Kastner's momentary softness. The Jewish political functionaries naturally recognised this practice of mine soon; therefore they spoke to me in full frankness about their worries and distresses. They would not have done this with a petty crime-official because they rightly could not presuppose any understanding of it and would have therewith irritated an impatient mediocre official with a narrow field of vision.

I gave Krumey the order to start the search for Mrs. Kastner through lieutenant colonel Ferenczy and also to approach the Chief of the Hungarian Secret Police – I think he was called Peter.[42] With the latter we managed very well until the Hungarian Secret Police got wind through their own information channels of the fact that we had, behind the backs of the Hungarian authorities, allowed Jews to emigrate abroad and that to a certain extent – since the arrival of the Standartenführer Kurt Becher, about whom I shall speak more later – material goods were exchanged for the emigrations. It was quite logical that the Hungarians were furious about that and our cooperation suffered particularly due to this. For a while the situation became so pointed that we no longer visited one another and for a while no longer participated in any discussions. Then it was reserved for me to discuss the entire problem with the Senior Police Chief in Hungary, General Winkelmann, and the Reich representative, Veesenmayer, to whom I had to report several times. But finally I obtained a resolution with the secretaries of state Baky and Endre, whereby the latter especially made it very easy for me to sort out the matter. Afterwards the relationship of our Hungarian Secret Police became once again bearable, but never again as comradely as before. With the advance of the Red Army, the relations in Hungary became more chaotic, whereby the illegal transports of Palestine-immigrants arranged by me and Kastner stopped.

When now the Hungarian Secret Police learnt of Kastner's arrangements with us, it took control of Mrs. Kastner to sound her out. Through Endre I demanded her release, for I did not wish that the wife of my Jewish negotiation partner be bothered or harassed in some way because the capability of my partner would suffer from it. With Endre a quick solution could come about inasmuch as there existed a warm

---

42   Peter, Chief of the Political Police in Budapest, Chief of the Hungarian Secret
      Police.

personal friendship between us. As an outward sign of that I had gifted Endre my own automatic pistol with the approval of the senior SS and Police chief. I had been a guest many times in the estate of his parents in Kiskunfölinháza, some 150 km south of Budapest, even after Endre had married the countess Croy in Budapest. As secretary of state he could give the appropriate orders to the Hungarian police with the instruction to inform the Ministry of the Interior of the current abode of Mrs. Kastner. And that happened. I do not remember any more today where the Hungarian gendarmerie or state police had taken Mrs. Kastner; to my impatient representations Endre said to me with his Magyar emphasis of the German language: "Look – I cannot give you Mrs. Kastner at the moment; she must be healed for some more days since she has received a beating." In fact Dr. Kastner came with his wife to me after some days and expressed his gratitude for the fact that I had given him his wife back. He now knew that no German office had anything to do with it, but that it had been a purely Hungarian action caused by his commercial transactions with the Germans to enable the Jewish illegal emigration through Romania.

When Kastner said to me that the Jews in Hungary were sacrificed like lambs instead of receiving help from the Jewish or pro-Jewish side, I explained to him that I would rather pursue my religious studies than have Jews be deported here but I have received this order. We did not live in the deepest peace, and sometimes I still believed in our victory. Kastner replied to me that he was certain that Germany would win the war. Then it was clear to me that he was lying to me exactly as I to him, for in that time I certainly no longer believed in our military victory. But Kastner never lost sight of his chief task; even when he informed me of the disappearance of his wife he used the opportunity to say to me: "Obersturmbannführer, I have seven hundred persons there; please release them to me!" I answered him as so often: "Agreed, Kastner, have them escape through Romania and regulate the details with Sturmbannführer Krumey!" *In this way even at this point in time several transports emigrated illegally from Hungary.* I cannot say for sure, but *it could have been altogether 18,000, perhaps even 20,000 Jews.* These transports were not checked by us; they were Kastner's own matter, it was only a question of how many Jews he could arrange to transport and the necessary money to take them to Palestine. That was Kastner's chief task, everything beside it a game for which he deployed his emissaries abroad in order to be able to fulfil the demands of a financial and material sort that Standartenführer Becher, for example, placed on him according to the instruction of the SS Reichsführer.

How this *illegal emigration* proceeded I know roughly because I had allowed it *not only in Budapest but everywhere in Hungary*. Only in Hungary did I dare, based on a certain independence, to circumvent, within the scope of the special command, the prohibition of the SS Reichsführer against Jewish emigration. In general the emigration proceeded as follows: The Jewish functionaries collected a contingent of selected Jews who were concentrated in a place chosen by the Jewish leadership. Occasionally we placed the supervision with SS members in Hungary so that some third office could not intervene at the last moment. The Jewish political organisation prepared well in advance the financial as well as the transport possibilities. On the target date the transit offices of the border police were informed by me and were instructed to allow these transports to pass freely and unhindered. Then they passed out of our sphere of power; afterwards they had to try to smuggle themselves through further. Naturally, the necessary provisions were made by the Jewish organisations, for example, in Romania, so that these emigrant contingents were concealed from the public. The chartering of the steamers was prepared well in advance, which were anchored or awaited in the concerned receiving ports; then the port authorities had to be deployed – certainly not without a large bribe – until finally the embarkation could take place. The Romanian port in Konstanza on the Black Sea was used by preference. Everything was illegal with these emigration groups; sometimes they did not possess any papers at all. They crossed through Romania in the dead of night and, insofar as Romanian offices declared themselves to be ready to cooperate, this doubtless cost a lot of money. In the Mediterranean, there were many small ships which always sailed as long as they were appropriately paid. The German war ships were instructed of the fact that these transports had been approved by us. However, if these emigration ships encountered Italian or units of other nationalities, this was a decided misfortune.

I know that *some transports were captured by the English Mandate authorities*. But after these emigrants had been taken into custody for a short or long time, they finally received the permission for Palestine. To what other country could the Mandate authorities send them? In Palestine, the Zionist organisations operated a reception and distribution service. They also had to be aware of where the British Mandate authorities showed gaps on the coast in order to land the ships with immigrants at these places. Once landed, the same service had to distribute the new arrivals over the territory.

The Deportations From Abroad

Hungarian Jews being transported by the Gendarmerie in Koszeg.

Kastner complained bitterly about the low number of Jews in Palestine, where illegal immigration was limited. Already at that time, and even today, I am convinced that there were probably, among the English Mandate authorities, people to support and promote illegal immigration for idealistic or financial reasons.

Even before the outbreak of war, Dr. Löwenherz had, in his great efforts to make possible emigration for as many Jews as possible, chartered, through the mediation of a travel agency in Germany, a steamer which then just set sail from a German port with six hundred or eight hundred Jews on board. This ghost ship did not allow me to sleep at night; this boat cruised the ocean; *no country on earth declared that it was ready to accept the human cargo of this steamer.* It cruised for weeks and weeks at high sea and was turned back everywhere. It was the most unsuccessful attempt of an illegal immigration, which already at that time confirmed to me that, *of course, almost all the governments of the world raged against the National Socialist Jewish measures and used our project against us through propaganda but nevertheless were in no way ready to bend even their little finger to alleviate this distress that was so tearfully bemoaned by them.*

For this first attempt at an illegal transport I had of course obtained the approval of my superior, the Inspector of the Sipo and SD, Dr.

Stahlecker, but nevertheless I was the expert and success was expected of me. The ghost ship generated a series of complaints and made me also wary of taking illegal emigration transports lightly.

The illegal transports organised by Dr. Kastner with my approval could, as mentioned, have included around 20,000. But the numbers could have also been much higher, for I can well imagine that Kastner did not keep an exact count of the respective figures, especially since I never had him checked and an exact contingent number was never mentioned; It was a matter of "around 700", "around 2,000", so that he always rounded it up upwards as far as it was technically possible. I estimated therefore around 20,000 persons, if Kastner followed the agreed numbers. If I had been directed by hatred, I would perhaps have been mean. But I wanted a political solution – and after the SS Reichsführer had himself relaxed his original prohibition of emigration, I did not need to be more papal than the Pope. These transports were trade and counter-trade in expectation of the chief trade of a million Jews for ten thousand cargo lorries.

Kastner's return service for this illegal emigration to Palestine consisted in – to repeat – the fact that he guaranteed peace and order among Hungarian Jewry and the systematic progress of the evacuation and also fulfilled the material conditions negotiated with Standartenführer Becher. Since Kastner himself had constant contact with the neutral foreign countries and with Palestine in order to carry out the transport preparations and obtain foreign exchange from abroad, and moreover had a number of emissaries at his disposal who could with my permission freely leave Hungary – everything without the knowledge of the Hungarian authorities, it is understandable that Kastner was precisely informed of everything that happened outside the Hungarian border and maintained through a sort of courier system in extremely close contact with all possible people. It is indeed possible that this courier and information network was used also for anti-Reich operations, perhaps for espionage. But what sort of espionage could an individual Jew conduct in Hungary when half of Hungary was already occupied by the Soviets, and many Hungarians themselves conducted espionage and senior officers had crossed over to the enemy?

After the assassination attempt on the Führer of 20 July 1944, it was indeed clear that the enemy derived his information from the primary source, Bendlerstraße. Never did even one office, say the commanding officer of the Security Police in Budapest, the senior

SS and Police chiefs or indeed the SS Reichsführer, give even the least hint in this direction. At that time we no longer needed to see that caution was exercised; on the contrary, everything indeed happened on the instruction of the SS Reichsführer. I would never have dared to go on my own course to any extent against orders. I adhered strictly to an order and always maintained everything in file notes, just to maintain face before my own subordinates from whom I demanded a clear implementation of my orders. If I had not myself carried out the orders that I had received from my superiors, I would have been a bad SS chief, and I believe that I was a good one.

Kastner conducted himself in exactly the same way with regard to his superiors. If I am asked today if Kastner received some instructions or the agreement of the most senior chief of the Zionists, Chaim Weizmann, for his "dealings" with me through which he traded valuable Jewish men for – as he intended – worthless Jewish human material, I cannot answer yes or no. It seems to me to be obvious that Kastner checked with his superiors because I conducted myself likewise in my sector. *From the Jewish side significant deliveries were sent from abroad to German offices*, and therefore Kastner must naturally have dealt with the senders, that is, his Jewish superiors. *When these Jews sent their supplies they thereby declared themselves automatically in agreement with Kastner's project and actions. If Kastner had undertaken this important cooperative work on his own or indeed against the instructions and wishes of involved Jewish organisations which indeed appeared later at the head of the Israeli government*, these personalities would never have had such a dignified burial granted to him as was the case.

I cannot say *what sum of foreign exchange was involved*, for it did not interest me. I only know that it was *considerable amounts* and I once learnt that Kastner and a companion came with a bag which was given over to a departmental head of the commanding officer of the Sipo; I think that the latter worked on "espionage and counter-espionage" in his department and plainly needed foreign exchange for his aims. I sometimes saw the content of the bag: so many bundled dollars. I have said many times that Kastner belonged to the Mapai party and later, I think, became a representative of this party in Israel, to which Ben Gurion, Golda Meir and many other official personalities also belong – many people who doubtless knew accurately of Kastner's activity in Budapest in its every detail.

Kastner must have had direct contact with Chaim Weizmann, for I remember that, on the order of the SS Reichsführer or of my immediate superior Gruppenführer Müller, I induced him to have his chief Dr. Chaim Weizmann come, on the promise of safe-conduct, to Berlin as guest of the Reich government.

I had put forward the same proposal to Dr. Löwenherz earlier. I myself hoped for very much from such a visit for the solution of the Jewish question. If we had had this possibility already before the war exactly as during the war, we would doubtless have been able to regulate much in a beneficial manner through direct negotiations with the most senior leader of Zionism. Kastner answered my suggestion at that time tired and resigned: "He will not come – he will not come." "Why not?" "Because he cannot come." "What does 'cannot come' mean?" "That I do not know, but he will not come, because he cannot come." I still do not know what Kastner meant by that, if it was impossible for Weizmann, as chief of the international Jewish organisations, to travel to Germany during the war, especially since he had indeed declared war on the German people, or that he could not come because he was prevented in some way from doing so. It was certainly unusual to invite the leader of a people who had declared war on the German people to Berlin with safe-conduct. That could perhaps have only been an idea of the SS Reichsführer, who at this time made all possible attempts to solve certain problems.

The SS Reichsführer ordered me to get into touch with Kurt Becher, it must have been shortly after my arrival in Budapest. Becher had settled with a small unit of the Waffen SS in Budapest in order to attempt, under the direct orders of the SS Reichsführer, to obtain certain financial advantages in exchange for a relaxation of the Jewish regulations. In Hungary, we found ourselves in a country with an autonomous government and could not demand from it what was possible in other countries where the German authorities had a free hand. Becher had received different individual commissions from the SS Reichsführer which I do not remember today; perhaps I did not know them very precisely even then because they did not concern me, for I was not in charge in this matter.

Becher belonged to the SS "Florian Gezer" division and negotiated directly with Kastner, who was the most prominent Jew; all the others belonged to the "second rank". I remember very clearly that Standartenführer Becher – naturally on the commission of the SS

Reichsführer – dealt with Weiß,[43] the Chief of the large metal concern in Hungary. Weiß was something like the Hungarian "Krupp" and concluded a sort of gentleman's agreement with Becher. According to this, this big industrialist could fly to neutral foreign countries with a special plane and 30 or 40 relatives and take, besides, millions of amounts in foreign exchange. Somehow I received written instructions regarding this and could incorporate them into my files so that, on my side, no more doubts stood in the way. I only had to put my signature under the final arrangements so that the matter went to the SS Reichsführer and I could close my "Weiß and consortium" files. The factories and properties of Weiß were transferred to the administration of the SS: Becher was thereby the mediator.

At first I was not completely at ease with Becher; I communicated my doubts to Gruppenführer Müller, who inquired of me about Becher in great detail and gave me to understand that he was thinking of taking him into custody; I wanted to be very friendly to him and request him to come with me to Gruppenführer Müller in order to be able to discuss this exchange trade business. During this discussion Müller would then send him to a concentration camp. To be truthful, I must say that I neither stressed Müller's order especially nor represented it as urgent, but mentioned it rather incidentally, for I wanted to tolerate Becher at that time and was glad that he did not accept Müller's invitation.

A little while later an incident took me by surprise. Becher had a sort of orderly, an SS Rottenführer, who was the owner of the Hotel Carlton in Preßburg. When once I, along with Dr. Kastner and one of his transactors, entered Becher's office, sandwiches and liquor were served by his orderly. Without any immediate reason, Becher rose to an artificial rage and shouted at Dr. Kastner: "If you do not provide me before such and such a date (some sum of dollars), I shall say to my comrade Eichmann that he has to gas ten thousand Jews!' Then I recognised Becher as an actor, for he knew quite precisely that neither Eichmann nor the Sipo gassed anybody. He knew quite precisely that an individual person could not at all decide on that. And he knew further that this was a secret matter of the Reich and that no mention should be made of it at all. *Moreover, he played this theatrical scene at a time when already the cow-trade – a million Jews for ten thousand cargo lorries – was under way and for that reason the liquidation measures in Auschwitz had been discontinued on the orders of the SS Reichsführer.*

43   Weiss, Jewish industrialist in Hungary, Martin Weiss Company in Budapest.

After the war, I found both the theatrical act of Becher as well as the criminalist's instinct of my immediate superior Gruppenführer Müller confirmed when I read that Becher travelled with Kastner after 1945 through Germany and was exempted from any discriminatory measure because "it was said to be due to him that some thousand Jews were able to be protected from gassing".

It may have been autumn 1944 when I was summoned along with Becher to the SS Reichsführer. At first we travelled separately, then together. Then Becher showed me under an oath of silence a precious gold chain in a beautiful case and remarked that this had been traded from Jews. He had to give it over to the SS Reichsführer, for it was "destined for a small woman with whom the SS Reichsführer has a child". When Himmler received Becher extraordinarily warmly in my presence, I inferred from it that every counteraction against Becher would from the start be destined to failure since he had the personal confidence of the SS Reichsführer. So I kept quiet, did my service and tried to manage with Becher as well as I could. In this way was explained the fact that even Müller could not institute anything against this man and Becher could allow himself with impunity to threaten the "gassing" of ten thousand Jews in an artificial outburst of rage.

Who the originator of the idea of the exchange of "one million Jews for ten thousand cargo lorries" was I can no longer ascertain with certainty; it can have been the SS Reichsführer, Gruppenführer Müller, Becher, Kastner, Brand or I myself. But it stands certain that I could make and made such a proposal only with the approval of my superiors. It is also certain that Himmler definitely wanted to motorise the 8th and 22nd SS division and required these cargo lorries for that. 10,000 cargo lorries with trailers, winterised, for a million Jews, that was clear to me; for here it was a matter of preserving German blood. I never proceeded with dollars or foreign exchange, for money meant nothing to me. But winterised cargo lorries for the eastern front was certainly worth my support and effort.

If I am told that it is certainly true that Joel Brand flew with this commission on 15 May 1944 to a neutral foreign country, then this could mean that I myself initiated this trade, even if it sounds astonishing to me even today that such a fundamental initiative stems from me. But if the above date is right, then I had not yet been to the SS Reichsführer and must have made this offer at my own discretion. But even today, thirteen or fourteen years after the event, everything does not seem quite credible to me. If I were the author of this trade, then I hold fast to it, as I would like to explain expressly. It is also possible that I indeed arrived at this idea but then presented it to my immediate superior Gruppenführer Müller first during a professional trip to Berlin and then received the approval for it. Even the SS Reichsführer can have known some weeks earlier that such a trade was planned. So, during my report in his field commando office, he may have said to me confirming in a way: "... and above all motorise the 8th and 22nd division for me!" Whatever may have happened, it is certain that the proposal was made. To exchange Jewish human material for dead inventory, that was an incentive for them – and moreover such offers of Jews and to the Jews did not take place for the first time in Hungary but were made already before in the Protectorate, in Austria and in the Old Reich. On that I can report details continuously: money and goods run like a red thread through the entire Jewish matter. That begins with the procurement of fee monies from abroad, for only with that could the Jews emigrate. *The receiving countries, not we Germans, demanded "money for blood" in order to accept Jews at all.* It was an enormous work to raise the many million dollars to allow the many hundred thousands of Jews to emigrate abroad. Every "head" cost around 250 dollars, that amounts to 250 million dollars in the case of a million Jews. This money the Jews had to be able to show; the individual Jew did not receive it in his hands but the travel conductor did. Then the trade proceeded further, for *the receiving countries demanded,* along with the levy of "fee monies", *also the evidence of professional training in technical or agricultural fields.* That was mostly only a business for the receiving country. *This circumstance obliged me to create training places in the technical and agricultural sector.*

In Herzl's work I had been able to read how close this training lay to his heart; I copied it and quickly transformed it into reality. The Zionist organisations strove to develop, especially for the eastern Jews, a number of small training places. On this basis I now trained Jewish locksmiths, carpenters, gardeners, farmers, millers, paper workers, etc. on a large scale. In this way the receiving countries received trained workers who were not accepted for charitable reasons or through compassion but for work in sectors that functioned defectively in the country itself. The immigrants had to prove what they could do; the fee money was to see to it that they did not in the first months become a burden to the receiving countries. That was the *"blood for goods" trade – long years before the war. These efforts towards an exchange trade continued during the entire war;* I shall be able to provide more detail on it in the course of these explanations. For this reason the story of the 10,000 cargo lorries was nothing extraordinary and I did not consider it to be so.

I presented this proposal to the Jewish functionaries, first to Kastner; it may be that Brand accompanied him. That I received Brand alone I would doubt, for I did nothing in Hungary without Kastner. It is certain only that I considered Brand as a subordinate colleague of Rudolf Kastner's and, after the matter was settled, commissioned Krumey to take Brand to Vienna in the official car to get him the necessary documents through the State Police office in Vienna and then to charter a courier plane to Istanbul. It may be that Himmler determined the number of cargo lorries and I that of a million Jews, for I was an idealist and generous with regard to the Jews according to the motto: "If we are going to do something, then let us do it". This seems to have been the case and I cite here as chief witnesses, first, Standartenführer Becher and, second, my then regular representative, Sturmbannführer Krumey to whom I doubtless communicated these things. It is clear that I could never get from Hungary alone a million Jews, for there were not a million Jews there. On the other hand, I knew that, in the Auschwitz concentration camp – I do not know in which other concentration camps for I have indeed not seen them – very many Jews were used as armaments workers. So I could immediately suggest that I would be able to get a million Jews in all. It is tragic that international Jewry was not able to obtain acceptance possibilities for this one million Jews. Perhaps international Jewry did not want it at all? Perhaps the price of a million Jews was just right to whip up compassion in the world and to obtain with its help the political intentions of Jewry, the founding of the state of Israel in the homeland declared by Balfour, and, on the other hand, to pressure Wall Street economically in such a way that just for pecuniary reasons it was worth writing off a million Jews completely and attaining material goals through them?

From the moment in which this cargo lorry matter proceeded, the SS Reichsführer naturally ordered a halt to the liquidations. If the trade had gone well, I would have had to produce a million Jews in perfect condition, and indeed not a randomly collected million but – as Dr. Kastner indeed repeatedly demanded and I assured him as well – *a million "valuable" Jews because Kastner indeed refused to accept all old and assimilated Jews.*

The Jewish Socialist Dr. Kastner may have possibly proposed another man for this trip to Vienna and Istanbul, but probably he would have been a Socialist too. Brand was a Jewish idealist like his master Kastner, and was perhaps even a nuance sharper, but of a primitive nature. Kastner was the intellectual superior, the master, and Brand was his chief companion. Kastner hoped for the realisation of this project exactly as I did and the accommodation possibility for a million Jews. Neither Kastner nor I nor anybody else could suppose that international Jewry or the Zionist organisations would not bring enough commitment to realise it. Nobody could believe that Brand's mission would go badly. Doubtless Kastner heard of this fiasco much sooner than I, for I was indeed dependent on Kastner's communications. For weeks he kept quiet about it; I would have done so also in his place in order to rescue what there was to be rescued. Anyway, at that time the thought may have for the first time come to Kastner that he too would under circumstances be sacrificed one day like an indefinite number of Jews if it was a question of the final political and economic goals of the Jewish central authorities. At that time, Kastner may have had doubts about his future fate. He then emigrated, after the war, to his beloved Erez Israel. He also became a representative; he immediately wrote a book and straightaway raised self-accusations against himself when he heard what was being whispered about him in his own camp. I would have done the same. And finally he was, even before the proper legal judgement, shot down on the street by people who were even more fanatical than he.

As mentioned earlier, I was able to carry out the Hungarian commission with great success because I could count on the unrestricted cooperation of the two secretaries of state Endre and Baky. The Arrow Cross movement existed in Hungary long before our invasion and, if people like Endre and Baky identified themselves with this movement, from whose ranks they had emerged, it is easy to conclude that they attempted long before to get rid of the "Jewish cancer". Endre, for example, belonged during the time of the Bolshevist terror regime of Béla Kun to those especially elite officer companies of Admiral Horthy which were recruited to the last man from voluntary officers who approached their task with the greatest élan; Endre pointed proudly to his bravery decorations, just as Peter, the Chief of the Hungarian Gestapo, did. The Bolshevist terror of Béla Kun was a clear stimulus to the anti-Jewish currents among the Hungarian people. Up to my presence in Hungary I had no idea of the fact that there were Magyar circles which positively longed for operations against Jewry. Endre related to me that, under Béla Kun, 18 or 19 out of 20 Communist functionaries were Jews. There were only a few Hungarian traitors with them, by and large however they were Jews and more Jews; for that reason he was thankful that he could render to his fervently beloved homeland the service of freeing it from the Jews.

The Eichmann Tapes

What was undertaken in Hungary against the Jews did not happen under the influence of the Germans, but as retaliation for the suffering that the Jews had inflicted upon them. Already when I met Endre for the first time in the guest room of his county house in Budapest, I encountered the Hungarian nationalist consciousness in a markedly emphatic manner; Endre announced to me the gratitude of the Hungarian government that it would now finally be rid of the Jews, and could deliver them to the German Reich. He offered to do everything to reach this goal as quickly as possible; thereby he assured me that it was the task of the Hungarian government to initiate everything that was necessary from the legislative and executive standpoint. The quicker the better, he only requested that all Jews be evacuated, for Hungary's sake. I could promise this to him, for my order from Berlin was to that effect.

It made a strong impression on me that Endre, as I heard, after the end of the war, had fled to Austria. He was captured on Hungarian territory and sentenced to death by hanging.

It was very difficult in to seize the Jews because of the disproportionately large number of assimilated Jews in Hungary. In Hungary, there was a broad aristocratic stratum, particularly officers of the former Imperial and Royal Army, among them sons of impoverished families who, as lieutenant or lieutenant-colonel, had, on marriage, to place a deposit, following the then army principles; so many of these officers had married rich women who could place the deposit and therewith gilded their coat of arms; a large part of these women were of Jewish origin. Obviously these Jewesses tended to assimilation and not only they but their entire clan, which was now bound with the scion of a noble family or officer dynasty. For that reason it could hardly be determined how great *the number of Jews in Hungary* precisely was; I would like to estimate it in sum at *500,000-600,000*.

When I was in those days commanded to Gestapo Office IV, my first activity there consisted in effecting the re-development of the two Jewish national funds which had been forbidden before my entry into office. It was a matter of the Jewish national funds and the Jewish construction funds which I then allowed to operate in order to obtain a financial base for the emigrating Jews. It is understandable that the Jewish funds that were no longer, or hardly, operating in Hungary sensed new life when I went there. They began to operate on their own; for they felt certain from the start of my tolerance and support. I did not know the individual directors or secretaries of these funds and deliberately never received them personally. My Jewish colleagues in Budapest received protective identification cards from me which they had to present to the German and Hungarian authorities to avoid all harassments and restrictions, which proved to be very useful with the Hungarian Gestapo and the gendarmerie in the individual counties and also with regard to the confusion in our German official apparatus and assured the success of my procedures.

After I had to personally carry out for the first time in Hungary what my "advisers" or representatives had been doing for years, according to orders, in the foreign countries occupied by us or under our power, I had every reason not only to extend my experience and practice but also to *set an example* for personal reasons. I wanted to prove how work can be performed if people stood behind me with their full support, in contrast to the "slow motion speed" which was to be observed wherever people somehow wished to sabotage a little.

It was, besides, conceivable that, after Hungary, it would be the turn of still more countries of Europe in a similar way. *If now my chief, Gruppenführer Müller, said: "We shall send the master himself ...", then I wanted to conduct myself like a master* by dealing with the fundamentals and transporting Hungarian Jewry to the Reich in lightning speed in spite of various kinds of resistance.

Rounding up and loading was done – as mentioned – by the Hungarian gendarmerie. Although it is maintained now that the first trains rolled already in April, I cannot believe that. I am rather more of the opinion that they worked from east to west zone by zone and the first loadings took place at the earliest in the middle of May. I insisted that – as always – Jews with foreign citizenship be strictly exempted and not included in the deportation. Obviously, the Reich representative Veesenmayer knew nothing of it in detail, but I reported the situation to the senior SS and Police chief in Hungary, who in turn informed Veesenmayer. In every zone I made available to the Hungarian gendarmerie an adviser; together with a liaison man of the German embassy, Jews with enemy or neutral citizenship were accommodated in eastern Hungarian camps and indeed in special accommodation. If one points to the fact that, according to the documents, a travel-plan conference took place on 4 May 1944 with representatives of the Reich railway, the Sipo and the Hungarian gendarmerie, this does not mean anything more or less than that these travel-plan conferences lasted three or four days and then at least ten or fourteen days more passed before the trains could be made available, so that one could not *begin with the transports* in any way before the *middle of May*. Perhaps Endre gave to the Hungarian gendarmerie through his colleague Baky the necessary orders to carry out the deportations as quickly as possible, no matter under what circumstances. If Endre expressed to me his impatience with regard to the speed, which I considered to be rapid, that is not to be wondered at. Perhaps these Hungarian offices wanted to definitely prevent the entire matter from being thwarted by some intervention. It may be that they therefore wanted to evacuate as many Jews as possible in a great hurry.

The fact is that the rounding up and loading of the Hungarian Jews led to many complaints. Wisliceny reported to me that the Jews in individual counties were driven and loaded "like cattle". Instruction with regard to rounding up and transport had been expressly issued through the Hungarian executive agencies, but we had only very limited possibilities of intervention on Hungarian soil and essentially only through the Hungarian agencies. Only on reaching Reich territory did the allotted lieutenant of my transport command have authority and could therefore instruct the station-master to halt the train so long until, for example, a fresh water supply was provided and the rubbish buckets were emptied and cleaned as well. Where we had sovereign rights my guidelines for the implementation of the evacuation were maintained, naturally apart from individual cases of exceptions that are to be found everywhere.

I never saw the loading on the part of the Hungarian gendarmerie because it was a subordinate matter for which I had no time; in addition, the Hungarian gendarmerie would have considered this to be an interference in their area of responsibility. They had to load the transports and to provide supplies for so many days as was discussed with the state secretaries. I had a regular police of some 300 men at my disposal and ordered, on the basis of my guidelines, that every transport train was to be accompanied by a lieutenant or senior staff-sergeant with 30 men. That was all that I had to do with it. But the two secretaries of state Endre and Baky were likewise human beings and took full notice of the deportation guidelines that existed already long before the Hungarian episode. Their principle was to avoid all avoidable hardships. Perhaps they were altered somewhat according to the Hungarian mentality, but perhaps they also adhered to it a hundred percent; I could not worry about that because this would have represented an interference in Hungarian sovereign rights.

The Deportations From Abroad

In every county I had one of my chief captains who had enough experience from other countries, people like Wisliceny, Burger, Brunner and others. In the regions they worked together with the Hungarian gendarmerie. If some uncertainties emerged, the gendarmerie could accept the opinion of my people or approach their superior office, that is, Endre of Baky. In a few cases my men were completely shocked; for example, when Wisliceny, pointed out to me that such methods had not occurred in his earlier deportation experience. It could be that Wisliceny's inborn goodness prompted him to use the expression "driven like cattle" when citing some individual cases. Because I never arranged anything orally, I recorded these complaints for the information of the secretary of state Endre and in my files. A consultation with the secretary of state was required many times, whereby I basically pointed out that the individual Jew should not be "punished" but that a "political solution of the Jewish problem" had to be found. I know that Endre for his part, like me, repeatedly called these matters to the attention of Major Ferenczy, liaison officer of the Hungarian gendarmerie, to the fact that the "guidelines" were to be adhered to; nevertheless there came about repeatedly individual cases of *insufficient rubbish buckets, or there was too little drinking water; also the food was sometimes bad, or it was stolen; or it was missing, and the wagons were overcrowded.* The Hungarian gendarmerie perhaps received from their superiors the summary order to load everything somehow so that the camp should be emptied as quickly as possible; after 240 km, the border was reached, then the Germans could consider how they would deal with it.

From Auschwitz I received constant protests from Höß or Liebehenschel; I also had to go there myself and heard then from the doctors that many transports from Hungary arrived in a desolate condition. Obviously it could not be in our interest to accept, instead of human material fit for work, sick people and to risk the protests of the WVHA. Besides, we had to keep in mind the transaction of 10,000 cargo lorries for which I had promised a million healthy Jews for emigration.

Pohl himself complained to me once in Berlin; I could only reply to him that not we but the Hungarian gendarmerie were responsible for the rounding up and transport, moreover I had approached the secretary of state Endre for that reason and instructed my advisers in the individual counties that the escort command should henceforth make the departure of the transports according to the prescribed regulations. As in Poland and other countries, the Jewish council of elders had been involved in the rounding up which the Hungarian police undertook; certainly the officials gave all the possible assurances to facilitate this work; I do not know if these were maintained, since even this lay outside my responsibility. Endre was very active, seldom to be found at his desk and was frequently on the road, even in the Reich, where he studied many things in order to introduce them then in his country too, adapted to Hungarian conditions, and not least the involvement of the council of elders in the rounding up of the Jews.

If I hear now that the Hungarian Reich administrator had protested most strongly against the deportations of the Hungarian Jews, I can respond only that I did not observe any of that. I cannot remember any more if Endre and Baky were already secretaries of state when the first transports rolled from Hungary. In any case, they already possessed the appropriate authority for the implementation of the deportation. What Horthy ordered did not need to interest me, but only the forced evacuation of the Hungarian Jews desired by Baky and Endre. The Reich plenipotentiary, Dr. Veesenmayer, had discussions with Horthy. I met the former only occasionally, perhaps eight times in all, when it was a matter of essential questions, whereas I visited the senior SS and Police chief, Winkelmann, almost daily. If difficulties really arose from the highest Hungarian offices, Dr. Veesenmayer would certainly have given me a stop order. Exactly the opposite occurred; for the two Hungarian secretaries of state never requested a restraining tactic but the most rapid procedure. It is however conceivable that Horthy wanted to ensure his position as Reich administrator; it would not have been an easy matter to revoke the deportation measures because it was Horthy's own Hungarian gendarmerie who undertook the rounding up and loading with some thousand men in the individual counties. An intervention of Horthy's I can remember only in a few cases, as, for example, Göring also did it.

It is unthinkable for me that the secretaries of state Endre and Baky as senior officials went against the instructions of their own government. My special command in turn stood under the senior SS and Police chief, General Winkelmann, and he in turn under the Reich plenipotentiary Dr. Veesenmayer, so that in this way all important decisions of the highest Hungarian state office became publicly known: naturally, everybody would have learnt of a general objection of Horthy's! The commanding officer of the Sipo and SD was subordinated to me insofar as it concerned my sector; I could give him instructions with regard to this, provided that these were signed by my office chief. In Hungary I worked once as a consultant in the RSHA, which to a certain extent gave the individual orders by itself, but on the other

Unknown Jewish couple wearing the yellow star, Budapest, Hungary.

hand as a consultant of the Sipo and SD in Hungary, whereby I, as chief of the special commando, reported to the commanding officer of the Sipo and SD. It was rather like, but naturally on a smaller scale, the position of Heydrich at a higher level, who, as Deputy Reich protector in Bohemia and Moravia, gave his orders for the Security Police by himself.

From my official position it is clear that Endre and Baky had never received orders from me, likewise Major Ferenczy, who was an outstanding officer, and who treated me as an equal ranking comrade but never as a superior. It was thus fully out of the question that I could have undertaken anything, even in the least, against the ordinances of Horthy; even with Veesenmayer I would have had reservations.

In general, before I dealt with one of the secretaries of state on any measure I always obtained from the senior SS and Police chief a clearance certificate and the latter himself requested such a thing from his superior, the Reich plenipotentiary, Veesenmayer. If I obtained the "clearance", which could also be given as an oral consent, then I knew that no foreign political damage would arise to the Reich from this or that action. If Reich administrator von Horthy had set himself decisively against any measure, then neither Winkelmann nor Veesenmayer would have approved this. Naturally, it is quite possible that Horthy or the prime minister wanted to carry out interventions, but did not really undertake these in general but only in individual cases, and that was only later. If it is said to me now that Prime Minister Sztojay or indeed the Reich administrator was "afraid" of me, I must remark that my office did not go beyond that of a departmental head so that I was never in the position to get around Gruppenführer Müller, indeed not even my friend Kaltenbrunner, who was himself very warm-hearted. To maintain the opposite can only be described as a Jewish invention.

I can only confirm that the Hungarian government was thankful to "get rid of" the Jews through us. One day the Hungarian prime minister Sztojay[44] gave a meal to the senior SS and Police chief Winkelmann or perhaps to the Reich plenipotentiary Veesenmayer, to which I did not receive a direct invitation but was, as it were, invited by General Winkelmann; before and after the meal I spoke with the prime minister. I remember very precisely that he expressed to me his gratitude for my efforts. As was so common, the host collected all possible representatives of his government around himself, it was a public meal as in peace time with lackeys on the stairs. Although the Minister of the Interior was very probably present at the meal, I quite honestly cannot say today what his name was and what he looked like. He was not active, he had almost nothing else to do once he was in agreement with the powerful procedure of Baky and the forceful bravado of Endre. It is possible that I was once or twice with the Hungarian Minister of the Interior in the company of Baky or Endre, but certainly then it was a matter only of courtesy calls, whereby no official matters were discussed. If Minister of the Interior Weiner has maintained that "increasingly brazen things occurred", then I must say to that that I have never seen this Weiner officially, and I can also add not even privately; for, otherwise, I would remember it. I was seated at this meal between the Hungarian War Minister and the wife of one of the present gentlemen. The atmosphere of cooperation with the Hungarian authorities marked this meal. If therefore I am told now, from the post-war literature, that at that time circles of the Hungarian gendarmerie or of the army had taken a sharp position against my mission, then I ask, citing the hundred year old famous Hungarian gallantry: Why did they not simply transfer me? I did nothing for my personal protection; my peace at night in the Budapest

---

44   Döme Sztójay (1883-1946) was prime minister of Hungary from March until August 1944. At the end of the war he was tried by a Communist People's Trial in Budapest and executed in 1946.

Quartier was "watched over" by only some eight policemen. The entire, post-war literature prompts in me the question, why in fact an assassination attempt was never made against my life. In my opinion I had at that time no enemies among the Jews; for I already stressed that I fought with them with an "open visor"; they knew where they stood in their dealings with me. The Jews with whom I had to deal did not think of any assassination attempt because they wanted something from me exactly as I from them. I received threatening letters in large numbers so that I received even in Prague a special guard in front of my house. The threatening letters indicated that I must be transferred, my days were numbered if I did not disappear immediately, etc. But I never worried about threatening letters.

In spite of all interventions, of which I hear only now, the deportations continued regularly. Therewith I had fulfilled the order of the SS Reichsführer; everything else was of no interest to me. I must further declare that in Hungary I never let a single train turn back: I turned back a train only once in my life; that was in the case of Denmark. Naturally it is easily possible that in an underhand way some dozens or indeed hundreds of men were brought back, but that is of no *fundamental* importance.

It is possible that, in June 1944, one or two trains were sent daily; likewise it may be right that, on 8 July 1944, the last official deportation train left Hungary. But it is most unlikely that I *evacuated 434,000 Jews in 53 days* from the middle of May to 8 July. *The number* was certainly high, but *not possibly higher than 300,000*. For the most part they went to Auschwitz, but also to the Burgenland and Straßhof. Of these *only a very small number were sent for physical liquidation*, insofar as they were *not fit to work*. All other deportations were held ready for the ten thousand cargo lorry exchange deal. Even though I was not responsible for the Jews from the Generalgouvernement, I declare that it went best for the Jews from Hungary in comparison to the former as well as to the Jews of other countries.

Many times I turned up the speed for the deportation from Budapest. My commission in Hungary was to carry out a lightning operation. Only in that way could I prevent partisan battles from arising in eastern Hungary with Jewish support – at the rear of the front. Thus I indeed began with the evacuation even there. In the west a success would have been much easier and numerically greater. In western Hungary or in the southwest stood our SS divisions and I would have been able to use the element of surprise fully with regard to Budapest.

Western Hungary I knew very well even from the peace time, but I was bound by my order: I had to prevent any partisan formation; how I did that was left to me. Anybody else would have begun in the west, and for that reason too Jewry had not anticipated that I would begin in the east. To scour everything from the east was the most difficult thing for me, not only because I had to send my people into fully unknown areas but also because I had to request Endre and Baky to bring the Hungarian gendarmerie to be deployed first in these broad, scattered, impassable areas.

In the Budapest ghetto naturally something similar could have happened as in Warsaw, but this ghetto stood under the Arrow Cross people, whose mentality was basically different from that of the German supervisory agencies in the Warsaw ghetto: the Arrow Cross people still had something of a revolutionary recklessness such as we had gradually lost or worn out after 1939. For that reason we did not need to worry so much about the Budapest ghetto; for the Arrow Cross people would have certainly intervened with iron discipline, especially since the Warsaw uprising was a warning sign even for them.

In order to deport from the capital I had to take into consideration many administrative technical steps. Even though Endre was determined to dismantle the Budapest ghetto, the difficulties were great; perhaps I did not obtain any transport trains on the determined date because they were lacking or more necessary elsewhere or the track was destroyed.

When the first V-1 was fired at London, Secretary of State Endre showed me a Hungarian morning newspaper with the announcement that the retaliation had begun, and wallowed in these words: "Victory is ours." Endre and Baky believed with strengthened vehemence in the final victory and I avoided dampening their enthusiasm.

It may be that the internal political development for the protection of the Jews from the Budapest ghetto through the manoeuvre of obliging them to a so-called fatigue duty was speeded up; for Endre and Baky had an important say in the Hungarian Ministry of the Interior. After Horthy's fall, the ghetto in Budapest was enlarged not by the German offices but by the Hungarian Arrow Cross people. During the scouring of the eastern territories of Hungary a certain percentage of Jews could escape from the grasp of the gendarmerie and go into hiding in the Jewish community of Budapest. This too, again, with some exceptions. Originally the Budapest Jewish community had consisted of around 150,000 Jews; it rose now very quickly to 200,000. The missing percentage of the Jews in the eastern counties was therefore very precisely determined, because there the Jew was predominantly orthodox or Zionist in contrast to the western counties and the provincial capital, where the assimilationist Jews predominated. For this reason I mentioned in my concluding report the figure of around 200,000 a figure which I received from the Hungarian side. During this entire time Brand's mission regarding the exchange of a million Jews for 10,000 cargo lorries continued. In Budapest, in the meanwhile, every office strove to obtain everything possible thing from the Jews. I can imagine that these offices always said as a final threat: "Now 'the wicked Eichmann' will come ..." Those, like Dr. Kastner, who were better acquainted with the situation knew better. If Kastner wished to send a contingent of illegal emigrants abroad, it was free for him to deal with whomever he wanted; but he could send them over the border only he if received the final consent from me. On the other hand, I could deal with whomever I wanted.

I must repeat: The operation in Hungary could have started only at the end of May 1944, that is what my painstaking calculation shows. If it is maintained that more than 3,000 Jews were transported in a train, that is not correct for either Hungary or for any other country, for there was never a train with more than 3,000 Jews, and very often with far fewer persons. If the Hungarian gendarmerie gave the figure of "615,378" deported Jews that is the usual exaggeration to declare the highest possible "success figures". It may have been about the 300,000 who were deported in Hungary, and nobody should maintain that they were "all gassed" for out of them countless Jews survived. After the war, I have seen with my own eyes how there were Hungarian Jews everywhere, and in large numbers. From where did these Jews come?

For me Kastner was the most important man and Joel Brand was one of his colleagues. If it is now related to me that Brand maintains the opposite in his book, then I have the following to say to that: Kastner and Brand were close friends. When Brand learnt that his friend Kastner was pilloried in the public opinion of the new state of Israel, that he literally had to fight for his life and the trial requested by himself against himself clearly did not produce the expected result, he considered that the time for intervention had come. Brand could prove that during the time in question he was active abroad and had, in the real sense of the word, struggled for a million Jews with Jewish and non-Jewish offices, with the English Minister for the Near East and with all possible economic and political leaders. Brand could therefore demonstrate before the Jewry of Palestine an alibi of positive service and dare to take his friend Kastner, who had got involved with the Gestapo, under protection by turning the tables and making himself Kastner's superior. Through that, undreamt of possibilities of a reasonable escape opened up to Kastner.

Today – after fourteen years it is sometimes extraordinarily hard to remember individual details, especially since I have no assistant who could give me some help. I had at that time sent Krumey and Wisliceny to Hungary as advance guard; Wisliceny, the more skilled negotiation partner, had the task of seeking out people among whom I could then make a choice and build up the framework of Jewish political functionaries. Naturally, it is probable that, already before Kastner, this or that person came into view and I dealt with him. The entire matter was under way in the first days after 20 March 1944 and I do not wish to maintain that I entrusted the standard activities from the start to Kastner. It is possible that, even before that, a Jew called Brand was presented to me; from many things that have been read out to me from his book it appears that Brand must have been with me often. But I see him in my memory as always being instructed by Kastner and I cannot get rid of this recollection in spite of having listened to the opposite opinion. Only one thing would be thinkable and explain the situation: when I conducted discussions in the beginning with Brand, he could have offered Kastner to me, to a certain extent as a substitute for the time of his absence. After then I had many negotiations with Kastner weekly, I knew no other negotiation partner than him, through whom also all the matters with Brand passed. I placed Hungarian Jewry totally under Dr. Rudolf Kastner, who at that time became the typical representative of Hungarian Jewry and he meant as much to me in Hungary as the then chief of the World Zionist Organisation, Chaim Weizmann.

Kastner had colleagues who worked on all branches of Jewish life in Hungary; I did not worry about smaller matters myself and therefore had it relatively easy. It did not interest me which cross-connections my people used officially; they had my trust and my authority and never misused these in all the many years. I trusted them completely and thereby always fared very well. So much more incredible is everything that I had to learn after 1945 about these people; in numerous cases I can only confirm as the truth the complete opposite of their explanations, which were no doubt extorted from them by coercion and pressure.

It was exactly the same with Kastner: I had no time to worry about his colleagues, especially since in Hungary I had, for the first time in my life, to affect a certain public image. In the central agency I never needed that to maintain my prestige; for, there I had to represent not myself but the executive of the Greater German Reich. In Hungary, I did not need to worry about any subordinate colleagues, for I had Kastner for that. His assistance was offered to Krumey. I myself had only to do with the chief of Hungarian Jewry who had been recognised and authorised by me.

Between Kastner and me there existed a mutual relationship of trust. Now, whom he deployed to carry out his intentions was, in all honesty, not known to me, and also it did not interest me at all. Therefore I do not know today many names from that time in Hungary, and I never got to know them. Perhaps Krumey knows them, who indeed had to deal with the details more than I. For me it only mattered that I reached the goal ordered to me: the removal of the Jews from Hungary and the exchange business of a million Jews for ten thousand winterised cargo lorries. How the goal was reached was a matter of indifference to me as regards the details, just as the circumstance whether one Jew more or less passed through the green border, with or without the approval of my office.

Kastner had all conceivable channels at his disposal and had his representatives everywhere; he could not have enough connections in order to somehow carry out the tasks set by me, for example, the exchange business which was to serve Jewry as well as the German Reich. The more irregular ways Kastner chose to achieve his goal the more I was ready to support him, for his goal coincided to a certain extent with my goal. Both the final goal and my position ordered me to help Kastner. Therein lies a difference which is to be maintained; for physical liquidation is a clumsy sort of operation, with which the RSHA, thus the Gestapo and SD, never had anything to do. We rather, as instruments, had to conduct the battle on the world-view intellectual field. Kastner had understood this basic position immediately, as emerges from our frequent long discussions on the future of Jewry.

There is another reason why I am reluctant to acknowledge Joel Brand as the most senior chief of Hungarian Jewry at that time: I know that I never dealt with a Jew called Brand but, from the beginning to the end, with a Jew Dr. Reszö Kastner. If Brand now claims that he was the chief of the whole matter and only after his departure did Kastner emerge to a certain extent as his substitute, I can only say that I would never have sent such a man abroad. I would have shown myself to be an amateur in the secret service, for it contradicts every rule to get rid of the most influential man. For this foreign mission Kastner would have without doubt been a more skilled "letter-carrier" than Brand, but he was the chief, whom I naturally would never have released at that time for that. By "letter-carrier" I do not in any way mean a simple person, for Brand was doubtless a person positioned in the midst of Jewish life, idealistically disposed and obviously capable; otherwise Kastner would not have entrusted him as his representative with this extremely delicate mission. I estimate Joel Brand to be a man who, originating from a relatively primitive intellectual environment, became acquainted early with the idealistic efforts of Jewry and became a sort of fanatic. I shall express it in other words: Brand had the conduct of a railway conductor in comparison to the "director general" Kastner. From newspaper reviews of Brand's book it emerges that he got on the nerves even of the female secretaries in the different Jewish central agencies and was dismissed as a grouch on account of his dogged excuses for the failed mission. Later, Brand went away from Israel deeply disgruntled and dissatisfied with himself and the world and dictated his story – apparently to a Weißberg.[45]

If it is said to me now that Brand expresses in this book his fear of the revenge of the SS Obersturmführer Eichmann against his family, I must reply to this the following: During my entire career it never occurred in any case that I "took revenge" in any form on wives, children or other family members of my negotiation partners. That would have beneath my dignity. Brand's family relationships were unknown to me, I never met his wife. Moreover, I committed myself most intensively to freeing Mrs. Kastner from the hands of the Hungarian gendarmerie, as I describe in another section. I was precisely informed about Kastner; he often came to the negotiations with his wife. She was a small, clever, communicative woman who sometimes even negotiated alone with me. Today she lives – as far as I know – in Palestine.

Not a single measure was taken against the family of Joel Brand that remained behind; they were not watched and would have been able to emigrate through Romania without my knowledge. And why should there be supervision or indeed "revenge"? We were equal discussion partners and idealists – we understood each other, only we were

---

45   Joel Brand's story was published by Alex Weissberg as *Advocate for the Dead: The story of Joel Brand* (André Deutsch, 1956).

political opponents and sought to negotiate: businessmen negotiate and politicians negotiate, and I was here as a police officer. Already for many years I was no longer a member of the Waffen SS but a police officer, thus a political leader of the SS in the secret service of the Greater German Reich and I had to conduct myself accordingly; I had to treat the partners whom I chose appropriately; for otherwise neither of the two sides would have had the advantage he hoped for.

Further, it is to be denied that Brand or Kastner ever participated in a "drinking session with the Germans". If I had found that out – and I would have known that if it had been a question of my colleagues – I would have pilloried them exactly as I had in other cases. After all, war had been declared against us by Chaim Weizmann, and therefore I could never have tolerated that my people celebrated with Jews. Whether in other offices or with Standartenführer Becher such carousals took place I do not know.

Moreover, I cannot answer the question whether the exchange business of a million Jews for ten thousand lorries represented, in May 1944, a means by which the SS Reichsführer could enter into dialogue with the Allies, perhaps influenced by Schellenberg. When we consider today the history of that phase of the war, it is possible that Himmler wished to explain to the English through a hint that: We have no interest in fighting against you, the western Allies, for these 10,000 cargo lorries will be deployed only against the east. It is possible that for the SS Reichsführer it was a matter less of the 10,000 cargo lorries than of the psychological interpretation of this offer, but I have no proof of that.

In the Nuremberg Trial, Obergruppenführer Berger is said to have claimed for himself the idea of the exchange business. This entire story of the exchange business is anyway like a crutch to which everybody seeks to press forward in order to be able after 1945 to demonstrate to a certain extent a moral alibi or even a service rendered to Jewry. It is certain that it was Himmler who gave the order to attempt this business and at the same time issued the order to Pohl to discontinue the physical liquidation in Auschwitz.

If it is maintained today that I felt this exchange business as a repulsive trade and committed myself to it because I had received the order for it but I never "had my heart in it", that should mean that I would rather have killed the Jews. Now, I never "had my heart in it" with the enemy; I would naturally have seen every enemy of the Reich dead rather than alive; for "only a dead enemy of the Reich is a good one". Moreover I always carried out every order that I received, and I am still proud of that; for thereby I fulfilled my oath. But in the Jewish question I always championed a bloodless solution. Why should this trade have been repulsive to me? I had, besides, another personal reason to urgently wish for the realisation of this exchange business: my best friend in those war times was Zehender, commander of the 22nd SS Cavalry Division.[46] I knew how he bent over backwards to defend his couple of square kilometres. We had become acquainted as junior leaders, and I helped him wherever I could when he, along with his division, was treated in a bad way apparently because there was nothing more to give. Then when I received the order of the SS Reichsführer: to "Motorise the 8th and 22nd divisions through an exchange deal of one million Jews for 10,000 cargo lorries", I suddenly saw a possibility of providing 5,000 of those ten thousand lorries to my friend for his division. I never asked my "heart" and also did not have to. I had to worry about Germany – that was my heart. Even my superior, Gruppenführer Müller, had the same attitude towards this trade as I. If we could exchange a number of enemies of the Reich for military advantages, then any trade is worth carrying out.

I am convinced of the fact that we would have given up even two million Jews for 10,000 lorries. The required number of Jews was indeed present, even if the opposite is maintained today. It is unimaginable what sort of advantages both sides, Jewish as well as non-Jewish, would have derived from this trade. Even Kaltenbrunner saw the matter from the same standpoint. For among us it was a matter of how it would benefit the nation. So it was purely professional with us, as everywhere in the world. If we had inquired about the right and wrong every time, then we would have been able to just go to sleep. Unfortunately this happened in other offices and that is why we lost the war.

That passage from Brand's book was expressly read out to me where Gross says to Brand: "Joel, you are blind as a child, do you really believe that Eichmann wants to free a million Jews to obtain dollars or cargo lorries? The Nazis know that they have lost the war, and Himmler wants to enter into dialogue with the Allies. I had the task to establish contact with the English and Americans for a separate peace. Your entire Jewish matter was only an incidental question, an offshoot of my mission here, but for us the most important." Gross scolded the Zionist leader wildly.

---

46 August Zehender (1903-45) was a Brigadeführer and Major-General of the Waffen SS. He was killed in action in Budapest in February 1945.

Hungarian soldiers round up Jews in Budapest 1942.

Brand then added that, after the experiences of a decade, he saw many things in another light. From knowledge I can only declare: people who were connected to the secret service tend to the overestimation of their own importance, the paid agents more strongly than the unpaid. They have no idea at all of the sober, dry as dust daily routine in the secret service central office. There are perhaps adventurers who seek to trim their activity with ideal motives but also ruthless guys who undertake their task only on account of the payment. Gross may have belonged to these. Brand would now, after ten years have elapsed, see many things differently, especially since he has read enough, among other things also about the efforts of the SS Reichsführer to enter into dialogue with the Allies. But if Brand fled in May 1944, that was still before the time when the SS Reichsführer was the Minister of the Interior, before the time when the assassination attempt against Hitler took place. At that time, Himmler had not yet thought of starting an "excursion" to make a pact with the enemy. These are things which only a mediocre brain like that of Brand or Gross compiled afterwards, out of thin air or out of other books, as line-fillers.

Before Brand took up his mission abroad, I apparently said to him: "Mr. Brand, do it quickly, come back, or else your people here will be finished." Such turns of speech and expressions do not belong to my communication style. Not a single word of that can have come from my mouth. If Brand speaks about a pistol on my writing desk, I should say to that that I never removed the weapon from my person. An old saying was hammered into us: "The German who keeps a spear farther than at arm's length is dishonourable." In our service, along with the concept of honour stands the desire for defence and self-preservation. I laid aside my belt only when I sat behind the desk; then, instead of in my pistol holster, my gun was kept close at hand in a stand below the writing table-top. If I hung my belt behind the armchair, then I had a second or third pistol ready at hand in a built-in trestle on the left or right. In Berlin, the pistols lay in the right drawer of the writing desk. Moreover, Brand thus apparently gives circumstantial evidence that he and his associates still trusted my word in 1944. If I let a Jew go abroad and said to him, his family was under my protection, I certainly did not mean by it that they were hostages. Around that time generally the Jews were rounded up and deported by the Hungarian police; "under my protection", that meant that the relatives of a man who had been sent on Jewish matters abroad remained untouched during his absence. The Jews knew that they could depend on that; not a single one was disappointed. But if Mrs. Brand was apparently imprisoned, that was an individual case due to the responsibility of the Hungarian police which had nothing to do with the general rounding up. Hungary was a sovereign state; the German Gestapo did not have to be informed of what the Hungarian police undertook.

Krumey had the order from me to regulate the details of Brand's mission. Brand was supplied generously with foreign exchange and taken to Vienna in the company of Krumey in an official car; there he looked around the city and lodged in a very decent hotel. He received the necessary papers and a place in a German courier plane to Constantinople, where he made contact with Jewish and English circles. Then he travelled to different countries, was taken into custody by the English and investigated whether he was a German spy, and finally came before the English Minister for the Near East. The latter asked him how he communicated to me: "Mr. Brand, how do you imagine that generally? Where would I go with a million Jews?" That was a particularly insulting question. Brand, who was an experienced negotiator, replied during this or another discussion with the English that "... the English said that they did not have sufficient shipping space to transport a million Jews. But if the Germans were ready in the difficult situation of their defensive battles to transport a million Jews by rail outside Hungary, then indeed the powerful British global empire and its allies must be in the position to come up with the ships for the transport of a million Jews."

The Deportations From Abroad

It was an order of the SS Reichsführer to conduct the deportations further even after Brand's travel abroad, in spite of the negotiations initiated, but with the addendum – which was not communicated to the Jews that the SS Reichsführer issued to the chief of the head office, Pohl, the instruction to stop the physical liquidation and to send the deportees for work deployment. Kastner gave me a continuous report of Brand's mission, his difficulties, his detention as a German spy. When now weeks and weeks passed, I made increasingly severe reproaches and demanded an explanation. Kastner answered me either that Brand was at the moment detained here or there or was in negotiations in Palestine and was scurrying around half the globe. He asserted everything on his word of honour. Kastner gave me his word of honour many times. He was an idealist and himself hoped for a positive outcome of Brand's mission. I surely pointed out occasionally that Brand's family had to remain here until his return, as it was agreed, though that did not in any way mean the slightest retaliation. In this way I was always kept in suspense by the prospect of Kastner's credible reports, which I expected.

On 1 July 1944, the scouring of eastern Hungary was finished; in addition to it, around 300,000 Jews were evacuated from western Hungary. If I am now confronted with an "Interim agreement between Jews and Germans, I can say to that that the Gestapo did not have anything to do with it. Possibly it was a matter of an arrangement which Standartenführer Becher, had made with the Jews, doubtless following the approval of the SS Reichsführer.

About the different attempts of individual offices to extract money or other material advantages from the Jews in Budapest I can basically affirm only that: numerous members of the offices in Budapest strove to rescue as many Jews as possible from Auschwitz. Army people, Sipo officials or members of some other agencies who could produce evidence of it after 1945 registered as a rule many plus points for their judgement as police officials and in this way made their life easier. It is clear that I was summoned together with Standartenführer Becher on this Budapest matter twice to the SS Reichsführer; there this trade was agreed upon. My representatives managed the details, but only the details; for Wisliceny was not authorised to deal with essential matters, not even manage details in an authoritative way. That was done by my regular representative in Budapest. If it is maintained now that I had, in the middle of June 1944, agreed to Kastner to take 30,000 old Jews to Austria for a payment of five million Swiss francs as advance payment for the Brand Mission but to expressly exempt therefrom "vital and productive Jews from the Carpathians or Siebenbürgen", I can only describe that as nonsense. I scoured Hungary from east to west and did not at all worry in particular from where the Hungarian Jews who were indeed chosen for the exchange trade came. Everything that Brand either does not wish to, or cannot, remember he places in my mouth whereas in reality he heard it from some people in the information service with the commanding officer of the Sipo, or from some Hungarian Gestapo man.

I, the representative of the German Gestapo, am supposed to have said all this. To Kastner I always spoke only of a hundred thousand Jews who would be available immediately if Brand could report the positive course of the negotiations by telegram. There was generally no talk of another contingent, either of 30,000 or of more Jews. Naturally it is possible that the people who wished to obtain foreign exchange deviously from Jews made irresponsible promises and threatened them with the "wicked Eichmann".

At the beginning of June 1944, the affair of a group of Jews from the Klausenburg ghetto who wished to emigrate to Palestine is said to have taken place. If now this description is read out to me from Brand's book, how Eichmann, raving mad, put his foot down and related to Wisliceny in the company of his colleagues that Major Ferencz had flatly "swallowed" one of the stories fabricated by him about a "Zionist conspiracy", I can only dismiss that as a crude lie! I know of no single case, even in Hungary, and as little do I know that a "Zionist conspiracy" would have appeared opportune.

It would therefore surprise me extraordinarily if a man like Kastner actually maintained that I dished up to the Hungarians a "fantastic story" about a "Zionist conspiracy". For, around that time I imagined myself to be at least as good an expert on the Zionist matters as Kastner himself. There is indeed only one possible explanation: some foreign exchange story had been launched by Becher and I had to defend the matter before the Hungarians. Becher did not come in contact with the two secretaries of state but they had accused me. It would have been very unpleasant for me if others had thought that I "played false". Precisely to Endre I often openly said: "You, Laczy, look, in this matter the Reich can rake in foreign exchange which can be used for the state or something else important; the SS Reichsführer already knows the purpose. The money likewise benefits Hungary also indirectly. Perhaps you will not have anything against it?" Naturally, Endre had nothing against it, but Peter had something against it; for, as an enraged

Hungarian nationalist, he wanted to do "business" only for Hungary. In this sense it is possible that I backed up Becher's "spin" before the Hungarians. But naturally I thereby told Endre the plain truth; this I would like to establish clearly so that none of the nationalistically thinking Hungarians, whom I esteem very much, might get the idea that I had done "business" with the Jews in favour of the German Reich at the cost of the Magyars. That was never the case!

To return to Klausenburg: This city indeed lies in Romania, and it would have been clear madness to, to a certain extent, "hold in reserve" Romanian Jews in Hungary for an illegal emigration to Palestine! How should Jews from Romania be brought to Hungary, where the opposite was always done?

Even before Endre was named secretary of state, we decided to travel together for a couple of days to eastern Hungary. He made a car available, a driver and a uniformed lackey. If I recall rightly, even his wife travelled with us. Even Wisliceny requested that he be included. It was a purely private trip which was to familiarise myself with the landscape of eastern Hungary. If there was time somehow for it, we wanted also to go into the Carpathians for bear-hunting. This trip helped me to deepen my contact with Endre, and so it was for me, to a certain extent, an official trip. The Carpathians offered a magnificent view; in an enormous wood there stood a beautiful hotel which belonged to the government. There we spent the night after we had enjoyed an eastern Hungarian national meal.

I must deny, as regards myself, that during this trip some "concentration places in brick-yards" were visited. And if such "experts in the subject" mention, "... Eichmann convinced Endre to send the eastern Hungarian Jews, for whom there was no place in the interior of the country, rather to Germany ...", that is once again simply a statement that suits the authors' books. It was a matter of an excursion, nothing more, and Endre made himself free for a couple of days, to visit some counties. Whether we accidentally passed by some brick-yards and perhaps sat there together I really do not know any more, but deportation matters were certainly not discussed; for they were already established earlier. During the first dinner with Endre in Budapest I had already mentioned that the programme for the prevention of any partisan activity behind the front included the scouring of the Hungarian territory from east to west and deportation to the Reich territory. If now so-called authors mention so casually that I said to the Jewish council, "Endre would like to eat the Jews with paprika", I must have been a downright dolt to make such a statement, and that about my friend Endre! This entire nonsense of the authors can indeed hardly be believed; they all say false things.

I remember well another group of 700, but not the 600 Jews whom Kastner wanted to send to Palestine illegally with my agreement; these 700 Jews were placed in Budapest under the watch of members of the "Florian Geyer" division, to protect them from any seizure. They were rounded up by Kastner in lists and were definitely not to be deported through Germany. Illegal transports never went through Germany, but all through Romania to Palestine. From where Kastner got these seven hundred Jews was unimportant to me. He declared them to be "700 young people", and I granted their emigration. I never checked such transports. Why should I have bargained so much in this case? I was always for short negotiations with Jewish functionaries; depending on the importance of the matter it was a matter of five minutes or half an hour. Perhaps also occasionally something more, but never two hours. If Kastner approached me – which he did often – to have some contingent of emigrating Jews approved, I granted the permission offhand, as it were; the details were to be discussed with Krumey. The entire story of Joel Brand is a mixture of fiction and truth; for actually I can remember even today the following sentence: "... then I must guard the camp ..." The guarding then actually came about in the described manner. It seems that the author here is trying to conjure up an exciting moment in his lines and, in addition, to rinse out the artfulness of the Jewish negotiators like a grease stain on a water surface. In reality all these negotiations took place in a much more sober and shorter manner. Never did Dr. Kastner make the statements put in his mouth, not through fear, but because his personal propriety would have forbidden that to him. Besides, how is it possible to believe that Wisliceny dared to call me by my first name during a negotiation in the presence of Jews?

As I hear now, Kastner seems to be criticised that he spent too much energy on this transport and even sheltered all his relatives and friends. I did not know that at that time; moreover he could transport whom he wanted. In the different illegal transports there could have been even Jews who were influential or dangerous for the Reich. But to weigh how far active and dangerous Jews could have indeed become dangerous to us in the relatively short time and if we would have obtained the 10,000 cargo lorries only late through a tedious check of the emigration contingents was the task of the SS Reichsführer. The really influential or dangerous Jew had enough contacts and relationships at his disposal; he passed into the general chaos which ruled in Hungary, as well as over the green border, often with the help of Jewish Hungarians who made it their pleasure to be able to get back at the Germans or of others who did everything for money or acclaim. Hungary was, during the entire war years, not so cordoned off on all sides that a clever Jew would not have had the possibility of fleeing over the green border. How should I have checked and sorted out these 700 people whom Kastner mentioned to me – as was customary in the case of Kastner's statistics, it was certainly in reality more than a thousand Jews who emigrated in this way to Palestine – and therewith make troubles for myself with the Hungarian gendarmerie? Just imagine: the Brand mission may have been successful, that is, a million Jews or at first also only the "advance section" of 100,000 would have been evacuated. How could I have investigated all of them for their "potential danger"? What interest did I have in one transport of 700 or 7,000 Jews in comparison to the scope of my task – my commission to scour Hungary from east to west demanded no great expenditure of energy because Dr. Endre pressed me to have the Jews rounded up by the Hungarian gendarmerie evacuated as quickly as possible; they were more than Pohl could accept in the concentration camps. My obligation was limited to taking over the Jews; I was responsible only for that. What happened before and after that was fully outside my power; for that I had no official powers.

It may have been around this time, in *June 1944*, when Dr. Kastner requested me to stop *"the liquidation machine in Auschwitz"*. Since I knew, on the one hand, that he was precisely informed through his information apparatus and, on the other hand, the already described incident with Becher had doubtless remained in his mind, I thought it right to explain to him fully the scope of my duty and the remit of the WVHA under which the concentration camps stood. In the presence of my secretary, I said to him that I had nothing at all to do with liquidation measures. Neither the Reich Security Head Office nor department IV-B4 in particular had to do with the liquidation. I said to him: "Kastner, you know as well as I that neither I nor the Chief of the Sipo are responsible for the "liquidation machine" in Auschwitz. You know as well as I that this is a matter of the SS Economic and Administrative Office which stands only under the SS Reichsführer.

When the ten thousand cargo lorries with trailers are here, then the "liquidation machine" in Auschwitz will be stopped. But not because

I want it but because the SS Reichsführer has ordered it so." Naturally, the Jews did not need to know that the SS Reichsführer had given the order in relation to this a long time ago, that is, when the exchange business was in progress, which coincided chronologically with the "Weiß works" affair.

If Brand writes that I said to Kastner: "If Brand does not return in three days, then I will have the mills in Auschwitz start again", I must counter that even the word "mill" is generally not familiar to me in this context. What I said to Kastner is explained in this manner: it was a general explanation of the responsibility of my Gestapo Office IV-B4. I also ask myself if one considers me to be such a sort of fool that I could expect from a man whom I had sent out after weeks of negotiations that he would be able to come back from distant Constantinople within three days?

My free discussion with Kastner on the office responsibilities can be interpreted as a disclosure of a secret matter of the Reich. I must admit that, but I was accustomed to speak with an open visor with my Jewish negotiation partners of the rank of Kastner. In addition, around that time all the foreign countries had already written and smeared us regarding the concentration camps in newspapers, pamphlets and other articles.

Finally, it is to be stated: If Brand's mission was successful, then the SS Reichsführer would have been immediately ready to transfer a million Jews abroad. Who knows how everything would have proceeded afterwards if the discussions which my representatives and I had with the Jewish functionaries on this account had led to a positive outcome. I am certain that the SS Reichsführer would, according to that, have handled the entire Jewish matter quite differently, just as all the Jews imprisoned in concentration camps up to the prohibition of emigration were immediately released if they could show an emigration permission from any country.

I would have been able to carry out the transport of a million Jews in spite of the war situation: citing the 10,000 lorries for the troops I would have "squeezed out" the necessary trains from the Reich Transport Ministry and had the Jews partly sent in a bloodless and unobjectionable way directly from Hungary to the nearby Romanian border, and partly sent from the concentration camps from the Reich territory to France. If they did not reach Spain, still France, where international Jewry would have been able to accept them.

The Deportations From Abroad

From Joel Brand's book I learn about a conversation between the English plenipotentiary for the Middle East and the emissary Brand in Cairo roughly around the same time that Kastner and I in Budapest worried about the outcome of the Brand mission. The Englishman asked Brand what now would happen if he returned to Budapest with a promise. Brand replied: "That is much simpler than you think, Sir, *a single order of Eichmann's is sufficient to stop the deportations*; thereafter he will give us the commission to compile lists for the transport of a million Jews. Perhaps the first transport will leave for Spain with only 20,000 men, but the life of these 20,000 will be saved." Thereupon the English High Commissioner asked: "But will Eichmann release them without having the guarantee that we will deliver the goods?" to which Brand answered: "Eichmann will give the go-ahead if the "Jewish Agency" accepts the offer. Whether you English then honour the word of the Jewish Agency, whether you deliver the Germans lorries, food or nothing at all, that does not interest me anymore, if only these first perhaps only 20,000 men are saved." Brand apparently explained later that the tragic delay for which exclusively Jewish offices were responsible cost the life of some hundred thousand men. *Now, they were perhaps transported to Auschwitz, but by far the majority remained alive*; Brand perhaps knows why he speaks about these "hundred thousand". I only know that I would, as proof of a credible business conduct, have sent 100,000 Jews to the Romanian or Spanish border even without the delivery of a single cargo lorry, if only the least news had reached us that Brand's mission had a chance of success. This message did not come. Brand will know why it did not come! As in all the years previously, even in this matter there was no office on earth that would have been ready to accept the Jews. Neither these one million nor these hundred thousand!

Kastner is dead and cannot speak any more; whether his wife today is still ready to speak out the truth, or whether she stands under certain influences and would form her statements opportunistically I do not know. But Brand is gradually becoming increasingly more important as chief witness even for the Israeli government, which wished up to now to dismiss him as absurd. For, it did not escape my observation that Brand's efforts in the English camp met with an understanding of the "exchange trading". Even though the cunning Brand pointed out to the English Minister for the Near East the German transport difficulties in order to obtain in this way the granting of English sea space, and the English state minister finally declared that he did not know where he would accommodate a million Jews, just the fact that the allies of the Soviet Union during the war embarked on negotiations with Brand as envoy from the German side is sufficient

After 1945, newspaper critics have apparently, as a result of this matter, magnified Stalin's mistrust of the Allies. According to the newspapers, the Swedish diplomat Wallenberg has apparently been missing up to this day because Stalin gave free rein to his wrath and from the start considered and judged everything that came from Hungary and had to do with Jewish matters with suspicion. It is not known if Wallenberg was killed in the first outburst of rage of Stalin's or perhaps even today scrapes out a life as the wreck of a man in some Soviet concentration camp. Wallenberg was in very close contact with Kastner; for Wallenberg could only really become active under the latter's aegis. On the one hand, he enjoyed the support of the Jews, on the other hand, that of the Gestapo and could, in this way, send considerable contingents of Jews in Budapest to foreign soil.

Today the extreme left in Israel criticises the then Jewish functionaries in Hungary that they had supplied to Wallenberg only such Jews who were chosen according to their social and material position, whereas the poor Jew without wealth was taken into consideration neither by their own political functionaries nor by Wallenberg. The rage regarding that extended at that time so far that conspiratorial organisations emerged in the Budapest ghetto, even if they could not accomplish anything until the invasion of the Soviets. Wallenberg had had several houses designated as "extraterritorial", on which he had boards with the Swedish coat of arms mounted; after the invasion of the Soviets, certain Jewish elements took action precisely against these houses.

Kastner assured me that Brand would return. Even though he did not return, the German Gestapo never took advantage of his family, even if Brand maintains that this fear impeded him in his negotiations.

Through a coincidence of fate Brand was raised to a certain importance; now he may, for his part, be striving to derive from this activity a certain halo of immortality because he was held as a Nazi spy in English custody and therewith wishes to play the "martyr" for Israel. But, in contrast to him, Dr. Kastner or even his wife have, in reality, been suffering idealists ready for sacrifice.

The importance of this matter and the tragic fate of many people obliges me to comment clearly on it: For the stopping of the deportations with immediate effect I had the authority of the SS Reichsführer. *So a clear difference should be made between deportation and physical liquidation.*

Hungarian Jews arrive in Switzerland in 1944 organized by Rudolf Kastner.

Although the Brand mission was under way for the exchange business of "1,000,000 Jews for 10,000 cargo lorries", the deportation had to continue: These Jews however were rounded up in camps to be ready on call all the time for the transport. If Brand had returned with the information that the "matter" was completed and five or ten thousand cargo lorries would roll, I would have allowed 100,000 Jews to be transported to some neutral border immediately as an advance group; for, I had the authority for that. But I would have also allowed 10,000, 15,000 or 20,000 Jews to travel through Romania to Palestine or even through France to Spain. That would have happened quite quickly. Delays would have occurred mostly in the acceptance by the Jews themselves; by me the evacuation of 20,000 Jews would have been completed in two days, but then at least two, three or four weeks would have passed before international Jewry had built the necessary acceptance establishments so that a second transport of 30,000 or 40,000 Jews could roll. The first contingent would have lasted very much longer than the fourth, fifth or sixth, because the organisation would have proceeded smoothly later. I had the authority to pledge my word of honour to the Jews in this case, and they had the right to believe it. It was naturally important for us to motorise two SS divisions at one stroke. So it was worth pledging my word of honour.

The Eichmann Tapes

As emerges from Brand's own report, it was to him a matter of indifference whether something was achieved through the business – the blame for failure would then lie with the Englishman. For Brand the main thing was that the Jewish Agency hand him a certificate on the basis of which he could prove to me that the trade was completed. Thereupon I would have naturally allowed 20,000, 30,000 to 100,000 Jews to leave; for it was arranged in this way and I had approval for that. After two or three weeks at most, it would then perhaps have transpired that the English did not come up with the cargo lorries and then I – as probably also the SS Reichsführer – would have said: "After me the deluge".

On 20 July 1944, I was in Hungary and heard in Budapest of the assassination attempt on the Führer. We took no security measures in Budapest; for we had good influential friends inside the Hungarian government so that no danger threatened us from this side. We needed as little to watch German military offices; for, in contrast to other countries where, as I heard later, members of military offices were imprisoned, we had in Hungary a good contact with them, so that nothing of that sort happened. I was personally surprised by the circumstance that an attempt in general could be organised and carried out; for I thought that the army was in the best hands, namely in those of the expert on the "national opposition" in Gestapo Office IV, Sturmbannführer Huppenkothen.

If the post-war "expert literature" states that I was endowed with the title "BDS Hungary" (Commanding Officer of the Security Police) and, in addition, it is maintained that that is in the personnel files, that claim is a downright nonsense. The commanding officer of the Security Police in Hungary was the already often mentioned SS Standartenführer Dr. Geschke, a good friend of mine for many years. He was earlier director of the Dresden State Police central office and was transferred from there through Mauthausen to Hungary. In my personnel files there cannot be such a "title" even by mistake.

One day, it may have been late summer or early autumn 1944, my friend, the commanding officer of the Sipo in Hungary, Dr. Geschke, said to me "This afternoon at 2 o'clock report to me for receipt of an order". Even though we adopted no strict official tone between ourselves and a good relationship existed between us, I was however officially so super correct that I groomed myself all buckled up according to regulations and with helmet, as I had learnt with the troops, in the antechamber of the adjutant and had myself announced. I was allowed in immediately, greeted and announced: "Obersturmbannführer Eichmann reports for the receipt of orders". The order originated from the SS Reichsführer and it said that I with my command – someone called it the "Eichmann special command" was to go to the Hungarian-Romanian border area of Arad and New Arad and there extract 10,000 ethnic Germans from the grip of the Soviets. If it is maintained that: "Eichmann disappeared on 23 August from Budapest in a condition of deepest depression, he very probably went to Romania ...", then the precise opposite was the case. It had a really redemptive effect on me to be finally able to get out of this entire confusion in Budapest and help ethnic Germans. This commission offered me extraordinary joy and in no way "deep depression".

From my friend Zehender, commander of the 22nd SS Cavalry Division, I had received ten or twelve 8 cm. grenade launchers, a unit of the Waffen SS half a company strong or even a little more and, in addition, I had my own members of the Sipo. On my march route there was a property of the Endre family which had already been abandoned on account of the nearby front. I had a litre of milk given to me by the administrator and paid him – one needs to be proper. Afterwards, Endre laughed at me about that; for the entire property would indeed have been at my disposal!

New Arad and Arad were in the hands of the Red Army, and the Hungarian Honved divisions were to start an attack. Until the latter decided on this, I let my people do exercises with the grenade launcher and other weapons. Arad is an old Hungarian county capital gone to Romania after the last war through a peace treaty. It is divided from New Arad by a small river. Around that time New Arad was a Romanian sovereign territory, some hundred metres away from the Hungarian border. When finally the Hungarian Honved divisions started the attack without any German support, they threw the Soviets several kilometres back so that the area became free. On a Sunday forenoon I drove through Arad. There a liberation celebration was taking place in the large square, because this area had fallen some hours or a day before once again into the hands of the Hungarians.

In New Arad there was a German army hospital in Soviet hands. The Russians constantly evacuated infantrymen and Red Cross personnel. Here I wanted to make an advance in order to liberate and gain the hospital. Since I could not carry out the original order for the evacuation of the 10,000 ethnic Germans, because this area was still in Soviet hands, I decided on my own to get the hospital inmates at first. We drove in the direction of New Arad and met on the way a German Red Cross sister who could not give sufficient expression to her joy at the rescue of the hospital. Already the previous night the Red Army men had partly evacuated transportable wounded persons; I had a discussion with the senior staff doctor of the hospital that the entire personnel were to be set marching in the direction of Budapest; I had the necessary means of transport at my disposal. The senior staff doctor had all the instruments packed and the two or three hundred wounded report; all who could up to then hardly crawl were suddenly in a position to go; the senior staff doctor said that even the seriously wounded now needed no more medicine; liberation was the best medicine. Because I dealt on my own authority, I later received from my superior Obergruppenführer Müller a reprimand but from the SS Reichsführer, on the contrary, the Iron Cross, second class.

We then travelled once again back to the property where I waited further for the Hungarian attack. In the meanwhile, the Hungarian senior commander of the division, a field-marshal whose name I cannot remember, had summoned me to him through his adjutant. But I evaded this order; for the field-marshal had already explained the reason for it through his adjutant: The evacuation of the ethnic Germans from a living area so important for the Hungarians would cause the resistance of the Hungarians including that of its own troops to wane. As to that I would only have been able to answer the field-marshal that the order of the SS Reichsführer said: *to extract 10,000 ethnic Germans from the Soviet grip.* When the Hungarian attack was successful, the ethnic Germans were evacuated. My colleagues were trained in this matter and could load everybody and set them marching in the direction of Budapest with the greatest speed, with the exception of those ethnic Germans who stubbornly refused to abandon their property or their land. A few days after the conclusion of this action, the Red Army had once again occupied the entire area with an energetic counter-attack; but we had saved the lives of the majority of the ethnic Germans.

Among the evacuees there were naturally some who at that time cried murder but later apparently they set up in their churches of the Virgin Mary a candle of thanks for the fact that I had remained hard and drew them out of this area. Today perhaps they live once again respectably, partly with the support of the federal government and with pensions on the basis of proven properties. Years later, after the war, I once met someone from this group of ethnic Germans who said to me how thankful they were to the man who had at that time taken them forcibly out of the area of New Arad. I did not reveal my identity but with inner joy and satisfaction I ascertained that the mission with which I was sent at that time to the Hungarian-Romanian border had been realised successfully.

During these months I travelled many times through Budapest to Berlin. My Budapest office was, during my absence, led by Krumey. In Berlin, I stayed eight to fourteen days and then drove back to my command, which had remained on the property and was exercising there.

From the Hungarian side it was insisted that, after the overthrow of the Reich administrator von Horthy, the deportations should be started again. But, on the other hand, the Allied bombers had practically smashed the railway network. Then somebody had the idea: *If the Allies smash the railway stations and the railway lines, then their allies, the Jews, should indeed march.* We set up, along with the Hungarians, the programme of *letting as many Jews march daily as we would have otherwise loaded onto trains.* The Hungarian gendarmerie rounded up the Jews and accompanied them in the Hungarian sovereign area; at the border, they were taken over by the German police. The impatience of Secretary of State Endre, for whom the deportations of the Jews anyway went far too slowly, gave birth to the idea of this foot-march. In spite of the pressure of the Hungarian government in all matters of the Jews, even this measure had to first obtain the approval of the German offices; such a foot-march would make the world opinion sit up and take notice. Doubtless I placed this matter to my immediate superior in the form of a written note with the request for acknowledgement and instruction. To do otherwise is unthinkable.

During the entire time of my Hungarian command, I travelled almost every four, at most every six, weeks to report to Berlin; for this purpose I had at my disposal a 3.4 Mercedes which was also made for quick night travels. During this time, for the receipt of essential orders, I was summoned many times by means of telegram to Berlin, to Müller. My immediate and direct superior Chief of Gestapo Office IV of the RSHA, SS Gruppenführer Heinrich Müller, was as cautious and pedantic a bureaucrat as I, who never neglected to go through the correct channel to get an instruction. That was called "covering"; I remember it because, within the scope of the many questions which have now been posed to me, I also heard once that I always "covered" myself; some author used that word. I wish to explain it in greater detail: It was not a "covering" externally, with regard to the enemy or neutral offices, but with regard to one's own superiors, with regard to possible dispute within the central authorities of the Reich. Dispute meant trouble with other German and non-German central offices from which unpleasantness could arise for the Reich. Thus also constantly the request for acknowledgements, communication of decisions and instructions. I can dare to maintain that the constantly cautious Müller and even his immediate superior, the often anxious and many times even undecided Kaltenbrunner, often did not decide themselves but requested the decision of the SS Reichsführer.

There existed a decision from the highest office for the foot-march of 10,000 or 15,000 Jews. That is to be seen from the fact that no authority was in the position to prevent or indeed halt this march. Since the decision had come down from the highest place on the German side, it was obvious that even the senior SS and Police Chief in Hungary, General Winkelmann, could not change anything in it. In the entire matter it was less about the 10,000-18,000 Jews, even though Endre was always behind me with the greatest impatience and did not even grant me rest at night, in a friendly form naturally; for he was one of the best friends that I have ever had; it was really about saying to our then enemies: It is no use for you to bomb or destroy the railway junctions on our way to the eastern front, for the consequences have to be borne by your own allies, the Jews – they are indeed your allies, because their general spokesman declared war on us. So leave these things which are of no use to you!

As far as I can remember, the Hungarian gendarmerie never needed to organise such a foot-march again. Today I can no longer declare with absolute certainty if the Jews for the foot-march were rounded up by the Hungarian gendarmerie in the counties or came from the Budapest ghetto. However, I think remembering that there were no evacuations at all from the ghetto, with the exception naturally of those contingents which Kastner diverted to Erez Israel in opportune age-groups, whereby it was naturally not a matter of all Jews of those age-groups; for he could not at all have accommodated these. But I cannot swear if some Hungarian office however did not, without the knowledge of the German offices, remove Jews from the ghetto.

For the foot-march, one of my colleagues was assigned to the Hungarian gendarmerie officer at that time. Following a sort of general staff plan, the marches were calculated for certain kilometre stretches per day, which however were constantly reduced with the increase in the marching days. Appropriate provision and drinking water depots were set up on the Budapest-Vienna highway. If it is said to me now that during this march many Jews were left lying as corpses on the way, I would have certainly learnt that at that time. I never heard anything about it! That one or two people fell out on such a march is explicable. For, on what march is there not someone who falls out?

Even though I do not think that I spoke personally with the Swede Wallenberg, I remember his name. Since I gave free rein to Krumey and did not worry about anything, it is possible that he dealt with Wallenberg on the march provisions and things of that sort for the march. In itself the provisions and equipment for the march were not the task of my office, but they were determined and supplied by the operations department of the Hungarian gendarmerie. If these gave a free hand to Wallenberg, he was indeed the person responsible; but if the Hungarians had a supply officer for it, then it was his duty.

The Jews were expected urgently as a welcome supplementary workforce for the Lower Austrian population, who were managing badly together and with whom, shovel to shovel, they were to dig anti-tank ditches as defensive measures against the expected offensive of the second Ukrainian front. When they arrived at the front, they were received by the Lower Austrian Gauleiter, doubtless according to the defence order.

If it is maintained by the Jewish side that, on 25 November 1944, Standtartenführer Becher, on Kastner's instigation, was able on account of this foot-march to move the SS Reichsführer to issue the order for the discontinuance of the physical liquidation, for the blowing-up of the gas-chambers and for making the commandants of the concentration camps personally responsible for seeing that even sick and frail people should be respected, I can only say to that the author does not speak the truth. I was twice or three times with the SS Reichsführer along with Becher, and already the first time Himmler mentioned that the physical liquidation would be stopped. The foot-march was the last that we undertook; for, already in October, the Soviet shelling of the Hungarian capital was very strong. Around this time, the Russians hammered at the suburbs, with the exception of a few weeks. Then even the evacuations stopped. If the SS Reichsführer had not given his order already, all Hungarian Jews would have been deported; but then the matter of the 10,000 cargo lorries was sufficient for that order. Besides, even today numerous Hungarian Jews live who were supposedly sent to be liquidated. For that we have the proof that my date for that order coincides approximately with Brand's departure; in between were May, June, July, August, September, October; that is six months; in these six months there was some evacuation and then nothing at all for many weeks. Apparently Brand himself writes that I had "disappeared" for months. That is the Jewish "art of discovering the truth", through a quite simple change of date to move the stop-order of the SS Reichsführer to the last possible date, that is, after the foot-march, to arrive at an enormously high number of evacuated Jews.

From where then should we have got a million Jews for the exchange trade? Naturally we would have had far more than a million, but valuable young men were promised to Kastner, and so we needed these to be immediately available and ready for transport in Budapest; in addition, there was a certain "risk figure".

Since it has been read out to me from certain publications that even 14,000 women had to take part in the foot-march, the corpses lined the streets in piles and other nonsense, I feel obliged once again to summarise the entire story of the foot-march in greater detail. Here really too much rubbish has been spoken by people who wish to make themselves interesting for some opportunistic reasons and, after 1945, sought to derive personal advantages for themselves.

When the air fleet of the Allies had destroyed the Györ railway station and many others on this route through bomb attacks, no more transport was possible – either for civil persons or of soldiers and war materials or evacuees. Consequently, even the Jews transferred by the Hungarian executive for evacuation could not be transported. It was ordered by the highest offices of the Hungarian and German side that around 10,000 Jews, be rounded up in the local counties, possibly also a small percentage from the Budapest ghetto, and should be taken by foot-march to the Lower Austrian border; in Lower Austria they were assigned to work-service deployment in the digging of anti-tank trenches. The order came from the Chief of the Sipo and SD to my office, thus through the customary channels; it is obvious that I could never have issued such an order on my own responsibility! Who first expressed the idea of the foot-march I no longer know; but it is possible that it was me. We had at that time to find a solution; for I was responsible to the SS Reichsführer for seeing to it that Hungary – at first placed immediately behind the battle front, later itself a war-zone – did not in any way become a "large partisan territory" insofar as it was a question of the Jewish partisan danger. Clearly Himmler had learnt from the terrible events in Warsaw and recognised the danger of a determined enemy willing to do everything possible against us.

I therefore set this contingent of Jews marching according to orders. It may have been some 180 km from Budapest to the border. The marching plan was discussed thoroughly in advance with the commander of the Hungarian gendarmerie; the details were conveyed to the relevant officer in charge among the Hungarians, Major Ferenczy. The daily marches were divided into at first longer, later ever shorter kilometre marches. I think that we calculated that, in 10-12 days, the head of the column should reach the Hungarian-Burgenland border. The Hungarian gendarmerie established provision depots in the respective overnight stations. The most possible care was taken in sanitary and hygienic respects. Naturally, we were living in war times and had no great claims to demand a high living standard. In spite of the emergency situation, further sharpened by the transport chaos and the destruction of the most important transport possibilities, everything that was possible was undertaken to send this procession of ten thousand to the Burgenland border. *I personally once drove along the stretch and can confirm that I saw only two corpses, those of old Jews, on the entire stretch.*

What of the "forced marches" after 1945, when incomparably larger contingents of Germans from the east were "evacuated"? Were any provision depots, sanitary and hygienic installations, set up considerately for these Germans after the completion of the daily march? Who did that? German thoroughness ordered that for the foot-march of the Jews at the end of 1944, so that the Hungarian gendarmerie carried it out according to the agreed plan.

It was fourteen years ago that I was first asked about the exact number of that contingent. Naturally, I cannot declare with certainty 10,000, it could also have been 15,000; but in any case I can authoritatively declare that it was in no way above 20,000, perhaps below 15,000. When these contingents arrived at the border, they were not, as originally agreed with the WVHA and the travel plan office, loaded onto trains, but taken over by the local group leaders, to help German women, children and old people dig anti-tank ditches with spades. The Gauleiter of Lower Austria took care of the provisions.

In this way, and not differently, did this episode transpire. It has however been connected with a lot of other things by the "fortune-hunting" authors of the post-war period because it seemed somehow opportune to them. Perhaps they calculated that all the participants were dead or the survivors had to scrape out an existence wretchedly and preferred to be silent. Today the time has come when I can speak about it.

So, for example, in November 1944 I wanted to have the Budapest ghetto evacuated – at least 200,000 person. On the basis of the Warsaw experiences, this ghetto stood under the strictest control and could not indeed become dangerous as a resistance breeding-ground. Certainly, the Arrow Cross people, above all Secretary of State Dr. Endre, would have seen the disappearance of the Budapest ghetto sooner rather than later, but the SS Reichsführer would never have issued an order for such a senseless measure. At the time in question, an evacuation of such masses was in general no longer to be thought of; as little could it be taken into consideration for some "exchange business" since even Jewish circles had to realise that the catastrophic transport situation in Hungary prohibited something like that. To send 200,000 or even only 100,000 persons on a foot-march would have been utter madness; for they would have all perished on the way. One can ask anybody who has already had practical experience with human masses under the most adverse circumstances, for example, my Soviet colleague, General Serov,[47] who would purely professionally have to agree with me in this matter, or the deportation experts of a Tito or the experts who worked in the territory of Czechoslovakia; they will all confirm the same thing.

If now I am told that, during this seven-day march, 1,200 men, among them also eighty-year-old women, died, this figure would have made up some 10% of all those taking part. The march, which I had carried out on orders received, naturally showed a fraction of a percent of natural losses. The foot-march was prepared in every detail and cost me much more work than if I had to organise five hundred transport trains to Auschwitz. We had to demonstrate that, in spite of the destructions of our railway transport lines, we were determined to carry out our systematic plan, in a form which was suited to the situation created by the Allies. The senior SS and Police chiefs or even the Reich plenipotentiary Veesenmayer informed me that these routes were bombarded to stop the Jewish transport.

---

47   Serov, Soviet General, MVD, responsible for deportations. Ivan Serov (1905-90) was head of the KGB between 1954 and 1958 and of the GRU (Soviet foreign military intelligence) between 1958 and 1963. He organised the deportations of Hungarians after the Hungarian revolution of 1956.

The Deportations From Abroad

The order said that only persons capable of marching were to be picked out; for us those who were capable of marching were the age-group of 16-50, and under certain circumstances also up to 60 years of age, for, according to one's energy, a forty-year-old may not be able to march but perhaps a sixty-year-old can. What the Hungarian gendarmerie understood by capable of marching did not have to interest the German offices. In the counties I had my advisers who were at the disposal of the Hungarian gendarmerie; these forwarded the order of the SS Reichsführer in all its details; that meant that in the Hungarian territory, as everywhere avoidable harshness's were to be avoided. I remember precisely that I had demanded for the foot-march expressly only persons capable of marching, that further the senior SS and Police Chief in Hungary, General Winkelmann, personally travelled along the stretch as, moreover, also the Hungarian Secretary of State, Dr. Endre, and certainly many others, even Höß and possibly SS Obergruppenführer Jütner. Many gentlemen of the WVHA inspected this march because it was originally planned to load this march on German soil and make it available to the WVHA. But when I hear now that Obergruppenführer Jüttner explained in Nuremberg that he saw columns of Jewish women, up to sixty years old, lying on the street and the senior SS and Police Chief Winkelmann had said to him that he was powerless and Eichmann alone was responsible, then I wish to declare regarding that: If a report of Jüttner's really exists and is not a lie, I can only say that I understand not a word of it: What is said there flouts every truth. It would have made my superior Gruppenführer Müller gasp if this foot-march had been a fiasco. Not once from the very sensitive Chief of the Security Service, Dr. Kaltenbrunner, did I ever hear even the least complaint. General of the Police, Winkelmann, himself of a sensitive nature, also likewise did not make the least representation to me; and none of them would make himself so ridiculous as to maintain that he had been placed somewhat "under pressure" by Obersturmbannführer Eichmann. According to rank and office, I had to click my heels before these people.

If one wishes to brand me a "Caligula", then the period before the end of the war is chosen most unfavourably; all these gentlemen strike themselves with their own hands if they wish to maintain that they had allowed themselves to be tyrannised in the least, before 1945, by an Obersturmbannführer, Eichmann, by a departmental head. What nonsense that they were "powerless" with regard to me! Never in my life did I have a written special power of the SS Reichsführer or of the Chief of the Sipo, I had nothing special at all. But within the humble official scope of my rank I always worked one hundred percent, thought through everything and with a demand of precise implementation. I carried out my service exactly and correctly, so that Gruppenführer Müller once said to me: "If we had had 50 Eichmanns, then we would win the war automatically!" That was not based on the substantial losses of the enemy because I had nothing to do with it, but strictly on implementation ability and unconditional loyalty in the implementation of received orders.

And so I cannot at all understand that there were German officers who quibbled over received orders and interpreted them as it suited them. With that we were sure to lose the war, and so it is understandable also that, already since the victory parade of Bock on the Champs Elysées, I was pessimistically inclined. One thing is certain: the SS Reichsführer never called me to account on the basis of the foot-march, as little did the Chief of the Sipo or my immediate superior, the police general Winkelmann. Reich plenipotentiary Dr. Veesenmayer as well as Dr. Endre congratulated me on the good implementation. I can indeed remember that, on account of all sorts of interferences, I gave, in a sonorous voice which I can sometimes adopt, and in an emphatic manner, the proofs that this or that statement was false. Then it did not matter to me if the person concerned was a Gruppenführer or Obergruppenführer. In spite of all the other discipline and subordination, I could denounce injustice with the strength of my conviction and my standpoint of justice. But these people, who represented higher ranks and offices, would never have allowed such a tone to arise if I had not been able to demonstrate to them with police precision that their information – mostly from hearsay – was false and incorrect. I could fall into almost the same rage even today if I think back on it.

I ask: Why then did they not institute any proceedings against this small Obersturmbannführer and small departmental head in the RSHA? Proceedings could indeed have been started easily at that time against somebody on account of some small matter by high, and the highest, of ranks; it would have been very easy for the senior SS and Police Chief Winkelmann and even for the commanding officer of the Sipo and SD, Standartenführer Geschke. Why was I congratulated instead?

Whether sick persons were kept back on this foot-march to Budapest I do not know; that is completely possible. I demanded of the advance commando of the Hungarian gendarmerie that daily marches be adhered to and always to obtain overnight stay possibilities. Naturally, that did not mean that Pullman mattresses were supplied; for, after all, the eastern front fighters had been fighting already for years without having warm food in their stomach. "Immediate work deployment" of these people in the anti-tank ditch construction did not mean that the men from the foot-march who arrived at 10 o'clock took a shovel in their hand at 10.15. What actually happened was upon their arrival, they were first separated. Then the Gau leadership provided food, and only then were the work implements taken up. In this way a long span of time passed before the first spade would dig up soil – in any case, much more time than hundred thousand eastern and western front fighters had in order to get some fresh air between arrival and immediate battle deployment, and in any case much more time than remained to the German women, children and old people driven together with a bayonet in just occupied villages and cities before *their* work deployment. It is the sheerest nonsense if it is maintained now that I threatened Wisliceny with court-martial on the basis of the return of a large number of sick people to Budapest. Thereby it was in no way a matter of deportations but of defence service against the pressing Red Army. So it is also absurd to maintain that Wisliceny had had a large number of sick Jews returned to Budapest during this march for work-deployment. What should sick Jews do in the digging of anti-tank ditches?

One who wishes to maintain that the foot-march had been a crime against humanity I can only counter with the fact that, in that, we allowed ourselves to be led by the example which the enemy gave us. The Jews were among these, for they had, through their highest spokesman, Dr. Chaim Weizmann, first declared war against us. The examples of the enemy determined the harshness of our measures – *at that time we heard how corpses of German women and girls were discovered between whose thighs the bases of wine-bottles still stuck out. At that time, we did not lie any more! At that time, we were no longer squeamish; we no longer worked with glacé gloves. At that time, everything was ordered, calculated and carried out. That I would like to have confirmed in this context.*

I repeat that Endre remained in office until our departure from Hungary; I visited him often in his Ministry, even in July and August 1944. In the summer – perhaps in mid-summer – he married, I remember. I also visited Endre during the time when I waited on the horse-farm of the Bechers for the deployment at the Romanian-Hungarian border area for the purpose of the evacuation of the ethnic Germans, that is, on the occasion of my travel to Berlin which passed through Budapest. When I obtained the Iron Cross for the liberation of the army hospital in New Arad I was also with Endre. Endre then rented a house close to me. At that time, the Soviet bombers were attacking Budapest, then I was often at Endre's, because he wished to be informed of the military situation. In the Ministry, Endre had a rack standing with two or three suits, as I ascertained at this time, summer 1944, and there was no question of an "abdication".

In September/October I had to vacate my house, which, I think, was on Utnov Street, to accommodate one of the senior army officers, and I received a sort of summer house which belonged to someone from the Manfred Weiß concern, significantly smaller, but that was not important to me. In this house I arranged a meeting to which General Winkelmann and Secretaries of State Dr. Endre and Baky, who still had their office and status, were invited, and also a baron, representative of the BMW works, Krumey, perhaps also Wisliceny, Dr. Geschke, the personal secretary of Dr. Endre and Peter from the Hungarian Secret State Police. But I had no hostess and therefore requested an aristocrat to perform these functions. She was the owner of a large steel mill which the army was to explode because it lay in the field of fire of the artillery; for this reason she did not accept my invitation at that time. All that must have been in 1944. I had no mistress in Budapest, as it is always represented so "finely"; perhaps I went out sometimes to dinner with a nice acquaintance, with whom however I never had intimate relations. On my search for a hostess for the mentioned evening I obtained one in the person of the charming bride of the representative of the German Information Service.

I relate all this so fully because it happened precisely during the time when – according to the post-war literature – Baky and Endre were supposed to have been shunted off on a "sidetrack". Perhaps Endre related to me that he occasionally had difficulties with his own countrymen, but because I never worried about Hungarian internal matters, I remember just as little the supposed "disarmament" of the Hungarian gendarmerie. It is right that Endre once made a two-week trip to Germany, but normally we met almost every evening, with Baky once a week. So I still know that a son of Endre's received the Golden Bravery Medal; if Endre really had had difficulties, he would not have hidden anything from me.

It may have been midsummer 1944 when the Jewish council of elders of Budapest came to me – with long faces; for some of their members had fled over the green border to Romania. In depressed tones they reported this to me and clearly expected at least a collective punishment. And I said to them: "Sirs, one who has "absconded" has "absconded" ... we cannot do anything about that ... It is not at all a matter of one person more or less ... If they are lucky and go over the border, then they should continue and keep going"; and therewith the matter was for me at an end. Apparently my conversation partners were stunned by this decision. Such decisions had the consequence that the enemy never knew how he stood at the moment with me, and could never feel very secure. Of course, Kastner, Löwenherz, Eppstein, etc. always knew; for they had spoken with me during hundreds of negotiations, so naturally they knew me.

Sometime later I had to visit the Chief of the Hungarian Gendarmerie for official reasons; I no longer know if I was ordered there or had myself requested a conversation through Lieutenant Colonel Ferenczy as a sort of liaison officer. Between Ferenczy and also his adjutant, Captain of the Gendarmerie Nagy, a primitive but faithful servant of his lieutenant colonel, and me there existed a very warm relationship. With the BDS[48] Dr. Geschke I was once invited to Ferenczy's vineyard estate, where a sort of snack in Hungarian style was offered to us consisting of pieces of meat and lard, and, with that, onions that were skewered on rods. The wine came from the vineyard of the lieutenant colonel; Nagy served us. So it was easy for me, through Ferenczy's mediation, to be allowed into the house of the Chief of the Hungarian Gendarmerie. I still remember his study, sober in its furniture maintained in a style that lay 30 or 40 years in the past. The gendarmerie in Hungary was an elite corps exactly as in the former Czechoslovakia. When I entered, the chief stood up, embraced me with genuine Hungarian enthusiasm, and informed me in an effusive way that, after the victorious war, certainly the time would come when a monument would be erected to me in a public square. Now, I knew the Magyars, and myself had relatives in Hungary; in their enthusiasm they are unrestrainable. But, nevertheless, I was surprised to hear that he went over a few days later to the Soviets and enemy leaflets showed his likeness on one side and, on the other, the invitation to surrender and to resistance against the German "occupation power". Such things also happened.

---

48   Commanding Officer of the Security Police and Security Service.

The Eichmann Tapes

In contrast, it made a deep impression on me when I heard of the fate of the father of my good friend Endre. It may have been around the same time – September/October 1944 – when the Russians pressed forward towards the region where his parental property lay. The old magnate was requested to flee and to take himself to safety, but he refused; he went once again on his fields and then shot a bullet into his heart, because he would not bend, as he said, to the "Jewish tyranny of the east", but rather wished to lie on his own land. His son refused to kill himself like his father; for he was a pious Catholic. He allowed himself to be taken prisoner instead of fleeing to German territory, because he did not wish to leave Hungarian soil. These convinced Hungarian patriots preferred to die on Magyar soil. He was hanged.

The situation in Budapest became increasingly more chaotic, the pressure of the Soviets stronger by the day. One day my friend Zehender, Chief of the 22nd SS Cavalry Division, ran out of munitions. He lay on the eastern border of the city, his division's command post was in the immediate vicinity of the tramway final stop; his supplies depot many kilometres to the west, his munitions depots also. He knew that the Russians were preparing for an attack on his division, but could not intervene because he had nothing more to fire, even though he had gathered together everything that he could scrape up – and that was a hundred pipes within his division. In view of his desperation, I made a proposal to him of forming a human chain from his munitions depot to the tramway with some thousand Jews, passing grenades, loading them into the trams and in this way transporting them to the eastern final station, where a command of the division could pick them up. I think that he discussed this also with Kastner. My colleagues were deployed, and a five or six hundred-long chain of Jews was formed; in an astonishingly short time one loaded tram after another travelled right across Budapest to Zehender. Full of joy, he said to me that he could now "explode a hundred pipes" and did not need any more to save munitions.

From the hostile post-war literature I have learnt that the "Eichmann Einsatzgruppe" was to take up 90,000 Jews to some brick-yards in August 1944 and that diplomatic protests prevented this. To that I can only say again that the entire literature which appeared from the ill-fated days of 1945 up to today represents a hotchpotch of fiction and truth. There never was an "Eichmann Einsatzgruppe", one only spoke of an "Eichmann special command"; about the taking of any Jews to some brick-yards I can only repeat that, in Hungary, German police officers were not in control but the Hungarian executive. The

Hungarian gendarmerie, associations of the Arrow Cross people, could "undertake" something within the Hungarian territory without my being able to intervene. If I was informed, that happened subsequently, but the Hungarian government was not obliged to inform the senior SS and Police chiefs or even me of everything that they planned in terms of police measures. It was not my affair if and which Jews the Arrow Cross people, the Hungarian gendarmerie or the Hungarian police listed, allotted or liquidated. My special command according to its commission – I cannot repeat that often enough – to free the Hungarian territory of those elements which, according to the opinion of my superiors, could, through their remaining further, make Hungary and especially eastern Hungary into a partisan area of the first rank immediately behind the front, whereby it was a matter of getting this group of people from the Hungarian government itself for evacuation. That was my order. I would never have been able to carry out even a single rounding up action with my few men.

My activity consisted especially in administration work. Beyond that, I obtained from the Reich Transport Ministry the trains for the transport and allotted to them at any time a regular police force of around 30 men as guard. What local precautions or measures the Hungarian offices took up to the loading did not interest me; I was also not involved in it in any way; for it was a question of a sovereign country.

I had a good relationship with the commanding officer of the Sipo and SD in Budapest, Dr. Geschke, but nobody, even no Hungarian office, had the least idea of that. Because my special command was relatively large, it demanded its own spacious building, whereas the immediate aides of the Commanding Officer of the Sipo and SD with a five or six man personnel could naturally be accommodated in a few rooms within the building of the BDS.

I explain bluntly that I lost control in Budapest in October 1944. That happened the moment no more evacuations could take place and therefore my responsibility for everything that was connected with it diminished; for indeed I did not have the least responsibility for other measures in Hungary. There were no more rounding-ups, and transports, because there did not exist any travel-plan any more; the trains ran irregularly, the Russians fired into Budapest, advanced once up to Csepel and were thrown back again in a short time, but then the ring around Budapest drew ever tighter. I still know that Standartenführer Becher took away at that time very many valuable materials, silver objects and such, from Hungary; whereto I do not know. In these last months, Becher drew my areas of responsibility ever more to himself – he had from the start striven to take the Jewish matter from my hands. He did not succeed fully in that; for he could not give any State Police instruction; no office would have accepted an order from him. The petty official may accept instructions for his field of responsibility if it is clear to him that they come from his official superior, but never from a person standing outside. Becher got involved everywhere; for example, he conducted negotiations with the Jews, so that I often inquired of Gruppenführer Müller in relation to this if Becher was authorised to do this. Here Himmler himself was to blame. He was somewhat unsteady in his decisions; it could happen that one heard in the forenoon a certain decision, which however was changed or turned to its opposite a couple of days later through another relating to the same matter. Himmler also often personally decided in individual cases and in this way overturned any general ordinance that he himself had issued. It was enormously difficult to find one's bearings in the different decisions of the SS Reichsführer; a talented man like Becher was able to get sometimes this and at other times that concession. Just the fact that Himmler dealt with Becher on Jewish matters meant a further decentralising of the treatment of the Jewish problem in Hungary. I had no control at all on what Becher negotiated with Kastner and other functionaries. Conversely, Becher also had no control over my negotiations; for I was not at all instructed to inform Becher of all my measures and discussions. I had a very good relationship with Becher, but I was once extremely annoyed with him, and indeed in the case of the already mentioned "theatrical act" in front of Kastner and his colleagues, because Becher in his feigned outburst of rage encroached on State Police matters and imputed measures to the Gestapo which in no way fell within our responsibility, and this in the presence of the enemy.

If I now hear that, on 1 September 1944, Kastner had obtained from me approval for a journey to Switzerland, that is completely possible; but I do not remember that and even less that a Hauptsturmführer accompanied him. Kastner had not only the permission to travel abroad when it seemed opportune to him for his efforts regarding the Jewish emigration, but he could also send Brand and other colleagues abroad. This happened in so many cases that I cannot recall this or that particular occasion. If Kastner travelled with Becher to Prague to meet Jewish delegates there I no longer know; but my consent could hardly have been solicited for that since this would have exceeded the scope of my powers. Becher could have obtained the approval directly from the SS Reichsführer; but in this case I would have at least heard

Soviet soldiers capture Hungarian troops, Budapest, December 1944.

something about it, especially since some important decision for the Hungarian Jews might have resulted. I repeat that I myself worried about only everything essential, my regular representative Krumey, on the other hand, about the details. Occasionally I was aware of these too, if I had signed them myself. The chief task of my deputation to Hungary consisted in accomplishing the rounding up of the Jews of this country by its own government and in motivating the central authorities. This demanded a teeming mass of preparatory work such as, for example, numerous conferences so that, from the start, all the details, insofar as they generally fell within the responsibility of IV-B4, lay with Krumey.

Naturally, I remember the "acquisition of foreign exchange" well; as I already reported, Kastner came to my office one day in the company of one or two Jews with heavy crates full of foreign exchange for the information department of the Commanding Officer of the Sipo and SD. At that time, I wondered that suddenly all possible offices had been involved in this "business"; even the army defence perhaps had discussions with Kastner, perhaps even with Wisliceny. It was naturally inevitable that the Hungarian Secret State Police, whose office lay only a few steps away from mine, discovered the apparently mysterious processes and that their leaders were involved doubtless with the knowledge of their superiors. I learnt from Kastner that he supplied foreign exchange to the Hungarian Gestapo.

Whether emigration permissions were sold to Slovak Jews in Hungary whose proceeds were destined for the family support of Waffen SS members I do not know; if it was a matter of a commission of Becher's I cannot anyway have been informed of it, as I have already explained, even if I also knew generally that he made many economic or financial agreements, and was also for a while, to a certain extent, a trustee of the Czepel works of the Weiß concern, where he diverted wares for the SS but certainly not of his own accord. I had nothing to do with that; for me it was sufficient to know that Becher also had to deal with Jews on a high-level mission.

Naturally, I was aware that Kastner was "tapped" from many sides. At first he reported everything to me, perhaps out of fear that he was being watched. In fact I had not had Kastner watched for even a single hour. In his different efforts to exploit his contacts and his mediation I gave him a free hand, but warned him of "subterfuges" and reminded him of his chief task of worrying about the accommodation of the Hungarian Jews. Kastner was moreover much too cautious to expose himself; on the other hand, I never heard, either at that time in Hungary or later, that any of our people had enriched himself personally through Kastner or other Jews; such a thing would have reached my ears, since the different offices were interwoven with one another in many ways so that someone somewhere would certainly have talked about it.

In Budapest, there lay a small German flotilla of the navy. Inexplicably somebody in the army heard that I had an intention of crossing the Danube with my amphibious vehicle some time. In any case, the chief of this flotilla offered to give me one or two safeguard boats. After I had determined in this way that already a certain group of people knew of my plan, I gave it up and limited myself thereafter to testing the vehicle in a small pond.

To comment further on the "reports" from the post-war literature: It is not true that Endre and Baky were dismissed at the end of 1944 from the government service. Endre was certainly secretary of state until 24 December 1944 when I left the city; I even heard rumours that he had become Foreign Minister. When I left, there was no underground movement in Hungary. No Jew would have dared to raise even a knife, let alone a firearm.

Some days before Christmas Eve, the entire German police received the order to move to Ödenburg.[49] Only one unit of the Gestapo under the leadership of a Sturmbannführer and government councillor was to remain in Budapest on the ordinance of the SS Reichsführer. I wanted to spend a couple of hours more with my friend Zehender of the 22nd SS Cavalry Division instead of waiting inactively in Ödenburg for further orders from Berlin. In Budapest, a desperate resistance was organised. Units of the Hungarian regular police, the gendarmerie, the Honved troops, the 8th and 22nd SS Cavalry divisions and the Gestapo Major with his unit were all involved.

As a symbol Himmler ordered the continued presence of the SS and police units in the Budapest castle. They all fell, even my friend and comrade Zehender; fighting with a submachine gun as the commanding officer of the division, he was fatally shot in the vicinity of the castle. Later I learnt of the anxiety of the police because I was considered for a while to be missing. With my chauffeur I remained until three o'clock in the afternoon on Christmas Eve 1944 in Budapest and then departed as the last member of the German police. For days an unbroken trek of civilians had already congested the streets up to the last square metre from Budapest in the direction of Vienna. Without warning the Red Army burst out, not from the east to Budapest but through the Schwabenberg. The street leading to Ödenburg lay under constant fire.

It was a very beautiful full-moon night on Christmas Eve 1944. Everything was covered in snow. On the street there stood a car in the middle of the road which blocked it. I went to the car and wanted to shout at the driver because he was blocking the street. I opened the door – a Honved soldier, dead and heavy, fell against me. I was shaken. My chauffeur was perhaps a hundred steps away, I was alone with the dead man and I set him back in the driver's seat. He was already frozen stiff. I banged the door shut. The saying of Götz[50] - "Me surrender?" gave me courage. Then I said to my chauffeur: "There is a dead soldier sitting in there, we must drive around through the field".

---

49   Sopron, in Hungary

50   Goethe's first version of his drama *Götz von Berlichingen* (1773) contained a saying of Götz's that is to be found in his autobiography: "Me surrender? ... Tell your captain ... he can lick my arse." The editions of the play after 1774 truncated the last sentence.

The Eichmann Tapes

I already pointed out that the Hungarian gendarmerie partially did not adhere to our deportation regulations which demanded that all avoidable harshness's should be avoided. On account of some Hungarian transports in very bad condition there were vehement protests of the camp commandant to which, I replied: I clarified that rounding up and the organisation of transport fell under the responsibility of the autonomous Hungarian government, but that I would approach Secretary of State Endre. The transport escort personnel were instructed to take care of the hygiene and sanitary arrangements, for which however the Hungarians, as I must stress once again, were responsible.

Around 130,000 inhabitants were in the beginning sent to the Budapest ghetto by the Arrow Cross people, but the number rose constantly until it reached around 200,000 because of a strong influx from the surrounding counties who wished to avoid the grasp of the gendarmerie. From here, as mentioned, there were hardly any evacuations; however, the Hungarian executive seems to have occasionally taken some Jews out without our knowledge in order to fill the transports. Moreover, Kastner looked here for a majority of his illegal Jewish emigrants who were then sent to a special camp; besides, I had to have ready at call, even here, a certain contingent for the oft-mentioned exchange business.

If Brand maintains in his book that only about a quarter of all Hungarian Jews survived the war, this figure is really too low: we can today ascertain how many supposedly "gassed Jews" are still present; indeed it is often enough sarcastically remarked: "There goes another gassed Jew!" I myself bought after the war beer and angora wool mostly from "gassed Jews". Without being able to prove it, I would like rather to suppose that – *at a very high calculation! around a quarter of the so-called 500,000 Jews could have died, three fourths however are still living.*

If one takes 500,000 as the base and in addition assumes that they had all been evacuated, then 125,000 would be a quarter of this number; *but it is fully impossible that, between at the earliest the middle of May 1944 and 8 July, the day that the hostile sources cite as the departure date of the last transport train from Hungary, thus in somewhat more than 50 days, 434,000 persons (according to the same sources!) could be transported.* Then daily, including Saturday and Sunday, 10,000 and more must have been transported. Moreover the large majority survived.

It was a regulation that escort personnel of 25 to 30 men accompany every deportation train. I had around 250 men at my disposal. If the figures of the hostile sources were right, I must have had a thousand men at my disposal – a sheer nonsense! Even the commanding officer of the Regular Police in Hungary would have been lucky if he had a thousand men at his disposal for such a task. Even a large reserve of trains would have been necessary; for, while the first people journeyed, more would already have had to be loaded. From Hungary to Auschwitz they took two days; thus two days to and some two days back – it was my constant battle to obtain trains in general, still more in the decisive days of the war of early summer 1944, where just the invasion and the Soviet offensive made that number of free trains fully impossible, even if one reckons that every train would have journeyed with a maximum of 3,000 men. What the post-war literature taken together says about Hungarian evacuation figures is therefore more than nonsensical. Even today it can be very easily ascertained in the files of the Reich Transport Ministry that at most 250,000 to 300,000 Jews in total were evacuated to Auschwitz as the final station.

The implementation of the transports extended, in my memory, not over seven weeks, but over some four months, and that was, considering the difficulties existing then, already an astonishingly short time for the human masses in question. But even in this time period it was impossible to transport the supposed 450,000 or even 434,000 persons since there were often no trains. As soon as the transports reached the Auschwitz final station, they were no longer my responsibility; the German escort team of the Regular Police packed their bags and travelled back on the next train to Budapest to their garrison. If I estimate 300,000 as the evacuation figure, then that is a very high absolute maximum. It can be clearly ascertained who among those were still alive in 1945 at the end of the war, but who would compile such a list?

If I should give a round figure for the Hungarian Jews sent to a final solution, whereby *"final solution"* refers *naturally* as much to *illegal transports, illegally approved emigration, unobstructed escape and life in ghettos*, I would estimate that at half a million. For a fit person without any great baggage – whether a Jew or non-Jew – it was absolutely not difficult to flee over the Hungarian-Romanian border, as is the case with other borders; we did not prevent this; for, *anyone who was outside our territory was "finally solved"*. Apart from the 200,000 ghetto Jews, one can reckon also around 100,000 Jews living scattered in the counties and in hiding who were not evacuated.

Today, I estimate that the last transports left for Auschwitz in September 1944, but already long before, and beginning with the order of the SS Reichsführer that a million of Jews were to be exchanged for 10,000 cargo lorries, Himmler discontinued the physical liquidation, because the inmates were first deployed for work and second had to stand in readiness in case Brand's mission led to success.

If Brand actually left on 15 May 1944 and it is certain that, on 5 May, the first travel-plan discussion for the evacuation took place, the first transport cannot have left before the middle of May; then somewhere in the second half of the month of May the order of the SS Reichsführer to halt the physical liquidation was issued. *And this order Himmler did not revoke until the end of the war.*

Young Jewish girl and children in the Lodz Ghetto, Poland.

WOHNGEBIET DER
JUDEN
BETRETEN
VERBOTEN

An auxiliary Jewish police force kept order in the Lodz Ghetto.

IV

After the End of My Deportations

The Changed Situation in Berlin

When I returned from Hungary to Berlin, I received unpleasant news regarding my Jewish functionaries. From 1938 to 1945 I had as a regular representative an extraordinarily reliable comrade, a man of bee-like industry who read through hundreds of files in hours-long painstaking work and daily dictated fifty to sixty letters. During the party's battle-time he had had a difficult time; his entire body showed the marks of different fights. He was hard and forbade to himself any personal approach to the Jews, whom he held always "at an arm's distance", as his own people too did, besides. The orders he issued came in a barrack yard tone, clear and hard, even though he never spoke loudly. He hardly tolerated contradiction.

In 1938 he came to me in Vienna as Hauptsturmführer and was later promoted just once to Sturmbannführer; a refusal to marry prevented further promotion. In an SS leaders' school he won an arrow bordered in red which was to be attached to the armband, whose exact significance I do not know. Even though he was a Hauptsturmführer, and I was at that time still Obersturmführer, he was allotted to me already in 1938 as regular representative and remained that, on the ordinance of the Chief of the Sipo and SD, also later in Berlin. We could not choose our regular representatives ourselves but were allotted them. During this visit to the "Central Office for Jewish Emigration" Heydrich had spoken to and examined not only me but also him.

There was no more an expert than him and therefore he was recognised even by the old police officials who were "wed" to their files. If a government official with eighteen or twenty years of service in his central authority office recognises a colleague not from the police then that means a great deal. He had worked all the years under my thumb as well as that of his immediate superior. As a consequence of my commission to Hungary, he was now independent for several months. He used my absence to dismiss many of my closest Jewish colleagues including commercial councillor Storfer. I heard of this in autumn 1944 during a short stay in Auschwitz. The camp commandant Höß related to me that an inmate called Storfer had appeared often referring to the fact that he was a close colleague of mine. He wished that I be informed immediately, for I would certainly not be in accord with his present situation.

I had him come immediately. Storfer arrived beaming with joy, and I asked him: "Yes, my friend, what then are you doing here?" Then he explained to me: "Obersturmbannführer, I made a mistake; I wished to escape because you were no longer there and I got scared. Thereupon I was caught. But you know however that I have never done anything bad and always did my work." I explained to Höß that Storfer had always worked with me in an orderly and good way without ever betraying another Jew. It was very hard to be released from a concentration camp ever since the order of the SS Reichsführer was issued, so I requested Höß to give Storfer only easy work and respectable food, and I promised to apply to the Chief of the Sipo and SD in Vienna, Dr. Ebner, to get him released. Storfer further complained that he was in a room with a couple of hundred men and suffered at night from anxiety. He requested to be able to sleep alone. Höß allowed that too, for he was in no way the suggested "brutal concentration camp commandant" but he had a human understanding for human needs. Naturally, he was bound by his orders; if I had by chance to fill his post, I would have also adhered to the same orders. Höß had Storfer do only light cleaning work with a broom and sleep alone in some corner. At that time I thought to myself that nothing much would befall him anymore; the yard work could not harm him, and he was to receive respectable food. Höß made me this promise in the presence of his retinue; they also saw how I gave Storfer my hand, spoke to him in a friendly way and encouraged him, with a pat on his shoulder, to be courageous.

Dr. Eppstein was the almost Prussian lawyer who spoke succinctly and was chairman of the Reich association. In Theresienstadt with its very mild supervision control I needed a hard Jewish hand, a man who was capable of leading a mass organisation and to show character even with regard to me. The "Reich Association of Jews" had become almost insignificant; therefore I sent Dr. Eppstein to Theresienstadt to take up the leadership there along with Rabbi Dr. Baeck, the Austrian general Sommer, Murmelstein and others. When I came from Hungary through Prague, I heard that Eppstein had been transferred to Auschwitz at the behest of my regular representative.

It may have been some issue which caused my regular representative, as the representative in charge with the corresponding authority, to get rid of those persons with whom I had worked all those years, precisely during my single long absence from the office, and without asking me. I think that my superior Gruppenführer Müller, who is even today very respected by me, was completely capable of playing this "trick" on me because my way of dealing with and treating the Jews was not pleasant to him. My regular representative could naturally not decide such sorts of matters by himself but channelled it through Gruppenführer Müller.

If I had been in Berlin, I would have had the entire matter revoked after consultation with Müller. When I learnt *that not only Dr. Eppstein but also Storfer, Weiman and Edelstein from Prague had been shot in Auschwitz*, I did not hold back my rage either before my regular representative nor before Gruppenführer Müller. As "reason" for it I was told that now – that is, at the beginning of 1945 – the situation corresponded to my lasting pessimism and that these Jewish functionaries with whom I had worked for so long, "knew too much" and therefore had to die. My answer to that was: "There are hundreds of other Jews who know the same thing; for everything indeed is recorded in file notes in the Jewish religious community in the 'Reich Association' everywhere! The entire working staff of these people know exactly as much as they." Besides, I emphasised that the promise given to the enemy could not be broken; I always kept my promises towards the Jews: now to these people I had promised that they would remain free and emigrate, just as I also promised and enabled emigration to Palestine to Dr. Rothenburg, or fulfilled Dr. Löwenherz's request to be able to go to his wife in England. Now it was too late and it was a great vexation to me.

I had worked with Dr. Eppstein from 1935 to 1943, around eight years, and with Storfer from 1938 to 1944, that is six years. Naturally, it was a different situation than 1942/43; for the Russians had advanced on Vienna at the end of 1944, much was relaxed in view of the menacing situation; only in this way can I explain that my regular

Dr. Eppstein Jewish community elder of Theresienstadt, was in Eichmann's absence, shot on 27 September 1944. His wife was killed in Auschwitz in October 1944.

representative could "tend to" his "worries" on account of my Jewish colleagues who "knew too much", and thereby get rid of some of them through an act that I considered to be arbitrary. My department knew no arbitrariness, and therefore I felt openly rebuffed. Doubtless executions took place at that time in different concentration camps, but my regular representative could naturally not give an instruction to this effect to any concentration camp, and I also as divisional head could not have done so. Gruppenführer Müller signed a decree on that and it was forwarded to the WVHA.

The Surrender is Foreshadowed

At this time there came to my office a letter from the Personnel Head Office or perhaps of the SS Leadership Head Office, but certainly not from the RSHA, which was sent out to all SS chiefs with an attachment of six or eight pages in large format with around 60 questions. The letter said that the addressed officer would certainly be surprised to deal with such a matter when, according to the order of the SS leadership, only work important for the war was to be settled and everything else put off until the end of the war. Further, it said that the SS Reichsführer was convinced of the enormous importance of this questionnaire and, for reasons which were explained in details that I no longer remember, it was imperatively important to answer these questions exactly and to return them at a given time through official channels. Along with me, many other SS chiefs flung this letter to a corner of the desk in an initial outburst of rage; but after some days, I then pulled this form out and set about filling it in. On the questionnaire everything was listed: birth, parental status, number of children, promotion dates, date of award of the Death's Head Ring of the SS Reichsführer[1], of the dagger, sword, work assignment, commands, foreign travel - in short everything. Already at that time I pondered over this remarkable matter, but anyway it did indeed come from one's own associates.

When I later heard that the enemy was very well informed about the life of every individual SS chief, I had doubts and I said to myself that the concerned office had doubtless rendered a service to the enemy. The opposite can hardly be proved. There remains no other explanation; for, according to orders, we had to lay aside more important things as not important for the war in order to avoid waste of paper and personnel as well as unnecessary claims of individual SS chiefs.

This questionnaire, whose answering cost many hours, was only possible if someone of a high rank had made the matter plausible to the SS Reichsführer, perhaps with a suggestion that files of the SS Führer would be lost in a bomb-attack or something. So the SS Reichsführer allowed himself to be "lulled". I cannot with the best will in the world imagine it differently, and I openly express my personal conjecture. When I heard that in this way the files fell into the hands of the enemy, I thought that it must indeed be investigated as should the tatooing of the blood-group on the arm of SS men was "suggested" long in advance.

Some months before the end of the war, it hit me like a blow that my personal friend Ebner, Sipo officer from Vienna, had been sentenced to death. He was an incredibly good-natured, tender hearted man, for whom all hardness of soul was abhorrent and who suffered personally under every energetic measure which he had to order. I visited him once on my travel through Vienna; on this occasion he related to me that the actor Hans Moser[2] who was much loved by us wanted to meet his wife, who was a Jewess; he lived separated from her, she

---

1   The SS Ehrenring, also called Death's Head Ring, was a personal gift bestowed by Himmler on SS officers who distinguished themselves in service.

2   Hans Moser (né Johann Julier, 1880-1964) was an Austrian actor who acted mostly in comic films. He was married to the Jewess Blanca Hirschler.

German officers and female auxiliaries from Auschwitz pose on a wooden bridge in Solahütte about 20 miles from Auschwitz. This photograph was presumably taken prior to 1941 when Hitler ordered the mass murder of the Jews in the camps.

had a laundry in Budapest. When I applied for permission for that, Kaltenbrunner and Müller were gladly ready to fulfil Moser's request. The couple met each other at the border and, afterwards, Moser with tears in his eyes wanted to thank me personally. Naturally, I exempted his wife in Budapest from every action. Ebner's attitude to the war I knew, it was like mine; on account of that we had to a certain extent sought and found each other out.

Whereas I expressed my thoughts only to my superiors, my comrades of equal rank or immediate subordinates, and indeed not as a criticism but through concern for the Reich, very candid words fell from Ebner in his nice circle of friends, partly in front of persons who did not belong to the Sipo. There a sort of "salon" politics was conducted, and from there perhaps was Ebner's attitude betrayed; a trial was set up for him and he was sentenced to death. When I heard that, I ran filled with fear to Gruppenführer Müller and explained to him that the news was totally incomprehensible to me and, with the statement that he was my best friend, I requested permission to visit him. Müller refused it. I stood up energetically for Ebner and indeed did not need to exaggerate; for he was in every respect a praiseworthy man. It was incomprehensible to me that he was punished so severely on the basis of words which were impelled by concern for the Reich and fell among his closest circle. Not only I but also Dr. Mildner and Huber stood up very energetically for Ebner, and Müller consoled me and said that he would have the sentence lifted. Ebner was then not hanged; he apparently lives freely today, and rightly so.

The commissions which, for example, Standartenführer Becher received in the last months of the war from the SS Reichsführer I do not know in detail. If he actually had received the order regarding all the concentration camps, I did not need to know anything about it; for I had nothing to do with the concentration camps. Now I had myself been an ear and eye-witness to how Becher maintained a very easy manner of speaking with the SS Reichsführer and could certainly have an influence on the latter, as is indeed understandable in the case of a man who was privy to the most private matters of the SS Reichsführer. But if it is maintained that Becher, etc., had arranged for the surrender, without a battle, of the Theresienstadt camp to the Russians, I can only state regarding that that, in Theresienstadt, a battle could never have taken place.

It is completely possible that Gruppenführer Müller discussed with the responsible offices the measures that were to be realised in case the Allies came up to the vicinity of a concentration camp. On my journeys I saw under way some of these marathon treks – inmates as well as guards – which crept tiredly along. I have heard here for the first time of an ordinance to blow up concentration camps, or indeed of Danube boats loaded with inmates that drowned. If I had been responsible even marginally for that, Müller should have informed me of such matters. I can neither confirm nor deny that Becher gave up the Bergen-Bergen camps to the English against the will of the military command offices. It would be understandable in human terms but not everybody is indeed so disposed to buy a "life-insurance policy" for himself at the end and to grant support to the enemy for that. The Jews belonged to the "enemy side" that I have often repeated, that was our obvious principle ever since Chaim Weizmann had declared war against the German nation.

If it is right that Becher finally received the entire concentration camp system on orders from the SS Reichsführer, the concentration camp commandants obviously would have followed his instructions and added a corresponding note to their files.

After the End of My Deportations

It was in the very last period of my stay in Berlin, in spring 1945. Gruppenführer Müller then said to me: "Yes, if we had had fifty 'Eichmanns' then we should have won the war." I was proud. My department was one of the few that was not destroyed by bombs; for I had spurred my colleagues to track every fire-bomb, and naturally took part in this hunt myself, in order to eliminate the damage immediately. My office in Berlin was still intact, but later the State Police directors moved in and ousted me. Every day there was a departmental head there who had hundreds of writing papers with diverse printed letterheads. Each of the gentlemen of Gestapo Office IV could now access files that declared where he had worked in the last few years and which official commissions he had carried out, also other statements and certificates with which he could disguise himself. We were perhaps 30 departmental heads in Gestapo Office IV, and the entire nation scrambled now to the "uncle" who noted down all "wishes".

In the relatively small space I played music with my subordinates: my assessor played the piano, I myself the second violin, my junior officer the first violin, for he could play much better than I. Even though the room was not large, there remained so much place at the back that Gruppenführer Müller stood separately with me; then he asked me: "So, Eichmann, what wishes then do you have?" Since I had returned from Hungary, I carried no longer the Walter but the Steyr army pistol. I had provided myself with two, one always in the haversack or bag and the other on my belt, for it has the same ammunition as my 9 millimetre submachine gun, and so it was simpler. My answer to Müller was: "Gruppenführer, I do not need these "certificates"; for you see" and there I pointed to my "Steyr" "that is my certificate; if I am completely at a loss, then this is my last medicine; everything else I do not need." That is the truth – of all the departmental heads of the Gestapo Office in Berlin, I was the only one for whom these false certificates would not have been valid, and Müller may have thought: "So he was the right person, and I have not been disappointed in him." So I was proud of myself.

On 17 April 1945, there was a heavy bomb attack on Brixlegg in Tyrol. Because I should have really died there, I remember the date; so I know precisely that I had shortly before reported for the last time to the SS Reichsführer. We were alone; the SS Reichsführer assessed the situation optimistically on the basis of reasons that were incomprehensible to me. He said: "We will have a better peace than the Hubertusburg, we will have to make concessions, but this peace will get better." He related to me that he had dealt with Bernadotte and had at least a hundred of the most prominent Jews in our territory in complete security; I suppose that he thought of "playing off" these hundred prominent Jews. On the other hand, I cannot imagine that only hundred Jews could, in such a serious political discussion and "negotiation", really play a great role and indeed tip the scales. But it must have been something similar, for the SS Reichsführer had also had the enormous, white-painted Swedish cargo trains, which travelled through Germany in kilometre-long columns, come in and released thousands of Jews to Bernadotte. He did not mention any individual names among these hundred prominent Jews; indeed, we had a large number in Theresienstadt, and also in different concentration camps, where they had been accommodated in a preferential manner. I think that among these were also Léon Blum,[3] an Austrian general, as well as a large number of people who had either been ministers or had occupied a high function, whose names were partly internationally renowned and the majority of whom were of European significance. The name Bernadotte was not new to me; he had been mentioned already when I reported last in Berlin in autumn 1944 along with Standartenführer Becher; Himmler had obviously prepared the entire matter in advance. Then the SS Reichsführer remarked once again: "I was never so optimistic, never. We will have a better peace than the Hubertusburg, and I tell you something, Eichmann, if I have to do it again, I will set up the concentration camps according to the English model. I made a mistake, I must set them up on the English model ..." I could not understand anything of that since I never directed a concentration camp. I thought at that time of the Boer concentration camps of the English, but perhaps the SS Reichsführer was thinking also of the entire English police system.

My later meeting with Kaltenbrunner in Altaussee and his statement: "It will be very pleasant to the SS Reichsführer to know, if he now negotiates with Eisenhower, that Eichmann is in the mountains, and our enemies know precisely that Eichmann with his men will not give himself up" I explain that to myself now as that the SS Reichsführer, during my last visit, not only wished to discuss the hundred prominent Jews but in the end especially wanted to be sure of me. Naturally I had only been a cog in the wheel, in a game which the SS Reichsführer thought he was playing; for I indeed ascertained later that he really "played", for which reason the Führer also degraded him and finally outlawed him. Then the Führer named somebody else, I think the

---

3   Léon Blum, French (Jewish) politician, Socialist Party of France, French Prime Minister.

Breslau Gauleiter Hanke,[4] as chief of the SS. This last visit took place in the old Ziethen castle north-east of Berlin.

For the accommodation of those hundred prominent Jews I travelled to Tyrol. In Linz I met SS Oberführer Dr. Pifrader,[5] inspector of the Sipo and SD in Hungary and the Upper Danube; Gauleiter Hofer[6] did not receive me; so I set to work "seriously"; for it was a matter of an SS Reichsführer order. At Brenner I picked out two places of accommodation and returned to Salzburg, where I met my representative from Berlin at the State Police office. He reported to me that, during my absence, he had received an order from Müller to go with the "acts of foundation" to Salzburg and to deposit them somewhere in the mountains. The acts of foundation are, among other things, the acts of the former Prime Minister Hermann Göring from the time when, for the first time, a Secret State Police was established. I travelled on to Linz and heard that Dr. Piffrader had fallen victim to a frightful bomb attack. In Prague I then sought the secretary of state of the Reich Protector, Gruppenführer K.H. Frank, who said to me that I could not proceed, in Berlin there was nothing more, Müller was away and also Kaltenbrunner, the Russians had broken through somewhere.

I received the order by telephone to go to Altaussee. This was the end of April or the beginning of May 1945, where I visited the Chief of the Sipo and SD. Sturmbannführer Gscheitler, Kaltenbrunner's adjutant, was a long-time comrade of mine. He received me warmly and announced me later to Kaltenbrunner. I was led to a room where Kaltenbrunner sat behind a large table. Kaltenbrunner had the field-shirt of an Obergruppenführer, almost wedge-shaped ski trousers and wonderful ski boots. Even though I was in a mood of the downfall as "in the last days of Pompeii", I observed all these details. Kaltenbrunner had taken a cognac after the meal, but I knew that he preferred beer. When he was still senior SS and Police chief in Vienna, I once went to him and saw how in the evening he ate his Upper Austrian soup and, in addition, drank a beer. He dealt out a game of solitaire and when, as the first to speak, I asked him: "Well Gruppenführer did it go well?", his answer was "No, badly". That was really nothing new to

---

4   Karl Hanke, Gauleiter of Lower Silesia in Breslau Wrocław.

5   Humbert Achamer-Pifrader, SS Oberführer, chief of an Einsatz group in the Baltic, later active in the Reich Security Head Office.

6   Hofer, Gauleiter of Tyrol in Innsbruck.

me, everything had to end badly. At the window the white snow from the Lohser slope shone in. In spite of my gloomy mood, the cognac tasted excellent to me: Kaltenbrunner asked me: "Yes, what are you doing now?" I answered: "I am going to the mountains ..." Thereupon he told me of the planned discussion between the SS Reichsführer and Eisenhower[7] Besides, he gave me the assignment to offer protection to the Romanian government chief Horia Sima[8] and his people and to take them along with me. Therewith the official part was completed. I formally took my leave of Kaltenbrunner, without any personal tone on his side. He remained sitting behind the table but his look betrayed his goodwill.

Gscheitler accompanied me out, and I went to the large hotel in the place where my people were. Even years later the owner of this hotel spoke of the "dog Eichmann" who confiscated his hotel and had his "hordes" come in who supposedly ravaged everything and caused great material damages. That was the fabrication of a wretched creature, a beneficiary who wanted to feather his nest through some hoped for compensation.

After the senior staff doctor of the neighbouring hospital in Altaussee had beseeched me to leave the place with my battle troops so that he could declare Altaussee an "open city", he informed me how many and what sort of wounded persons were staying in the Altaussee district. Then I granted the request of the senior staff doctor; even before the major part of my battle troops had vacated our hotel, I saw how Red Cross sisters cleaned room after room and floor after floor: the hotel was established as a military hospital station. Apart from the known people of my office, my battle troop was constituted of Waffen SS members and later even HJ youths.

In Altaussee some of Schellenberg's SS unit, and Office VI were stationed. I think they themselves had set fire to the Kremsmünster monastery and, earlier, hauled out some cargo lorries of a special sort, whose load consisted of tropical and other uniforms but contained nothing of winter and ski equipment. Though they did have masses of down sleeping-bags and emergency rations of chocolate, hard-cured sausage and similar goodies which we had not seen for a long time. They also possessed a coffer, an iron casket which was filled with dollars, pounds, and bank-

---

7   Dwight Eisenhower, General, President of the USA.

8   Horia Sima, Leader of the Iron Guard in Romania.

notes. All this stuff, along with the team, I had to take over on the orders of Kaltenbrunner; besides, again on orders from Kaltenbrunner, I had to organise the resistance in the Höllengebirge mountains. On the Blaa-Alm I wanted to set up a base, on a saddle which had, on the one side, Ischl im Tal below it and, on the other, Altaussee. From Altaussee this march towards the mountain lasted a couple of hours. In Altaussee I ordered 150 HJ youths – there was nobody else there – to shovel up the snow which was partially 1-2 metres high, so that I could go through with my fleet of vehicles, at least to the Blaa-Alm.

I reported to Horia Sima and informed him that I had an order from the Chief of the Sipo and SD to take charge of him and bring him with his staff to the mountains. Horia Sima was visibly delighted at that and, even more so, his cabinet chief and the other seven or eight ministers and generals. From the stocks of Office VI I had paymaster uniforms handed to them; with the exception of Horia Sima, who remained in civilian clothes. Some soldiers, armed and unarmed, were already returning home, from Bad Ischl, where the Americans were already based. In the market-place girls danced with the "conquerors". We were frightfully angry at that. That must have been in the first days of May; the 3rd or 4th. There was strong snowfall, and the weather had turned to winter. Naturally, there lay even deeper snow above on the Blaa-Alm, but the meadows below, near Altaussee, were already free of snow, and the Alm stream bubbled. Everything was now again covered by the snowfall, and the street had to be shovelled clear.

We arrived at the Blaa-Alm. I occupied a room in the sole inn and had a weapons room set up and the "uniform collection" stored. I was warned about the host that he was a treacherous "black-listed" person, and it would best to "get rid of" him. It was the time when everybody wanted to get rid of everybody else. When I looked at the "sausage" of a host, I thought to myself: "You need not get rid of him – he is not doing anything anyway." Among the motley things thrown together from the Kremsmünster camp was also a barrel of red wine. I placed it on the street, and every infantryman who went homewards from Ischl through the mountains could drink here a glass of wine and continue on. More than five minutes' stay was not permitted. So the barrel became empty and my own people did not become drunk. The coffer, with the dollar and pound notes as well as the gold coins, I gave over to councillor Hunsche with the instruction to make a precise inventory, for as a councillor, he was even in these days the best guarantee that these things would be administered in an orderly manner. I myself camped in the inn.

Horia Sima and his people I had accommodated near my quarters. His War Minister requested arms. I complied with his request, and now all the Romanians once again wore field uniforms, insofar as the stocks sufficed. The War Minister or another general came with me to the "weapons room", a part of the room in the inn, where, to my great surprise, he picked out an FN and with the astute eyes of an expert, ascertained something that had escaped me because I had not yet looked at the weapons room thoroughly and was also not a weapons expert: it was a silencer which he attached to his pistol in a trice! The thing now looked like a semi-flame-thrower; I said to him that silencers were forbidden, but he replied to me: "... but it silences the sound." These Romanians still had drive and I found myself very bound to them.

Among my equipment there was also a complete radio car. On the first day, when the sun rose, a Hauptsturmführer from Office VI reported with an order of Obergruppenführer Kaltenbrunner according to which he had to pick up emergency rations. I replied to him that I needed the emergency rations myself. Then he became overbearing and Obersturmführer Burger asked me: "Should I get rid of him?" But I waved him off and let him take a half-coffer full of dried sausages and chocolate. As I figured out later, he naturally bolted with these things somewhere, perhaps to Switzerland. A red-haired SS Oberscharführer came to me some three or four times, always with a piece of paper with Kaltenbrunner's signature, which I knew, and seemed to me to be genuine, and the instruction that rolls of "Napoléons d'or" should be handed over to the bringer. A roll contained 50 pieces; I had no reason to investigate the genuineness or lack of it of Kaltenbrunner's signature, for us in the mountains money and gold meant nothing, on the other hand bread and emergency rations everything. I therefore graciously had councillor Hunsche pay out the money rolls against a receipt and the demands, which had been signed by Kaltenbrunner, placed in the files by Hunsche; but perhaps he put the receipts also into the coffer. Obersturmführer Burger informed me that he had made a precious find in the cargo lorries of Kremsmünster, that is, some down feather sleeping-bags of the airforce; they had all already been discarded but he was able to save one for me. Later this sleeping-bag served me well during my imprisonment.

On the next morning I heard a loud scream and looked through the window at how Burger was beating a civilian with blows to the ear, left and right. I ordered Burger to come to; he reported that this was a teacher from some valley village who wanted to plunder the stocks in a cargo lorry, so he had given him a rough lesson. I answered Burger that an officer does not beat. One who plunders is placed before a court-martial and shot, but not beaten. The teacher was naturally not shot. I had the radio car driven to a clearing in the woods. Horia Sima requested me to keep in touch constantly with the outside world and there the radio car offered the possibility of quick information on all possible wavelengths; especially among the Romanians there were many highly talented people for this work. Hardly had I given the order for the placement of the radio car than a loud detonation occurred; it was reported to me that the radio car had been blown up by a demolition bomb. I had the fool, a Untersturmführer, who was responsible for that come to me: I could not lock up the guy because I had no prison; the deed was not sufficient for shooting, and I could also not drive him away; for he could have betrayed us. So I just shouted at him and threw him out. I thought to myself: "What rubbish-heap have you gathered together here?" Men of the Waffen SS and such as were just released from the hospitals and were once again assigned to some unit, men who were scraped up by the Sipo, then this fully insubordinate heap of the Office VI, some sluts, my own people, 150 HJ men and, in addition, the Romanians ... And with this heap I was now to conduct a war in the Totengebirge. I had weapons, even the most modern; I had never before seen an assault rifle, and now I had them in huge quantities, ammunition, rocket-propelled grenades, everything in large quantities.

Somewhat higher than the Blaa-Alm lay the Rettenbach-Alm. My best skier was Burger, whom I sent out with a man as companion, to check the snow conditions and accommodation possibilities. Then I gave the order to vacate the Blaa-Alm for the immediate objective of Rettenbach-Alm. All weapons that we did not need I had smashed and made unusable, and they were then thrown into the river flowing near the Rettenbach-Alm. Not a single arm was to be thrown into the river in a usable condition. This work lasted an entire forenoon. After I had assured myself that no single weapon remained that we could not drag up to the Rettenbach-Alm, I, as the last person, left the Blaa-Alm and clambered up to the Rettenbach-Alm. Here I had allocated, through an advance command of the Romanian government in exile, some shepherd's huts where even the remaining units could be accommodated. After the blowing up of the radio car, I had let go the majority of the people, because I saw that discipline had suffered very much. Besides, Ernst Kaltenbrunner sent an ordinance to me on the Blaa-Alm with a handwritten order on writing paper which bore the letter-head "Chief of the Sipo and SD". This letter said: "The

SS Reichsführer orders that the English and Americans should not be shot at." I had to counter-sign, and then the order was passed on throughout the valley.

I can no longer for the life of me recount the exact course of events those last days; for I lived in a state of shock, and the will to live also failed me. Almost everything was a matter of indifference, even if I had been placed against the wall. Many felt that way at the time; they had fought, worked, worried about and feared for the Reich – and now it collapsed; there was no will to live any more.

After the Surrender – Together with Horia Sima

So we knew nothing of Himmler's dismissal, only that he was in north Germany; he was certainly somehow in touch through radio with Kaltenbrunner; for, at the Loser-Hang, there was a radio facility under the control of a Sturmbannführer from Office VI; from there I obtained the situation reports in the last days. Hunsche wanted to go once again to Altaussee to visit his family, which I granted to him. When he returned, he reported to me that during his absence the American tanks had rolled in there. He had returned backwards through the garden, through field after field, to the Blaa-Alm.

I do not think that the order that "the English and Americans are not to be shot at" was a private initiative of Kaltenbrunner's; for in that case he would not have written "By order of the SS Reichsführer". And then Kaltenbrunner would not also have said: "It is good that Eichmann is based in the mountains; for Himmler wants to negotiate with Eisenhower."

Today, all this seems so childish, to go to the mountains with such a ridiculous bunch and to want to play at war there like a mountain spirit with a couple of boy-scouts. But if the leadership had remained rational, we would have been able to build up a resistance line and, if there were more "partisan chiefs" up there, then it would also have come to a "partisan war" which would have hindered the enemy at least some weeks and prepared difficulties for them, since we could have simply inhibited the collapse. If one knows those mountains, nothing is easier than to block the road from Bad Ischl to Aussee with a couple of men. We would have retreated more and more. At first the attacker would have had large losses, for all advantages were to be found naturally on the side of those with a knowledge of the mountains. Indeed we would not have attacked but only observed without being able to be observed. Naturally this war would inevitably come to an end, for reasons of food-supplies; for, at that time, up there it was all deeply snowed in and, if the enemy had sent up a mountain-troop battalion, they would have very soon mastered the situation. But we would have still been able to survive for a couple of months. Today, all this naturally seems like madness; perhaps the SS Reichsführer recognised this and therefore gave the order not to shoot at the English and Americans.

I think even today that the Oberscharführer collected the gold bars by using counterfeit papers. Kaltenbrunner could not hand over that entire "rubbish" to me and encumber me almost at the same time with individual ordinances, for he could not know what order I had issued with regard to the coffer. I would not have considered this in the case of any other superior, but in the case of Kaltenbrunner I indeed had to suppose that he left me largely with a free hand. The emergency rations had only served to tide these gentlemen from Office VI through the "dry period"; then they went to Switzerland, where the gold coins offered a better bread. As I heard later, these people from Office VI cleared off to Switzerland with gold and money and death and the devil.

Somewhere in his book the Jew Joel Brand maintains that I once said to him in Budapest that I had provided for my family. I indeed pardon him this "poetical licence", but such a statement I never made. Unfortunately I did not generally "provide for" my family, not even when I went to Altaussee. In the post-war years, when I did not give any news of myself, I did not know how my wife would have to struggle with the CIC. If I had known that and not lived in those days in Altaussee in a mood of world-collapse shock, then I would have "provided for" my family exactly as some gentlemen of Office VI did. And really I would have been able to do it even better, for, instead of leaving behind my family without means, I would have been able to cover them with foreign exchange and gold. That I would not even have had to do myself: a Kastner, a Brand, a Löwenherz, and whatever else their names are, would have brought me foreign exchange and gold with the greatest gratitude to any country that I mentioned to them. If I had promised to them a special privilege for that, I could have had my family sent to the most distant and neutral country in the world. But I did not do that; in Altaussee I gave my wife as a last gift a briefcase full of grains and a half-sack of flour. And poison capsules, one for every child and for my wife, and to her I said: "If the Russians come, then you have to bite on them; if the Americans or the English come, then not". That may have been the end of April or beginning of May 1945. That was my only "provision". Today I regret it on the one hand; for I could have made it easier for my wife and children but, on the other hand, I say to myself – "Thank God I did not become the murderer of my children!"

On the Blaa-Alm therefore I dismissed, as I mentioned, the entire team insofar as it was a question of the regular people, to each I had 5,000 Reichsmarks paid out through Hunsche and against their signature; for, in the coffer there were also Reichsmarks. An SS assistant implored me to take her with me, she did not know where to go and had nobody. But I was at that time hard, and instead of a reply I only said to the councillor Hunsche: "Pay out five thousand marks and – Next!." I was at that time tethered fast so that everybody who heard that I did not need him any more gladly disappeared.

On the Blaa-Alm there remained not a single weapon, only large stocks which were not important for any attacks and could not therefore harm us. The uniform collection, for example, remained there and the rolls of cloth, the linen and the shirts which Office VI had remarkably sent up so that I seemed like an old trader and thought to myself: "These have been the operations of Office VI decisive for the war." It was a hoarding for one's personal economy, perhaps partly destined for the Office V people; and I even accepted that.

On the Rettenbach-Alm I first visited the Romanian government in exile, because they had been placed under my protection. The Romanians thanked me for the provisions; I then saw that they had been accommodated well considering the situation, had a roof over their head, were not hungry and their mountain equipment was good.

Even Oberscharführer Slavick was with me. In Budapest he was my house-guard, responsible for the security of the house in which the senior police chiefs had quartered me. On the Rettenbach-Alm he emerged as a cook. Slavick was by profession a butcher, always cheerful, optimistic and well-fed, because he always sat at the source. Here he had found a wooden shed in a shepherd's hut where he had hay and even some straw brought in. As a child of the big city he had no idea what a disaster he had set up; on the straw he had placed peppermint containing hay. Because I was dead tired I lay down without checking, with the result that I woke up the next morning with a maddening head-ache.

Columns of German soldiers after their surrender to US forces in May 1945.

The Eichmann Tapes

To the Romanians and my own people I conveyed the order of the SS Reichsführer not to shoot at the English or Americans; the reply to that was mostly the Götz expression. Already around us crept armed "homeland defenders" with red-white-red armbands, all "anti-Piefkes" and simple people who probably had shouted loudly in 1938 with calls of "Heil Hitler", but who later wanted "to have been no part of it". Then I set up a trap circuit and had warning signboards brought, even on the so-called hunting strips which stand in the high mountains for the free use of every forester, worker, forest assistant. The warning signboards said that any approach without warning would be fired upon. Apart from my fat Slavick, I had among my Austrians many sharpshooters by whom I had "nests" laid. I do not know if they went off, for at that time there were explosions in all corners and ends. No report was brought to me, but also not about mutual actions, so that either the warning signboards were respected or my protective nests worked well.

I came to an understanding with Horia Sima that since we lacked radio contact, and on account of the latent danger of being overrun by the enemy, to pitch our camp higher. First I sent my chauffeur Polanski to Altaussee and let Hunsche know that he had to give him the necessary money. I urged Polanski to buy up the entire bread stock at a baker's, for better or for worse, but certainly on payment; for we had only rusk and biscuits. After a few hours Polanski came back with a hundred loaves of fresh bread. In the high mountains I needed no car, so I sent away Polanski, who had been my faithful chauffeur for years, at his request, with a cargo lorry to Bad Ischl. I hope he was lucky!

On the next day we moved our base some hundred metres higher; with the exception of Horia Sima we all took part in bringing the food, blankets and such on a rope which rose upwards at a 45 degree gradient. We spent this night in the open air on the snow crust. Naturally we were awake all the night. On the following day Burger said to me: "Obersturmbannführer, we have discussed the order that we should not shoot at the English and Americans, the Russians are not coming here. You will be sought as a war criminal, not we.[9] If therefore you go away and would name another commandant, you would do a service to your comrades."

---

9   Reitlinger, *Die Endlösung*, Colloquium Verlag, 1956, p.187: "... and the commandants of Theresienstadt were taken from the Eichmann staff. The three commandants following one another, Siegrfied Seidel, Anton Burger and Karl Rahm, stood trial together with the deputy commandt Wilhelm Schmidt in 1946/47 and were hanged. With the exception of Seidel, whoose trial took place in Vienna, they were sentenced by the court in Leitmeritz."

I considered that my war task was fulfilled, and said then: "People, I now leave you alone on the Rettenbach-Alm ... The war is over, you cannot shoot ... See how you can come through ..." My antechamber policeman for many years Jänisch reported immediately and requested that he be able to go with me. We all drank one more schnaps together. Horia Sima and his ministers also wore civilian clothes now; we promised to see one another somewhere in western Germany, and indeed as pseudo-patients in the waiting-room of some doctor. Sima gifted me one more golden fountain pen in farewell. In this way we parted.

In US Captivity

When Jänisch and I, it was I think in the first half of May 1945, were apprehended by an American patrol, we went to a small American prisoners' camp. There I passed myself off as airforce Obergefreiter[10] Bart. That was the name of a shopkeeper in Berlin-Britz where I had always shopped in the thirties. After I had studied the psychological attitude of the American CIC, I decided to change my identity from a member of the airforce to a member of the SS. So I became Untersturmführer Otto Eckmann and advanced my date of birth one year to 19 March 1905 in Breslau. This figure I could easily remember, and even the signature was fluid so that I would hardly have fallen victim to any fiasco through a momentary distraction during a necessary signing.

After crossing a camp we were led into the large Weiden collection camp in the Oberpfalz. My Obersturmführer Jänisch was grouped with me; he possessed the daring to give his own rank and his own name. At that time it was very opportune "to be modest", but Jänisch could not be brought to that and even gave the Security Service as his unit.

In Weiden, after a while, so-called work squadrons were demanded by the Americans. I reported for that and, since I passed myself off as an Untersturmführer, I was assigned as a train driver to the Ober-Dachstetten camp in Franconia, while Jänisch went with his unit to a work-camp at Degendorf on the Danube. This must have been around August 1945; I remained there until the beginning of January 1946.

Often Jewish commissions came to the camps to "visit" their "friends"; we all had to come forward and then they looked over to see if they

---

10   Corporal

discovered familiar faces. All around stood Americans to protect the operation. Gradually these commissions became burdensome to us prisoners of war and, when once again cars advanced to the barbed wire and some Jews stepped out, someone – I think that it was an Obersturmführer shouted at them: "Scram, you dogs!" All laughed and howled. The Americans did nothing against that. At that time it was not really pleasant for me but basically everything was "a matter of indifference" for me. Only I had firmly decided that, if it would go badly for me, I would not pass into eternity without an "order".

Once we even had to watch a film on the Jewish liquidation, but we revolted and then did not have to see it. At that time I requested Jänisch to get me some poison, for foolishly I had thrown my capsule over the latrine. The eternal hearings at the CIC became too stupid for me; I thought: "It is all the same, I will get warm water and a razor blade." Then Jänisch said to me: "Well, that you could have done yesterday, then we would have had more peace now." That made sense to me; then there was another hearing, and then I took the razor blade and shaved with it. When thereafter I was in the Oberdachstetten camp and had already withstood the CIC, we were to have Poles for our guard. And again I said to myself: "Here you will not escape – or you must kill a couple of Americans, and that also serves no purpose."

In the camp there was a chemist from somewhere in the Warthegau, a Unterscharführer. I said to him – he knew about me: "You know, one does not get out of here; I still have some morphine with me, around four to five decagrams. Is that enough? I will get together some red rag, make a swastika flag for me and eat the morphine." But I was a cautious man and wished to know how the thing worked; I had never yet had anything to do with morphine. Since I was a layman in the field and also did not possess any syringe, I wanted to swallow the thing; I thought to myself: "If you lie there like that, you must die", but the chemist said to me: "You know, with 300 grams you already have enough, you do not need to gulp it at all, much less is sufficient, but perhaps you will be violently sick; then you will vomit the thing, and it would have been of no use." Then he said further that only one person had troubles with it; even that made sense to me, and so I said to myself, one has to go on one way or the other.

At that time everything was a matter of indifference to me. When I was dragged to the hearings in Ansbach, in the forenoon there was a hearing and in the afternoon there was a hearing and then locked up in a cell and again pulled out, I wondered: it was my fate. But the "sergeant" wanted to have his work squadron together and fought with the CIC so that they would bring back this guy – me – to him. Then I lay once again in a tent with two or three other comrades. There was a doctor with us who said to us: "I am there because I have 14 more days to live." He mentioned his illness to the American doctor; I inquired of him how one could indeed escape from there. But we were again loaded on; I thought it was going again to the hearing, but we were on the way back to Oberdachstetten. I had wanted to make an end, but it did not go well. So what more should I do?

In the meantime, we were taken a couple of times more to Ansbach for hearings which caused me no further difficulties. But when I could in this way roughly calculate how and at what time any suspicion could be raised against me and I could accordingly have been taken back to Ansbach or Oberdachstetten, I decided to get out. We were nine or eleven officers in our camp, and therefore I could not of my own accord "make a getaway", but requested the camp director for a discussion with the officers. Up to that moment, it was around December 1945, I had not declared anything to him. When I now began to make my escape preparations, I gave him my name, rank and office. Then he said: "My dear comrade Eckmann, I have known that already for a long time, for your Obersturmführer Jänisch informed me of that on oath of secrecy, but since you did not declare anything to me I have kept it to myself." I described to the director of the camp the necessity of my absconding and requested him to arrange a discussion so that I would receive the approval of my officer comrades for this escape insofar as he considered it necessary.

It was an unwritten code of honour that an officer can only escape if all officer comrades, or the responsible German camp officer, issued the approval for it, because under certain circumstances reprisals for the comrades remaining behind were to be feared. The discussion with the officer took place and, without declaring my intentions to the individual comrades, I described to two officers the necessity of my escape because I would be prosecuted on account of political activity. At that time, not much was asked; I could never imagine that in any SS camp the agreement to that would have been refused to a chief who had to escape. To two officers with whom I had been close friends I said that I wanted to try to get through to the Grand Mufti, who was at that time living in Egypt. This was a very vague plan, but I indeed needed a destination. I then carried out my escape in one night according to plan; I left the camp with the papers prepared by me under the name of Otto Henninger.

My Years In Germany After My Escape

I lived in West Germany after the war almost five years in all and saw much with my own eyes, among other things also that there were Hungarian Jews everywhere. For, after I had escaped, I was constantly on the road. So I travelled to Hamburg, from there to the Rhineland and from the Rhineland to the Lüneburg Heath. In the Lüneburg Heath I lived near Bergen-Belsen. Everywhere smelt of garlic. I traded wood and eggs there with the Jews and said to myself: "God, and we are supposed to have killed all of them?"

It must have been either in summer 1946 or in summer 1947 when, on the edge of the Lüneburg Heath, I got possession of an entire stack of old newspapers whose articles dealt with, among other things, me under titles like "Mass-murderer Eichmann", "Where is the mass-murderer hiding?", etc. I was perplexed when I read that the "infamous mass-murderer Eichmann stayed last under the name of Lieutenant Eckmann in the Oberdachstetten camp"; besides the date of my escape from the camp was right, and it was added that "he was trying to go to the Grand Mufti via a secret route known only to him" And I said to myself that I had clearly escaped at the right time. Naturally I pondered from where the CIC could have obtained the name "Eckmann". There were only two possibilities: the Lower Saxon thickhead Jänisch, who gave his own name and his service assignment in the questionnaire, had been through all the years very good and useful for his administrative duties; seen in purely human terms he was a person little capable of resistance, and if the CIC had "correctly" questioned him, the discovery of the name Eckmann was no longer surprising. It seemed to me unlikely that the CIC questioned the camp director after my escape and the latter possibly said: "The man has now for a long time disappeared behind "the seven mountains"[11] and, if the CIC proves in some weeks the opposite of my present statements, my camp can only expect troubles from it, so I speak the truth."

Every policeman has his own method of making inquiries. So I know that, in the first years after 1945, I was sought by the police – obviously by the Allied police, but later also by the police of my homeland. If what the newspapers report is right, Wisliceny was promised his life

---

11   A German expression derived from the fairy-tale of Snow White and the Seven Dwarfs.

on the condition that he get me alive or dead. For years I preserved an extract from the extreme left *Oberösterreichische Zeitung* in which it could be read that a Jewish officer whose name I unfortunately have forgotten, but who occupies today a high rank in the Israeli army, had explained that he had gone with a Jewish commando unit to Altaussee, where they had located Eichmann, who was surrounded by many very sharp watchdogs. After they had struck Eichmann down with truncheons and had made him unconscious thereby, they loaded him onto a jeep and drove him to a clearing in the woods. In the meantime, he had awoken from his unconsciousness and was then asked: "Are you Obersturmbannführer Eichmann?" Thereupon Eichmann said: "Yes … what do you want from me?" The Jews had then struck Eichmann down; the officer added: "Eichmann died remarkably respectably." Thus at least one innocent man fell victim to this Jewish search for me. I know also that a wanted person who has not been found after five years is struck off from the search list; today I have not been sought for a long time.

In the woody heath region of Celle district I worked for many years as a woodcutter and poultry breeder. The work was hard, but there was a good comradely relationship; through keen savings I succeeded in collecting over the years the necessary monies for an overseas journey; finally, in 1950, I left the old continent and travelled through Italy to South America. Since my arrival I have not left this large as well as generous South American country any longer and undertook an occasional change of job only within its borders.

For a trial against me "*in absentia*" there is indeed not enough; I have spent so to speak half my life as a police man and therefore know of what a difficult nature the charges are and that the files can only be weighed in hundredweights so that a conviction "*in absentia*" cannot be made straightaway, especially since the opposition expects great material advantages from a trial against me.

How I See My Own Case

I am gradually getting tired of living like an anonymous wanderer between two worlds. No man can escape from the voice of his heart – it whispered constantly to me to seek peace. I would like to find even peace with my former enemies; perhaps this belongs to the German character. I would be the last one that would not be ready to place myself before the German courts if I had not to consider that the political interest in the Jewish question is however still all too great to lead the materials to a clear, objective conclusion. I do not wish to doubt the efforts to reach a right verdict in a German court, but I am not so clear about the legal status of a former recipient of orders who on the basis of an official oath had carried out orders and instructions received.

After a serious examination I must declare that I myself am innocent, and under certain circumstances I can stand before a legal evaluation with a pure conscience. This may be forgiven me and not considered as a show of arrogance, from which I do not suffer anyway. Before my conscience I have been nothing but a faithful, correct, hard-working, paid member of the SS and the Reich Security Head Office, filled only with ideal impulses for my fatherland. I was never a "basic swine". After conscientious self-examination, I must declare that neither I nor the members of the department IV-B4 directly under me were murderers.

Up to now I have not yet heard that my "deportation colleagues" in the non-German world were prosecuted on account of complicity in killing or were accused of that. In that they deported not only Germans but also innumerable members of other nations, with a very high percentage of fatal results. The number of deportees goes far into the millions, partly even during the war, mostly indeed after the war. In the post-war literature there is a considerable number of proofs of that. None of my colleagues "from the other side" were prosecuted on account of these possible crimes, neither under "crimes against humanity" nor "complicity in murder". Probably their subjective attitude to those events is somewhat the same as mine. Equal justice and equal punishment for all, that must be the principle.

To stick to the truth with finicky precision, I could be prosecuted of complicity in killing during the war because I passed on the transportation orders, supervised their compliance and had known that a proportion of these deportees were killed, even if by another entirely different unit and by an entirely different head office. This circumstance is widely known; I therefore will not fall into the suspicion of saying something that could penalise this unit or this head office anew. If any of the deportees were killed, who they were or how many I did not know, for this did not fall within my sphere of duties.[12] My attitude to these matters was founded on my belief in the "national emergency" announced by the leadership of the Greater German Reich. To that belongs my belief in the necessity of a total war when faced with the possibility of the downfall of the German nation. This belief was strengthened and confirmed by Kaufman's and Morgenthau's declarations. With this attitude, with a pure conscience and trusting heart, I did the duty ordered of me. I think that this is likewise obligatory for all patriots. The more and the more intensively I observed matters from my field of responsibilities the clearer did my own conviction become that I am not guilty of any crime, not even according to the present-day legislation. From the demands of the state and the fatherland, I have no need to declare myself guilty of being an "accomplice in killing" during the war. That is true for me as it is for my "colleagues" on the other side. For they, like me, carried out orders.

The actions and thoughts of a man are determined by the spirit of the times in which he lives. My actions and thoughts were determined by the situation of my people, as it was brought about by the ignominious treaty of Versailles. My thoughts and actions were also determined by the official oath which bound me.

When, after the death of Prime Minister von Hindenburg, I did active SS service in a battalion, we were sent by train to Munich; there I swore the new oath to the Führer and the Reich Chancellor, Adolf Hitler. The oath was obviously voluntary. When I was transferred in 1934 from the troops to the SDHA, I swore a second oath, the official oath to the SD. When I was commandeered in 1940 from the SD to the Gestapo, I swore anew an official oath which, as in the case of the SD, declared secrecy and strict observance of orders. When, in 1941, Heydrich informed me that an order of the Führer had ordered the physical liquidation of the Jews, this was for me at that time a law; for, orders from the Führer had legal force – that was true for all German national comrades. I was active as a civil servant; there is no

---

12   This repeated statement on always the same subject was left in, since it may be of some psychological significance.

authority among civil servants but every civil servant, whether junior or senior, from the detective to the Chief of the Sipo, had to carry out instructions and orders according to existing laws, ordinances and decrees; there was and is no alternative among civil servants. In an official apparatus nobody can do and permit what he wants, but everybody acts according to orders.

What the oath of allegiance means and what it enforces is, by and large, well known independently of nationality. *Because they stood under an oath of allegiance, soldiers and officers of the Allied air forces killed German women, children and old people and turned their dwellings into rubble and ashes, and even dropped atom-bombs without previous warning.* They all acted on orders, did their duty, obeyed. To call upon the individual air fleet chiefs to answer would be as absurd. After the war, millions of German civilians were killed in the east and hundreds of thousands in the Sudetenland forcibly evicted. War in future conflicts will doubtless be even more total – and even then no statesman will be able to imagine working with those who refuse to obey orders or with traitors. Against such individuals the responsible state chief must apply the full force of the law. Precisely Zionist Jewry and the other political currents among the Jewish people within their new state will least be able, surrounded by patent and latent danger, to exclude this way of thinking. A patriotic character must reject as immoral any "punishment" for obedience in the implementation of received orders.

No Russian, no Israeli, no Englishman, no American and no Frenchman was punished even in a single case if he, in an official position or in fulfilment of his oath of allegiance, carried out his orders, however "criminal" these actions may have been in themselves. *Why should the gallows or jail be valid only for Germans?* Of course: all killing and wounding is painful. Nevertheless, in a fatefully difficult time, the one who refuses an order, no matter of what nationality, is in my eyes, as well as in those of many Germans and non-Germans, not a loyal citizen since he has not adhered to his oath of allegiance.

Thus two oaths bound me: the oath of allegiance to Adolf Hitler and the oath to the SS Reichsführer. These two oaths bound me completely. The oath is the highest obligation which a man can enter into; all had to obey it, be this with friends or foes. In order to accomplish their goal, both sides deployed conventional and unconventional methods. One killed directly, unlocked the levers of their murder machines in the air as well as on the sea and on land and gave free rein to death; the

A German girl mourns over her dead mother, murdered by Polish troops in 1939.

other contributed to it in some form: among friends and foes the same picture, on water, on land and in the air. And an oath bound all of them.

And the lesson? The lesson of Auschwitz and Nagasaki, of nights of phosphorus fires in the German Reich and the refugee marches of Germans that were lined with piles of corpses even after the war? Are there two sorts of "morality": a religious, a war morality, a morality of "right or wrong, my country", a morality of the instinct for survival and a morality such as the Old Testament describes quite horribly? Could a "cog in the wheel", in the gearbox of one's own or of the enemy's murder machine during the war break out of that which was imposed on him? The recipient of orders could think what he wanted, but he could not express it, unless he had felt suicidal impulses. The Socratic wisdom is subjected to the law of the state, and indeed unconditionally, so did the humanists teach us. The law threatened the death penalty against the philosophers. Socrates should have been able to escape it, but the law did not allow him; he drank the poison.

316

The Eichmann Tapes

My attitude, in the years of the second World War, was not very complicated; I found the parallels for myself simply in nature. The oath of allegiance did not prohibit me independent thought, not even when the result of my thought and seeking would have turned out in a negative way, and if I had disapproved of the will and goal of the government which I was under. The more I listened to the events, the less injustice I found in the demands of my government. Everybody was actually right from his point of view. What other legions of seekers recognised I also found confirmed: The fate that had always been present, that was always immovably the same, of all organic life, and its law of the survival instinct, which is stronger than every so-called moral demand. The ants in their "cities", the termites in the tropics, the bees in the broad circle of our earth, they teach us subordination to a cruel law with a compelling logic. From the bacilli under the microscope to the sun of our solar system everything is ruled by a law.

The law orders and demands integration to it; only the sick or degenerate constitutes an exception. I have to obey so that a greater community can live and I in it. Before the the rule of law personal feelings must capitulate. In this way did I carry out the orders of my superiors faithful to my oath and according to the best of my knowledge and conscience. And without any Pilate gesture, I declare: I am not guilty before the law and before my conscience, exactly as little as the circle of persons subordinate to me were during the war. We were all small "cogs in the wheel" in the gearbox of the huge chain of the murdering Moloch. In order to speak the full truth, however, I declare: If my superiors had through an order or a decree demanded from me the killing of enemies of the Reich, I would have had to follow this order without default mindful of my oath. If this had ever been the case, I would go into the question of guilt only if the accomplices in killing of our former enemies, or of the countries which, from the end of the war to the present day, prepared and carried out wars and killed or ordered killings, would also be subjected to questions of morality and guilt.

Who then was an accomplice in killing? That is a large field. An example: The war of the German Reich against Poland. It would not have been necessary if those envious of the German nation had not wanted to have it, because they feared the "experiment of successful National Socialism" and its effects which were dangerous to them.

Already the most recent historical research demonstrates the absolute avoidability of this war. Poland certainly did not want this war and

German victims from the Allied bombing of Hamburg, a city that was of no strategic or military importance.

Germany neither. The curse of Versailles burdened Europe, but if the great General Pilsudski[13] had still lived, it would never have come to an armed encounter between the two nations. Not for nothing did German soldiers, during the occupation, stand on an unbroken guard of honour before the last resting place of this great Pole.

In 1940, I accepted an invitation of the Chief of Office V in the RSHA, the Chief of the Reich Criminal Police, SS Gruppenführer and Lieutenant General of the Police, Reich Criminal Police Director Arthur Nebe, who later, on the basis of his involvement in the attempt to assassinate Hitler on 20 July 1944, was sentenced to death. Quite confidentially he showed me and many of my colleagues an exhibition of the victims of the "Bromberg Bloody Sunday":[14] the *corpora*

---

13   Jósef Pilsudski (1867-1935) was Chief of State of the Second Polish Republic established in 1918 and First Marshal from 1920. His major foreign political aim was to break up Imperial Russia and the Soviet Union into their constituent nations.

14   On September 3 1939, two days after the German invasion of Poland, there occurred a massacre in Bydgoszcz wherein around 200 or more ethnic Germans were killed by Polish troops. In the German reprisals that immediately followed, hundreds of Poles and Jews were killed.

delicti[15] were shown cleanly prepared, with complete criminal police objectivity, including the statements of the witnesses and photographs of the crime scenes. The skulls of the Germans living in Bromberg and murdered in this city of their homeland showed clear entry and exit-wounds or skulls obviously smashed with sharp-edged objects or ordinary clubs. Further, there were there photos of crime scenes of Germans beaten together who were thrown into a pond, where they drowned miserably. Others again were murdered in a Bromberg street or in a pub. In my field of vision lay a small skull which radiated something feminine; it was pierced with a Dum-Dum bullet with a relatively small entry-wound and an exit-wound as large as a palm which had fully torn apart one side of the skull. Nearby, there was the picture of this woman standing in the midst of her children, a family picture from happier times; even today I see this picture before me.

This "exhibition" of the Bromberg Bloody Sunday gave me for the first time the right to be hard and unpitying with regard to the enemies of the Reich. All this was years before my chief said to me that the Führer had ordered physical liquidation. Already at that time the feeling of vengeance was awakened in many Germans by this, the fury and the burning outrage against all those who had attacked German blood. The children in the picture were my children, the young mother was a part of the future of my people.

Nebe was an ice-cold criminologist and described to me and my subordinates the events in that way. I, who saw all that, had been impulsive, Nebe was cold. I wished that I had been as cold in feeling in police matters as Nebe, then I would have had a lighter inner life today. Perhaps Heydrich had arranged this visit to this "exhibition" in his Jesuitically providential way, whereby the word "Jesuit" does not at all signify for me a disparagement but is an expression of my great respect for the Jesuit system. I summarise: The murders of the Bromberg Bloody Sunday tore the hypocritical masks from the face of the enemies of our Reich and revealed their inveterate hatred.

An Attempt at a Historical Reckoning

Who had ordered these murders? Who had carried them out? Were orders, instructions, decrees, ordinances present? Were the guilty at that time punished by the Polish government or by an international

---

15   The evidence of a crime having been committed.

24 March 1933 the Jews launch their campaign against Hitler and National Socialism.

tribunal? Versailles was a pause in the war, here in Bromberg I saw the beginning of the second stage. Who had prepared the war and brought it about? Germany? Had Adolf Hitler not warned repeatedly? Hitler had said in January 1939: If international Jewry were to succeed in triggering a war against Germany, this time Jewry itself would have to pay for it.[16] They successfully saw to it that a German-Polish settlement did not prevent the war.

Dr. Chaim Weizmann as speaker of the Jews, and the leader of the World Zionist Organisation, had in 1933 declared war against the German nation in the name of Jewry. The answer of the Führer and Reich Chancellor was not late in coming: However the war may go, one thing is certain: the losers would in any case be Jewry. Today we know that Hitler was wrong - the statistics on the Jewish population alive today prove it. Moreover, the Jews established their own state, Israel. The tribute in blood which the former Jewish enemy of Germany had to offer during the war is, in comparison to the number of Jews in the world, not greater, often even smaller than the blood tribute of other nations.

---

16   In his speech to the Reichstag on January 30, 1939: "If the international Jewish financiers in and outside Europe should succeed in plunging the nations once more into a world war, then the result will not be the Bolshevization of the earth, and thus the victory of Jewry, but the annihilation of the Jewish race in Europe!"

But still more questions force themselves on the observer. Who killed millions of German women, old people and children in Hamburg, Berlin, Dresden and in the other cities of Germany in the north and the south, east and west? Who hunted with aeroplanes men who were working on the fields, riding on the streets on their bicycles? Who shattered them with explosive bombs, who burnt them with sulphur and who baked them into mummy-like shrunken men? Who ordered this, who carried it out, and according to who's orders? Who rendered assistance for that? Have the guilty then or today been punished by their governments or by international tribunals? Was that really not necessary because the victims were only Germans? Seven million Germans have been killed during the war, so says an expert on the matter, Churchill, in his memoirs. And, at an international conference, he maintained that thereby enough space was created to "transfer" at least the same number of Germans driven from their living places. The Germans only needed to be driven from the eastern territories and already everything was again in balance. This expulsion cost the German people millions of lives, especially old people, women and children. Soviet authorities carried it out, the Polish authorities were their accomplices, likewise the Czech, Hungarian, Yugoslav and Romanian authorities of the post-war period. Orders and instructions were doubtless present: indeed they were specified in a large conference.[17] Stalin even discussed shooting 50,000 German officers as a "bonus action".

Who carried out the million-fold murder of German blood? Have the guilty been punished? Nothing happened: The victims were only Germans; there were no murderers responsible there. There was apparently also nobody there who "abetted murder". For the most part there existed unequivocal orders and decrees from the responsible offices, and therewith everything went in an orderly manner. After all one had sworn an oath of allegiance and had to obey. But why should this not be valid among the Germans? Should we have faced our enemies singing psalms and hosannas? What crimes against humanity and mass murders were carried out in North and South Korea, in Indo-China, in Morocco, in Algeria, in Red and Nationalist China, in Cyprus, in the course of the Mau-Mau rebellion in Africa? Why indeed did only German field-marshal generals and German ministers swing from the gallows? Why only German officers, junior officers, men, officials and employees at the gallows or before the shooting squads? Why were the allies of Germany hanged or shot, Japanese, Croats, Slovaks,

---

17   The Yalta Conference between Roosevelt, Stalin and Churchill, where the forced deportation of Germans from eastern Europe was decided upon.

An Attempt at a Historical Reckoning

Two British soldiers, Sergeants Clifford Martin (left) and Mervyn Paice, murdered in Palestine by the Jewish terrorist organization Irgun.

Hungarians? Why did they kill, and why do they still persecute all those who believed then in one Europe with one Reich as its centre? I think of the SS volunteers from Flanders, Wallonia, France, the Netherlands, Denmark, Norway, Sweden, Romania, the Cossacks and all those, no matter whence these idealists may have come from, who served in their divisions and offices, loyal to their oath, an idea, the idea of a united Europe?

The post-war laws of Nuremberg were valid only for Germans and their allies. After the Germans had been silenced and therewith the "only disturber of the peace on earth" was neutralised, were there no more preparations for war, no wars and genocides, no crimes against humanity? One may count how many wars have raged since the gallows of Nuremberg! The Germans were not involved in any of these events. So I ask myself: Where then are the gallows for war criminals and crimes against humanity? Are there no more of them? Was Nuremberg valid only for us Germans? Or has one, in the hurry

322

of events and in the rage, forgotten that, in 1945, at Nuremberg a new international law was created? Or were the gallows of Nuremberg and the paragraphs on which they were based rather an injustice?

As soon as I seek to find clarity about whether, and how far, I have been an accomplice to events during the war, my search for guilt and atonement is suddenly interrupted. Israeli tanks and armoured cars roll firing and burning through the Sinai, Israeli air force squadrons dropped bombs on peaceful Egyptian villages and cities, Israeli bayonets startle Egyptian families from their peaceful sleep. For the second time since 1945! And England's and France's war colossi entered North Egypt. An entire army gave their fiery blessing to that peaceful delta in the land of the pharaohs. Who are the aggressors here, who are the war criminals, who are the accomplices in murder? Were the guilty punished by their governments? The victims are Egyptians, Arabs, Muslims.

There is no doubt that Israel is the principal aggressor and principal war criminal against the Arab peoples. Who brings Israel to justice? Or must the Egyptian people pay for the fact that it has the insolence to live on its own ancestral soil? Do the German people really believe that, after the declaration of war by Chaim Weizmann, Jewry living all over the world have sought peace? To the historical researchers it will become increasingly clearer why the American envoy in London, Kennedy,[18] wrote in his diary on 3 September 1939: "The Jews finally have their war." Besides, even today details are partially known why, since the Middle Ages, lasting disagreements have arisen between the Jews and their host peoples.

There is no justification at all to declare me "guilty" in the sense of being an accomplice, while the "other side" does not show the same readiness. I do not know if I will receive justice in the West. Perhaps the real reason for the situation lies in the circumstance that the Christian Bible to which a large part of western thought is bound expressly states that all salvation comes from the Jews. It is possible that for political reasons it has not yet been considered opportune to consider me and others like me from that time other than as guilty. Such a verdict I will never acknowledge; for it is without any parallel. It would represent an international legal impossibility; against it I protest that I am a man who stood under an oath of office and allegiance and had to serve his fatherland, in a hard battle.

---

18   Joseph Patrick Kennedy Sr. (1888-1969) was U.S. ambassador to the United Kingdom from 1938 to 1940. He was the father of President John F .Kennedy.

An Attempt at a Historical Reckoning

In contrast to many former comrades, I must speak and scream to the world: We Germans who only did our duty are not guilty. You, 360 million Muslims, with whom much binds me and those of you who find in the Koran and in the writings of your fathers more truth, I call upon you to judge me; for you, the children of Allah, know the Jew longer and better than the West. Your jurists may stand in judgement and pass a verdict on me!

Eichmann Absolves Himself

In these explanations I have not spared or minimised anything, I have totally affirmed the responsibility that fell upon me. I have spoken the full truth, even when it incriminates me, even where it was easy to find an escape or to bring forward a lie. Precisely because I never baulked at incriminating myself, it is no empty declaration when I say today: *If I had been appointed as the one commissioned for the final solution of the Jewish question rather as a Reich commissioner, then certainly hardly a single drop of Jewish blood would have flowed, then hardly one Jew would have found a violent end, then one of those comprehensive "political" solutions would have been arrived at into which I rushed at that time with veritable ardour and which I sought to realise in spite of my deficient powers, repeatedly hindered by all possible offices and unpleasantness.*[19]

---

19   Eichmann's italics.

CPSIA information can be obtained
at www.ICGtesting.com
Printed in the USA
BVHW041327261221
624769BV00003B/114